MEMRISTOR AND MEMRISTIVE NEURAL NETWORKS

Edited by **Alex Pappachen James**

Memristor and Memristive Neural Networks

http://dx.doi.org/10.5772/66539
Edited by Alex Pappachen James

Contributors

Xinjiang Zhang, Runmiao Li, Huang Anping, Yu Chi, Yao-Feng Chang, Cheng Chih Hsieh, Ying-Chen Chen, Chih-Yang Lin, Meiqi Guo, Fei Zhou, Burt W. Fowler, Ting-Chang Chang, Jack C. Lee, Jason Eshraghian, Kamran Eshraghian, Herbert Ho-Ching Iu, Carlos Sanchez-Lopez, Illiani Carro-Pérez, Victor H. Carbajal-Gomez, Miguel Angel Carrasco-Aguilar, Francisco Epimenio Morales-López, Atsushi Tsurumaki-Fukuchi, Masashi Arita, Yasuo Takahashi, Luis-Miguel Procel-Moya, Henrique Gomes, Stefan Meskers, Dago De Leeuw, Alex James, Timur Ibrayev, Olga Krestinskaya, Irina Dolzhikova, Dietmar Fey, Lukas Riedersberger, Marc Reichenbach, Yao Shuai, Geetika Khurana, Nitu Kumar, James Scott, Ram S. Katiyar, Aigerim Tankimanova, Fatih Gul, Yunus Babacan, Abdullah Yesil, Yasin Oğuz

Published by InTech
Janeza Trdine 9, 51000 Rijeka, Croatia

Publishing Process Manager Dajana Pemac
Technical Editor SPi Global
Cover InTech Design team

First published April, 2018
Printed in Croatia
Legal deposit, Croatia: National and University Library in Zagreb

Additional hard copies can be obtained from orders@intechopen.com

Memristor and Memristive Neural Networks, Edited by Alex Pappachen James
p. cm.
Print ISBN 978-953-51-3947-8
Online ISBN 978-953-51-3948-5

For EU product safety concerns:
IN TECH d.o.o., Prolaz Marije Krucifikse Kozulić 3, 51000 Rijeka, Croatia,
info@intechopen.com or visit our website at intechopen.com.

Meet the editor

Alex Pappachen James received his PhD degree from the Queensland Micro- and Nanotechnology Centre, Griffith University, Brisbane, QLD, Australia. He is internationally known for his contributions on memristive networks, neuromorphic computing and image processing. Currently, he is chairing the Electrical Engineering Department at Nazarbayev University. He is a mentor to several tech start-ups and co-founded companies in machine learning and computer vision hardware. He has been a founding chair for IEEE R10 Circuits and Systems Society Chapter and an executive board member of IET Vision and Imaging Network. He is the founding chair of IEEE Kazakhstan subsection, R8, and mentor to IEEE NU Student Branch. He was an editorial member of Information Fusion (2010–2015), Elsevier, and is an associate editor for HCIS (2015–present), Springer; IEEE Access (2017–present); IEEE Transactions on Emerging Topics in Computational Intelligence (2017–present); and IEEE Transactions on Circuits and Systems 1 (2018–present). He was a faculty senate chair of NU between 2016 and 2017. He received an award from the president of Kazakhstan for his services in the field of education in Kazakhstan in 2017. He is a senior member of IEEE, life member of ACM and senior fellow of HEA.

Contents

Preface IX

Section 1 Memristor Devices 1

Chapter 1 **Physical Models for Resistive Switching Devices 3**
Luis-Miguel Procel-Moya

Chapter 2 **Graphene Oxide-Based Memristor 19**
Geetika Khurana, Nitu Kumar, James F. Scott and Ram S. Katiyar

Chapter 3 **Emulator Circuits and Resistive Switching Parameters of Memristor 41**
Abdullah Yesil, Fatih Gül and Yunus Babacan

Chapter 4 **Nanoscale Switching and Degradation of Resistive Random Access Memory Studied by In Situ Electron Microscopy 63**
Masashi Arita, Atsushi Tsurumaki-Fukuchi and Yasuo Takahashi

Chapter 5 **Resistive Switching in Metal Oxide/Organic Semiconductor Nonvolatile Memories 93**
Henrique L. Gomes, Dago M. de Leeuw and Stefan C.J. Meskers

Section 2 Memristor Modelling 113

Chapter 6 **Memristor Emulator Circuit Design and Applications 115**
Carlos Sánchez-López, Illiani Carro-Pérez, Victor Hugo Carbajal-Gómez, Miguel Angel Carrasco-Aguilar and Francisco Epimenio Morales-López

Chapter 7 **Simulating Memristive Networks in SystemC-AMS 147**
Dietmar Fey, Lukas Riedersberger and Marc Reichenbach

Chapter 8 **Modeling of Coupled Memristive-Based Architectures Applicable to Neural Network Models 167**
Jason Kamran Jr Eshraghian, Herbert H.C. Iu and Kamran Eshraghian

Chapter 9 **Mathematical Modeling of Memristors 187**
Yasin Oğuz

Section 3 Memristor Neuromorphic Applications 207

Chapter 10 **Introduction to Memristive HTM Circuits 209**
Alex James, Timur Ibrayev, Olga Krestinskaya and Irina Dolzhikova

Chapter 11 **Review of Recently Progress on Neural Electronics and Memcomputing Applications in Intrinsic SiOx-Based Resistive Switching Memory 227**
Cheng-Chih Hsieh, Yao-Feng Chang, Ying-Chen Chen, Xiaohan Wu, Meiqi Guo, Fei Zhou, Sungjun Kim, Burt Fowler, Chih-Yang Lin, Chih-Hung Pan, Ting-Chang Chang and Jack C. Lee

Chapter 12 **Memristor Neural Network Design 249**
Anping Huang, Xinjiang Zhang, Runmiao Li and Yu Chi

Chapter 13 **Spike-Timing-Dependent Plasticity in Memristors 283**
Yao Shuai, Xinqiang Pan and Xiangyu Sun

Chapter 14 **Neural Network-Based Analog-to-Digital Converters 297**
Aigerim Tankimanova and Alex Pappachen James

Preface

The growth in internet of things, devices and systems has resulted in the need to develop energy-efficient near-sensor processing devices and circuits. This requires the development of alternative computing implementations such as neuromorphic computing, quantum computing and approximate computing. Memristor devices and their natural properties to change states can be used to mimic neural circuits and neural networks. It is estimated that these networks can be scaled in the future to create large-scale neurocomputing solution.

This book covers a range of models, circuits and systems built with memristor devices and networks in applications to neural networks. It is divided into three parts: (1) Devices, (2) Models and (3) Applications. The resistive switching property is an important aspect of the memristors, and there are several designs of this discussed in this book, such as in metal oxide/organic semiconductor nonvolatile memories, nanoscale switching and degradation of resistive random access memory and graphene oxide-based memristor. The modelling of the memristors is required to ensure that the devices can be put to use and improve emerging application. In this book, various memristor models are discussed, from a mathematical framework to implementations in SPICE and verilog, that will be useful for the practitioners and researchers to get a grounding on the topic. The applications of the memristor models in various neuromorphic networks are discussed covering various neural network models, implementations in A/D converter and hierarchical temporal memories.

This book is a response to the growing field of memristor networks and applications, providing insights into a collection of topics in memristor devices, circuits and systems. It is suitable for the introductory studies and equally useful for the researchers to discuss the emerging topics in the memristor networks.

Alex Pappachen James
Nazarbayev University
Kazakhstan

Section 1

Memristor Devices

Chapter 1

Physical Models for Resistive Switching Devices

Luis-Miguel Procel-Moya

Additional information is available at the end of the chapter

http://dx.doi.org/10.5772/intechopen.69025

Abstract

We present a classification and description of the principal resistive switching and transport mechanisms in chalcogonides materials. We classify the model according to how many material dimensions are involved in the resistive switching mechanism. In this way, we describe the phase change model (3D), the interface modulation model (2D) and models where the switching mechanism depends on the formation of a conduction filament (1D). Among the conduction filament models, we include the thermochemical oxygen diffusion mechanism, the oxidation/reduction mechanism and the quantum point effect.

Keywords: chalcogonides, resistive switching, physical models

1. Introduction

Typically, a resistive switching material changes its resistance between two states: High Resistive State (HRS or OFF-state) and Low Resistive State (LRS or ON-state). The most common structure for a resistive switching devices is an insulator between two metals or metal/insulator/metal (MIM) structure. One of the most important applications of these kind of devices is for non-volatile memories or Resistive RAMs (ReRAMs).

The metal elements of the MIM structure are called top and bottom electrodes. An electrical stimulus is necessary to apply between these electrodes to change the resistive state of the insulator material. In order to determine the resistive state (HRS or LRS), a low voltage is applied on the electrodes, and the current, which flows through the insulator, is measured (I_{HRS} or I_{LRS}). There are several orders of magnitudes of difference between I_{HRS} and I_{LRS} currents. The change from the HRS to the LRS is called SET process and the change from the LRS to the HRS is called RESET process.

Depending on the voltage polarity applied on the electrodes, there are two schemes to change the resistive state: unipolar and bipolar. On the one hand, in the unipolar scheme, the resistive state change does not depend on the voltage polarity and there are two threshold voltages: one for the RESET process (V_{RESET}) and one for the SET process (V_{SET}) with the same polarity as we can see in **Figure 1**. On the other hand, in the bipolar scheme, V_{RESET} and V_{SET} have different polarities (**Figure 2**).

There is no universal theory or model which explains the electron conduction in the two resistive states and the SET and RESET processes because there are many factors that affect the switching behaviour, such as the type of the insulator material, fabrication process, nature of the dielectric breakdown, among others. However, Waser and Wutting proposed a classification based on the type of the resistive switching mechanisms, such as nanochemical materials, ferroelectric tunnelling, electrostatics effects, phase change mechanism, thermochemical mechanism, redox-based effect, electrochemical effect, molecular switching effect and magnetoresistive effect [1].

Chalcogonides are one of the most used materials in the fabrication of resistive memory devices. The switching mechanisms related to these materials are: phase change memory effect, thermochemical memory effect, redox-based memory effect and interface defect modulation. The phase change mechanism affects the complete volume of the insulator material and it is considered as a 3D mechanism. A 2D resistive switching mechanism is the modulation of the defect density at the metal/insulator interface. Finally, when the resistivity material depends on the formation of a conduction filament (CF), 1D mechanisms are involved in the resistive switching process. Thermochemical diffusion of oxygen, reduction/oxidation of the CF and quantum point contact effects are typical 1D mechanisms.

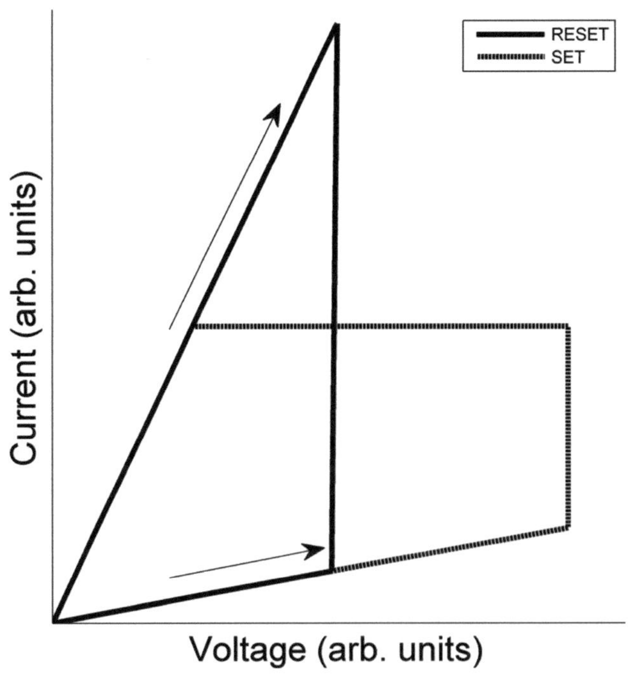

Figure 1. SET and RESET process for unipolar behaviour.

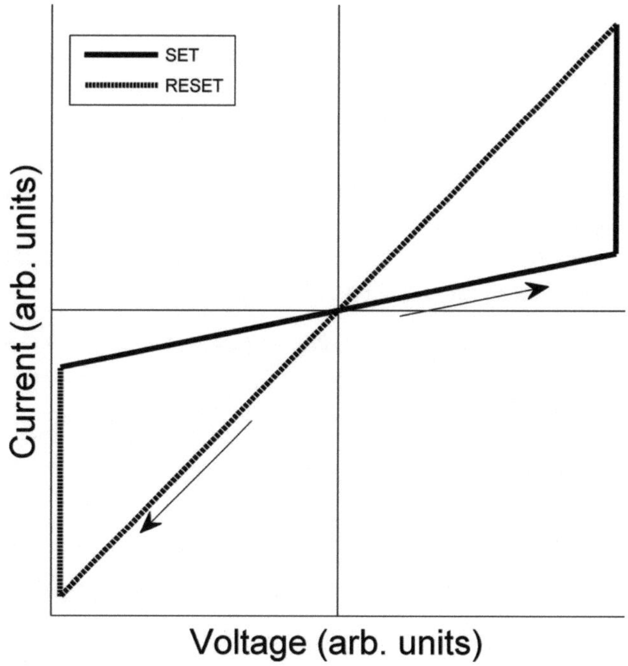

Figure 2. SET and RESET process for bipolar behaviour.

2. Phase change model

Heavier chalcogonides, such as tellurides and selenides, show different electrical and optical properties in their amorphous and crystalline phases (**Figure 3**). The resistive switching of these materials is unipolar. On the one hand, the amorphous phase of these materials has high resistivity and low reflectivity and, on the other hand, crystalline phase has low resistivity and high reflectivity [2]. These properties are being exploited in the development of optical storage

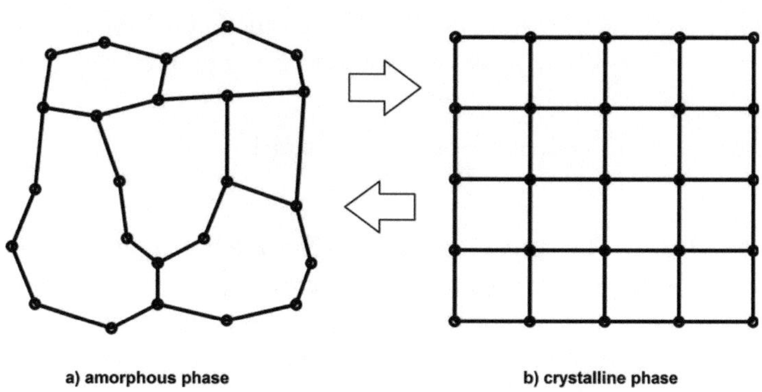

Figure 3. Phase change mechanism: the phase material changes from (a) amorphous phase to (b) crystalline phase (and vice versa) to have different resistivity and reflectivity.

products, such as compact disks (CD), digital versatile disks (DVD), high-definition digital versatile disks (HD-DVD) and Blu-ray disks (BR). The first kind of materials used for optical storage were good glasses, such as Te-based alloys like $Te_{85}Ge_{13}$ doped with Sb, S and P. These materials show good electrical switching properties in the amorphous and crystalline phases but the crystallization time was in the order of microseconds, too high to be considered for optical storage. The second generation of these materials shows shorter crystallization time and good optical properties. Among these materials, we have GeTe, $Ge_{11}Te_{80}Sn_4Au_{23}$, GeTe-$Sb_2Te_3$, GeBiTe and GeInSbTe. After, a third family of materials was later discovered which includes alloys of Sb_2Te doped with Ag, In and Ge [2].

There are two important temperature thresholds in these materials: the melting temperature (T_m) and the glass-transition temperature (T_g) with $T_m > T_g$. The process to change the material phase from crystalline to amorphous and vice versa is as follows [2]:

- To write a bit, a short high-pulse laser or current is applied on the crystalline material to reach T_m temperature.
- The material is cooling down rapidly with a rate higher than 10^9 K/s. In a very short time, the material reaches the amorphous phase without passing through the crystalline one.
- To erase the bit, a long short-pulse laser or current is applied on the amorphous material. The material temperature increases over T_g. There is an increment of the electron mobility and the material changes to the crystalline phase.

For electrical storage devices, the resistive switching property is fundamental and all these materials have it. However, not all these materials have the reflectivity switching property. To have this property, a very short time (few tens of nanoseconds) is needed for cooling down the material from the liquid phase to amorphous phase (step 2) [2].

When a low voltage is applied to the material in the amorphous phase, a very low current is measured due to the high resistance. When the voltage reaches a value around 0.7 V, the resistivity decreases and the material reach the so-called ON-amorphous phase [1, 2]. In these phases, the current increases significantly and enables enough heat to recrystallize the material. During the phase change, material defects play an important role. In the amorphous phase, the current is controlled by the Pool-Frenkel conduction, where carriers are trapped in defect sites according to the following equation (electron hopping mechanism) [1]:

$$I = 2qAN_T \frac{\Delta z}{\tau_0} e^{-(E_C - E_F)/kT} \sinh\left(\frac{qV\Delta z}{2kTt_h}\right) \tag{1}$$

where A is the contact area, V the applied voltage, N_T the integral of the trap distribution, Δz the intertrap distance, τ_0 the scape time for a trapping electron, E_F the Fermi energy, E_C the conduction band energy, q the elementary electron charge and t_h the thickness of the material. Because of the total conduction is presented in the complete material volume, this mechanism is called 3D. Experimental results show that the defect density in the material is very high and most of the defects are negative U-centres [1]. On the other hand, computational simulations show that in the crystalline phase, vacancy defects predominate with a concentration of 25% [1].

3. Metal/insulator interface modulation model

In this model, the resistive switching is presented at the metal/insulator interface. In other words, there is a contact resistance switching behaviour. This interface depending mechanism is presented in Peroskite oxides in which the material resistivity strongly depends on the interface area and the switching mechanism is always bipolar. A typical material that shows this behaviour is the Nb-doped $SrTiO_3$ [3].

The origin of this resistivity change can be understood by examining the metal/insulator interface band diagram as shown in **Figure 4**. The insulator oxide is usually doped with different metals. Depending of doped metal and its density, the insulator behaves as semiconductor at the interface. This provokes a Schottky barrier contact instead of a pure ohmic contact [3].

An electric field applied on the metal electrodes can electrochemically modify the oxygen vacancy density at the interface. For an n-type semiconductor, an increment of the oxygen vacancies density reduces the depletion layer, W_d, in the energy band diagram provoking an increment of the tunnel electron conduction and, therefore, a decrement of the contact

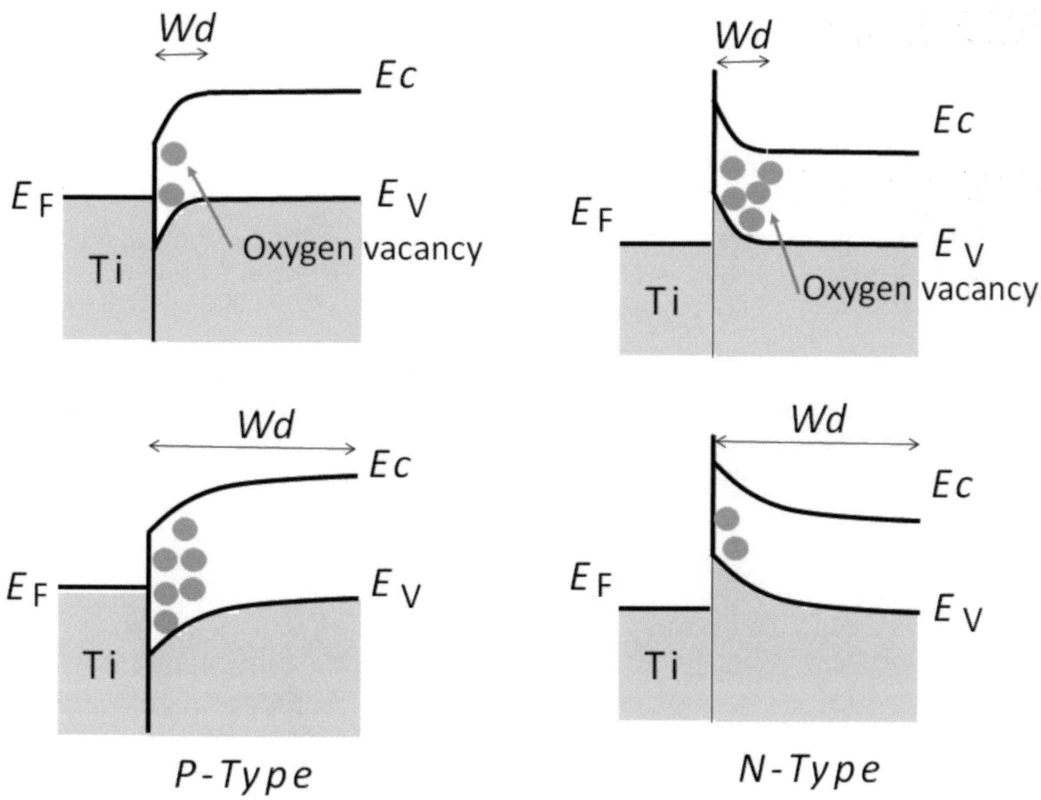

Figure 4. Band diagrams at the Metal/Insulator interfaces. For a p-type semiconductor, the presence of oxygen vacancies increases W_d. For an n-type semiconductor, the presence of oxygen vacancies decreases W_d.

resistance (LRS). If an electric field is applied on the opposite direction, the number of oxygen vacancies in the n-type semiconductor decreases and provokes an increment of W_d and, therefore, the contact resistance increases (HRS). On the other hand, for a p-type semiconductor, the increment of oxygen vacancies increases W_d and the contact resistance (HRS), and a diminution of the oxygen vacancies decreases W_d and the contact resistance (LRS). In this model, the metal work function plays a very important role because the band bending strongly depends on this parameter.

Sawa showed very good resistive switching results for Ti/$Pr_{07}Ca_{0.3}MnO_3$/$SrRuO_3$ (Ti/PCMO/SRO) cells, where SRO has metal properties and PCMO acts as p-type semiconductor. As well, the SRO/$SrTi_{0.99}Nb_{0.01}O_3$/Ag (SRO/Nb:STO/Ag) cell showed a good resistive switching behaviour where Nb:STO acts as an n-type semiconductor [3].

Another way to change the contact resistance is by adding a thin semiconductor layer of an oxide material between the metal and the insulator materials [3]. The semiconductor layer transforms the contact resistance from ohmic to a Schottky barrier. Without this layer, there is no switching resistance for some insulators. Sawa shows experimental results for Ti/$Sm_{0.7}Ca_{0.3}MnO_3$(n unit cells)/$La_{0.7}Sr_{0.3}MnO_3$/SRO (Ti/SCMO(n)/LSMO/SRO) where SCMO is a p-type semiconductor [3]. It was demonstrated that for n = 5 unit cells, there was a very good hysteresis in the I-V curve. As well, the SRO/$SrTiO_3$/$SrTi_{0.99}Nb_{0.01}O_3$/Ag (SRO/STO/Nb:STO) cell showed a resistivity changes but not a good hysteresis in the I-V curve [3].

4. One dimensional models for resistive switching materials

In several transition metal oxides, when a voltage is applied on the electrodes of a pristine MIM cell, the current measured is very low. When the voltage increases up to a threshold value, the electric field applied provokes a dielectric breakdown. When this occurs, a conduction filament (CF) is formed in the insulator as shown in **Figure 5**. The necessary potential to form this filament is called forming voltage (V_F). The CF is formed due to the Joule-heating effect, which leads a temperature increment in the insulator. The dielectric breakdown is driven by a thermal runway. When a voltage is applied on a transition metal oxide, the resistance

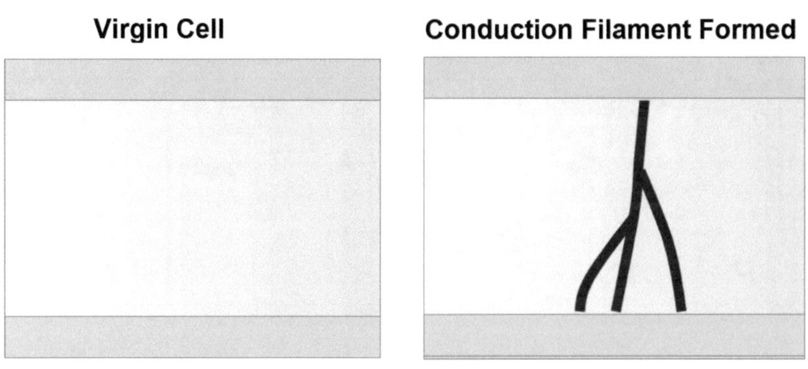

Figure 5. Left: virgin cell. Right: Cell with conduction filament formed.

starts to decrease but not in a permanent way. In this process, the material temperature increases up to certain value (related to a threshold voltage) when a local redox reaction begins and causes structural defects (grain boundaries or dislocations) [4].

The voltage polarity to change states in cells with CF can be unipolar or bipolar. For unipolar behaviour, the electron conduction mechanism is related to thermochemical changes in the filament due to the Joule-heating effect. On the other hand, for bipolar behaviour, the electron conduction through the CF depends on redox effects or quantum point contact effects. In both cases, the switching mechanisms (SET and RESET processes) are related to the thermochemical oxygen diffusion in the CF. We can consider the CF as a 1D parameter because the material resistivity is area independent. It is very important to note that in CF programmable devices, there exist a variability problem because not all filaments are equal or similar [5].

4.1. Thermochemical oxygen diffusion model

Ielmeni, Nardi and Cagli have been developed a physical model for NiO cells with very good concordance with experimental results [4]. In this material, the RESET process happens in small steps, whereas the change of states occurs suddenly during the SET process. The $V_{\mathrm{RESET}}$and I_{RESET} parameters depend on the resistance material in the HRS. I_{RESET} always decreases when the resistance increases. On the other hand, the V_{RESET} in function of R curve has an U behaviour. That is, for low values of R, V_{RESET} decreases when R increases, and for high values of R, V_{RESET} increases when R increases. For the RESET process, the CF temperature depends on the square of the applied voltage as follows [4]:

$$T = T_0 + \frac{R_{\mathrm{th}}}{R} V^2 \tag{2}$$

where T_0 is the room temperature and R_{th} is the effective thermal resistance. By using Eq. (2), we can obtain the V_{RESET} voltage:

$$V_{RESET} = \sqrt{\frac{R\Delta T_{RESET}}{R_{th}}} \tag{3}$$

where $\Delta T_{\mathrm{RESET}}$ is the critical temperature increment for the onset oxidation. The ratio R/R_{th} is almost constant according to the Wiedemann-Franz law for metals [4]. This means that V_{RESET} is almost constant and I_{RESET} decreases with respect to R. This is not true in experimental results. For explaining the increment of V_{RESET} with respect to high values of R, we have to study the size-dependent Joule-heating effect. The parameter R_{th} is the parallel of two resistances: R_{th}' and R_{th}'', where R_{th}' only depends on the CF and R_{th}'' depends on the rest of the material (bulk oxide). R_{th}' can be computed by considering the thermal nanofilament conductivity, k_{th}, as follows [4]:

$$R_{\mathrm{th}}' = \frac{t_h}{8k_{\mathrm{th}}A_{\mathrm{CF}}} \tag{4}$$

where t_{h} is the oxide thickness and A_{CF} is CF area. As R_{th} is inverse proportional to A_{CF}, for high values of A_{CF} (low resistance) R_{th} is approximately R_{th}'. On the other hand, for low values of ACF, we have that $R_{\mathrm{th}} \approx R_{\mathrm{th}}''$. As well, when k_{th} increases, R_{th}' predominates over R_{th}''.

For explaining the behaviour of the V_{RESET}-R curve for low values of R, we have to consider that the ratio R/R_{th} is almost constant in Eq. (3) and ΔT_{RESET} must increase in order to obtain a metal diffusion in the filament, which is a filament area dependent process. Hence, V_{RESET} increases for low values of R. This size-dependent diffusion is considering in following Arrhenius expression developed in Ref. [4]:

$$T_{RESET} = \frac{E_A}{k\log\left(\frac{t_{RESET}}{t_0}\left(\frac{\varphi_0}{\varphi}\right)^2\right)} \tag{5}$$

where E_A is the activation energy, k the Boltzmann constant, t_0 and ϕ_0 are constants, ϕ is the CF diameter and t_{RESET}= 1s is the reset time. Ielmini et al. showed very good results between their model and experimental data of NiO devices [4].

The electron conduction mechanism in the LRS strongly depends on the activation energy. For low values of E_A, the filament has a metallic behaviour and the resistance is given by:

$$R = R_{0m}(1 + \alpha(T - T_0)) \tag{6}$$

where T_0 is the room temperature, R_{0m} is the metallic resistant at T_0 and α is the temperature coefficient. On the other hand, for high values of E_A, electron conduction is driven by the Pool-Frenkel model in semiconductors and the resistance follows the following equation:

$$R = R_{0s}\exp\left(\frac{E_{AC}}{kT}\right) \tag{7}$$

where R_{0s} is the extrapolated resistance at infinite T, k is the Boltzmann constant and E_{AC} is the activation energy for conduction. Both conduction behaviours are related to position of Fermi level (E_F). Inside the CF filament, there are oxygen vacancies, whereas the bulk oxide is doped by oxygen. An insulator doped by oxygen behaves as a p-type semiconductor and, on the other hand, oxygen vacancies provoke an n-type behaviour. Therefore, the conduction filament in LRS behaves as an n-type semiconductor and the electron conduction is modulated by the concentration of oxygen vacancies, which is directly related to the E_F position. When the oxygen vacancies concentration is too high, the CF behaves as a degenerately doped semiconductor and E_F is very close or above the conduction band [4].

As was mentioned before, the SET process happens suddenly and it strongly depends on the resistance of the HRS (before the SET process). The HRS resistance can be described by the Pool-Frenkel model and is given by Ielmini et al. [4]:

$$R = \frac{kT\tau_0 t_h}{q^2 A_{CF} N_T \Delta z^2}\exp\left(\frac{E_{AC}}{kT}\right) \tag{8}$$

where τ_0 is the attempt-to-escape characteristic time for a carrier from a specific state, t_h is the material thickness (or filament length), N_T is the dopant density, A_{CF} is the filament area and Δz is the distance between positive charged defects. Ielmini et al. showed, from experimental data, that necessary power for the setting process (P_{SET}) is directly proportional to $R^{-0.5}$, which means that [4]:

$$V_{SET} = \frac{P_{SET}}{I_{SET}} = \sqrt{P_{SET}R} \propto R^{0.25} \tag{9}$$

$$I_{SET} = \frac{P_{SET}}{V_{SET}} = \sqrt{\frac{P_{SET}}{R}} \propto R^{-0.75} \tag{10}$$

The tendencies for V_{SET} and I_{SET} parameters in function of R were experimentally confirmed the Ielmini group in Ref. [4].

4.2. Trap-assisted-tunnelling model

In bipolar cells, the transition between the LRS and the HRS is commonly related to the formation and rupture of the CF. A typical material which presents a CF with bipolar behaviour is the HfO_2. As well as in unipolar cells, oxygen vacancies play an important role. The most accepted theory for forming the CF in a virgin cell is that the oxygen atoms migrate from the CF to the insulator/metal interface due to the Joule-heating effect. When the CF is already formed, to change from the LRS to the HRS, the CF is oxidized (oxygen atoms migrate from the electrode to the CF), whereas to change from the HRS to the LRS, the CF is reduced leaving oxygen vacancies and forming percolation paths (oxygen atoms migrate from the CF to the electrode).

Guan, Yu and Wong have developed a model for explaining the carrier conduction through the CF in bipolar cells where the principal transport mechanism is the trap-assisted-tunnelling (TAT). The continuity transport equation in the oxide region is given by Guan et al. [6]:

$$\frac{df_n}{dt} = (1-f_n)\sum_{m=1,\, m\neq n}^{N} R_{mn}f_m - f_n\sum_{m=1,\, m\neq n}^{N} R_{mn}(1-f_n) + (R_n^{iL}+R_n^{iR})(1-f_n) - (R_n^{oL}+R_n^{oR})f_n \tag{11}$$

where f_n is the electron occupation probability of the nth trap, R_{mn} is the electron hopping rate from trap m to trap n, R_n^{oL}/R_n^{oR} are the electron hopping rate from trap n to the right/left electrode and R_n^{iL}/R_n^{iR} the electron hopping rate from the right/left electrode to trap n. It is well known that oxygen vacancies contribute to the TAT. In quasi-steady state, Eq. (11) transform to [6]:

$$(1-f_n)\sum_{m=1,\, m\neq n}^{N} R_{mn}f_m - f_n\sum_{m=1,\, m\neq n}^{N} R_{mn}(1-f_n) + (R_n^{iL}+R_n^{iR})(1-f_n) - (R_n^{oL}+R_n^{oR})f_n = 0 \tag{12}$$

The current can be computed by evaluating the electron flow near the electrode:

$$I = I^L = I^R = -q\sum_{n=1}^{N}\left((1-f_n)R_n^{iL} - f_nR_n^{oL}\right) = -q\sum_{n=1}^{N}\left((1-f_n)R_n^{iR} - f_nR_n^{oR}\right) \tag{13}$$

The hopping rate can be computed by the Mott hopping model as [7]:

$$R_{mn} = R_0 \exp\left(-\frac{r_{mn}}{a_0} + \frac{qV_{mn}^H}{kT}\right) \tag{14}$$

where $R_0 \approx 10^{12}$Hz is the vibration electron frequency, $r_{mn} = |r_m - r_n|$ is the distance between vacancies n and m, a_0 is the attenuation length wave function, $V_{mn}{}^{H} \approx -F^H(r_m - r_n) \approx V^H(r_m) - V^H(r_n)$ is the barrier change due to an external electric field and $V^H(r_n)$ is the homogeneous component of the potential solution of the Poisson equation. The hopping rates from a trap to an electrode are [6]:

$$\begin{aligned} R_n^{iL,R} &= R_{\text{tunnel}}^0 N^{L,R}(E_v^+) F_{\text{in}}^{L,R}(E_v^+) T_n^{L,R,+} \\ R_n^{oL,R} &= R_{\text{tunnel}}^0 N^{L,R}(E_v^\bullet) F_{\text{out}}^{L,R}(E_v^\bullet) T_n^{L,R,\bullet} \end{aligned} \tag{15}$$

where e $R^0{}_{\text{tunnel}}$ is the tunnel coupling strength between a trap and an electrode, $N^{L,R}$ is the number of states at a given energy in an electrode and $E_v{}^+/E_v{}^\bullet$ are the energy of an empty/filled trap given by Guan et al. [6]:

$$E_v^{+,\bullet}(r_n) = E_v^{+,\bullet} - qV^H(r_n) \tag{16}$$

$T_n{}^{L,R,+\bullet}$ is the tunnel probability from the left/right electrode into a trap given by the Wentzel-Kramers-Brilloin approximation [6]:

$$\begin{aligned} T_n^{L+,\bullet} &= \exp\left[\left|\int_0^{x_n} \frac{1}{h}\sqrt{2m^*\left[E_C - E_{v0}^{+,\bullet} - qV^H(x_n)\right]}dx\right|\right], \quad E_v^\pm < E_C - qV^H(x) \\ T_n^{R+,\bullet} &= \exp\left[\left|\int_{x_n}^{L} \frac{1}{h}\sqrt{2m^*\left[E_C - E_{v0}^{+,\bullet} - qV^H(x_n)\right]}dx\right|\right], \quad E_v^\pm < E_C - qV^H(x) \end{aligned} \tag{17}$$

where x_n is the xth component of r_n, L is the oxide thickness and m^* is the tunnelling effective mass in the oxide. $F_{in}{}^{L,R}$ is the Fermi integral which represents the filled states in an electrode above $E_v{}^+$ and takes into account the inject electrons from the electrode into the trap n:

$$F_{in}^{L,R}(E_v^+) = \int_{E_{v0}^+ - qV(x_n)}^{+\infty} f(E - (E_F^{L,R} - qV^{L,R})dE = \int_{E_{v0}^+ - qV(x_n)}^{+\infty} \frac{1}{1 + \exp\left((E - (E_F^{L,R} - qV^{L,R})/kT\right)} dE \tag{18}$$

where $E_F{}^{L,R}$ is the Fermi level of the right/left electrode and $V^{L,R}$ is the applied voltage on the left/right electrode. On the other hand, $F_{out}{}^{L,R}$ is the Fermi integral which takes into account the number of empty states in an electrode bellow $E_v{}^-$ which can accept electrons from the trap n:

$$F_{out}^{L,R}(E_v^-) = \int_{-\infty}^{E_{v0}^- - qV(x_n)} \left[1 - f(E - (E_F^{L,R} - qV^{L,R})\right]dE = \int_{-\infty}^{E_{v0}^- - qV(x_n)} \frac{1}{1 + \exp\left((E_F^{L,R} - qV^{L,R}) - E/kT\right)} dE \tag{19}$$

According to Guan et al. model, the generation oxygen vacancies are given by [7]:

$$P_G(F^{eq}, T, t) = \frac{t}{t_0} \exp\left(-(E_a - \gamma|F^{eq}|)/kT\right) \tag{20}$$

where the time, t, is within the interval $[\tau, \tau + t]$, F^{eq} is the local electric field of an ion, $1/t_0 \approx 10^{13}$Hz is the oxygen vibration frequency, $E_a \approx 1$eV is a parameter related to the height of the potential barrier and γ is a coefficient which represents the local enhancement due to the electric field. This rate dominates the SET process.

On the other hand, during the equilibrium state (absence of F^{eq}), the oxygen vacancy recombination rate is given by Guan et al. [6]:

$$P_R^0 = P_G(F^{eq} = 0, T, t) = \frac{t}{t_0} \exp\left(-E_a/kT\right) \tag{21}$$

Therefore, the recombination rate for a non-equilibrium state is [7]:

$$P_R = \beta P_R^0$$

where β is a parameter related to concentration of oxygen ions which can be computed by the following approximation [6]:

$$\beta(x, t) = \beta_0 \exp\left(-\frac{vt}{L_p}\right) u(x, t) \tag{22}$$

where L_p is decaying length of ion concentration, $u(x,t)$ is a function related to the oxygen diffusion and can be approximated by the complementary error function. v is velocity of the oxygen ions waveform given by Yu et al. [7]:

$$v = \frac{a}{t_0} \exp\left(-E_m/kT\right) \sinh\left(q\gamma^{drift} F/kT\right) \tag{23}$$

where a is the lattice constant, E_m is the migration barrier, γ^{drift} is the enhancement coefficient related to the dielectric material and F is the electric field left by an oxygen ion. Eq. (13) is coupled with the solution of the Poisson equation to obtain the potential distribution in the cell:

$$-\nabla^2 V = \frac{\rho}{\varepsilon} \tag{24}$$

where ρ is the volumetric charge density and ε is the material permittivity. The border conditions for Eq. (24) are: $V(x=0)=V^L$ and $V(x=L)=V^R$. Guan et al. showed very god results of their model for experimental data of HfO_x devices [7].

4.3. Quantum point contact model

The complete quantum point contact (QPC) model was developed by Miranda and Suñe [8]. Originally, the model was developed for explaining the soft and hard-dielectric-breakdown in SiO_2. If the dimension of the narrowest point of the CF is in the order of the Fermi wavelength, λ_F, quantum point contact effects are presented. There are some experimental works, where the QPC model could explain well the transport conduction in the HRS and LRS for HfO_2 devices [9–11].

According to the QPC model, the first quantized sub-band behaves as a potential barrier for the incoming electrons as shown in **Figure 6**. We used a parabolic potential as potential barrier with the following physical parameters: Φ being the potential barrier height measured at the Fermi level, t_B is the potential thickness at the Fermi level, R is a series resistance external to the constriction, V is the applied voltage on the electrodes, q is the elementary electron charge and I is the filament current that flows in the x direction.

The potential barrier height is defined by the cross-sectional area of the constriction and determines two conduction states. For the HRS, the top of the potential barrier is above or inside the energy window and the dominant conduction mechanism is tunnelling (this description is valid only for low-voltages). On the other hand, if the top of the potential barrier is below the energy window, the cell is in the LRS and the conduction mechanism is essentially ballistic (transmission probability close to 1). The conduction in the LRS is independent of the

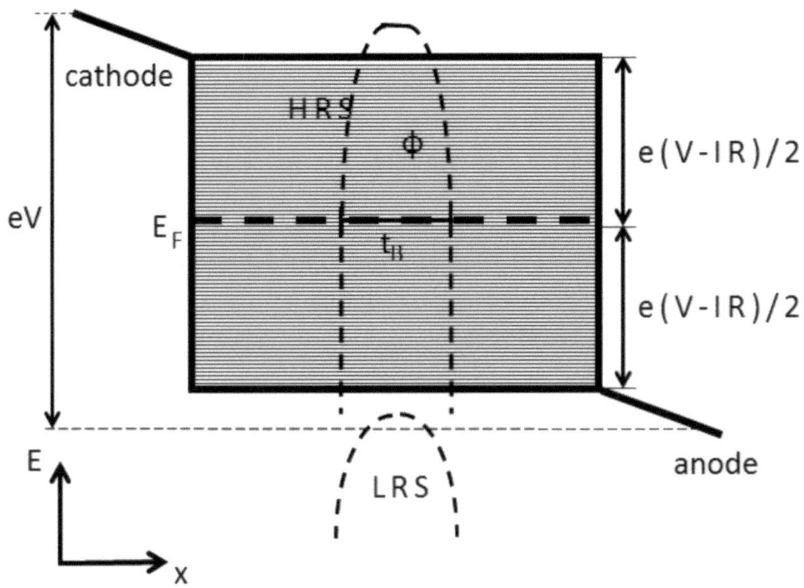

Figure 6. Energy band diagram of the narrow constriction, where V is the applied voltage on the electrodes, R is an external series resistance that takes into account the non-idealities of the model, I is the filament current, e(V-IR) is the energy window associated to the electron conduction (shaded region), EF is the Fermi level, Φ is the potential height with respect to EF, tB is the potential thickness at EF and e is the elementary electron charge. The conduction is in the x direction. The top of the potential barrier is above or inside the energy window for the HRS and below for the LRS.

potential barrier. By assuming a parabolic potential barrier in the narrow constriction and by using the Landauer formalism for 1D quantum conductors and the zero-temperature limit for the parabolic potential barrier, the current through the filament is [9, 10]:

$$I = \frac{2e}{h} N \int_{-e(V-IR)/2}^{e(V-IR)/2} T(E)dE \tag{25}$$

where *T*(*E*) is the electron transmission probability, *N* is the number of active channels in the filament and *h* is the Planck's constant. For a parabolic potential barrier, there is an analytical expression for *T*(*E*):

$$T(E) = \left(1 + \exp\left(-\alpha(E - \Phi)\right)\right)^{-1} \tag{26}$$

where α is a shape parameter related to t_B. By integrating over the total energy window, we have that the filament current is [9, 10]:

$$I = \frac{2eN}{h}\left\{e(V - IR) + \frac{1}{\alpha}\ln\left[\frac{1 + \exp\left\{\alpha[\Phi - e(V - IR)/2]\right\}}{1 + \exp\left\{\alpha[\Phi + e(V - IR)/2]\right\}}\right]\right\} \tag{27}$$

If we consider $V \gg IR$ and only one active filament for the HRS (not multiple filaments), we obtain [9, 10]:

$$I \approx \frac{2e}{h}\left\{eV + \frac{1}{\alpha}\ln\left[\frac{1 + \exp\left\{\alpha[\Phi - eV/2]\right\}}{1 + \exp\left\{\alpha[\Phi + eV/2]\right\}}\right]\right\} \tag{28}$$

For the LRS, we suppose an ideally ballistic transport that ($T(E) \approx 1$) and the current is [9, 10]:

$$I \approx \frac{NG_o}{1 + NG_oR} V \tag{29}$$

where $G_0 = 2q^2/h$ is the quantum conductance unit.

We show in **Figure 7** experimental results of I-V curves for the HRS and LRS and its fitting with the QPC model for HfO_2 cells. We have found in Ref. [10] that $\alpha \propto \Phi^n$ with $n = -0.35$. There is a QPC expression which relates Φ and α by considering t_B constant [9, 10]:

$$t_B = \frac{h\alpha}{2\pi^2}\sqrt{\frac{2\Phi}{m*}} \tag{30}$$

where m^* is the electron effective mass in the constriction. Moreover, the constriction radius, r_B, can be extracted by using another QPC equation [9, 10]:

$$r_B = \frac{hz_o}{2\pi\sqrt{2m * \Phi}} \tag{31}$$

where $z_0 = 2.404$ is the first zero of the Bessel function J_0. In Ref. [10], we have experimentally found that $r_B = 1.14$ nm with a standard deviation of 0.06 nm for bipolar HfO_2 cells, which

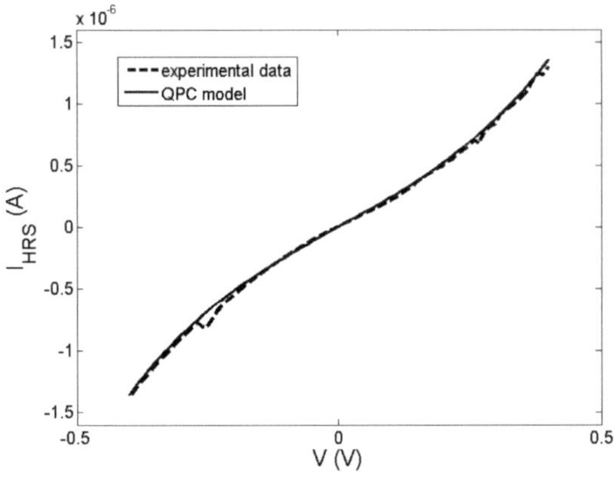

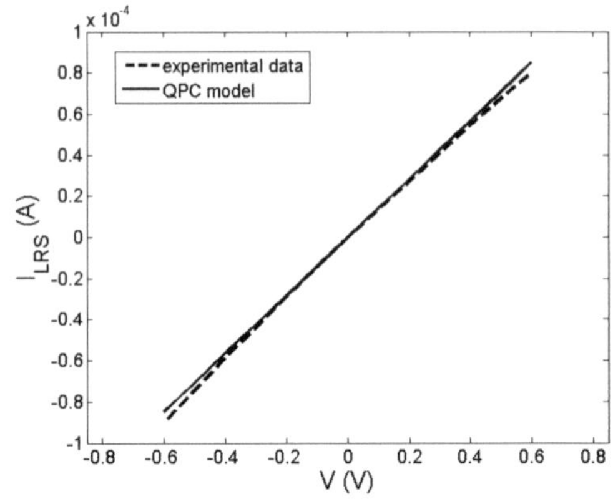

Figure 7. Experimental and theoretical I-V characteristics for the (a) HRS and (b) LRS. The QPC model (Eqs. (28) and (29)) was used for theoretical curves.

agrees with the quantum approach of this model. Miranda et al. showed that Φ has a linear dependence with respect to the temperature given by Avellán et al. [12]:

$$\Phi(T) = \Phi_0 - \gamma T \tag{32}$$

where Φ_0 is a potential height at a T_0 temperature (a given temperature) and γ is a temperature coefficient. For extracting γ, we can use the following expression [12]:

$$\frac{d(\log[I/1A])}{dT}\ln(10) = \alpha\gamma \tag{33}$$

This dependence has been probed in experimental results of HfO_2 cells in Ref. [10].

5. Conclusions

We have presented a classification of physical models for explaining the resistive switching mechanisms in chalcogonides materials. In the literature, there are many physical models proposed for explaining the electron conduction and switching mechanism in specific materials and fabrication process conditions. In the present work, we divide the models according to the number of material dimensions involved on the resistive switching mechanism. The phase change mechanism (PCM) is presented in some Te-alloys used an optical storage devices. In this switching mechanism, the material changes from the amorphous phase to the crystalline phase. Because of the resistivity affects the complete cell volume, the phase change mechanism is considered a 3D model. On the other hand, the modulation of the resistive contact is a 2D model because the defect concentration only affects the metal/insulator interface. This mechanism is presented in some perovskite materials.

http://dx.doi.org/10.5772/intechopen.69025

The principal component of 1D models is the presence of a conduction filament. The filament is formed in a virgin cell by applying a certain threshold voltage. Depending on the cell polarity, the transport mechanisms can be: thermochemical diffusion of oxygen, filament oxidation-reduction or quantum point contact. For unipolar cells (like NiO cells), the resistive switching and the carrier conduction are controlled by the thermochemical diffusion of oxygen in the CF due to the Joule-heating effect. For bipolar cells (like HfO_2), the switching mechanism is related to the oxidation/reduction of CF. If the CF radius at the narrowest part of the CF is in the order of the Fermi wavelength, the transport is driven by the quantum point contact effect, otherwise the transport depends on the oxidation/reduction of CF.

Author details

Luis-Miguel Procel-Moya

Address all correspondence to: lprocel@usfq.edu.ec

Instituto de Micro-Nanoelectrónica, Universidad San Francisco de Quito, Quito, Ecuador

References

[1] Waser R, Wuttig M. Function by defects at the atomic scale - new concepts for non-volatile memories. In: Proceedings of ESSCIRC; IEEE.org, USA. Athens, Greece. 14–18 November 2009. pp. 65-72

[2] Wuttig M, Yamada N. Phase-change materials for rewriteable data storage. Nature Materials. 2007;**6**:824-832

[3] Sawa A. Resistive switching in transition metal oxides. Materials Today. 2008;**11**:28-36

[4] Ielmini D, Nardi F, Cagli C. Physical models of size-dependent nanofilament formation and rupture in NiO resistive switching memories. Nanotechnology. 2011;**22**:254022-1-254022-12

[5] Degraeve R, Fantini A, Raghavan N, Goux L, Clima S, Govoreanu B, Belmonte A, Linten D, Jurczak M. Causes and consequences of the stochastic aspect of filamentary RRAM. Microelectronic Engineering. 2015;**147**:171-175

[6] Guan X, Yu S, Philip Wong H -S. On the switching parameter variation of metal-oxide RRAM—Part I: Physical modeling and simulation methodology. Transactions on Electron Devices. 2012;**59**:1172-1182

[7] Yu S, Guan X, Philip Wong H-S. On the switching parameter variation of metal oxide RRAM—Part II: Model corroboration and device design strategy. IEEE Transactions on Electron Devices. 2012;**59**:1183-1188

[8] Miranda E, Suñé J. Analytic modeling of leakage current through multiple breakdown paths in SiO_2 films. In: IEEE International Proceedings Reliability Physics Symposium. IEEE.org, USA; Orlando. USA. 30 April–3 May 2001. pp. 367-379

[9] Miranda E, Walczyk C, Wenger C, Schroeder T. Model for the resistive switching effect in HfO_2 MIM structures based on the transmission properties of narrow constrictions. IEEE Electron Device Letters. 2010;**31**:609-611

[10] Procel LM, Trojman L, Moreno J, Crupi F, Maccaronio V, Degraeve R, Goux L, Simoen E. Experimental evidence of the quantum point contact theory in the conduction mechanism of bipolar HfO_2-based resistive random access memories. Journal of Applied Physics. 2012;**074509**:074509 (1-5)

[11] Degraeve R, Roussel Ph, Goux L, Wouters D, Kittl J, Altimime L, Jurczak M, Groeseneken G Generic learning of TDDB applied to RRAM for improved understanding of conduction and switching mechanism through multiple filaments. In: IEEE International Electron Devices Meeting. IEEE.org, USA; San Francisco. USA. 6–8 December 2010. pp. 632-635

[12] Avellán A, Miranda E, Schroeder D, Krautschneider W Model for the voltage and temperature dependence of the soft breakdown current in ultrathin gate oxides. Journal of Applied Physics. 2005;**014104**:014104-1-014104-5

Chapter 2

Graphene Oxide-Based Memristor

Geetika Khurana, Nitu Kumar, James F. Scott and Ram S. Katiyar

Additional information is available at the end of the chapter

http://dx.doi.org/10.5772/intechopen.69752

Abstract

A memristor is the memory extension to the concept of resistor. With unique superior properties, memristors have prospective promising applications in non-volatile memory (NVM). Resistive random access memory (RRAM) is a non-volatile memory using a material whose resistance changes under electrical stimulus can be seen as the most promising candidate for next generation memory both as embedded memory and a stand-alone memory due to its high speed, long retention time, low power consumption, scalability and simple structure. Among carbon-based materials, graphene has emerged as wonder material with remarkable properties. In contrast to metallic nature of graphene, the graphene oxide (GO) is good insulating/semiconducting material and suitable for RRAM devices. The advantage of being atomically thin and the two-dimensional of GO permits scaling beyond the current limits of semiconductor technology, which is a key aspect for high-density fabrication. Graphene oxide-based resistive memory devices have several advantages over other oxide materials, such as easy synthesis and cost-effective device fabrication, scaling down to few nanometre and compatibility for flexible device applications. In this chapter, we discuss the GO-based RRAM devices, which have shown the properties of forming free, thermally stable, multi-bit storage, flexible and high on/off ratio at low voltage, which boost up the research and development to accelerate the GO-based RRAM devices for future memory applications.

Keywords: memristor, graphene oxide, forming free, multi-bit storage, flexible devices

1. Introduction

The memristor (contraction for memory resistor) acclaimed as the fourth fundamental circuit element together with already known the capacitor, the inductor and the resistor was theoretically predicted by Chua in 1971 [1]. But it attracted much attention in 2008, when a

TiO_2-based crossbar memory array was developed by the HP Labs, and the cross-point storage element was recognized as the memristor [2]. Recently, a rather deep analysis has been provided concerning memristors [3], which shows conclusively that the memristor is not the long-sought fourth circuit element but the memory extension to the concept of resistor. With unique superior properties, memristors have promising applications in non-volatile memory (NVM), artificial neural networks, programmable logic devices, signal processing and pattern recognition circuits. Random access memory (RAM) is an important form of computer data storage. However, due to the technological and physical limitations imposed by dynamic random access memory (DRAM), static random access memory (SRAM) and flash memory towards low power, small size, fast speed, high density and non-volatility, there is an urgent need of upcoming NVM technologies with low power, high density, high read/write endurance and scalability. In a memristor, a new memory device to solve these problems, a resistive random access memory (RRAM) is a good direction for the development of future memory technology. RRAM is a memory using a material whose resistance changes under electrical stimulus and can be seen as the most promising candidate for next generation memory both as embedded memory and a stand-alone memory due to its high speed, long retention time, low power consumption, scalability and simple structure [4]. Typically, RRAM is a two-terminal device that the switching medium is sandwiched between top and bottom electrodes (**Figure 1**) and the resistance of the switching medium can be modulated by applying electrical signal (current or voltage) to the electrodes. Appropriate value of programming voltage pulse can set the device from high-resistance state (HRS) to low-resistance state (LRS) known as SET or writing process. Similarly, switching back of the device from LRS to HRS using a voltage pulse known as RESET or erase process. Based on the voltage polarity used, RRAM can be categorized into two types: unipolar and bipolar resistive switching [5]. The switching operation is called unipolar, if the SET and RESET processes occur at the same voltage polarity. In the SET process, the current is usually constrained by current compliance. Whereas, the switching is bipolar if the SET and RESET processes occur at reversed polarity of voltages. In both switching modes, two resistance states are distinguished from each other at a small read-out voltage, therefore read operation has no influence on the resistance state. However, the attractive properties of RRAM are low fabrication costs, scalability into the nanometre regime, fast write and read access, low power consumption and low threshold voltages.

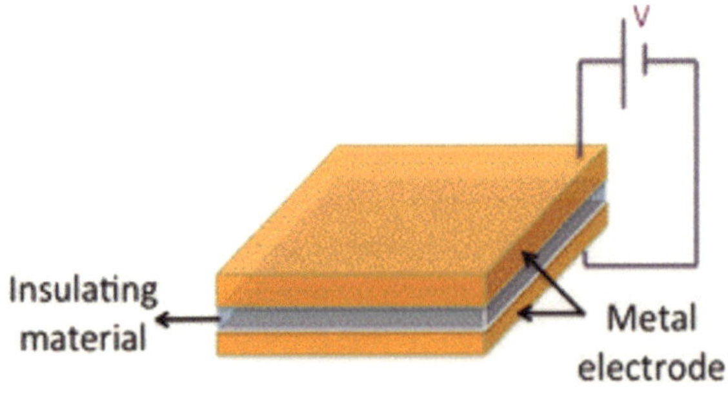

Figure 1. Schematic and electrical configuration of a two-terminal RRAM cell.

The resistive switching effect has been explored until now in several materials including transition metal oxides, perovskite oxides, organic materials and carbon-based materials. Carbon-based materials have been researched extensively as an important class of materials for many years to defeat the technological barriers of conventional semiconductor electronics [6–8]. Previously, the efforts have been made to fabricate the field effect transistor (FET) devices [9, 10] based on carbon materials. Therefore, it is highly demandable to fabricate carbon-based memory devices to integrate logic and memory devices based on same material. This chapter introduces RRAM properties of the carbon compound known as graphene oxide (GO). It is basically a wrinkled two-dimensional carbon sheet with various oxygenated functional groups attached to its basal plane and peripheries, with the thickness of around 1 nm and lateral dimensions varying between a few nanometres and several microns. Graphene oxide has been synthesized by various chemical methods, such as Hummers' method and its modification, Brodie method and Staudenmaier method. In contrast to the metallic nature of graphene, the graphene oxide is good insulating/semiconducting material, which can be readily obtained by oxidizing graphite with strong oxidants.GO sheets are heavily oxygenated, bearing hydroxyl and epoxide functional groups on their basal planes, in addition to carbonyl and carboxyl groups located at the sheet edges. Furthermore, the ability of these sheets to form covalent as well as non-covalent (based on interactions) bonds encourages the fabrication of a wide variety of hybrid structures such as transistors, sensors, optoelectronic and memory devices etc. [11, 12]. The two dimensionality of GO permits scaling beyond the current limits of semiconductor technology, which is a key aspect for high-density fabrication. Out of tremendous applications of graphene oxide, this chapter focuses on the memory device application. Graphene oxide (GO) with an ultrathin thickness is attractive due to its unique physical-chemical properties. GO can be readily obtained through oxidizing graphite in mixtures of strong oxidants, followed by an exfoliation process. The presence of these functional groups makes GO sheets electrically insulating, with characteristics comparable to other thin-layered oxide materials, with the advantage of being atomically thin, which makes GO the perfect candidate for the fabrication of memristive devices [13, 14]. As GO is water soluble which makes it facile to transfer onto any substrate in thin film form by simple methods of spin coating, drop-casting, Langmuir-Blodgett (LB) and vacuum filtration. The as-deposited GO thin films can be further processed into functional devices using standard lithography processes without degrading the film properties [15, 16]. Furthermore, the band structure and electronic properties of GO can be modulated by changing the quantity of chemical functionalities attached to the surface. Therefore, GO is potentially useful for microelectronics production.

2. Status of graphene oxide-based RRAM devices

Graphene oxide-based resistive memory devices have several advantages, such as easy synthesis and cost-effective device fabrication, scaling down to few nanometres and compatibility for flexible device applications. Reliable and reproducible resistive switching behaviour was first reported in graphene oxide thin films prepared by the vacuum filtration method by He et al. in 2009 [17]. They observed very low switching voltages and low on/off ratio of about 20 in

Cu/GO/Pt structure. Soon after that there were many reports published showing high on/off ratios in GO-based RRAM devices [18, 19]. Mechanism for the resistive switching characteristics in GO-based RRAM was found to be due to the oxygen migration, oxygen vacancies and the electrode diffusion [20, 21]. Furthermore, Jeong et al. presented a GO-based memory that can be easily fabricated using a room temperature spin-casting method on flexible substrates and has reliable memory performance in terms of retention and endurance [22]. Resistive switching effect was shown in Ni-doped graphene oxide by Pinto et al. [23]. Transparent non-volatile memory device based on SiOx and graphene was also reported which features high transparency, long retention time and low programming currents [24]. Zhuge et al. reported the forming voltage dependence on GO film thickness and on different top electrodes [20]. Forming process is the application of initial high voltages to the devices to initiate the switching process, which is detrimental to the device structure and operation. Forming-free GO RRAM devices having high on/off ratio with good retention and endurance properties are potential candidates for non-volatile RRAM. Therefore, in this chapter, we will be discussing RRAM properties of the GO-based devices, which are forming free, thermally stable, multi-bit storage, flexible, having high on/off ratio at low operating voltages that boost up the research and development to accelerate the GO-based RRAM devices for future memory applications.

2.1. Graphene oxide-based RRAM devices

Synthesis of graphene oxide presented in this chapter has been carried out by modified Hummers method [25, 26]. In brief, highly oriented pyrolytic graphite (HOPG, 2 g) was oxidized using potassium permanganate ($KMnO_4$, 7 g) in the presence of concentrated H_2SO_4 (50 ml) in ice bath. After the reaction, excess distilled water was added to the solution. With continuous stirring a 30 wt.% of hydrogen peroxide (H_2O_2) was added slowly until the gas evolution had stopped. Further 15 more-minute stirring was done to the resultant mixture, and then it was filtered through nylon membrane. Repeated washing was done by distilled water and 5% HCl solution until the filtrate was neutral. Finally, the obtained dark brown slurry was dried for 24 hour in a vacuum oven at 60°C. A colloidal suspension of GO was prepared in distilled water by sonicating graphite oxide in water for 2 hour. Such a solution of GO was used to fabricate the thin films by spin coating process on ITO/Glass substrate. To construct metal-insulator-metal (MIM) devices, platinum top electrodes with an area of 40 × 40 μm^2 were deposited by DC sputtering utilizing a shadow mask. The schematic representation of fabricated Pt/graphene oxide/imdium-tin oxide (GO/ITO) is shown in **Figure 2**.

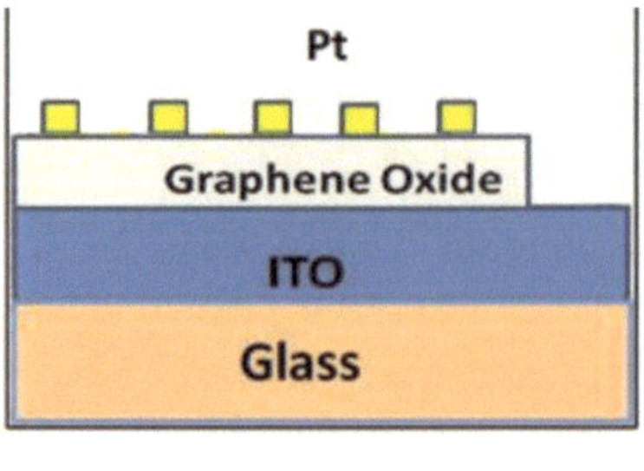

Figure 2. Schematic representation of GO-based MIM devices [26].

To observe the switching characteristics of the device, I-V measurements for the Pt/GO/ITO device at 300 and 500 K were performed as shown in **Figure 3a** and **b**). The Pt/GO/ITO device was found initially in low-resistance state having resistance value of ~40 ohm. **Figure 3** shows that as the positive voltage was increased, a sudden fall in current was observed at a voltage of ~3.2 V indicating abrupt increase in the resistance of the device. This is known as RESET process and device transformed from its initial low-resistance state (LRS) to high-resistance state (HRS) also known as OFF state.

The low-resistance state of GO-based MIM devices once obtained persisted even when the applied voltage was reduced to zero indicating non-volatility. In high-resistance state, when the voltage was swept a sudden increase in current was observed at a voltage of approximately −1.2 V indicating abrupt decrease in the resistance of device and switching from high-resistance state to low-resistance state as shown in **Figure 3a**. This is known as the SET process which switched the MIM device in LRS or ON state. The LRS of device remained preserved even when the applied bias voltage was removed. During this set process, current compliance was kept fixed at 100 mA to avoid the breakdown of GO film due to high current flow in low-resistance state. By repeating the set and reset processes over 100 cycles, it was observed that the reset voltage was larger than the set voltage and spread over a small window of voltage between ~3 and 3.4 V, whereas the set voltage had a spread between approximately −1.2 and −1.8 V. Thus, the device showed a typical bipolar resistive switching (BRS) behaviour with an on/off current ratio of 10^4 over 100 test cycles. Switching characteristics of the device were also studied at elevated temperature of 500 K (as shown in **Figure 3b**). Reduction in the value of reset voltage at 500 K was observed which could be attributed to enhanced diffusivity of oxygen ions at elevated temperature compared to that of room temperature. However, contrary to that we found increment in the set voltage at elevated temperature. Further at high temperature of 500 K, the on/off ratio of the device was found to decrease up to ~10^2 compared to its value at 300 K which was ~10^4; however, this ratio of high- and low-resistance states is sufficient for operation of memory devices. Low- and high-resistance states were stable up to 10^4 seconds and up to 100 cycles indicating good retention and endurance characteristics of the device at elevated temperature of 500 K.

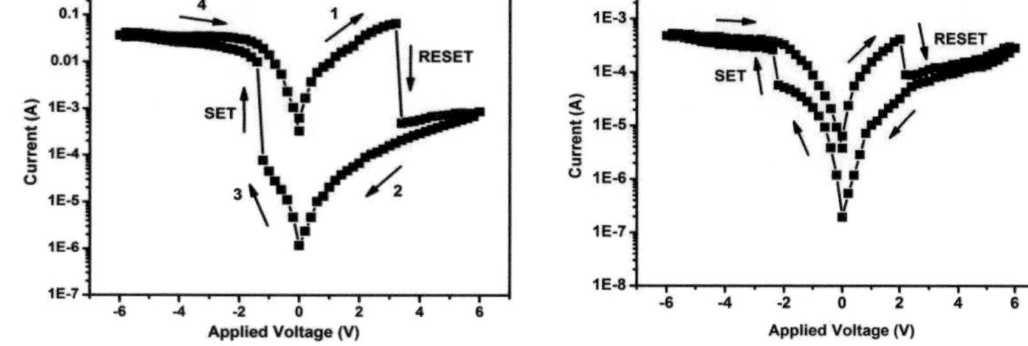

Figure 3. Current-voltage characteristics of the Pt/GO/ITO device at (a) 300 K and (b) 500 K [26].

Based on the conduction mechanism, it was observed that GO device contains conducting paths between top and bottom electrode perhaps due to the presence of oxygen vacancies and electron traps in graphene oxide layer forming electron hopping path [27]. Presence of oxygen vacancies in graphene oxide indicates partial reduction of GO and dominance of sp^2 character over sp^3 character providing high conducting channel in GO film and initial low-resistance state without any forming process. In Pt/GO/ITO devices, the bottom electrode ITO acts as a source/reservoir of oxygen ions [28]. To ascertain the presence of sp^2 and sp^3 characters of carbon, Raman spectroscopy measurements were carried out on the Pt/GO/ITO devices both in LRS and HRS and are shown in **Figure 4**. As can be seen in **Figure 4** that in case of as-grown device and the device in LRS, the presence of G peak signifying the sp^2 character is larger in intensity compared to the same peak when the device was switched into HRS by the application of suitable bias voltage. This indicates that the sp^2 character dominates in LRS. While in case of HRS, the sp^2 character is suppressed. These RRAM devices based on GO layer fabricated by a simple process of spin coating show a forming free bipolar resistive switching (BRS) in Pt/GO/ITO structure with high on/off ratio of 10^4 exhibiting good retention and endurance properties at room and elevated temperatures.

2.2. Graphene oxide-based multi-layer structures for high-density data storage

Organic memory devices have gained much attention as future information and storage components owing to their low weight, flexibility, inexpensive and facile fabrication methods [29, 30]. Recent reports have shown that organic memory devices have been developed through layer stacking [31] and using advanced memory architectures [32–35]. However, the most organic memory devices are suffering with slow switching [36] and low storage capacity [37, 38]. RRAM

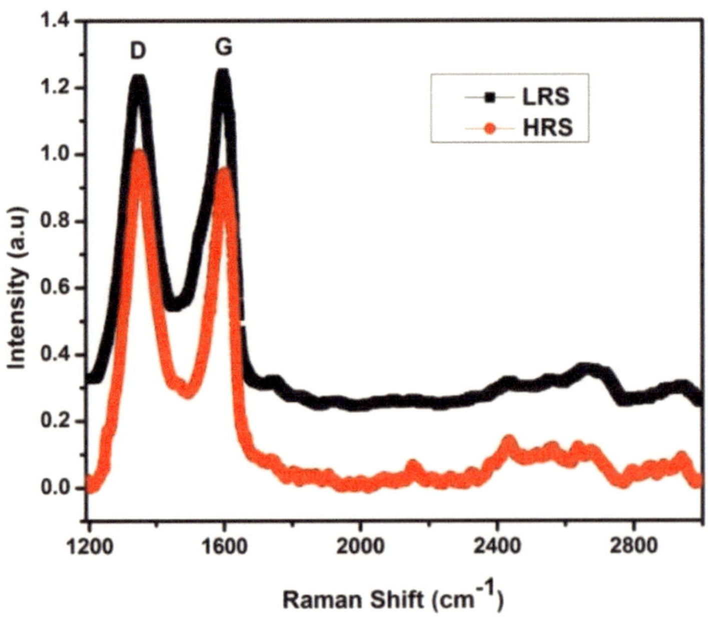

Figure 4. Raman spectra for Pt/GO/ITO device in LRS (upper curve) and HRS (lower curve) [26].

performance of the organic memories can be greatly enhanced by forming hybrid organic structures [39], organic/inorganic composites [40] or by dispersing nanomaterials [41, 42]. Among all other organic polymers, polyvinylidene fluoride (PVDF) was used due to its non-reactive nature, better heat resistance, flexibility and low weight. As mentioned above, hybrid structures of organic memory devices provide enhanced memory characteristics; therefore, heterostructure of PVDF was fabricated using a charge trapping element in it. In this study, reduced graphene oxide nanoflakes (GR) were used as a charge trapping layer owing to their unique chemical structure and exceptional properties [6, 43–47] that make it ideal for charge trapping [48] and storage [49] for memory applications. Also, the defects (vacancy, interstitial sites, etc.) present in GR also work as the charge trapping nodes [50]. Tri-layer structure was fabricated by assembling graphene nanoflakes (GR) between PVDF polymer layers [51] through spin coating process on ITO/glass substrate as shown in **Figure 5**. DC sputtering was used to deposit platinum top electrode having area (100 μm × 100 μm) through shadow mask to obtain devices from the stacked structure.

As the voltage was increased, multi-stage SET and RESET were observed in positive and negative polarities, respectively, as shown in **Figure 6a**. This process was repeatable for a number of cycles, which established the device as a non-volatile memory with multilevel conductance states. The multilevel SET process occurring in the device can be due to multi-channels formation as trapping sites in graphene bear different threshold potentials. Electrons occupied these trapping sites even if the applied voltage is removed, thus preserving the non-volatile nature of the device in ON state. When negative voltage is applied to the device, current firstly increases with voltage due to the presence of trapped charges in the nodes. At a particular negative bias, current jumps to low value due to the de-trapping of electrons from the trapping nodes which initiates the breaking of conducting channels. Further at a particular negative bias, when most of the electrons de-trapped and ejected back to ITO, the conducting path completely disrupts and the device transits to OFF state bearing high resistance. The multi-channel RESET process occurring in the device is also due to the same mechanism as discussed in the SET process. In brief, it may be due to the breaking of multi-channels at different potentials. Reports have shown that the intermediate stage present in the device revealing multi-level switching is due to the formation of multi-filaments [52] having different threshold potentials [53]. The device

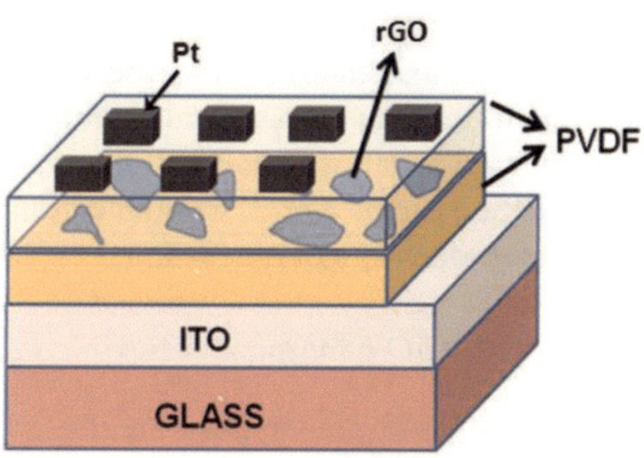

Figure 5. Schematic diagram of the layer-by-layer fabricated Pt/PVDF/rGO/PVDF/ITO memory devices. Top electrode of platinum (Pt) having area 100 × 100 μm^2 was deposited using DC sputtering [51].

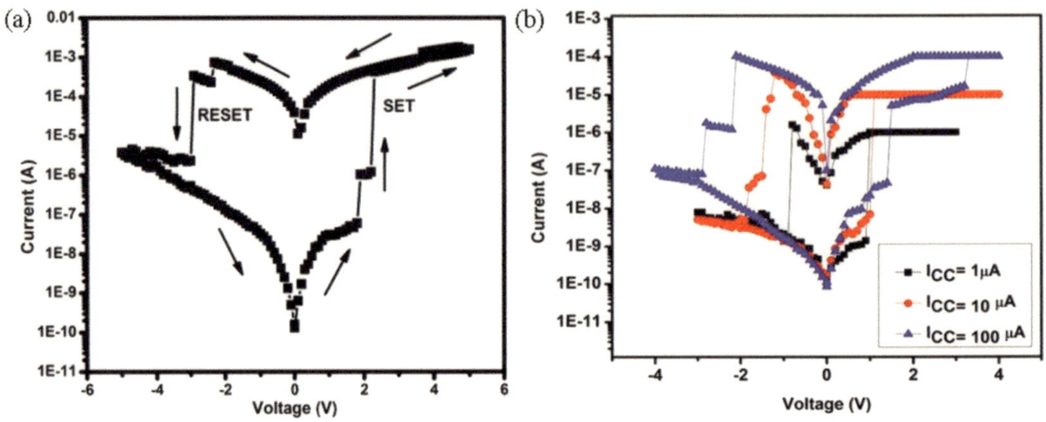

Figure 6. Typical I-V characteristic curves plotted in semi-logarithmic scale of Pt/PVDF/rGO/PVDF/ITO device (a) showing the presence of intermediate state. (b) Under different compliance currents of 1, 10 and 100 μA showing different low-resistance states corresponding to the compliance current applied [51].

was further subjected to different compliance currents of 1, 10 and 100 μA during the SET process and correspondingly obtained different low-resistance states as shown in **Figure 6b**.

When the highest value of ICC was imposed, the device was observed in lowest resistance state. However, the HRS value for different ICC was almost the same. All four different states including one HRS and three LRS were observed in the device. It was proposed that with the highest compliance current applied during SET process, maximum number of trapping nodes are filled and hence maximum number of conductive channels are formed resulting in the lowest resistance state, while with the application of the lowest compliance current, small number of trapping nodes are filled having less number of conducting channels, leading to higher resistance state. To observe the performance and stability of the memory device, its endurance and retention properties were studied. **Figure 7a** represents the endurance characteristics of the device for all the four resistance states tested against number of cycles. As can be seen from **Figure 7a**, the four different states including one HRS and three LRS (LRS1, LRS2 and LRS3) were stable with no overlapping of resistances tested over the 150 number of cycles. **Figure 7b** shows the retention properties observed in the device where the resistance of all four states were measured using a read voltage of 0.1 V over a period of 10^4 seconds. The graph shows well-differentiated resistance states of HRS and three LRS with no degradation in resistance values over the long time. These measurements for retention and endurance for the device showed that it has well performance and good stability. This tri-layer structure fabricated by simple spin coating method can be seen as a potential candidate for future memory devices qualifying the need for high-density storage media.

2.3. Graphene oxide composite with ZnO nanorods for flexible memory devices

Flexible RRAM devices have shown good potential for bendable memory systems [54–58]. These memories are in much demand due to the qualities of inexpensive, low weight, portability and user-friendly interfaces over conventional rigid silicon technology [59]. The substrates for flexible memories could not bear high temperatures used in growth techniques, this limitation

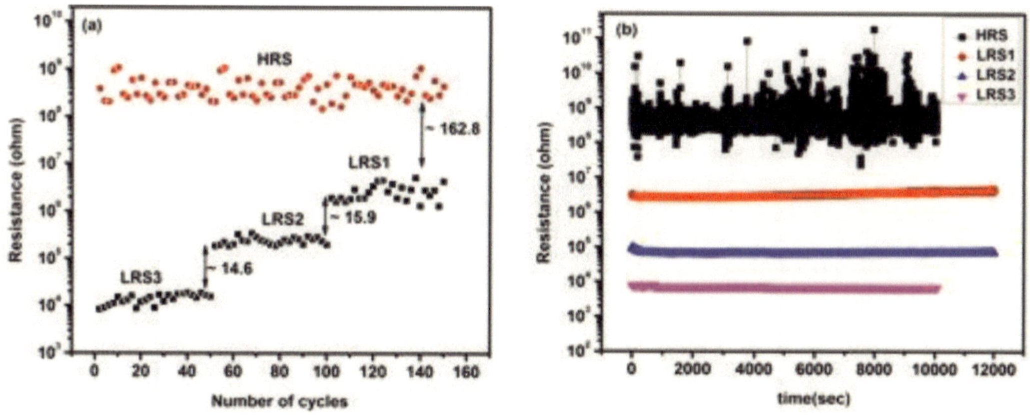

Figure 7. Resistances of the device in all LRS and HRS under different compliance currents of 1, 10 and 100 μA with read voltage of 0.1 V. (a) Endurance properties over 150 cycles with enough margin between the states. (b) Retention characteristics over 10^4 seconds for all four states [51].

demands for the need for materials which can be grown on these substrates at room temperature. Obeying this condition, GO is readily oxidizable and water soluble, which qualifies to be fabricated in thin films on flexible substrates at room/moderate temperatures. There are reports which have shown that integration of nanomaterials into oxides is helpful in enhancing the resistive switching properties of the devices [60–62]. In this work [63], ZnO nanorods (ZNs) were grown in horizontal direction on GO sheets to maximize the contact area between the nanorods and GO sheets [64, 65]. The consequence of this was observed in significant reduction in switching voltages in comparison to GO alone. The solution of GOZNs was spin coated to ITO-coated polyethylene terephthalate (indium-tin oxide on polyester film (ITOPET)) substrates to fabricate the films. Initially, the Al/GOZNs/ITOPET devices were in high-resistance state (HRS). In the very first cycle, a forming voltage around 5 V with current compliance of 2 mA was applied to activate these devices. Device showed SET and RESET processes on positive and negative voltages having non-volatile nature. To investigate the effect of ZNs addition into the GO matrix, another device Al/GO/ITOPET was fabricated following the same process except the incorporation of ZNs in it, and this device showed comparatively higher values of SET and RESET voltages.

I-V measurements performed on both devices, shown in **Figure 8**, have clearly shown that SET and RESET voltages in the device containing ZNs were severely reduced to approximately half in comparison to the device containing no ZNs. To further understand the effect of changing ZNs ratio in GO matrix on resistive switching, the I-V characteristics of different compositions (10:1, 5:1, 3:1 and 2:1) were studied and found that 3:1 was the best among all. In Al/GOZNs/ITOPET devices, we propose that the conducting filament formation during the SET process is due to the oxygen vacancies. Oxygen concentration gradient exists at the interface of GO, and Al has high oxidation tendency. Therefore, oxygen ions from GO move towards and react with Al forming a new interfacial Al oxide layer [66]; also this process induces the oxygen vacancies into the GO region. With the positive bias is applied to the top electrode, these induced oxygen vacancies are deeply inserted into the GO matrix and providing the conductive paths during the SET process. With the negative polarity these oxygen vacancies are pushed back resulting

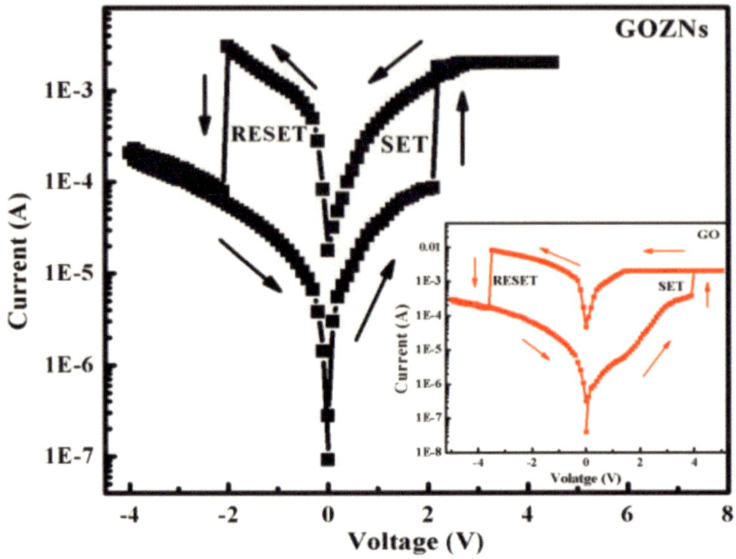

Figure 8. Typical I-V switching characteristics in Al/GOZNs/ITOPET devices. Inset shows the I-V characteristics for Al/GO/ITOPET device [63].

in rupture of the conducting channel during the RESET process. But with the incorporation of ZNs into the GO matrix, significant reduction in the switching voltages was observed and this is due to the desorption/adsorption of oxygen at the interface of GO and ZNs, which stimulates the formation/rupture of conducting paths on the application of suitable polarity voltages. This mechanism based on oxygen vacancies is well supported by the X-ray photoemission spectroscopy (XPS) measurements of these samples shown in **Figure 9**.

Figure 9a is the XPS graph for C1s peak in GO and GOZNs samples. The C1s graph of GO contains sp^2 and C—O—C peaks, whereas for the GOZNs sample, the C—O—C peak has disappeared having only sp^2 peak in the spectra. The XPS study showed the reduction in oxygen content with the disappeared C—O—C peak for the GO matrix having ZNs, which demonstrates that GO has become comparatively less resistive having sp^2 character dominant. However, ZNs are well known for chemisorption of oxygen at its periphery and it can be evidenced by the fitted O2 peak for O1s spectra in **Figure 9b**. Also, the peak positions for these O1 and O2 in GOZNs sample were found to be little shifted towards lower energy. Furthermore, a noticeable increment in the intensity of O2 peak was also observed in GOZNs in comparison to ZNs. The O1s peak was also found to be shifted to lower binding energy due to the additional oxygen absorbed by ZNs as shown in **Figure 9b** [67]. Further, the presence of excess oxygen can also be clearly observed in **Figure 9c** which shows the shift in the Zn 2p peak towards lower energy in GOZNs sample in comparison to ZNs sample [67]. The performance of flexible electronic devices can be tested through flexibility and mechanical endurance measurements. The flexibility measurements were done on the Al/GOZNs/ITOPET devices and the value of resistance was plotted as a function of bending radii as shown in **Figure 10a**. The resistance was measured up to the maximum bending radius of 4 mm and amazingly found that the LRS and HRS were widely separated and can be well distinguished. The mechanical

http://dx.doi.org/10.5772/intechopen.69752

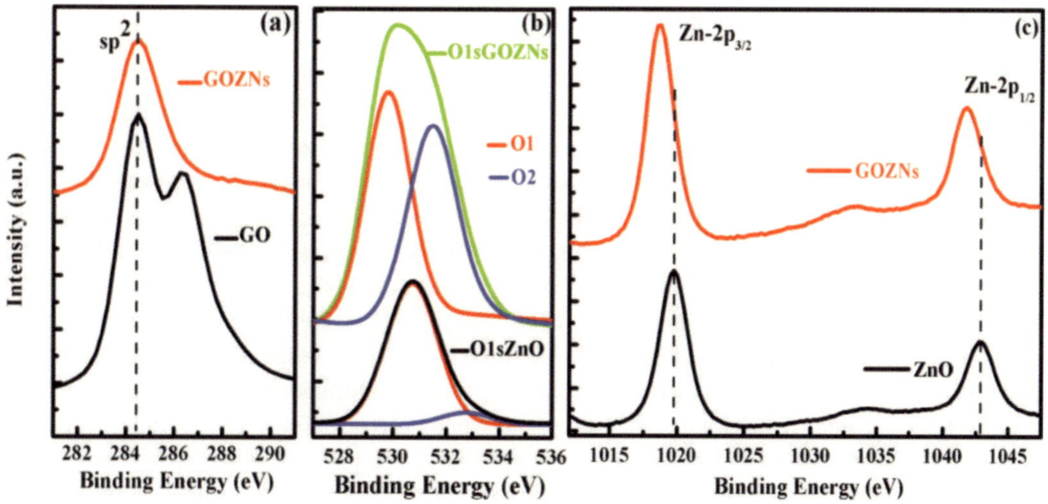

Figure 9. (a) Comparative XPS spectra of GO and GOZNs for C1S peak. (b) XPS spectra of ZNs and GOZns showing O1S peak resolved into two components O1 and O2. (c) Zn2p spectra of ZNs and GOZNs samples [63].

reliability test was also performed by constantly flexing the device many times to the bending radius of 6 mm and the resistance was plotted against number of bending cycles as shown in **Figure 10b**. The HRS and LRS resistances show no noticeable degradation even up to 1000 times of repeated bending. The measurements performed on the Al/GOZNs/ITOPET device show excellent flexibility and mechanical endurance results and provide the data which show that the devices are capable for flexible memory applications. This study shows that the devices based on ZNs embedded in GO are potential candidate for future flexible non-volatile memory applications.

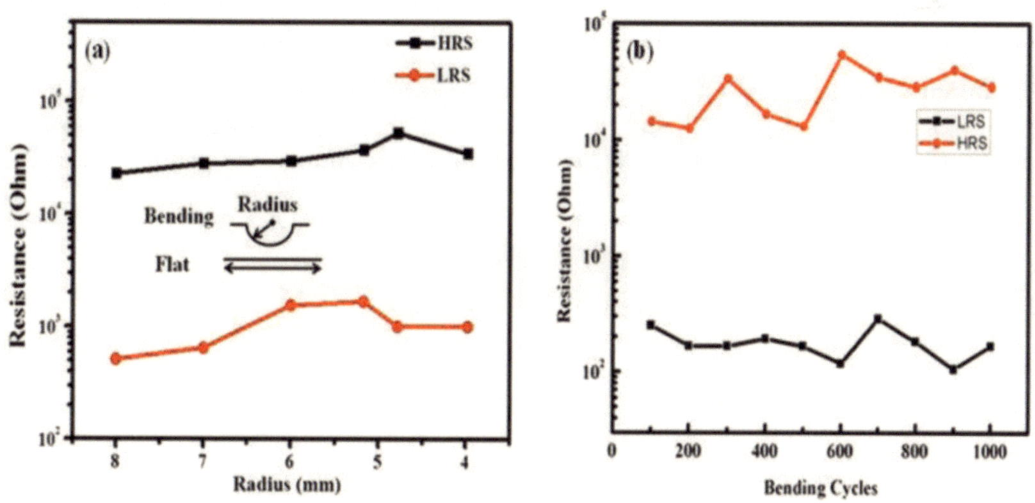

Figure 10. (a) Flexibility test for various bending radius on Al/GOZNs/ITOPET RRAM device. (b) Mechanical bending endurance of device at bending radius of 6 mm on Al/GOZNs/ITOPET RRAM device [63].

2.4. Nanoparticles embedded graphene oxide RRAM devices for low operating voltages and high on/off ratio

RRAM devices based on oxide have good switching characteristics, but still there are two major downsides with these memories: first one is the need of an initial forming voltage [68–70] to initiate the switching mechanism, which is detrimental to device performance, however, this issue can be resolved by manipulating the deposition and growth process and the other problem is the uncontrolled position of conductive channels formation during repetitive applied bias. To address the problem of initial forming in graphene oxide (GO)-based devices, we adopted the method of electrophoresis to deposit the device structure [71]. Reports have shown that the graphene oxide films grown by electrophoresis are conducted or reduced in nature [72, 73].As the oxygen functional groups attached to its basal plane get removed, the graphene oxide films become semiconducting having localized π-π electrons network. These functional groups can be eliminated by passing the current during electrophoresis deposition process, resulting GO to be reduced or semiconducting in nature. In this study, the films were deposited by electrophoresis and as deposited films were found to be in low-resistance state; therefore, no high forming voltages were required to initiate the switching process. To resolve the problem of confined conducting channels, we have to understand that there is random formation of conductive filaments at nanoscale with applied bias in un-doped films, and it is hard to confine their position precisely. The reports for RRAM devices based on transition metal oxides infused with metallic nanoparticles have shown enhancement in switching properties with the addition of metal nanoparticles [61, 74]. The present study is focused on improved switching characteristics of graphene oxide films embedded with gold nanoparticles (Au Nps), which helps to confine the conducting filaments during numerous sweep cycles. A colloidal suspension of GO with Au Nps was obtained by sonication. The films were deposited by electrophoresis process using the sonicated GO with Au Nps (GOAu) solution [71]. Electrophoresis was performed using a home-built assembly with a pair of ITO/glass as electrodes and a Keithley current source. GOAu films were deposited at room temperature by varying the current value ranging from 0.1 to 1.0 mA for 1–10 minutes having 1.5 cm distance between the electrodes as shown in **Figure 11**.

The thickness of deposited GOAu film was measured to be ~85 nm. The GO layers were in the size range of 3–5 μm and Au Nps were found in the range of 10–15 nm. The switching matrix constitutes the stack of GO layers with Au Nps. Aluminium (Al) top electrodes

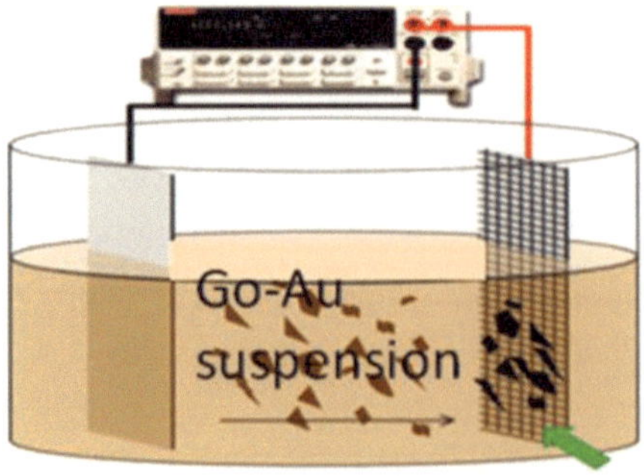

Figure 11. GO films grown by electrophoresis process.

were deposited by thermal evaporation method through a shadow mask having diameter of 200 μm. Thus, the device structure formed was Al/GOAu/ITO/glass. Another sample was also fabricated using GOAu solution by spin coating on ITO/glass substrate for XPS study. To know the chemical composition of as-grown GOAu films by electrophoresis, XPS study was performed as shown in **Figure 12**. These XPS measurements were done to illustrate the amount of oxygen functional groups present in electrodeposited GOAu films (**Figure 12a**) and spin coated GOAu films (**Figure 12b**) (XPS for spin coating films was performed to compare the amount of oxy groups). The peaks corresponding to C1s spectra as depicted in **Figure 12** are C—C, C—O and C=O which are at respective binding energies of 284.6, 286.5 and 288.4 eV. In electrodeposited film, the C—O peak has low intensity in comparison to the C—C peak which shows that the oxygen content is less in the film. The lower oxygen content or presence of oxygen vacancies is favourable for as-deposited films to be in low-resistance and hence eliminating the need of forming voltages. Inset of **Figure 12a** shows the presence of Au $4f^{7/2}$and Au $4f^{5/2}$ peaks at their respective binding energies of 84 and 87.5 eV.

To demonstrate the effect of Au Nps in GO devices, another film of GO having no Au Nps on ITO/glass by electrophoresis keeping same deposition parameters having Al top electrodes (Al/GO/ITO) was fabricated and measured its switching characteristics. **Figure 13a** shows typical I-V switching characteristics of Al/GO/ITO (inset) and Al/GOAu/ITO devices, respectively. The initial resistance of the devices was found 3.5×10^4 Ω with Au Nps and 1.3×10^6 Ω without Au Nps. Therefore, the initial resistance of the device incorporated with Au Nps was found to be 100 times lower than that of the pristine GO device. The on/off ratio between LRS and HRS in pristine GO devices is very low and that too at high voltages. GOAu devices have enhanced on/off ratio at very low switching voltages as compared to pristine GO devices which is due to the presence of Au Nps, which are working as charge trapping centres.

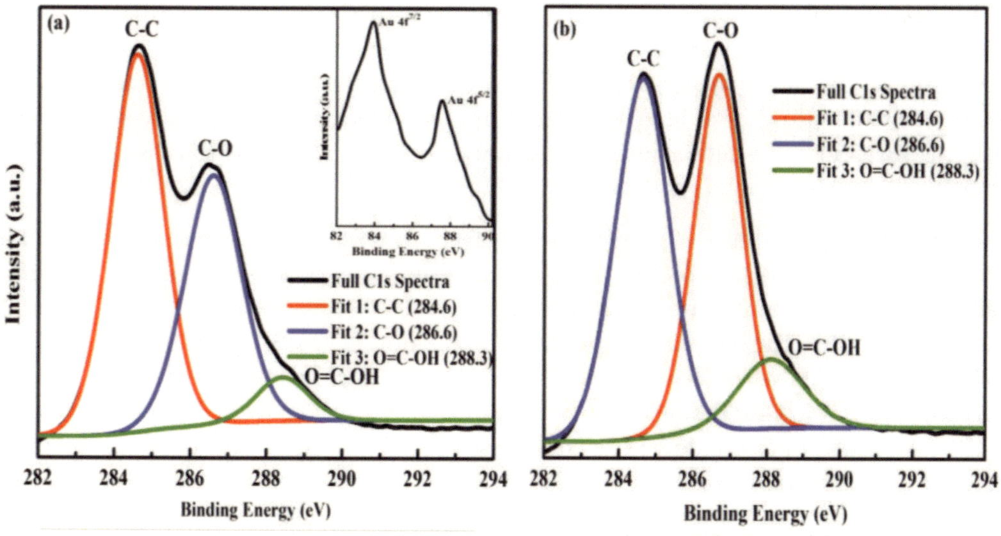

Figure 12. (a) XPS spectra for C1s peak of GOAu film grown by electrophoresis. Inset shows Au peaks for the GOAu film. (b) C1s peak of spin-coated GOAu film [71].

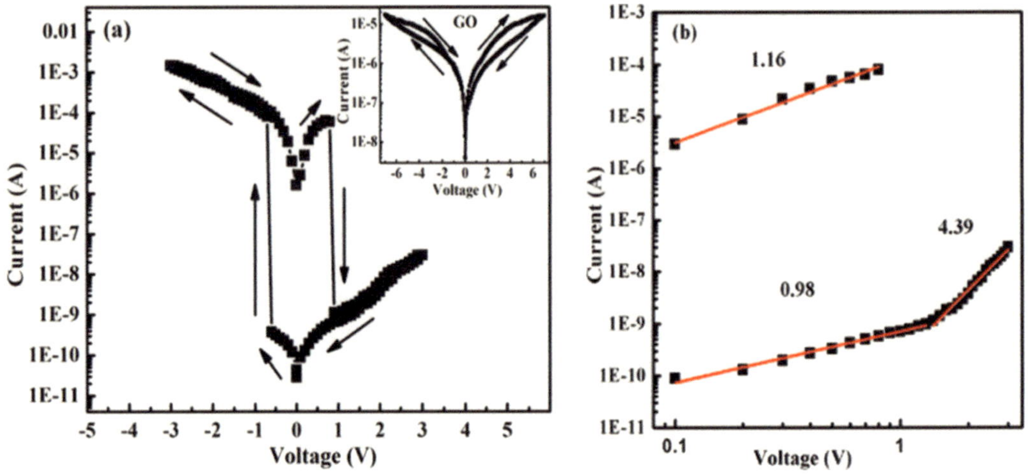

Figure 13. (a) Typical I-V characteristics of the Al/GOAu/ITO device in semi-log scale; inset shows I-V characteristics for the Al/GO/ITO device. (b) log-log I-V plot for the GOAu device [71].

The slope of the I-V curve in LRS was found to be ~1 as shown in **Figure 13b**; however, this linear current-voltage relationship need not be ohmic: It can be Schottky-limited conduction in the Simmons' limit of short electron mean free paths [75],while in the high voltage regime of HRS, the slope was found to be ~4.4, which reveals that a strong space charge limited current (SCLC) mechanism also known as trapped charge limited current (TCLC) mechanism is prevailing in the device [76]. The TCLC behaviour of the films is in agreement with the presence of Au Nps in the films, which are working as charge trapping centres. Hence the charges get trapped in one voltage polarity transiting the device to HRS and detrapped in the opposite polarity rendering back the device to LRS again. Therefore, the device shows bipolar switching behaviour exhibiting trapping/detrapping mechanism. GO sheets have different types of defects, such as oxygen vacancies, dislocations etc. [77, 78]. The defects and trapping nodes present in GO sheets play a significant role in switching behaviour. Initially, the device was in LRS due to the presence of large number of oxygen vacancies and the Au Nps. The device performed well in both states showing retention, endurance and statistical distribution over different cells as shown in **Figure 14a–c**.

As discussed above, Au Nps dispersed in GO layers trap the charge, resulting in capacitive behaviour of the devices. In order to test this scenario, capacitance-voltage (C-V) measurements were carried out. **Figure 15a** and **b** shows the C-V curves of the Al/GO/ITO and Al/GOAu/ITO devices. The measured capacitance was found to be ~3.4 pF in LRS and ~11.2 pF in HRS in GO device, whereas it was ~9 pF in LRS and ~350 pF in HRS in the GOAu device. It was observed that in both the resistance states, capacitance values were increased by a factor of ~10 in HRS/LRS in GOAu devices in comparison to GO devices, which is mainly due to the charge trapping process by Au Nps. In GO matrix having Au Nps, this can be explained as follows: the array of Au Nps induces the coupling capacitance and the trapping energy levels are set by the work function of Au Nps.

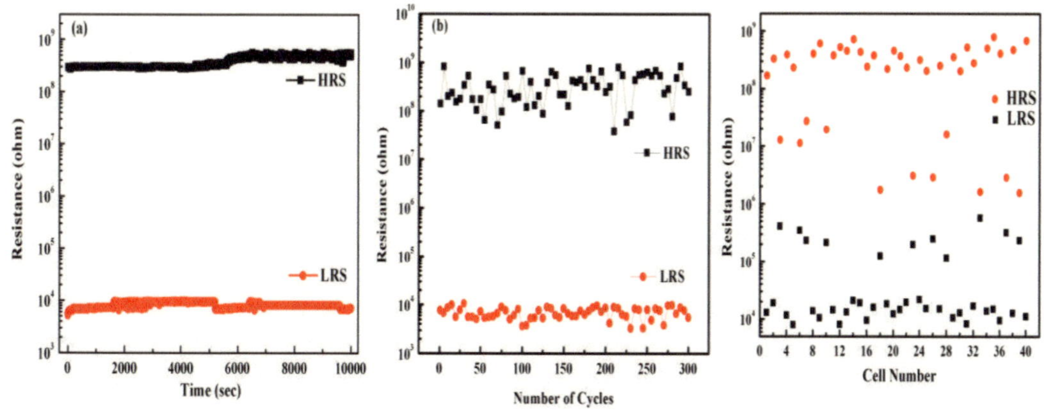

Figure 14. (a) Retention, (b) endurance properties and (c) statistical distribution over different cells of GOAu device in LRS and HRS [71].

Followed by an initial random charging, the charge carriers around a single Au Np may increase due to trapping process, which results in increasing the capacitive coupling and finally increases the coulomb repulsion. Au Nps embedded in GO matrix act as small capacitors having large capacitance due to their big surface/volume area and the associated interfacial polarization. An additional barrier will be created by these metal-island capacitors which prevent the movement of electrons in the matrix and the charge transfer through these small metal-islands, below a particular threshold voltage gets blocked (charges get trapped) leading to an increase in resistance as well. Therefore, in GOAu devices, achieving such a huge resistance in HRS can be attributed to the coulomb blockade effect imparted by the Au Nps which is associated to the quantum effect of metal nanoparticles [79, 80].

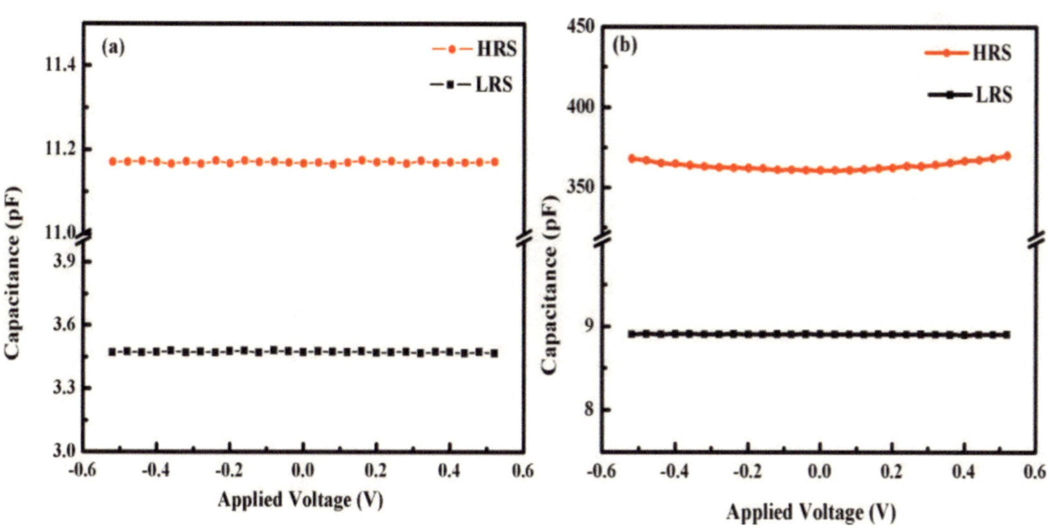

Figure 15. C-V curves of (a) GO and (b) GOAu devices in LRS and HRS [71].

3. Conclusions

In summary, graphene oxide is a promising material for RRAM devices due to its high scalability and unique physical-chemical properties. Fabrication of GO and its films, composites and heterostructures are very cost effective and opens up the direction for commercialization. Showing forming-free behaviour is an excellent property of GO devices over other oxide-based devices that require initial high voltages to start the switching process. Multi-level switching in GO-based heterostructures has the potential of high-density data storage, which is the need of future non-volatile memories. Flexibility and mechanical endurance observed in GO-based composite RRAM devices have prospects in portable and flexible devices which is advantageous over the rigid silicon technology. Gold nanoparticles embedded in GO have shown enhanced switching properties with very high on/off resistance ratio and very low switching voltages, which are suitable for low power resistive memory devices. The mechanism underlying the graphene oxide-based memories is the formation of conductive filaments due to the roles played by oxygen ions and vacancies. Therefore, GO-based RRAM devices have enough potential to become one of the important non-volatile memories due to their encouraging properties of forming free, multi-bit data storage and low power flexible devices. However, further research is still needed towards scaling of these devices below 10 nm node and that too having fast switching speeds to establish graphene oxide-based non-volatile resistive devices achieve a niche in memory industry.

Acknowledgements

The authors acknowledge the financial support from DOD Grant (AFOSR-FA9550-16-1-0295) and IFN-NSF Grant (EPS-01002410) for travel support.

Author details

Geetika Khurana[1*], Nitu Kumar[1], James F. Scott[2,3] and Ram S. Katiyar[1]

*Address all correspondence to: geetkhurana84@gmail.com

1 University of Puerto Rico, San Juan, Puerto Rico

2 Department of Chemistry, University of St Andrews, St Andrews, UK

3 Department of Physics, University of St Andrews, St Andrews, UK

References

[1] Chua LO. Memristor – The missing circuit element. IEEE Transactions Circuit Theory CT-18. 1971;**18**:507-519

[2] Strukov DB, Snider GS, Stewart DR, Williams RS. The missing memristor found. Nature. 2008;**453**:80-83

[3] Shan SD, Sheng CY, Xian CZ, Jun L, Young S. Toward the complete relational graph of fundamental circuit elements. Chinese Physics B. 2015;**24**:068402-6

[4] Chang TC, Chang KC, Tsai TM, Chu TJ, Sze SM. Resistance random access memory. Materials Today. 2016;**19**:254-264

[5] Waser R, Aono M. Nanoionics-based resistive switching memories. Nature Mater. 2007; **6**:833-840

[6] Novoselov KS, Geim AK, Morozov SV, Jiang D, Zhang Y, Dubonos SV, Grigorieva IV, Firsov AA. Electric field effect in atomically thin carbon films. Science. 2004;**306**:666-669

[7] Rueckes T, Kim K, Joselevich E, Tseng G, Cheung C, Lieber C. Carbon nanotube-based nonvolatile random access memory for molecular computing. Science. 2000;**289**:94-97

[8] Avouris P, Chen ZH, Perebeinos V, Carbon-based electronics. Nature Nanotechnology. 2007;**2**:1748-3387

[9] Wang XR, Ouyang YJ, L X. Li, Wang HL, Guo J, Dai HJ. Room temperature all-semiconducting sub-10-nm graphene nanoribbon field-effect transistors. Physical Review Letters. 2008;**100**:0031-9007

[10] Burghard M, Klauk H, Kern K. Carbon-based field-effect transistors for nanoelectronics. Advanced Materials. 2009;**21**:0935-9648

[11] Mao S, Cui S, Lu G, Yu K, Wen Z, Chen J. Tuning gas-sensing properties of reduced graphene oxide using tin oxide nanocrystals. Journal of Materials Chemistry. 2012;**22**: 11009-11013

[12] Zhang XQ, Feng YY, Tang SD, Feng W. Preparation of a graphene oxide phthalocyanine hybrid through strong pi-pi interactions. Carbon. 2010;**48**:211-216

[13] Liu J, Wang R, Cui L, Tang J, Liu Z, Kong Q, Yang W, Gooding J. Using molecular level modification to tune the conductivity of graphene papers. Journal of Physical Chemistry C. 2012;**116**:17939-17946

[14] Park S, An J, Potts JR, Velamakanni A, Murali S, Ruoff RS. Hydrazine-reduction of graphite- and graphene oxide. Carbon. 2011;**49**:3019-3023

[15] Eda G, Fanchini G, Chhowalla M. Large-area ultrathin films of reduced graphene oxide as a transparent and flexible electronic material. Nature Nanotechnology. 2008;**3**:270-274

[16] Cote LJ, Kim F, Huang JX. Langmuir-Blodgett assembly of graphite oxide single layers. Journal of the American Chemical Society. 2009;**131**:1043-1049

[17] He CL, Zhuge F, Zhou XF, Li M, Zhou GC, Liu YW, Wang JZ, Chen B, Su WJ, Liu ZP, Wu YH, Cui P, Li R-W. Nonvolatile resistive switching in graphene oxide thin films. Applied Physics Letters. 2009;**95**:232101-232103

[18] Kim I, Siddik M, Shin J, Biju KP, Jung S, Hwang H. Low temperature solution-processed graphene oxide/$Pr_{0.7}Ca_{0.3}MnO_3$ based resistive-memory device. Applied Physics Letters. 2011;**99**:042101

[19] Yi M, Cao Y, Ling H, Du Z, Wang L, Yang T, Fan Q, Xie L, Huang W. Temperature dependence of resistive switching behaviors in resistive random access memory based on graphene oxide film. Nanotechnology. 2014;**25**:185202-185207

[20] Zhuge F, Hu B, He C, Zhou X, Liu Z, Li RW. Mechanism of nonvolatile resistive switching in graphene oxide thin films. Carbon. 2011;**4**(9):3796-3802

[21] Wang Z, Tjoa V, Wu L, Liu WJ, Fang Z, Tran XA, Wei J, Zhu WG, Yud HY. Mechanism of different switching directions in graphene oxide based RRAM. Journal of the Electrochemical Society. 2012;**159**(6):K177-K182

[22] Jeong HY, Kim JY, Kim JW, Hwang JO, Kim JE, Lee JY, Yoon TH, Cho BJ, Kim SO, Ruoff RS, Choi SY. Graphene oxide thin films for flexible nonvolatile memory applications. Nano Letters. 2010;**10**:4381-4386

[23] Pinto S, Krishna R, Dias C, Pimentel G, Oliveira GNP, Teixeira JM, Aguiar P, Titus E, Gracio J, Ventura J, Araujo JP. Resistive switching and activity-dependent modifications in Ni-doped graphene oxide thin films. Applied Physics Letters. 2012;**101**:063104

[24] Yao J, Lin J, Dai Y, Ruan G, Yan Z, Li L, Zhong L, Natelson D, Tour JM. Highly transparent nonvolatile resistive memory devices from silicon oxide and graphene. Nature Communications. 2012;**3**:1101-5. DOI: 10.1038/ncomms2110

[25] Hummers WS, Offeman RE. Preparation of graphite oxide. Journal of the American Chemical Society. 1958;**80**:1339-1339

[26] Khurana G, Misra P, Katiyar RS. Forming free RS in graphene oxide thin film for thermally stable nonvolatile memory applications. Journal of Applied Physics. 2013;**114**:124508-124504

[27] Joung D, Chunder A, Zhai L, Khondaker SI. Space charge limited conduction with exponential trap distribution in reduced graphene oxide sheets. Applied Physics Letters. 2010;**97**:093105-093103

[28] Younis A, Chu D, Li S. Oxygen level: the dominant of resistive switching characteristics in cerium oxide thin films. Journal of Physics D: Applied Physics. 2012;**45**:355101-355106

[29] Sekitani T, Yokota T, Zschieschang U, Klauk H, Bauer S, Takeuchi K, Takamiya M, Sakurai T, Someya T. Organic nonvolatile memory transistors for flexible sensor arrays. Science. 2009;**326**:1516-1519

[30] Ling QD, Liaw DJ, Zhu C, Chan DS, Kang E, Neoh K. Polymer electronic memories: Materials, devices and mechanisms. Progress in Polymer Science. 2008;**33**:917-1012

[31] Kwan WL, Tseng RJ, Wu W, Pei Q, Yang Y. Stackable resistive memory device using photo cross-linkable copolymer. IEEE International Electron Devices. Meeting. (IEDM Tech. Digest 10-12 Dec 2007); pp. 237-240

[32] Cho B, Kim T, Song S, Ji Y, Jo M, Hwang H, Jung GY, Lee T. Rewritable switching of one diode-one resistor nonvolatile organic memory devices. Advanced Materials. 2010;**22**:1228-1232

[33] Song S, Cho B, Kim T, Ji Y, Jo M, Wang G, Choe M, Kahng YH, Hwang H, Lee T. Three-dimensional integration of organic resistive memory devices. Advanced Materials. 2010;**22**:5048-5052

[34] Asadi K, Leeuw DM, Boer B, Blom PW. Organic non-volatile memories from ferroelectric phase-separated blends. Nature Materials. 2008;**7**:547-550

[35] Cho B, Song S, Ji Y, Kim T, Lee T. Organic resistive memory devices: Performance enhancement, integration, and advanced architectures. Advanced Functional Materials. 2011;**21**:2806-2829

[36] Kim T, Oh S, Lee J, Choi H, Wang G, Park J, Kim D, Hwang H, Lee T. Effect of metal ions on the switching performance of polyfluorene-based organic non-volatile memory devices. Organic Electronics. 2010;**11**:109-114

[37] Ma LP, Liu J, Yang Y. Organic electrical bistable devices and rewritable memory cells. Applied Physics Letters. 2002;**80**:2297-2299

[38] Ramana CV, Moodley MK, Kannan V, Maity A. Solution-based spin cast processed organic bistable memory device. Solid State Electronics. 2013;**81**:45-50

[39] Braun S, Salaneck W, Fahlman M. Energy-level alignment at organic/metal and organic/organic interfaces. Advanced Materials. 2009;**21**:1450-1472

[40] Kim TW, Yang Y, Li F, Kwan WL. Electrical memory devices based on inorganic/organic nanocomposites. NPG Asia Materials. 2012;**4**:e18, 1-12

[41] Kim SS, Cho W, Ahn C, Im K, Yang J, Baek I, Lee S, Lim KS. Fabrication of fin field-effect transistor silicon nanocrystal floating gate memory using photochemical vapor deposition. Applied Physics Letters. 2006;**88**:223502-223503

[42] Ko SH, Yoo CH, Kim TW. Electrical bistabilities and memory stabilities of organic bistable devices utilizing C60 molecules embedded in a polymethyl methacrylate matrix with an Al_2O_3 blocking layer. Journal of the Electrochemical Society. 2012;**159**:G93-G96

[43] Geim AK, Novoselov KS. The rise of graphene. Nature Materials. 2007;**6**:183-191

[44] Zhang Y, Tan Y, Stormer HL, Kim P. Experimental observation of the quantum Hall effect and Berry's phase in graphene. Nature (London). 2005;**438**:201-204

[45] Balandin AA, Ghosh S, Bao W, Calizo I, Teweldebrhan D, Miao F. Superior thermal conductivity of single-layer graphene. Nano Letters. 2008;**8**:902-907

[46] Loh KP, Bao Q, Eda G, Chhowalla M. Graphene oxide as a chemically tunable platform for optical applications. Nature Chemical. 2010;**2**:1015-1024

[47] Muller M, Brauninger M, Trauzettel B. Temperature dependence of the conductivity of ballistic graphene. Physical Review Letters. 2009;**103**:196801-196804

[48] Rani A, Song JM, Lee MJ, Lee JS. Reduced graphene oxide based flexible organic charge trap memory devices. Applied Physics Letters. 2012;**101**:233308-233305

[49] Yang R, Zhu C, Meng J, Huo Z, Cheng M, Liu D, Yang W, Shi D, Liu M, Zhang G. Isolated nanographene crystals for nano-floating gate in charge trapping memory. Science Reports. 2013;**3**:1-7

[50] Cho C, Lee YG, Jung U, Kang CG, Lim S, Hwang HJ, Choi H, Lee BH. Correlation between the hysteresis and the initial defect density of graphene. Applied Physics Letters. 2013;**103**:083110-083113

[51] Khurana G, Misra P, Katiyar RS. Multilevel resistive memory switching in graphene sandwiched organic polymer heterostructure. Carbon. 2014;**76**:341-347

[52] Li C, Jiang H, Xia Q. Low voltage resistive switching devices based on chemically produced silicon oxide. Applied Physics Letters. 2013;**103**:062104-062103

[53] Younis A, Chu D, Li S. Bi-stable resistive switching characteristics in Ti-doped ZnO thin films. Nanoscale Research Letters. 2013;**8**:154-156

[54] Lee S, Kim H, Yun DJ, Rhee SW, Yong K. Resistive switching characteristics of ZnO thin film grown on stainless steel for flexible nonvolatile memory devices. Applied Physics Letters. 2009;**95**:262113-262115

[55] Kim S, Choi Y. Resistive switching of aluminum oxide for flexible memory. Applied Physics Letters. 2008;**92**:223508-223503

[56] Kinoshita K, Okutani T, Tanaka H, Hinoki T, Agura H, Yazawa K, Ohmi K, Kishida S. Flexible and transparent ReRAM with GZO memory layer and GZO-electrodes on large PEN sheet. Solid-State Electronics. 2011;**58**:48-53

[57] Seo JW, Park JW, Lim KS, Kang SJ, Hong YH, Yang JH, Fang L, Sung GY, Kim HK. Transparent flexible resistive random access memory fabricated at room temperature. Applied Physics Letters. 2009;**95**:133508-133503

[58] Kim S, Yarimaga O, Choi S, Choi Y. Highly durable and flexible memory based on resistance switching. Solid-State Electronics. 2010;**54**:392-396

[59] Kim S, Jeong HY, Kim SK, Choi SY, Lee KJ. Flexible memristive memory array on plastic substrates. Nano Letters. 2011;**11**:5438-5442

[60] Shi L, Shang DS, Chen YS, Wang J, Sun JR, Shen BG. Improved resistance switching in ZnO-based devices decorated with Ag nanoparticles. Journal of Physics D: Applied Physics. 2011;**44**:455305-455305

[61] Chang WY, Cheng KJ, Tsai JM, Chen HJ, Chen F, Tsai MJ, Wu TB. Improvement of resistive switching characteristics in TiO_2 thin films with embedded Pt nanocrystals. Applied Physics Letters. 2009;**95**:042104-042103

[62] Zhang R, Chang KC, Chang TC, Tsai TM, Chen KH, Lou JC, Chen JH, Young TF, Shih CC, Yang YL, Pan YC, Chu TJ, Huang SY, Pan CH, Su YT, Syu YE, Sze SM. High performance of graphene oxide-doped silicon oxide-based resistance random access memory. Nanoscale Research Letters. 2013;**8**:497-496

[63] Khurana G, Misra P, Kumar N, Katiyar RS. Tunable power switching in nonvolatile flexible memory devices based on graphene oxide embedded with ZnO nanorods. Journal of Physical Chemistry C. 2014;**118**:21357-21364

[64] Yang Y, Liu T. Fabrication and characterization of graphene oxide/zinc oxide nanorods hybrid. Applied Surface Science. 2011;**257**:8950-8954

[65] Kawasaki S, Fan HJ, Catalan G, Morrison FD, Tatsuta T, Tsuji O, Scott JF. Solution-process coating of vertical ZnO nanowires with ferroelectrics. Nanotechnology. 2008;**19**:375302-375305

[66] Panin GN, Kapitanova OO, Lee SW, Baranov AN, Kang TW. Resistive switching in Al/graphene oxide/Al structure. Japanese Journal of Applied Physics. 2011;**50**:70110-70116

[67] Khallaf H, Chai G, Lupan O, Heinrich H, Park S, Schulte A, Chow L. Investigation of chemical bath deposition of ZnO thin films using six different complexing agents. Journal of Physics D: Applied Physics. 2009;**42**:135304-135308

[68] Russo U, Ielmini D, Cagli C, Lacaita AL. Filament conduction and reset mechanism in NiO-based resistive-switching memory (RRAM) devices. IEEE Transactions on Electron Devices. 2009;**56**:186-192

[69] Chang WY, Ho YT, Hsu TC, Chen F, Tsai MJ, Wu TB. Influence of crystalline constituent on resistive switching properties of TiO_2 memory films. Electrochemical and Solid-State Letters. 2009;**12**:135-137

[70] Yang JJ, Miao F, Pickett MD, Ohlberg DAA, Stewart DR, Lau CN, Williams RS. The mechanism of electroforming of metal oxide memristive switches Nanotechnology. 2009;**20**:215201-215209

[71] Khurana G, Misra P, Kumar N, Kooriyattil S, Scott JF, Katiyar RS. Enhanced resistive switching in forming free graphene oxide films embedded with gold nanoparticles deposited by electrophoresis. Nanotechnology. 2016;**27**:015702-015707

[72] An SJ, Zhu Y, Lee SH, Stoller MD, Emilsson T, Park S, Velamakanni A, An J, Ruoff RS. Thin film fabrication and simultaneous anodic reduction of deposited graphene oxide platelets by electrophoretic deposition. Journal of Physical Chemistry Letters. 2010;**1**:1259-1263

[73] Chen Y, Zhang X, Yu P, Ma Y. Stable dispersions of graphene and highly conducting graphene films: A new approach to creating colloids of graphene monolayers. Chemical Communications. 2009:4527-4531

[74] Cui P, Seo S, Lee J, Wang L, Lee E, Min M, Lee H. Nonvolatile memory device using gold nanoparticles covalently bound to reduced graphene oxide. ACS Nano. 2011;**5**:6826-6833

[75] Scott JF. There's no place like Ohm: Conduction in oxide thin films. Journal of Physics: Condensed Matter. 2014;**26**:142202-142204

[76] Son DI, Park DH, Kim JB, Choi JW, Kim TW, Angadi B, Yi Y, Choi WK. Bistable organic memory device with gold nanoparticles embedded in a conducting poly(N-vinylcarbazole) colloids hybrid. Journal of Physical Chemistry C. 2011;**115**:2341-2348

[77] Khurana G, Kumar N, Kotnala RK, Nautiyal T, Katiyar RS. Temperature tuned defect induced magnetism in reduced graphene oxide. Nanoscale. 2013;**5**:3346-3351

[78] Rozada R, Paredes JI, Villar-Rodil S, Martínez-Alonso A, Tascón JMD. Towards full repair of defects in reduced graphene oxide films by two-step graphitization. Nano Research. 2013;**6**:216-233

[79] Lu J, Moon KS, Xu J, Wong CP. Synthesis and dielectric properties of novel high-K polymer composites containing in-situ formed silver nanoparticles for embedded capacitor applications. Journal of Materials Chemistry. 2006;**16**:1543-1548

[80] Feng Q, Dang Z, Li N, Cao X. Preparation and dielectric property of Ag-PVA nano-composite. Materials Science and Engineering: B. 2003;**99**:325-328

Chapter 3

Emulator Circuits and Resistive Switching Parameters of Memristor

Abdullah Yesil, Fatih Gül and Yunus Babacan

Additional information is available at the end of the chapter

http://dx.doi.org/10.5772/intechopen.71903

Abstract

Chua predicted the existence of the fundamental circuit element, which provides the linkage of flux (ϕ) and charge (q). The new circuit element that is called memristor (memory + resistor) was demonstrated by Hewlett Packard (HP) researchers in 2008. Researchers focused on memristor fabrication, modeling, and its application with other circuit elements. Researchers could not find the commercially memristor devices in the market because of some fabrication difficulties. For this reason, researchers focused on the memristor modeling to analyze its characteristics with other circuit elements. This chapter presents a review of the general information of memristor and its device parameters. The chapter is continued with the details of memristor mathematical and SPICE models and memristor emulators based on the other circuit elements.

Keywords: memristor, memristor models, SPICE, memristor emulator, active circuit element-based memristors

1. Introduction

Both active circuit elements and passive circuit elements are used in circuit design, and the first circuit elements that come to mind are passive circuit elements: resistor, capacitor, and inductor. Resistor, capacitor, and inductor define the relationship between the voltage and current, voltage and charge, and current and flux, respectively. Leon Chua from the University of California (Berkeley) showed the missing relationship as shown in **Figure 1** between flux and current in 1971 and 1976 [1, 2].

At the same time, Chua called the missing circuit element as a memristor (memory + resistor) and presented the mathematical equations of the new circuit element. But the seminal paper

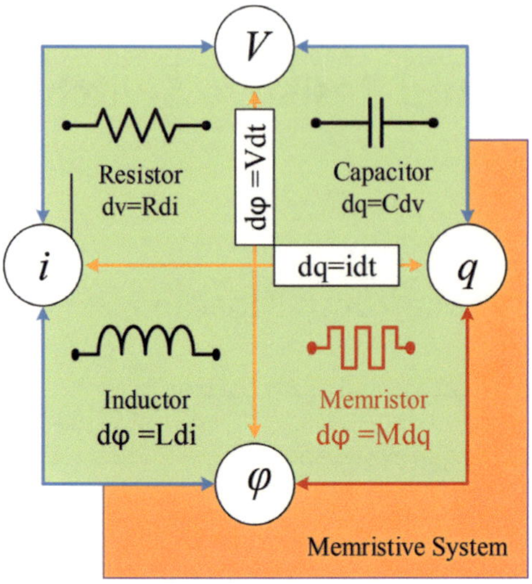

Figure 1. The fundamental two-terminal passive circuit elements.

Figure 2. The scanning tunneling microscope image of the memristor [4].

of Chua could not find attentions among the researchers because of the technical fabrication difficulties of the memristor. Therefore, researchers did not focus on the memristor and its application until its first fabrication of memristor by HP researchers in 2008 [3]. The first memristor is made from TiO_2 thin film and has crossbar structure as shown in **Figure 2**.

The HP research team also presented the mathematical model of TiO_2 memristor, and current-voltage relationship is defined by

$$V = [M(x_1, x_2, \ldots x_n)]I \tag{1}$$

where V is the voltage and I is the current. Here, M is the resistance of memristor and memristance and depends on x_i state variables. Memristance which performs nonlinear characteristics depends on frequency and applied input signal. The TiO_2 memristor consists of two main structures which are named doped and undoped region as shown in **Figure 3**, and the memristance changes the ratios of the doped region and device thickness.

Memristor acts as a conductor if the thickness of the doped region becomes wide as shown in **Figure 3b**. Undoped region becomes wide as shown in **Figure 3c**, and memristor behaves as a high-resistance element when the input signal applied in an opposite direction.

Memristance is as below:

$$M(x) = \left[R_{ON}\,x + R_{OFF}(1 - x)\right], \; \left(x = \frac{w}{D}\right) \tag{2}$$

The change of the x value is depicted:

$$\frac{dx}{dt} = \frac{\mu_v R_{ON}}{D^2}\, i(t) \tag{3}$$

The μ_v is the electron mobility, and w and D denote the doped area of memristor and thickness of the memristor, respectively. The resistances of the high and low dopant concentrations are symbolized with R_{ON} and R_{OFF}, respectively. Researchers added a function to the memristor mathematical model to take into account the nonlinear dopant effect [3, 5–7]. Equation (3) is rearranged as follows:

$$\frac{dx}{dt} = \frac{\mu_v R_{ON}}{D^2}\, i(t) f(x) \tag{4}$$

The first function which is called window function is presented by HP research team [3] as shown below:

$$f(x) = \frac{x(1 - x)}{D} \tag{5}$$

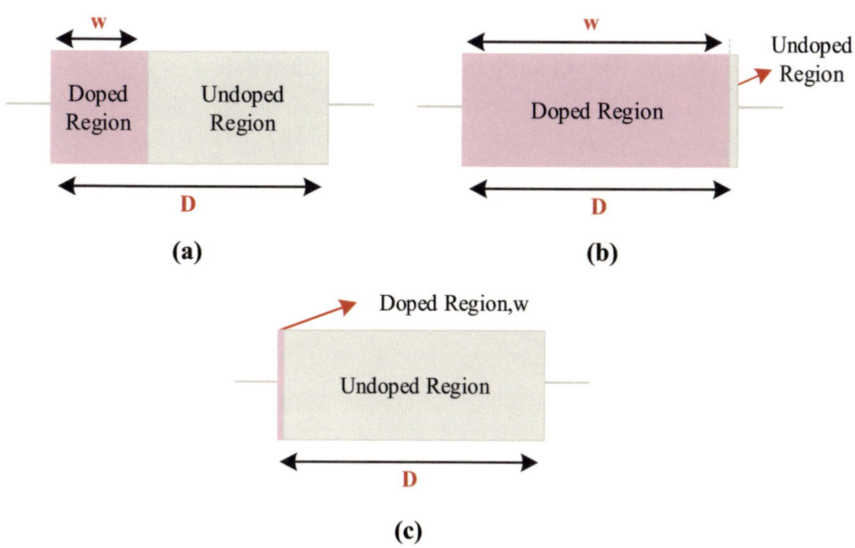

Figure 3. Memristor (a) initial state, (b) low-resistance state, and (c) high-resistance state.

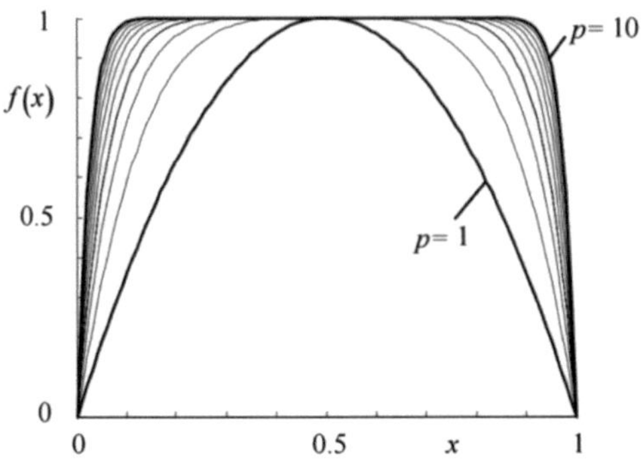

Figure 4. Window function presented by Wolf and Joglekar [5].

The HP model is linear and very simple; so Wolf and Joglekar [5] depicted the new window function as shown below:

$$f(x) = 1 - (2x - 1)^{2p} \tag{6}$$

The function is starting to similar the rectangular shape when *p*-value becomes higher, namely, dopant drift is decreasing as shown in **Figure 4**.

Biolek et al. [6] modified the model of Wolf and Joglekar:

$$f(x) = 1 - \left(x - stp(-i)\right)^{2p} \tag{7a}$$

$$stp(i) = \begin{cases} 1, i \geq 0 \\ 0, i < 0 \end{cases} \tag{7b}$$

The window function which is presented by Biolek is shown in **Figure 5**.

Prodromakis et al. [7] depict the versatile model as the following:

$$f(x) = j(1 - [(x - 0.5)^2 + 0.75]^p) \tag{8}$$

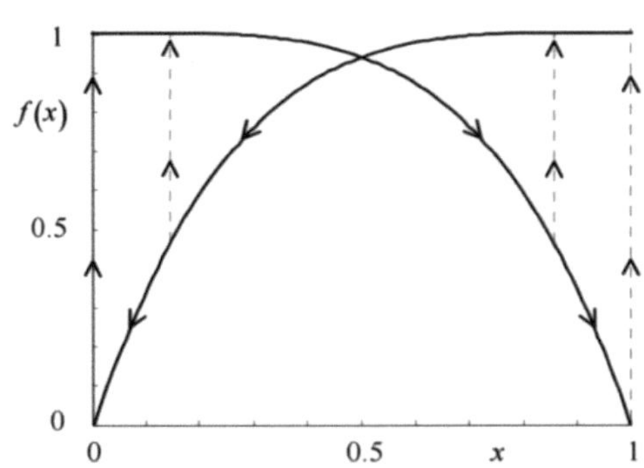

Figure 5. Window function presented by Biolek et al. [6].

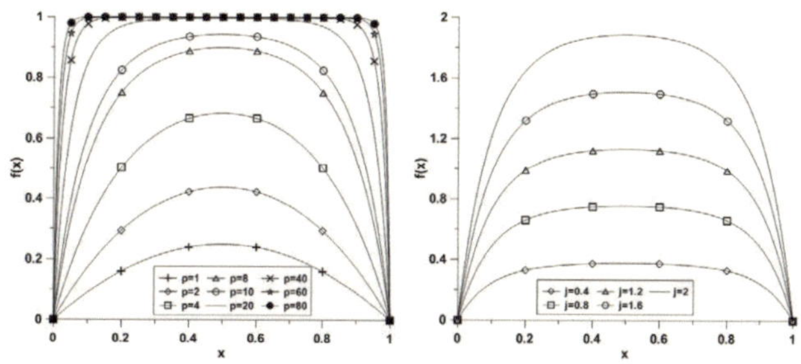

Figure 6. Window function presented by Prodromakis et al. [7].

Model function of Prodromakis et al. becomes higher than the value of 1 unlike previous window functions. The function depends on the various *p*-values shown in **Figure 6**.

Researchers suggested various mathematical memristor models such as nonlinear ion-drift model [8], Simmons' tunnel barrier model [9], and ThrEshold Adaptive Memristor (TEAM) model [10] different from the linear HP model. The chapter is continued with memristor device.

2. Memristor switching device parameters

The pinched hysteresis loops serve as a fingerprint in the characterization of memristors [11] as shown in **Figure 7**. It is to say that, if any two-terminal device is showing pinched hysteresis loop, a memristor regardless of the device material is accepted. Resistive switching (or memristive behavior) in metal-oxide semiconductor was first observed by Hickmott in 1962, but it was interpreted as the current anomaly [12]. As in resistive switching devices, a typical pinched hysteresis loop is seen at the first and third quadrants of the current-voltage (I-V) curves [13]. Put differently, all memristors can be accepted as resistive switching devices regardless of the operating mechanisms and the device material [14].

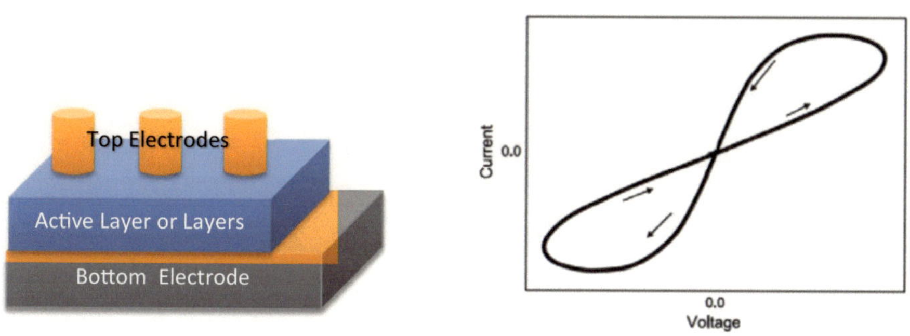

a) b)

Figure 7. (a) Schematic representation of a memristor device and (b) typical pinched hysteresis current-voltage loop of memristor devices.

2.1. Active layer material and top/bottom electrode

The semiconductor-based memristor devices usually consist of an active layer sandwiched between a top and a bottom electrode (TE/BE) depicted in **Figure 7**. The first physical implementation of the memristor was achieved by HP labs using TiO_2 metal-oxide active layer [3]. After that, several physical memristor devices suggested the use of different materials and production methods. Most metal-oxide semiconductors exhibit memristor characteristics, including TiO_2, ZnO, HfO_2, VO_2, TaO_x, and so on [13, 15, 16]. There are two types of contact in semiconductor: one is of Schottky (rectifying), and the other one is ohmic. Several electrode materials can be used as TE or BE including Pt, Au, Ag, Al, etc. In one diode-one resistor (1D1R)-type memory cell memristor device, one of the electrodes must be a Schottky contact [17].

2.2. Unipolar or bipolar operation

The unipolar and bipolar operation of memristor devices which are shown in **Figure 8** can be categorized in according with current-voltage characteristics. In unipolar operation characteristics depend only on the amplitude of the applied voltage, whereas bipolar operations are resolved by polarity and amplitude of the applied voltage [13]. Unipolar operation is more striking than bipolar operation in memristor switching devices, since it needs simple circuits. But then, bipolar operation has generally high uniformity and more endurance compared to unipolar operation [18].

2.3. Physical mechanism

There are two types of physical working mechanisms in the explanation of the time-dependent current-voltage characteristics, based on molecular or ionic models: the homogeneous interface type and the filamentary (conduction path) type [13, 16]. In the homogeneous type, the migration of oxygen vacancies as the majority carriers causes change of resistance. The filament-type mechanism is associated with the formation and rupture of conductive filaments

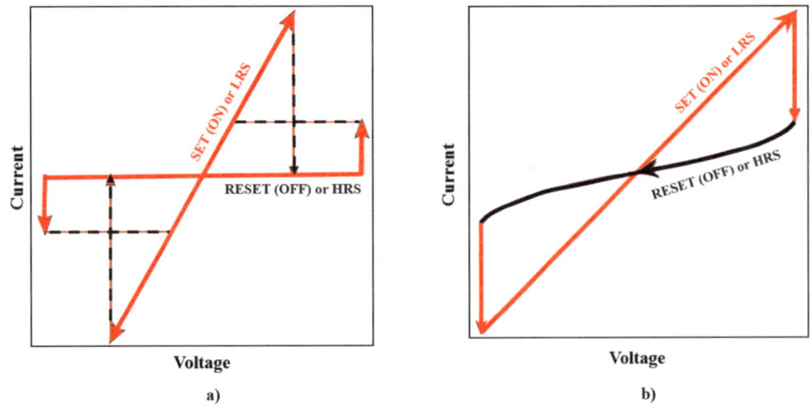

Figure 8. Typical current-voltage curves of memristor devices (a) unipolar and (b) bipolar.

in the active layer. Both types of mechanisms can be observed in the memristor devices as shown in **Figure 9** and depend on the material and fabrication methods [18].

2.4. Operation current-voltage

It is well known that reversible switching between a low-resistance state (LRS) or ON (SET) and a high-resistance state (HRS) or OFF (RESET) can be achieved by applying a certain voltage [18]. Operation voltage is also an important value for CMOS or other device integrations for memristor devices. Another criterion for the memristor devices is the power consumption related to the operation current. With the aim of escape permanent damage from over current, the compliance or limit current (CC) must be set in both unipolar and bipolar operations [13]. The compliance current is also related to power consumption of a memristor device [19].

2.5. ON/OFF ratio

The memristor has two states when used as a switching device: the high-resistance state (HRS) or OFF (RESET) state and the low-resistance state (LRS) or ON (SET) state [13]. The ON/OFF ratio defined as the proportion between resistances in HRS and LRS is some of the most important parameters when memristors are used as switching device [18].

2.6. Retention time and endurance

The time to hold ON/OFF state is an important criterion when memristor device used a resistive switching memory or ReRAM element [20]. It is expected that the memristor device's distribution of the HRS or LRS state which is shown in **Figure 10** has acceptable values besides its ON/OFF ratio [19]. Since the memory unit needs to be repeatedly read or written by the other control units, cycling endurance is one of the main importance of memristor-based memory devices [18].

Some of recent memristor devices which are composed of various materials are compared according to the some important parameters as shown in **Table 1** [19, 22–24]. The chapter is continued with memristor emulators based on the active circuit elements.

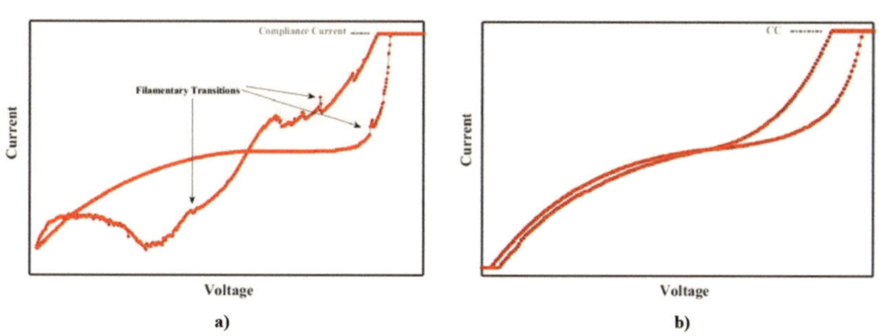

Figure 9. Typical current-voltage curves of memristor devices: (a) filamentary and (b) homogenous transitions on bipolar operation [19].

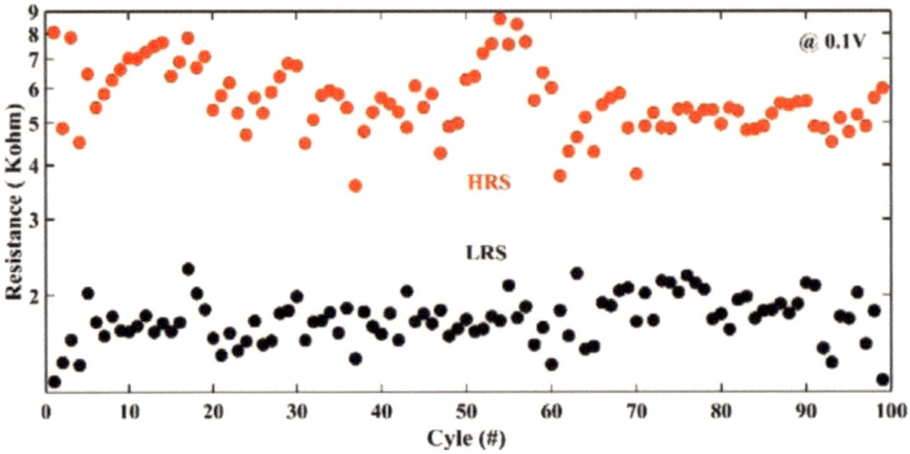

Figure 10. Typical endurance test of a memristor device @0.1 V for 100 cycles [21].

Active layer material	TE/BE	Operation mode	Operation mechanism	Operation voltage	ON/OFF ratio	Retention time	Endurance	Ref.
ZnO	Al/Al	Bipolar	Homogenous	−1.5 V/+1.5 V	5 × 10^1	N/A	100	[19]
TiO_2	Al/Al	Bipolar	Filamentary	−3 V/+1.5 V	8 × 10^2	N/A	10^{12}	[22]
HfO_2	Pt/Ti	Bipolar	Filamentary	−3.5 V/+2 V	10^3	10^4	1000	[23]
TaO_x	Pt/Pt	Unipolar	Filamentary	−1.5 V/+1 V	10^1	N/A	1000	[24]

Table 1. Comparison table of some recent memristor devices.

3. Memristor models and emulators

Many SPICE models and emulators are presented by researchers [6, 25–47]. The first and applicable memristor model has been presented by Biolek and co-workers [6]. This model takes into account the boundary conditions using window function, and the feedback-controlled integrator is used to implement memory effect of the memristor. The block diagram of memristor and its SPICE model is shown in **Figure 11**. All simulation results which are shown in **Figure 12** are completed using SPICE codes as shown below. Each curve is compatible with TiO_2 memristor, and boundary effects are taken into account (**Table 2**).

Researchers are not able to reach the memristor devices in the market because of some production problems of the memristor. For this reason, researchers focused on the designing of memristor emulators to use with other circuit elements. Yener and Kuntman reported full active device-based memristor emulator which is consisting of differential difference current conveyor (DDCC) [35]. The proposed grounded memristor emulator consists of four circuit blocks based on DDCC as shown in **Figure 13**. Furthermore, there are no experimental results; however, its SPICE simulation results are given.

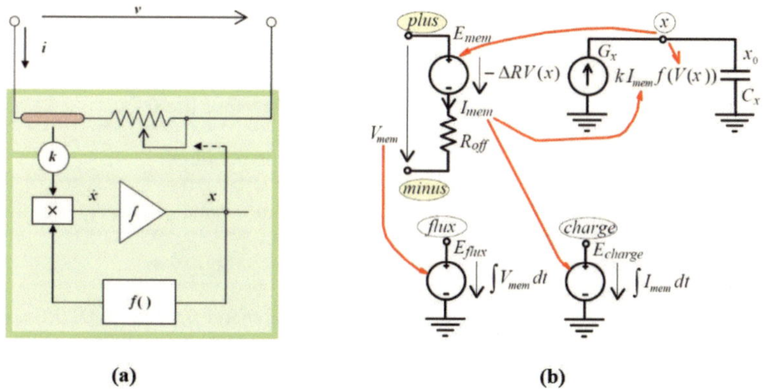

Figure 11. (a) Block diagram and (b) SPICE model of the memristor [6].

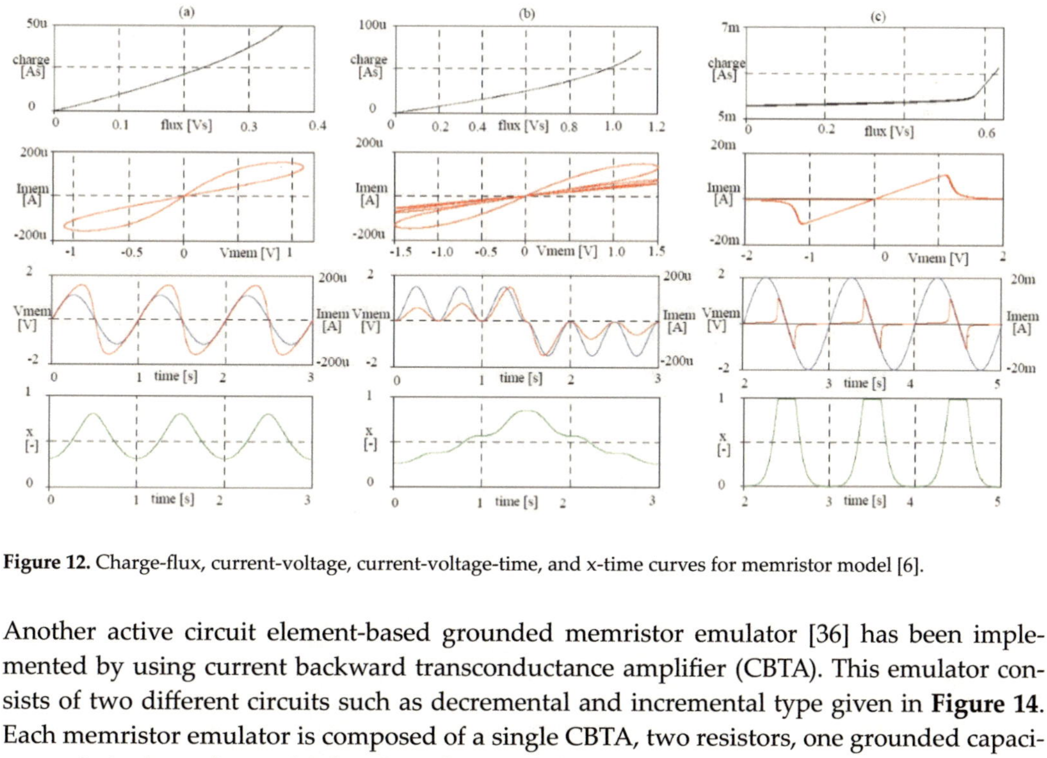

Figure 12. Charge-flux, current-voltage, current-voltage-time, and x-time curves for memristor model [6].

Another active circuit element-based grounded memristor emulator [36] has been implemented by using current backward transconductance amplifier (CBTA). This emulator consists of two different circuits such as decremental and incremental type given in **Figure 14**. Each memristor emulator is composed of a single CBTA, two resistors, one grounded capacitor, and single analog multiplier. In order to validate the feasibility of the presented memristor, only SPICE simulation results have been given.

The generalized mutator structure based on adder and subtractor has been proposed by Minaei et al. [37]. As far as connection ports are concerned, the generalized structure employs memristor, meminductor, and memcapacitor without using analog multiplier. By selecting an inductor to port 3, a capacitor to port 4, and a nonlinear resistor such as a diode to port 1, the generalized structure given in **Figure 15** is utilized as memristor. Nonetheless, so as to verify the workableness of the presented structure, the SPICE simulation results are given.

```
* HP Memristor SPICE Model
* For Transient Analysis only
* created by Zdenek and Dalibor Biolek
**************************
* Ron, Roff - Resistance in ON/OFF States
* Rinit - Resistance at T = 0
* D - Width of the thin film
* uv - Migration coefficient
* p - Parameter of the WINDOW-function
* for modeling nonlinear boundary conditions
* x - W/D Ratio, W is the actual width
* of the doped area (from 0 to D)
*
.SUBCKT memristor Plus Minus PARAMS:
+ Ron = 1 K Roff = 100 K Rinit = 80 K D = 10 N uv = 10F p = 1
**********************************************
* DIFFERENTIAL EQUATION MODELING *
**********************************************
Gx 0 x value = {I(Emem)*uv*Ron/D^2*f(V(x),p)}
Cx x 0 1 IC = {(Roff-Rinit)/(Roff-Ron)}
Raux x 0 1T
* RESISTIVE PORT OF THE MEMRISTOR *
*******************************
Emem plus aux value = {-I(Emem)*V(x)*(Roff-Ron)}
Roff aux minus {Roff}
**********************************************
*Flux computation*
**********************************************
Eflux flux 0 value = {SDT(V(plus,minus))}
**********************************************
*Charge computation*
**********************************************
Echarge charge 0 value = {SDT(I(Emem))}
**********************************************
* WINDOW FUNCTIONS
* FOR NONLINEAR DRIFT MODELING *
**********************************************
*window function, according to Joglekar
.func f(x,p) = {1-(2*x-1)^(2*p)}
*proposed window function
;.func f(x,i,p) = {1-(x-stp(-i))^(2*p)}
.ENDS memristor
```

Table 2. SPICE codes of modeled memristor [6].

Kim and co-workers presented the active circuit element-based memristor emulator [38]. This circuit is also implemented on the bread board using discrete circuit elements that are ADL1116PAL for NMOS transistors, ADL1117PAL for PMOS transistors, TL082 for OPAMP, and AD633 for analog multiplier and passive elements. There are three important tasks to implement memristor emulator: memory effect, frequency-/voltage-dependent characteristics, and nonlinearity. Memory effect and frequency/voltage dependency characteristics are implemented by using a capacitor like many other previous emulator circuits. Nonlinear characteristic of the memristor is obtained using multiplier circuit block. But each used block gives rise to extra power dissipation and more complex circuit (**Figure 16**).

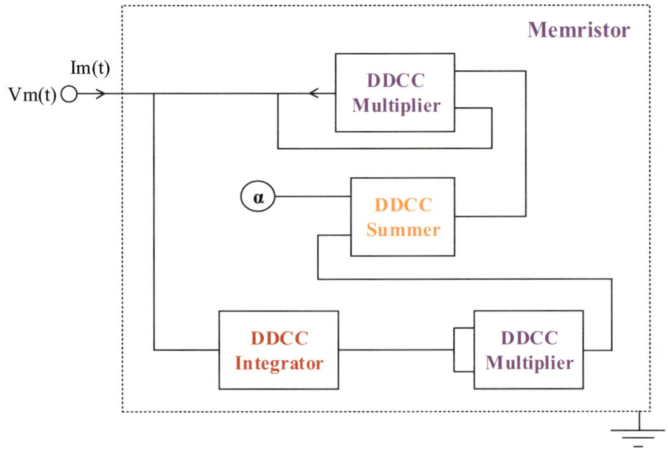

Figure 13. DDCC-based memristor emulator which is presented by Yener and Kuntman [35].

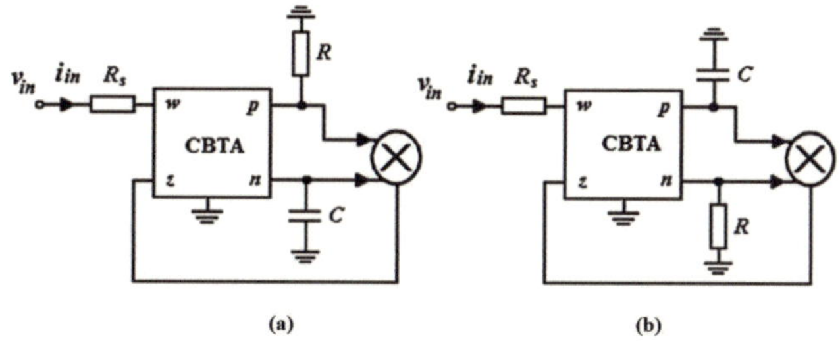

Figure 14. CBTA-based memristor emulator (a) decremental structure and (b) incremental structure [36].

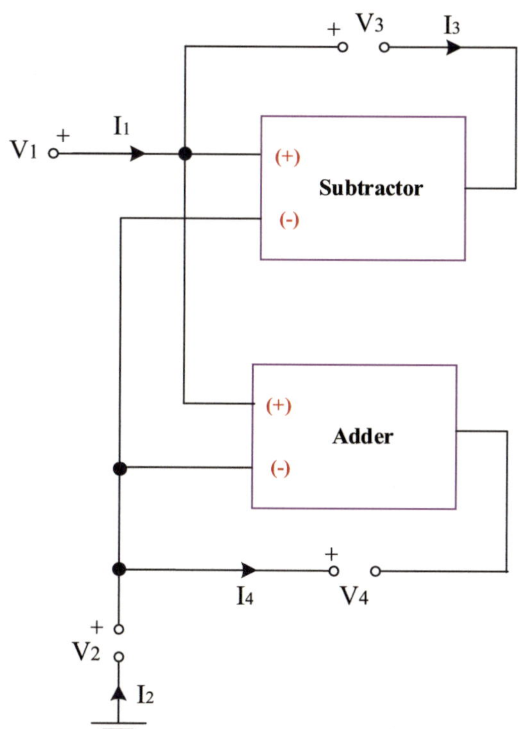

Figure 15. Generalized mutator structure based on adder and subtractor [37].

Another active circuit-based memristor emulators which are shown in **Figure 17** have been presented by Abuelma'atti and Khalifa [39]. Each emulator which is based on current-feedback operational amplifier (CFOA) enjoys operating two different types like decremental and incremental memristor emulators. This situation is a disadvantage of the emulator besides its grounded structure. Each circuit comprises three CFOAs, four resistors, two capacitors, and germanium diode without using an analog multiplier. Nonlinear characteristic is provided by germanium diode. CFOA which is an active element is modeled by AD844 commercially available active devices, and experimental results have been investigated.

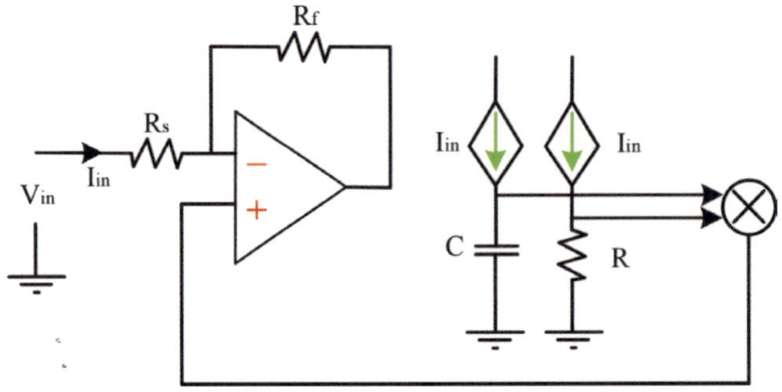

Figure 16. Voltage-controlled memristor emulator which is presented by Kim and co-workers [38].

Sánchez-López and Aguila-Cuapio proposed the charge-controlled memristor emulator circuit [40]. This circuit which is shown in **Figure 18** is grounded; hence, application areas of the presented memristor emulator are limited in circuit designs. Moreover, it is implemented with discrete circuit element such as AD844 and AD633 besides its disadvantages.

Babacan and co-workers presented new memristor emulator based on multi-output operational transconductance amplifier (OTA) [41]. This emulator shown in **Figure 19** is a derivative of the DDCC-based memristor emulator [42], but memristance value of this emulator

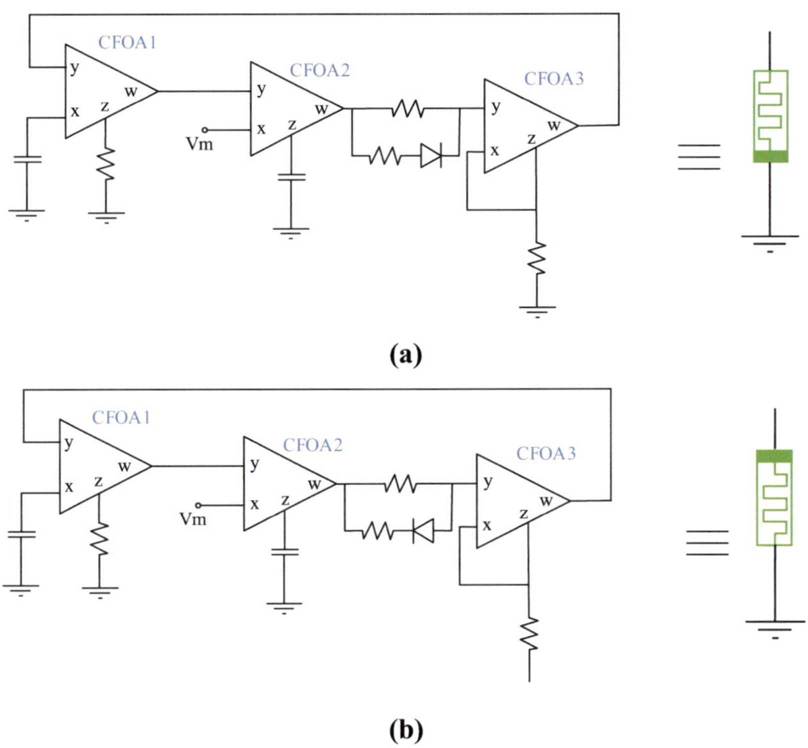

Figure 17. CFOA-based memristor emulator with (a) decremental and (b) incremental characteristic [39].

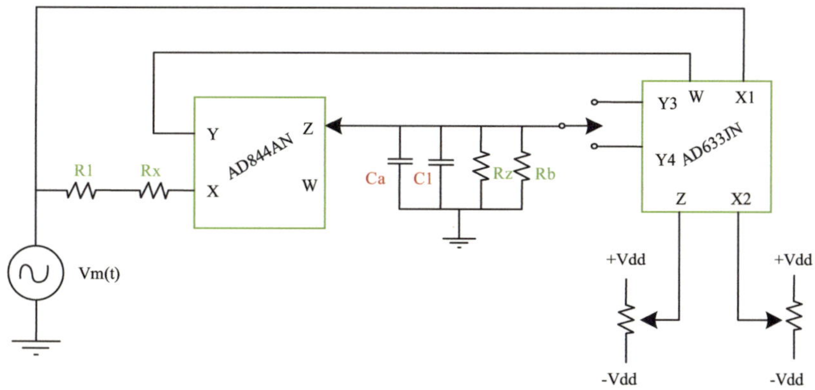

Figure 18. Memristor emulator based on AD844 [40].

can be adjusted by biasing current of the OTA. The change of the memristance value can be controlled by changing resistor (R) value. Average memristance value can be controlled using OTA-gm value because of the fact that OTA is used as controllable resistor by connecting the negative output terminal to the positive input terminal. In order to demonstrate the performance of OTA-based memristor emulator, both SPICE simulation results and experimental results have been performed. For experimental results, the memristor emulator is built using passive elements and commercially available active devices such as OPA860 for MO-OTA and AD633 for the analog multiplier.

Yesil and co-workers suggested only one DDCC-based memristor emulator which can be operated in high-frequency regions [42]. It is observed from **Figure 20** that the capacitor provides the memory effect and the multiplication of both capacitor and resistor voltages is connected to the Y terminal of the active device. The resistance of memristor emulator circuit decreases when the Z terminal of the DDCC device is chosen as positive terminal (Z_P). Consequently, the circuit shows decremental memristor characteristics. For another state, an

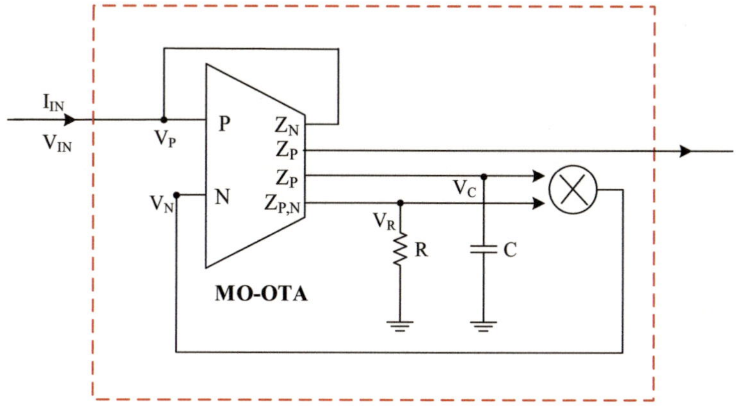

Figure 19. OT-based memristor emulator which is presented by Babacan and co-workers [41].

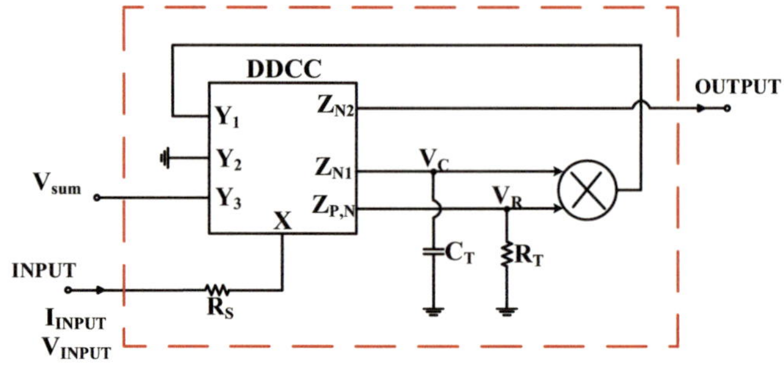

Figure 20. DDCC-based memristor emulator which is presented by Yesil and co-workers [42].

incremental memristor can be obtained when the Z terminal of DDCC is chosen as negative terminal (Z_N). This emulator consists of the third terminal (V_{sum}) to provide the floating characteristic. Serial connected memristors split applied voltage such as resistor if these memristors carry out a voltage; accordingly, the third terminal is connected to the output terminal. Just as DDCC-based [35], CBTA-based [36], and adder-and-subtractor [37]-based memristor, the performance of [42] is confirmed by SPICE simulations results.

Sozen and Cam proposed new floating memristor emulator based on OTA and CCII as shown in **Figure 21** [43]. This emulator is made up of three OTAs, four CCIIs, and seven passive elements. Both SPICE simulation results and experimental results of the presented memristor emulator have been given to confirm its workableness and feasibility. Commercially available active devices CA3080 and AD844 have been utilized instead of OTA and CCII, respectively.

Sánchez-López et al. proposed second-generation current conveyor (CCII)-based flux-controlled memristor emulator which is shown in **Figure 22** [44]. The presented emulator comprises of four CCIIs, a multiplier circuit, five resistors, and single grounded capacitor. AD844 and AD633 are used instead of CCII and analog multiplier in the flux-controlled memristor emulator, respectively. So as to indicate the performance of flux-controlled memristor emulator, both SPICE simulation results and experimental results have been exhibited.

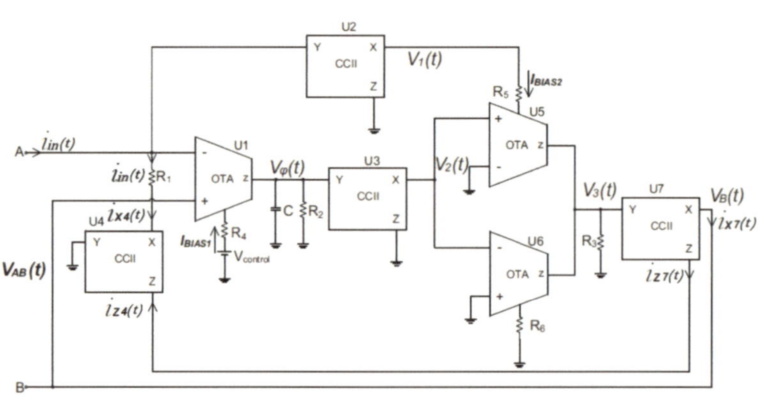

Figure 21. OTA- and CCII-based memristor emulator [43].

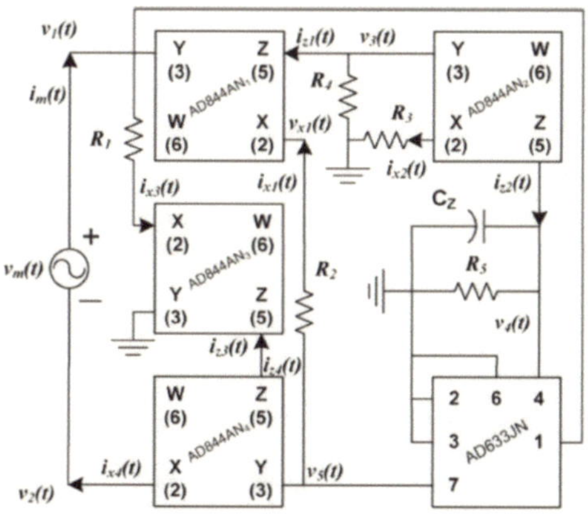

Figure 22. Floating flux-controlled memristor emulator based on CCII [44].

Babacan and Kacar suggested new memristor emulator which does not need any multiplication block as shown in **Figure 23** [45]. This emulator is also fully floating, namely, has two terminals, and input signal can be applied in both terminals. The nonlinearity is provided by transistors which are operated in the subthreshold region. The presented memristor emulator includes single-ended OTA, one grounded capacitor, and two PMOS transistors. Note that the bulk terminals of PMOS transistors are connected to drain terminals of relevant transistors.

The first memristor model which accounts for spike-timing-dependent plasticity (STDP) mechanism is proposed by Li and co-workers [46]. The model which is shown in **Figure 24** consists of five circuit models, and each model depends on the previous model so this model is complex and does not have any circuit implementation.

Babacan and Kacar suggested real-time fully floating memristor emulator which is accounted for synaptic activity [47]. Both memristive and STDP characteristics are obtained from the

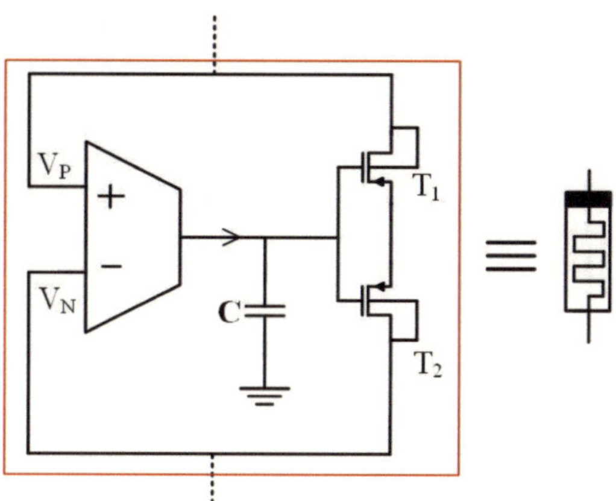

Figure 23. Fully floating memristor emulator based on OTA [45].

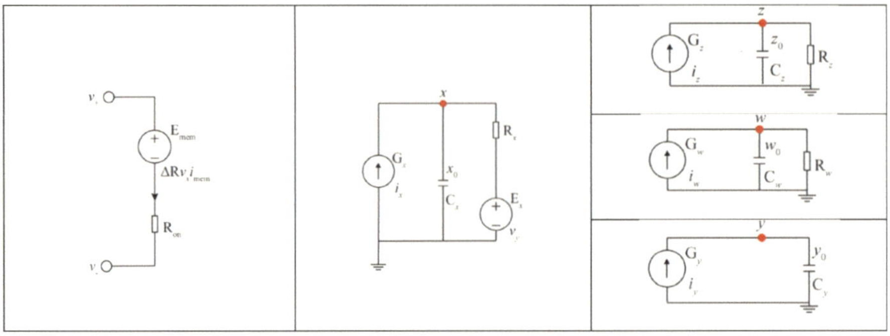

Figure 24. Memristor model which is accounted for STDP mechanism [46].

circuit which is shown in **Figure 25**. It is observed from **Figure 25** that fully floating memristor emulator consists of a few numbers of MOS transistors and capacitors without using analog multiplier. Furthermore, STDP is experimentally demonstrated in memristive devices [48–50].

In summary, the comparison of the memristor emulator circuits is according to some important design parameters such as used circuit elements, electronically controllability, power supply value, etc. Each emulator has superior properties among the other emulators. Researchers can prefer appropriate emulator circuit for their memristor-based circuit designs (**Table 3**).

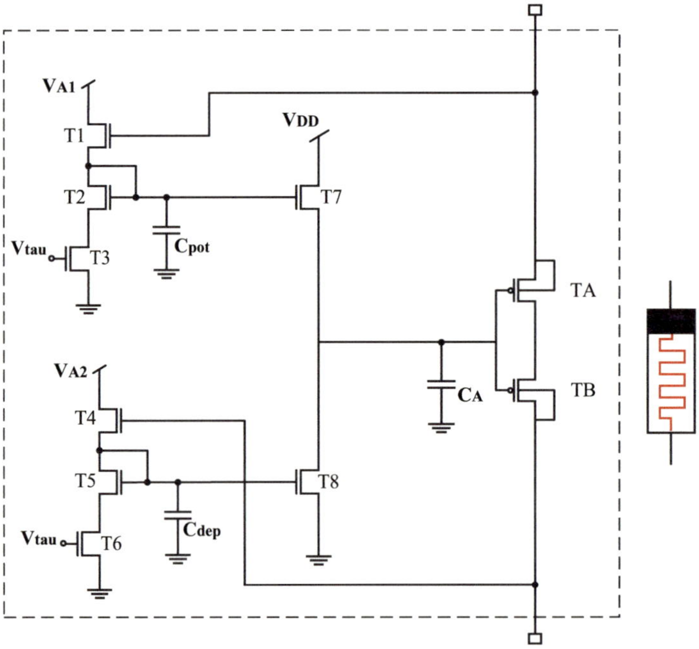

Figure 25. Memristor circuit which is accounted for STDP mechanism [47].

Reference	No. of floating passive elements	No. of active comp	No. of grounded passive elements	Sim./exp	Electronically controllable	Floating/ grounded memristor emulator	Power supply
[35]	—	10 DDCCs, 8 transistors	4 R, 1 C	Sim.	No	Grounded	±1.25 V
[36]	1 R	1 CBTA, 1 multiplier	1 R, 1 C	Sim.	No	Grounded	±0.9 V
[37]	1 L, 1 C	1 adder and 1 subtractor	1 D	Sim.	No	Grounded	±1.25 V
[38]	1 R	2 OPAMPs, 1 multiplier, 10 transistors	1 R, 1 C	Both	No	Grounded/ floating	±5 V
[39]	2 R, 1 D	3 CFOAs (AD844)	2 R, 2 C	Exp.	No	Grounded	NA
[40]	1 R	1 CCII(AD844), 1 multiplier (AD633)	1 C	Both	No	Grounded	±10 V
[41]	—	*1 MO-OTA, 1 multiplier*	*1 R, 1 C*	Both	*Yes*	Grounded	*±1.25 V/±5 V*
[42]	1 R	1 DDCC, 1 multiplier	1 R, 1 C	Sim.	No	Floating	±1.5
[43]	3 R	3 OTAs, 4 CCIIs	3 R, 1 C	Both	*Yes*	Floating	±15
[44]	2 R	4 CCIIs (AD844), 1 multiplier (AD633)	3 R, 1 C	Both	No	Floating	±10 V
[45]	—	1 OTA, 2 transistors	1 C	Sim.	No	Floating	±1 V
[47]	—	10 transistors	3 C	Sim.	No	Floating	—

Table 3. Comparison of memristor emulator circuits.

4. Conclusion

In this chapter, memristor devices, models, and emulators have been referred. Memristors have nonlinear characteristics; therefore, high-order mathematical equations should be used to create a mathematical model of the memristor. Active circuit elements are essential to build memristor emulators because of the fact that active elements are versatile and suitable for nonlinear circuit element designs. Nowadays, memristors can exhibit different characteristics when they are fabricated using various materials. Important characteristics such as switching mechanism, synaptic behavior, and operating frequency region are directly depending on the memristor structure. Hence, there is an essential to implement various models and circuits to emulate real memristors. Some emulator circuits exhibit hard-switching characteristics, other emulators exhibit smooth-switching characteristics, or some emulators account for spike-timing-dependent plasticity mechanism.

As a result, researchers are not able to reach real memristor easily so all emulator models and circuits are important to exhibit real memristors. Memristors are ultradense devices and consume very low energy; that is why it is not only important to emulate real emulator. Researchers need also emulator circuits which have minimum energy consumption and simple structure.

Author details

Abdullah Yesil[1], Fatih Gül[2] and Yunus Babacan[3]*

*Address all correspondence to: yunusbabacan@gmail.com

1 Department of Naval Architecture and Marine Engineering, Bandirma Onyedi Eylul University, Balikesir, Turkey

2 Department of Software Engineering, Gumushane University, Gumushane, Turkey

3 Department of Electrical and Electronic Engineering, Erzincan University, Erzincan, Turkey

References

[1] Chua LO. Memristor-the missing circuit element. IEEE Transactions on Circuit Theory. 1971;**18**:507-519. DOI: 10.1109/TCT.1971.1083337

[2] Chua LO, Kang SM. Memristive devices and systems. Proceedings of the IEEE. 1976; **64**:209-223. DOI: 10.1109/PROC.1976.10092

[3] Strukov DB, Snider GS, Stewart DR, Williams RS. The missing memristor found. Nature. 2008;**453**:80-83. DOI: 10.1038/nature06932

[4] William RS. How we found the missing Memristor. IEEE Spectrum. 2008;**45**:29-35. DOI: 10.1109/MSPEC.2008.4687366

[5] Wolf SJ, Joglekar YN. The elusive memristor: Properties of basic electrical circuits. European Journal of Physics. 2009;**30**:1-24. DOI: 10.1088/0143-0807/30/4/001

[6] Biolek Z, Biolek D, Biolkova V. Spice model of memristor with nonlinear dopant drift. Radioengineering. 2009;**18**:210-214

[7] Prodromakis T, Peh BP, Papavassiliou C, Toumazou C. A versatile memristor model with nonlinear dopant kinetics. IEEE Transactions on Electron Devices. 2011;**58**:3099-3105. DOI: 10.1109/TED.2011.2158004

[8] Lehtonen E, Laiho M. CNN using memristors for neighborhood connections. In: 12th International Workshop on Cellular Nanoscale Networks and Their Applications (CNNA). 2010. pp. 1-4. DOI: 10.1109/CNNA.2010.5430304

[9] Pickett D. Switching dynamics in titanium dioxide memristive devices. Applied Physics. 2009;**106**:74508-74514. DOI: 10.1063/1.3236506

[10] Kvatinsky S, Friedman EG, Kolodny A, Weiser UC. TEAM: Threshold adaptive memristor model. IEEE Transactions on Circuits and Systems I: Regular Papers. 2013;**60**:211-221. DOI: 10.1109/TCSI.2012.2215714

[11] Adhikari SP, Sah MP, Kim H, Chua LO. Three fingerprints of memristor. IEEE Tran sactions on Circuits and Systems I: Regular Papers. 2013;**60**:3008-3021. DOI: 10.1109/TCSI.2013.2256171

[12] Hickmott TW. Low-frequency negative resistance in thin anodic oxide films. Journal of Applied Physics. 1962 Sep;**33**(9):2669-2682

[13] Sawa A. Resistive switching in transition metal oxides. Materials Today. 2008;**11**:28-36. DOI: 10.1016/S1369-7021(08)70119-6

[14] Chua L. Resistance switching memories are memristors. Applied Physics A: Materials Science & Processing. 2011;**102**:765-783. DOI: 10.1007/s00339-011-6264-9

[15] Lim EW, Ismail R. Conduction mechanism of valence change resistive switching memory: A survey. Electronics. 2015;**4**:586-613. DOI: 10.3390/electronics4030586

[16] Strukov DB, Kohlstedt H. Resistive switching phenomena in thin films: Materials, devices, and applications. MRS Bulletin. 2012;**37**:108-114. DOI: 10.1557/mrs.2012.2

[17] Huang CH, Huang JS, Lin SM, Chang WY, He JH, Chueh YL. ZnO1−x nanorod arrays/ZnO thin film bilayer structure: From homojunction diode and high-performance memristor to complementary 1D1R application. ACS Nano. 2012 Sep 6;**6**(9):8407-8414

[18] Ielmini D. Resistive switching memories based on metal oxides: Mechanisms, reliability and scaling. Semiconductor Science and Technology. May 2016;**31**(6):063002

[19] Gul F, Efeoglu H. ZnO and ZnO1−x based thin film memristors: The effects of oxygen deficiency and thickness in resistive switching behavior. Ceramics International. 2017;**43**(14):10770-10775. DOI: 10.1016/j.ceramint.2017.05.090

[20] Akinaga H, Shima H. Resistive random access memory (ReRAM) based on metal oxides. Proceedings of the IEEE. 2010 Dec;**98**(12):2237-2251

[21] Gul F, Efeoglu H. Bipolar resistive switching and conduction mechanism of an Al/ZnO/Al-based memristor. Superlattices and Microstructures. 2017 Jan 31;**101**:172-179

[22] Boratto MH, Ramos RA, Congiu M, Graeff CF, Scalvi LV. Memristive behavior of the SnO_2/TiO_2 interface deposited by sol–gel. Applied Surface Science. 2017 Jul 15;**410**:278-281

[23] He W, Sun H, Zhou Y, Lu K, Xue K, Miao X. Customized binary and multi-level HfO_{2-x}-based memristors tuned by oxidation conditions. Scientific Reports. 2017;**7**:10070

[24] Lian X, Wang M, Rao M, Yan P, Yang JJ, Miao F. Characteristics and transport mechanisms of triple switching regimes of TaOx memristor. Applied Physics Letters. 2017 Apr 24;**110**(17):173504

[25] Benderli S, Wey TA. On SPICE macromodelling of TiO_2 memristors. Electronics Letters. 2009;**45**:377-379. DOI: 10.1049/el.2009.3511

[26] Zhang Y, Zhang X, Yu J. Approximated SPICE model for memristor. International Conference on Communications, Circuits and Systems, ICCCAS. 2009. pp. 928-931. DOI: 10.1109/ICCCAS.2009.5250371

[27] Biolek D, Biolek Z, Biolkova V. SPICE modeling of memristive, memcapacitative and meminductive systems. Circuit Theory and Design. European Conference on IEEE. 2009. pp. 249-252. DOI: 10.1109/ECCTD.2009.5274934

[28] Chen Y, Wang X. Compact modeling and corner analysis of spintronic memristor. In: International Symposium on Nanoscale Architectures. 2009. pp. 7-12. DOI: 10.1109/NANOARCH.2009.5226363

[29] Yang JJ, Strukov DB, Stewart DR. Memristive devices for computing. Nature Nanotechnology. 2013;**8**:13-24

[30] Yakopcic C, Taha TM, Subramanyam G, Pino RE, Rogers S. A memristor device model. IEEE Electron Device Letters. 2011;**32**:1436-1438. DOI: 10.1038/nnano.2012.240

[31] Williams RS, Pickett MD, Strachan JP. Physics-based memristor models. IEEE International Circuits and Systems (ISCAS). 2013. pp. 217-220. DOI: 10.1109/ISCAS.2013.6571821

[32] Pershin Y, Di Ventra M. SPICE model of memristive devices with threshold. Radioengineering. 2013;**22**(2):11-15

[33] Babacan Y, Kacar F, Gurkan K. A spiking and bursting neuron circuit based on Memristor. Neurocomputing. 2016;**203**:86-91. DOI: 10.1016/j.neucom.2016.03.060

[34] Mutlu R, Karakulak E. Emulator circuit of TiO_2 memristor with linear dopant drift made using analog multiplier. Electrical and Electronics and Computer Engineering (ELECO). 2010. pp. 380-384

[35] Yener SC, Kuntman HH. Fully CMOS memristor based chaotic circuit. Radioengineering. 2014;**23**:1140-1149

[36] Ayten UE, Minayi S, Sagbas M. Memristor emulator circuits using single CBTA. International Journal of Electronics and Communicatons (AEÜ). 2017;**82**:109-118. DOI: 10.1016/j.aeue.2017.08.008

[37] Minaei S, Göknar IC, Yıldız M, Yuce E. Memstor, memstance simulations via a versatile 4-port built with new adder and subtractor circuits. International Journal of Electronics. 2015;**102**:911-931. DOI: 10.1080/00207217.2014.942890

[38] Kim H, Sah MP, Yang C, Cho S, Chua LO. Memristor emulator for memristor circuit applications. IEEE Transactions on Circuits and Systems I: Regular Papers. 2012;**59**(10):2422-2431. DOI: 10.1109/TCSI.2012.2188957

[39] Abuelma'atti MT, Khalifa ZJ. A new memristor emulator and its application in digital modulation. Analog Integrated Circuits Signal Process. 2014;**80**:577-584. DOI: 10.1007/s10470-014-0364-3

[40] Sánchez-López C, Aguila-Cuapio LE. A 860 kHz grounded memristor emulator circuit. International Journal of Electronics and Communications (AEÜ). 2017;**73**:23-33. DOI: 10.1016/j.aeue.2016.12.015

[41] Babacan Y, Yesil A, Kacar F. Memristor emulator with tunable characteristic and its experimental results. International Journal of Electronics and Communicatons (AEÜ). 2017;**81**:99-104. DOI: 10.1016/j.aeue.2017.07.012

[42] Yesil A, Babacan Y, Kacar F. A new DDCC based memristor emulator circuit and its applications. Microelectronics Journal. 2014;**45**(3):282-287. DOI: 10.1016/j.mejo.2014.01.011

[43] Sözen H, Çam U. Electronically tunable memristor emulator circuit. Analog Integrated Circuits and Signal Processing. 2016;**89**:655-663. DOI: 10.1007/s10470-016-0785-2

[44] Sánchez-López C, Mendoza-López J, Aguila-Cuapio MA, Muñiz-Montero C. A floating analog memristor emulator circuit. IEEE Transactions on Circuits and Systems II: Express Briefs. 2014;**61**:309-313. DOI: 10.1109/TCSII.2014.2312806

[45] Babacan Y, Kacar F. Floating memristor emulator with subthreshold region. Analog Integrated Circuits and Signal Processing. 2016;**90**:471-475. DOI: 10.1007/s10470-016-0888-9

[46] Li Q, Serb A, Prodromakis T, Xu H. Memristor SPICE model accounting for synaptic activity dependence. PLoS One. 2015;**10**(3):1-12. DOI: 10.1371/journal.pone.0120506

[47] Babacan Y, Kacar F. Memristor emulator with spike-timing-dependent-plasticity. AEU-International Journal of Electronics and Communications. 2017;**73**:16-22. DOI: 10.1016/j.aeue.2016.12.025

[48] Jo SH, Chang T, Ebong I, Bhadviya BB, Mazumder P, et al. Nanoscale memristor device as synapse in neuromorphic systems. Nano Letters. 2010;**10**:1297-1301. DOI: 10.1021/nl904092h

[49] Berdan R, Xu HY, Li XH, Yu H, Liu YC, et al. Synaptic learning and memory functions achieved using oxygen ion migration/diffusion in an amorphous InGaZnO memristor. Advanced Functional Materials. 2012;**22**:2759-2765. DOI: 10.1002/adfm.201103148

[50] Li Y, Zhong Y, Xu L, Zhang J, Xu X, et al. Ultrafast synaptic events in a chalcogenide memristor. Scientific Reports. 2013;**3**:1619. DOI: 10.1038/srep01619

Nanoscale Switching and Degradation of Resistive Random Access Memory Studied by *In Situ* Electron Microscopy

Masashi Arita, Atsushi Tsurumaki-Fukuchi and
Yasuo Takahashi

Additional information is available at the end of the chapter

http://dx.doi.org/10.5772/intechopen.69024

Abstract

The metal-filament-type resistive random access memories (ReRAMs) with copper were investigated from the point of view of dynamical microstructure evolution in the repetitive switching operations using *in situ* transmission electron microscopy (*in situ* TEM). Through a series of experiments for uncovered solid electrolyte films, stacked devices, and nanofabricated cells, formation and erasure of the copper filaments and deposits were confirmed. The behavior of the filament and deposit depended on the switching condition and history. Based on these *in situ* TEM results, the switching schematics and the degradation process were discussed.

Keywords: *in situ* transmission electron microscopy, resistive random access memory, ReRAM, conductive bridge random access memory, CBRAM, memristor, conductive filament

1. Introduction

The resistive random access memory (ReRAM) has great potential as a candidate of the next-generation nonvolatile memory because of the high-speed operation, the wide memory window, and the high-density storage per cost [1]. In addition, its capability of the multilevel or analogue memory control and its hysteretic nonlinear current-to-voltage (I–V) characteristics are suitable for the operation of the artificial neural network hardware using memristors, and this research field is very active especially in these years [2–5]. Because of these advantageous properties, vast numbers of works on ReRAMs have been reported as described in numerous review articles [6–14]. In these years, highly integrated memory chips have been reported [15–17], and a 16 Gbits chip with 180 MB/s write and 900 MB/s read performance fabricated at the 27 nm node has already been demonstrated using the Cu-based ReRAM [18]. Commercialized or nearly commercialized ReRAM chips have also been reported [19–21]. However, there are still ambiguous issues of the switching and device degradation mechanisms, while basic principles of the ReRAM operations have been discussed using the electrochemistry of solid materials.

The ReRAM operation is performed by simply applying voltage to the device having a capacitor structure with a switching layer between the top and bottom electrodes (TE and BE) as shown in **Figure 1(a)**. The initial state of the device is typically the high-resistance state (HRS). It converts into the low-resistance state (LRS) by applying voltage (SET or "Forming" for the first SET). Subsequent voltage returns the resistance to HRS (RESET) as shown in **Figure 1(b)**. The *I–V* curves are hysteretic with the resistance ratio HRS/LRS typically 10^2 or larger (**Figure 1(c)**). The operation is called "bipolar" when the voltage polarity for SET and RESET should be reversed, while it is "unipolar" without polarity change. The ReRAM families energetically investigated have been the valence change memory (VCM) composed of a thin oxide layer between two noble electrodes, and the conductive bridging RAM (CBRAM; there are also other naming) composed of a solid electrolyte with an electrochemically active electrode (Cu or Ag) and an inactive electrode (Pt or TiN). In this report, we study some CBRAMs showing the bipolar switching as shown in **Figure 1(b)**.

The CBRAM operation has been explained based on electrical measurements and electronic and electrochemical discussions [8, 10, 14, 22]. Assuming that the TE is Cu, positive voltage to the TE generates Cu cations through oxidation of the electrode at the interface with the solid electrolyte. These cations move along the electric field and are metallized after receiving electrons at the BE interface. A Cu filament is formed there and grows toward the TE. When this filament connects two electrodes, SET switching is completed. Voltage reversal induces the opposite reaction, and the filament is ruptured (RESET). This simple model based on the results of the electrical measurements is plausible, which is an analogical model of electroplating. However, the switching details like filament evolution at SET/RESET and the behavior of the filament during device degradation are hard to be accomplished only with electrical measurements, which are important for usage of ReRAM with guaranteed reliability as the actual electronic device in the circuit.

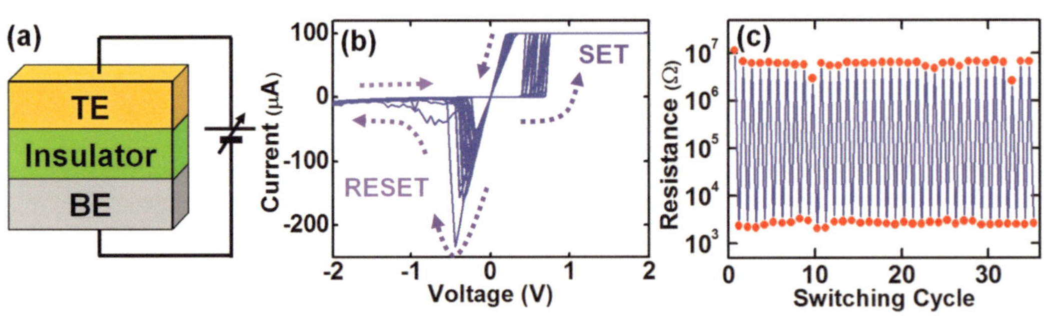

Figure 1. (a) Schematic structure of ReRAM, and typical experimental data of (b) an *I–V* switching curve and (c) a cyclic endurance graph of $Cu/WO_x/TiN$ CBRAM cells.

To overcome this problem, *in situ* transmission electron microscopy (*in situ* TEM) has been applied on a variety of ReRAMs [12, 14, 23, 24] including CBRAMs [25–29] and other families [30–37], which enable real space observations during ReRAM switching. In some examples, formation and erasure of a Cu or Ag filament were confirmed at quick switching of CBRAM [25, 27]. In another report, the filament growth scheme was categorized in terms of its dependence on the cation mobility and the reduction rate [38]. Comprehension of the filament formation has been much advanced with the sake of *in situ* TEM. On the other hand, *in situ* TEM works on RESET and the multiple operations are still rare, although they are quite important for development of reliable ReRAM devices.

For filling the lack of this knowledge, we have performed *in situ* TEM of SET/RESET and/or multiple switching cycles for an uncovered solid electrolyte, stacked CBRAMs, and nanofabricated CBRAM cells. In this contribution, we will review our work in these years [25, 29, 39–44] and discuss the role of the filament at SET/RESET, the filament growth/erasure mode influenced by the switching history, the CBRAM degradation, and the localization of the filament to achieve stable switching.

2. Experimental procedure of *in situ* TEM

A schematic diagram of the *in situ* TEM system is shown in **Figure 2(a)**. The TEM (10^{-5} Pa) was equipped with a home-made TEM piezoholder, a piezocontrol system, a current measurement unit, and a CCD camera system (30 frames/s) [45]. The Pt-Ir electrode set in the TEM holder is movable to select the location of the fixed ReRAM sample to be measured (**Figure 2(b)**). The TEM experiments were performed with the beam current density much less than the 170 fA/nm^2 (typical current density for our high-resolution TEM observations).

The *I*–*V* measurements were carried out using a source measure unit (SMU). The sweeping rate was typically between 0.3 and 1.6 V/s. The pulse switching operation (pulse width of

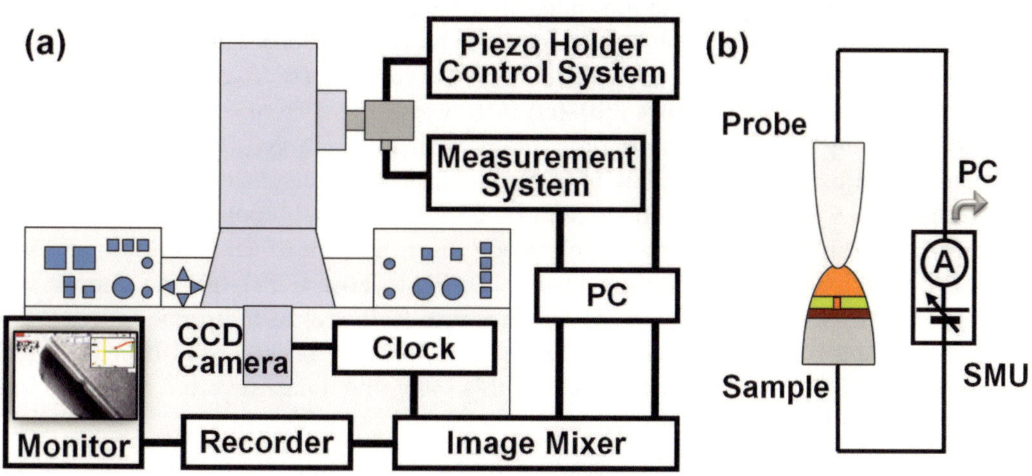

Figure 2. Schematics of (a) the *in situ* TEM system and (b) the geometry of the sample and the probe.

100–500 μs) was occasionally performed. The measurements were done with current compliance of SMU to prevent sample destruction. However, this current compliance was occasionally insufficient because of the parasitic capacitance of the system. In some cases, a MOSFET was installed in the piezoholder to control the compliance current (I_{comp}) strictly. To investigate the microstructural change, the TEM images were recorded simultaneously with the current measurements by using a charge coupled device (CCD) video camera. The video contrast was occasionally enhanced nonlinearly to enable a clear identification of the faint contrast. Frame averaging was also used to reduce the noise.

3. Filament formation and erasure in chalcogenide containing Cu

Filament formation and erasure will be demonstrated using GeS containing copper (Cu:GeS) [25, 39]. Though the switching speed and the retention property were not good enough for actual devices, this material is good for easy investigation of the filament evolution. The Cu:GeS thin film was sputter deposited at room temperature (RT) on a wedge-shaped Pt-Ir substrate that acted as the electrode. The film was 8–60 nm thick and was amorphous including Ge nanocrystals. A sharp Pt-Ir probe (the counterelectrode) contacted the Cu:GeS layer, and the *I–V* measurements were performed. The probe was grounded, and the substrate was biased. In this sample, the Cu ion source was Cu:GeS itself. The atomic composition estimated using EDX was Cu:Ge:S = 4:4:2. Though the PtIr/Cu:GeS/PtIr structure was electrochemically symmetric, it showed the asymmetric ReRAM switching (i.e., bipolar switching) because of the shape difference between the substrate and the probe.

3.1. *In situ* SET and RESET operation

The *I–V* curve is plotted in the left panel of **Figure 3**, where the current compliance was I_{comp} = 500 nA. Clear hysteretic curve was seen as investigated in other studies of solid electrolytes [6, 10, 46, 47]. TEM video images are presented in the right panel of **Figure 3** where each image corresponds to the states (a)–(i) marked in the *I–V* graph. There was no special contrast just before the voltage sweep started (**Figure 3(a)**). The current gradually increased until about 2.5 V, and a deposit-like dark contrast grew from the probe (cathode with this voltage polarity) (**Figure 3(b)–(c)**). Afterward, the current quickly reached I_{comp}. This is SET giving LRS. Correspondingly, the deposit was enlarged (**Figure 3(d)–(e)**) and contacted the substrate. In RESET with negative biasing of the substrate, there were sudden jumps at −0.5 and −2 V, which are abnormal with the usual bipolar switching. This is special for the sample without the Cu electrode (thus, amount of Cu is limited) and was neither conventional SET nor RESET [8, 10, 14, 22]. In **Figure 3(f)–(g)**, the deposit was contracted with negative voltage from the substrate (cathode) to the probe (anode). The deposit detached from the substrate in **Figure 3(h)**, and the resistance returned to HRS. This was the RESET switching. At the end of this cycle, the image reverted almost to that of the original (**Figure 3(i)**).

The deposit size and the current corresponded; therefore, this deposit is expected to act as the conductive filament. The polarity dependence may be attributed not to the electrochemical

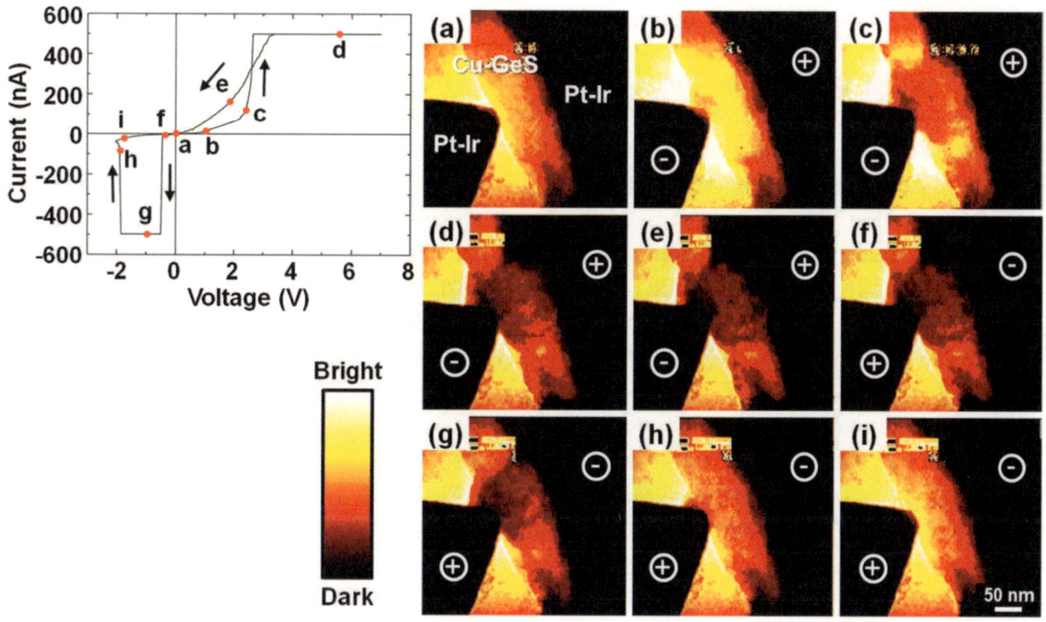

Figure 3. The switching curve (left panel) and TEM images extracted from a video (right panel) of a Cu:GeS film. The images (a)–(i) correspond to the states marked in the switching curve.

properties of the electrodes but to the asymmetry of the electric field caused by the shape difference of the electrodes. Because of the concentrated electric field, Cu ions accumulate at the probe when the substrate is positive. On the other hand, electric flux disperses toward the substrate when the polarity is reversed. Even though Cu is thought to accumulate at the substrate-film interface, its density is low for filament formation.

3.2. SAD and EDX of the conductive filament

Selected area diffractometry (SAD) and energy dispersive X-ray spectroscopy (EDX) were performed in real time during the operation (but other area than **Figure 3**). In this subsection, the results are briefly summarized. Detailed experimental data are seen in Refs. [25, 39].

The crystal structure of the filament was studied using *in situ* SAD. When a deposit was formed, sharp spots appeared in the patterns. They twinkled like stars. This indicates that nanocrystals were formed, and their orientation frequently changed during the voltage scan. The 1152 frames of the SAD video (35 s) were summed, and Debye rings were identified. The estimated *d*-values were those of Cu reflections. For the elemental analysis, the EDX of the filament was performed with voltage application (+1 V). The Cu peak was greatly enhanced relative to the initial state. The composition estimated using the thin foil approximation was Cu:Ge:S = 7:2:1, while the region containing no filaments showed 4:4:2. The filament was an agglomeration of nanocrystals with a relatively large amount of Cu; probably metallic Cu or its alloy with either Ge and/or S.

3.3. Decrease of the SET voltage and the residue of the filament

The SET voltage usually goes down after forming. This was considered to be caused by the wreckage of the filament [8, 10, 14, 22]. To understand this phenomenon, we performed three continuous SET cycles from the initial state. Because of a short retention of this sample, the deposit disappeared automatically without negative voltage. Thus, only the positive cycles were investigated. The SET voltage in the 1st, 2nd, and 3rd cycles decreased from 2.25 to 1.83 V (2nd) and 1.50 V (3rd). In this experiment, the probe position was changed as seen in **Figure 4**, where the arrows indicate the point where the probe hit in the 1st cycle. A filament appeared and disappeared at the probe in the 1st cycle (**Figure 4(a1, a2)**). Afterward, the probe was shifted as seen in **Figure 4(b1)**. When positive voltage was applied, a filament appeared elongating into the region where the 1st filament was formed. In the 3rd cycle, measurement was conducted without changing the probe position from the 2nd cycle (**Figure 4(c1)**). A filament was formed at the same place (**Figure 4 (c2)**). The region where the filament has been formed has priority in subsequent switching. Residuals of the filament should remain as extremely small metallic nanocrystals, which cannot easily be detected by SAD or conventional TEM. They are thought to act as nuclei of the filaments and to reduce the SET voltage.

3.4. Summary

The fundamental behavior of the conductive filament in Cu:GeS was demonstrated by using *in situ* TEM, *in situ* SAD, and *in situ* EDX. The switching scheme is understood as follows.

When the substrate is positively biased, Cu ions in GeS move to the cathode (probe) and a metallic deposit appears there. It consists of Cu-based nanocrystals. The deposit expanded and finally touched the anode (substrate), and the resistance state is LRS. Even in this stage, the microstructure changes with voltage application. The deposit dissolves by polarity reversal, and it shrinks from the cathode (substrate) to the anode (probe). This process gives HRS. The formation/erasure of the deposit clearly corresponded to SET/RESET. Therefore, the conductive filament must be formed in the deposit. This behavior of the filament follows the electrochemical model [8, 10, 14, 22]. With the continuation of the switching cycle, the SET voltage decreased. This is caused by the residuals (probably Cu nanocrystals) that remain even in HRS. These residues are thought to act as nuclei of the filaments.

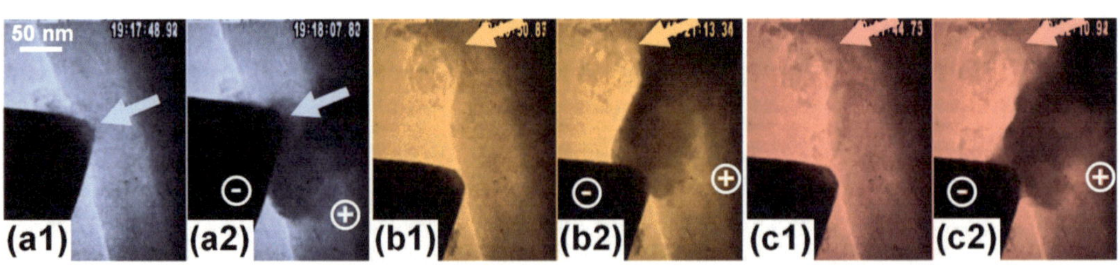

Figure 4. *In situ* TEM images of the (a) 1st, (b) 2nd, and (c) 3rd switching cycle of a Cu:GeS film. Images (a1), (b1), and (c1) are before the SET cycle, and those of (a2), (b2), and (c2) are after SET. The probe position was shifted between (a) and (b), while it was unchanged between (b) and (c). The arrow marks the potion where the probe was contacted in the 1st cycle.

4. CBRAM having the stacked structure with the Cu electrode

The special constitution of CBRAM was used in Section 3 for easy performance of experiments, such as a tip-shaped electrode and nonuse of Cu electrode. Operation was slow, and the current was much less than μA. This is satisfactory for a characterization of conductive filaments. However, to understand realistic operation, the multiple switching cycles should be achieved for multilayered CBRAMs. In Sections 5 and 6, MoO_x and WO_x sandwiched between electrochemically active Cu and inactive TiN electrodes are demonstrated. The dynamics of filament growth/shrinkage (Section 5) and device degradation (Section 6) are discussed through repetitive ReRAM operations with increase of the switching current.

The CBRAMs studied are $Pt_{(100)}/Cu_{(30)}/MoO_{x(50)}$ and $Pt_{(100)}/Cu_{(30)}/WO_{x(20)}$ on TiN/Si substrates, where the numbers denote the thicknesses in nm. Here, the TiN surface was oxidized due to the O_2 plasma treatment for cleaning. The oxide switching layers were prepared using reactive RF sputtering (Ar-20% O_2) of metal targets, while the others were by Ar RF sputtering. All depositions were done at RT without any heat treatment, and both oxides were amorphous. Typical TEM image and EDX map are shown in **Figure 5(a) and (b)**. The layer structure is clearly identified, and the overall switching area is observable. Samples for *in situ* TEM were processed using the ion-shadow method [48], where many cone-shaped small devices were formed. The device diameter was less than 500 nm as shown in **Figure 5(a)**. The current for switching was measured between the biased Pt/Cu and grounded TiN/Si. The current in the LRS was limited by the serially connected resistance of TiN/Si.

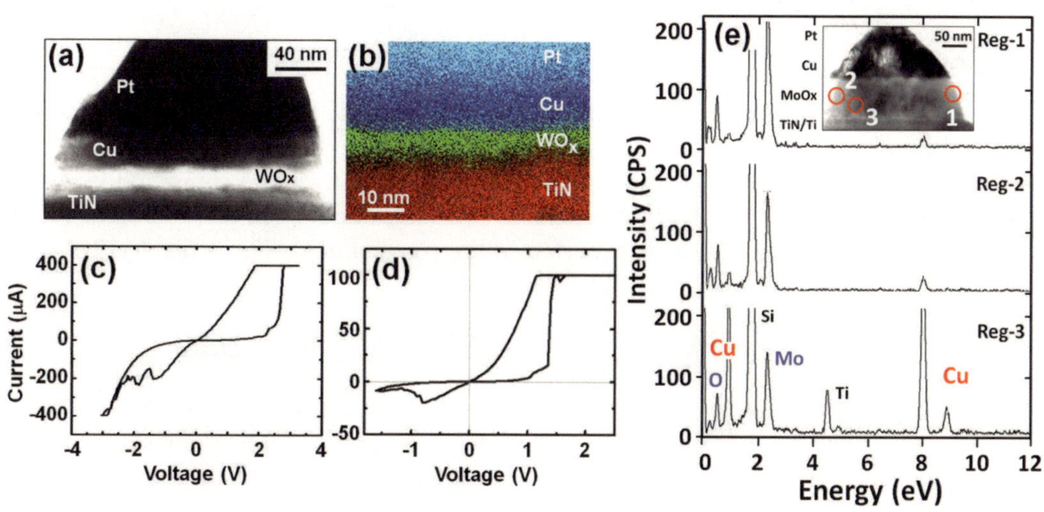

Figure 5. (a) TEM image and (b) EDX mapping of a $Pt/Cu/WO_x/TiN$ sample where clear layer stacking was seen. The *I–V* switching curve of (c) a TEM sample (size: 350 nm) and (d) a microdevice (size: 16 μm) of $Pt/Cu/MoO_x/TiN$. They corresponded well to each other. (e) EDX spectra from the MoO_x layer without the filament (Reg-1 and Reg-2) and the filament (Reg-3). Enhancement of the Cu signal was clearly seen in Reg-3. Inset is the TEM image showing the analyzed areas.

Multiple switching was realized during the TEM observation. An example of the *I–V* curve measured in TEM is **Figure 5(c)**. The current gradually increased with positive voltage, and then the resistance was quickly converted to LRS. In the negative voltage region, the current exhibited jumps giving HRS. This is the typical bipolar switching as seen in **Figure 5(d)** of a conventional CBRAM device fabricated on a Si wafer using the lithography technique. The similarity of fundamental features of these graphs indicates that the vacuum environment in the TEM and electron beam irradiation had no negative effects.

Checking *in situ* TEM videos, filament-like dark contrast grew in the SET cycle and shrank/vanished in the RESET cycle. Here, this darker contrast in the oxide layer is assumed to be the Cu-based conductive filament. This assumption was confirmed by EDX for regions with/without the filament (**Figure 5(e)**). The filament was made up largely of Cu.

5. Switching operation of stacked CBRAM

In this section, the filament dynamics and its mechanism are demonstrated. The CBRAM discussed here is mainly the device having the MoO_x [29, 41, 43, 44].

5.1. Filament formation in the SET process

An example of the SET cycle is shown in **Figure 6**, where the *I–V* graph (**Figure 6(a)**) and the TEM video images (**Figure 6(b)–(g)**) are compared. The initial resistance was 40 MΩ, and thus the Cu inclusion level in MoO_x was small. For initialization, 15 positive/negative cycles were done, and the resistance decreased to 500 kΩ. Clear SET/RESET switching started after this treatment. Here, the gray contrast on the right of the image is unrelated to the switching because it showed no change of note. Increasing the voltage from state-(b), the current increased gradually. In **Figure 6(c)**, a slight change was seen near the central area. The current increased greatly at 3 V (state-(d)), and a dark contrast appeared abruptly in a wide area from the Cu electrode (**Figure 6(d)**). This gathered to be a clear contrast and connected two electrodes in **Figure 6(e)–(f)**. Its growth direction was from the anode (Cu) to the cathode (TiN), and this is opposite to the direction expected in the conventional electrochemical CBRAM

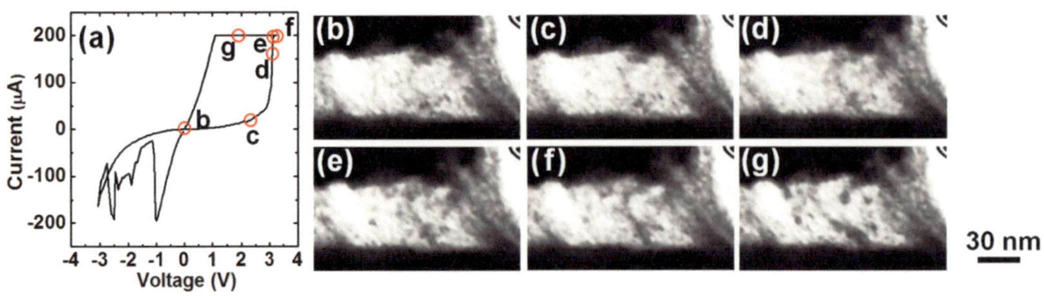

Figure 6. (a) The SET curve and (b)-(g) corresponding *in situ* TEM images of a Cu/MoO_x/TiN device with little Cu inclusion. The filament quickly grew from TE to BE.

model [8, 10, 14, 22]. This behavior has been observed in other switching materials like SiO_2 [28], ZrO_2 [27], and WO_x [42] that are thought not to dilute much Cu (or Ag). During the additional voltage application (over-SET named in this report), the filament grew further and changed its contact position with the Cu electrode toward the left (**Figure 6(g)**). Even after bridging, the filament shape continued to change. Finally, the resistance changed from 500 to 8 kΩ. The LRS retention time was longer than 5 min.

The growth direction reversed in the subsequent SET cycle (**Figure 7**). The switching started at states-(c) and (d). At this moment, there was no dramatic change in the TEM image (**Figure 7(b)–(d)**). When the current increased rapidly at state-(e), a small dark contrast appeared near the cathode (TiN). This is thought to be the nucleus of the filament. It grew, and a 35 nm thick filament bound two electrodes (**Figure 7(f)–(g)**). After the nucleus appeared, the bridging was completed within 200 ms. The resistance decreased from 750 to 8 kΩ.

To discuss the filament growing direction, five images sequentially extracted from the video (30 ms intervals) are shown in **Figure 8**. The nucleus of the filament appeared near the BE (TiN, cathode) and grew toward the TE (Cu, anode). This fits well with the electrochemical switching model [8, 10, 14, 22]. Based on the discussion in a previous report [38], the Cu ion mobility must be high in this case. This was the SET cycle after **Figure 6** (and RESET). Thus, tiny Cu residuals were expected in MoO_x at the starting of this SET. It may influence the Cu ion mobility. In addition, the Joule heat also can increase the ion mobility since large compliance current of > 10^2 A was used here.

The growth scheme from the cathode to the anode was seen also in another sample having Cu deposits near the MoO_x/TiN interface in the initial state. In this case, the initial resistance was small (700 kΩ), and Cu dissolution had happened already in the initial state. This may be caused by a temperature increase during ion milling for TEM sample preparation as seen in heat-treated Cu/SiO_2/BE [49].

Three *I–V* curves from the initial state are shown in **Figure 9(a)**. The nonhysteretic curve of the 1st cycle started to be hysteretic in the 2nd cycle. Though the resistance decreased to 400 kΩ, there was no change in the video image. In the 3rd cycle, a clear hysteresis was identified, the resistance decreased to be 30 kΩ after SET, and RESET occurred. Corresponding images (**Figure 9(b)–(d)**)

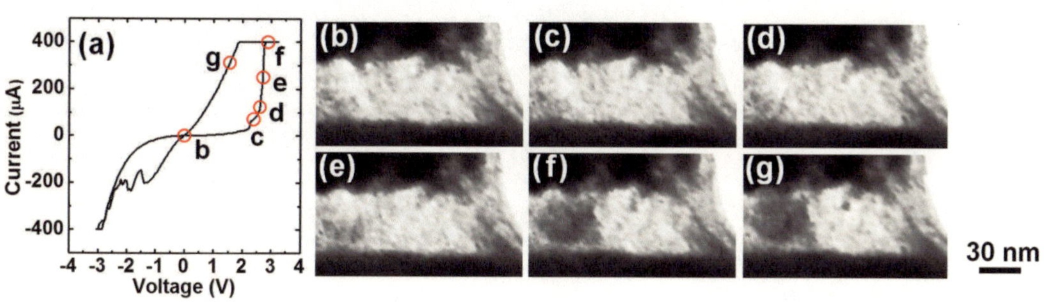

Figure 7. (a) The SET curve and (b)-(g) corresponding *in situ* TEM images of a Cu/MoO_x/TiN device when the switching layer was expected to contain a certain amount of Cu dissolution after the cycle in **Figure 6**.

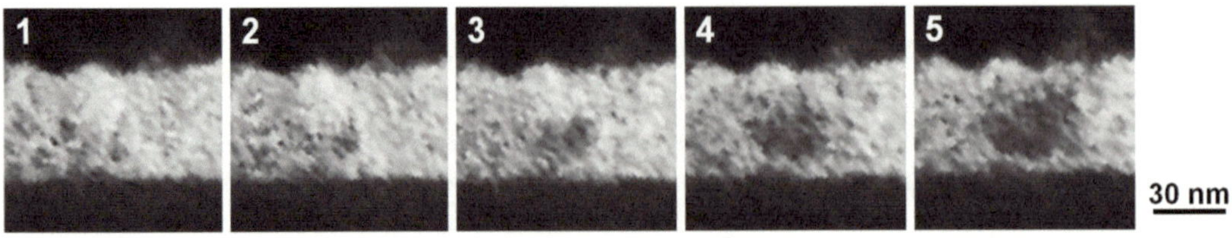

Figure 8. Details of the SET process in **Figure 7**, where the subsequent TEM video frames (images-1 to 5) were shown with the interval of 30 ms. The image-2 corresponds to **Figure 7(e)**. The Cu filament grew apparently from BE to TE.

showed a slight contrast change. The Cu deposit near ox-TiN/TiN (arrows) grew during SET (**Figure 9(c)**), and it disappeared during RESET (**Figure 9(d)**). This Cu deposit must play an important role in ReRAM.

Clear and abrupt current jumps began after the 4th and 5th cycles. The SET operation in the 6th cycle is shown in **Figure 10(a)** compared with the *in situ* TEM images (**Figure 10(b)–(g)**). A Cu deposit that grew in the 5th cycle (round contrast) was identified when the voltage sweep started (**Figure 10(b)**). There is an abrupt current jump at states-(c) and (d). However, the deposit did not show a clear change (**Figure 10(c)–(d)**). It then grew from the cathode (TiN) to the anode (Cu) with the current flow after the SET switching (over-SET) (**Figure 10(e)–(g)**). The deposit did not bridge two electrodes, although the resistance was reduced much.

Summarizing shortly, there were two SET modes with filament growths from the cathode or from the anode depending on the amount of Cu in the MoO_x layer.

5.2. Filament shrinkage and erasure in the RESET process

The RESET process after **Figure 10** is shown in **Figure 11**, where the filament had not bridged. At the states-(b) to (d) in **Figure 11(a)**, the TEM images (**Figure 11(b)–(d)**) maintained the contrast just after SET. A clear RESET switching occurred between states-(d) and (e), but the deposit shrank only slightly (**Figure 11(e)**). Continuing current flow (over-RESET named in this report),

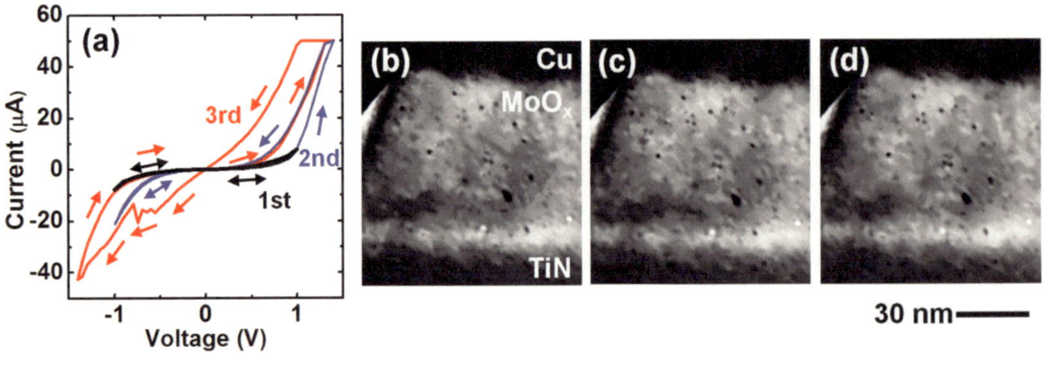

Figure 9. (a) Three *I–V* switching cycles and (b)–(d) TEM images in the 3rd cycle of a MoO_x CBRAM. The images showed appearance/disappearance of a deposit as indicated using arrows in (b) before SET, (c) after SET, and (d) after RESET.

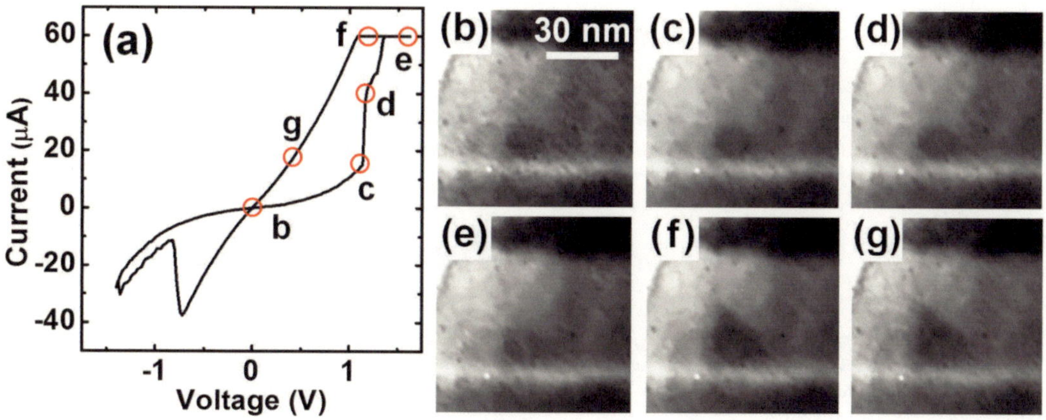

Figure 10. The 6th SET cycle performed after **Figure 9** (Cu/MoO_x/TiN). (a) *I–V* switching curve and (b)–(g) corresponding video images. Growth of the filament from BE to TE was identified.

it continued to shrink (but still not large change), toward the anode (TiN), giving roundish contrast (**Figure 11(f)** and **(g)**). The shrinkage direction fits the filament model [8, 10, 14, 22].

Figure 12 is another example of RESET with nonbridging (or weakly bridging) filament. In this example, the filament vanished due to large negative current (−600 μA, **Figure 12(a)**). The image at starting of the voltage sweep (**Figure 12(b)**) was not changed by RESET switching at state-(c) (**Figure 12(c)**). At state-(d) during over-RESET, an unexpected negative SET with large current occurred, and the filament began to shrink (**Figure 12(d)–(e)**). The filament vanished from the cathode (Cu) to the anode (TiN) (**Figure 12(f)–(g)**). Dissolution of the Cu filament was seen not only at the apex. A small precipitate near the Cu electrode (left of the images) also vanished in **Figure 12(g)**. The current spread widely and contributed to the erasure of the filament and the precipitate nearby. Although the negative SET was abnormal, we can conclude that the large negative current was required for a complete erasure of the filament.

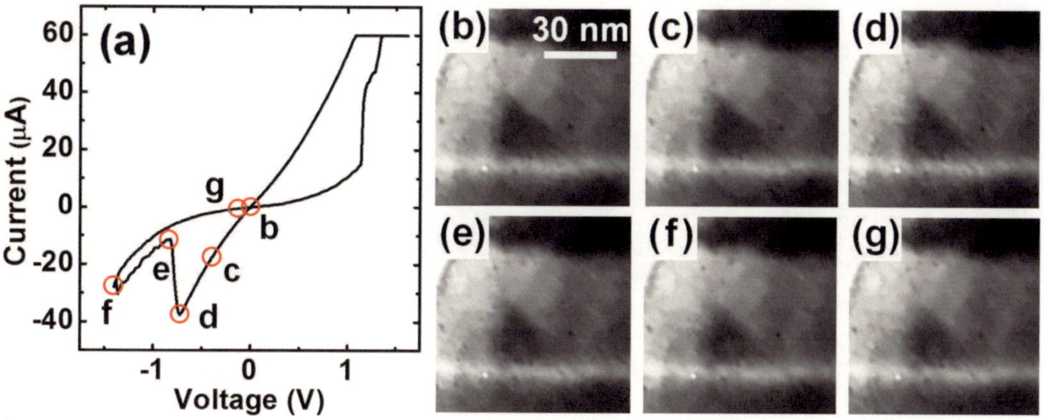

Figure 11. The 6th RESET cycle performed just after **Figure 10** (Cu/MoO_x/TiN), where the filament did not connect to the Cu TE. (a) *I–V* switching curve and (b)–(g) corresponding video images. Shrinkage of the filament from TE to BE was identified.

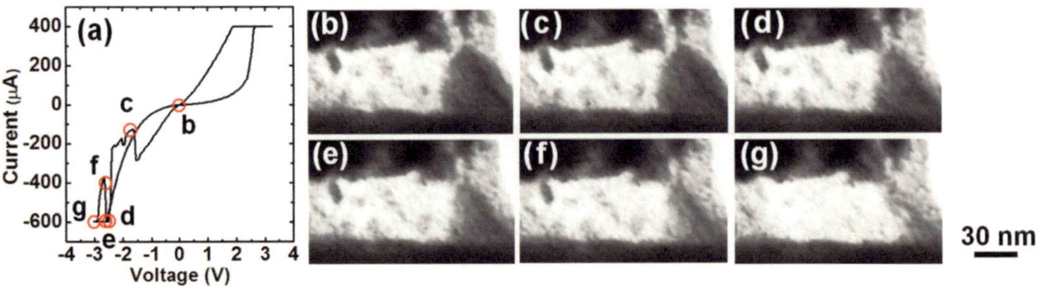

Figure 12. The RESET operation of a Cu/MoO_x/TiN where the filament did not show clear connection to the Cu TE. (a) *I–V* switching curve and (b)–(g) corresponding video images. The filament was overall erased from TE to BE during over-RESET while it did now show any change to note at the moment of RESET switching (state c).

Figure 13 is an example to show what happens for the bridging filament, which is the RESET process of **Figure 7**. With negative voltage sweep, the LRS was weakly changed by RESET before (c). The resistance further increased after another weak RESET between state-(c) and (d). However, the image of **Figure 13(d)** did not change from **Figure 13(b)–(c)**. This suggests that the RESET switching occurred locally in the filament, probably at the ends of filaments touching the electrodes [50, 51]. Through over-RESET with large negative current, the filament started to shrink (**Figure 13(e)**) and was diminished in **Figure 13(f)**. It was erased in **Figure 13(g)** although some residuals remained. A clear hysteresis was seen, and the resistance changed from 9 to 200 kΩ. The details are shown in **Figure 14** with 30 ms intervals. The filament shrank from the anode (TiN) to the cathode (Cu). This behavior did not fit with the reported filament model [8, 10, 14, 22]. The TiN surface was oxidized in this experiment, which must have higher resistance than the filament. The Joule heat concentrated in this region may assist the Cu dissolution there, and the Cu ions moved along the electric field and are adsorbed by the Cu TE.

5.3. Switching power and filament size

The current flow during RESET is an important factor to control the filament. This is true also for SET to form the conductive filament. The filament size is a key factor to affect the resistance

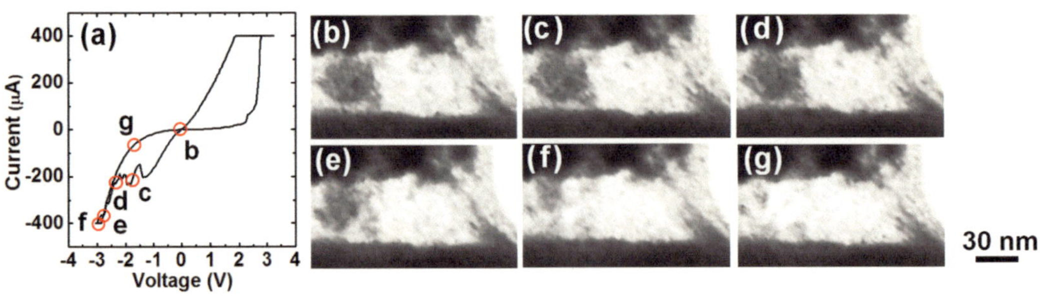

Figure 13. The RESET operation of a Cu/MoO_x/TiN when the filament bridged two electrodes. (a) *I–V* switching curve and (b)–(g) corresponding video images.

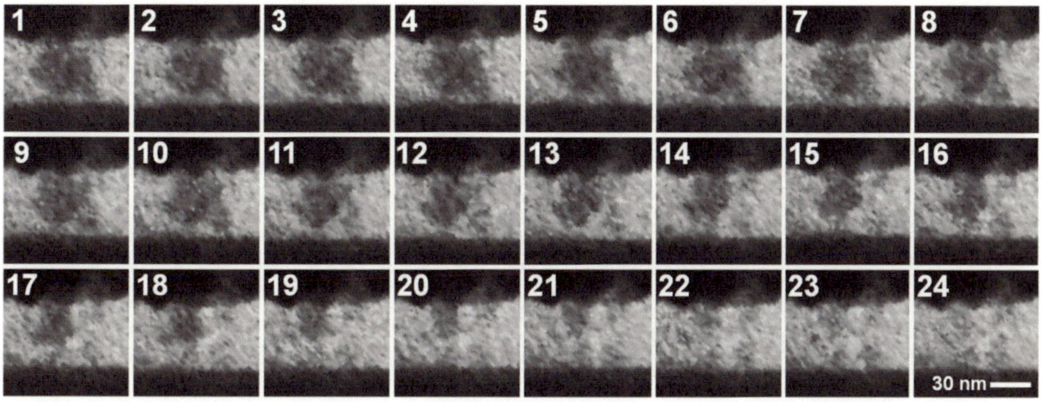

Figure 14. Details of the RESET process in **Figure 13**, where the subsequent TEM video frames (images-1 to 24) were shown with the interval of 30 ms. The Cu filament shrank apparently from BE to TE.

as well as the data retention of LRS. In this subsection, the relation between the switching power at SET and the filament size will be discussed using *in situ* TEM results.

To investigate the filament growth, five successive SET/RESET cycles were measured (**Figure 15**), where the over-SET process was gradually strengthened with increasing I_{comp}. Here, almost no over-RESET was used to prevent shrinkage of the filament. As identified in **Figure 15(a)**, the resistance gradually decreased. Corresponding TEM images acquired after SET operations are shown in **Figure 15(b)–(f)**. The filament grew step-by-step from the cathode (TiN) to the anode (Cu) with the increase of the injection power at SET. Though the resistance did not show drastic change even when the filament reached the Cu TE, it was because the resistance of TiN/Si serially connected to the switching layer limited the current.

There is a set of data with large SET current in **Figure 16**, where enough over-RESET was done to erase the filament in each cycle. During SET/RESET cycles, I_{comp} was stepwise increased to 1 mA, at which the device was destructed. **Figure 16(a)–(d)** shows the TEM images taken just after each SET. The filament in the 1st SET with I_{comp} = 200 μA was thin, and it became thick with I_{comp} (**Figure 16(e)**) as expected earlier [51, 52].

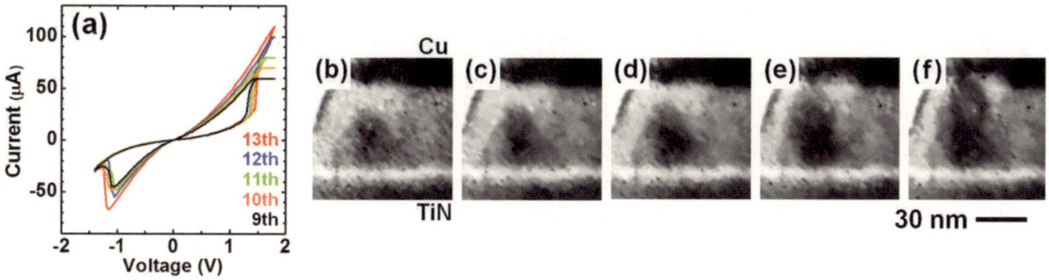

Figure 15. The 9th to 13th SET operations with increasing the compliance current (Cu/MoO_x/TiN). (a) The switching curves and the video images after SET in the (b) 9th, (c) 10th, (d) 11th, (e) 12th and (f) 13th cycles. The filament grew step by step, and the resistance decreased.

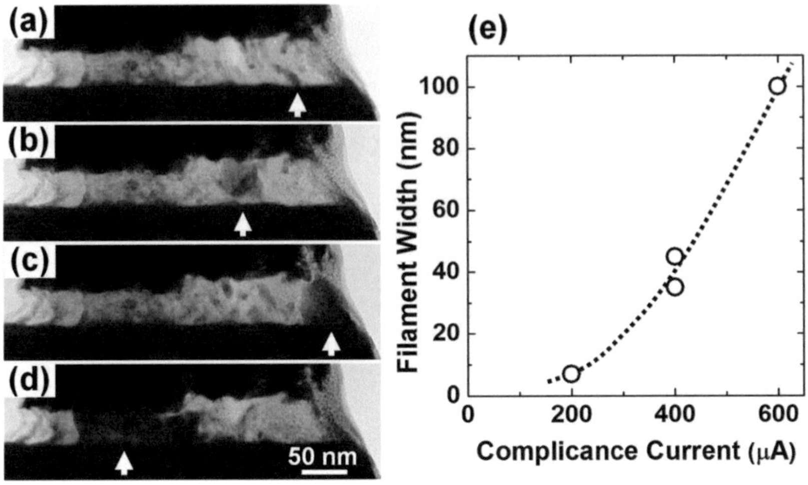

Figure 16. (a)-(d) *In situ* TEM images after SET with increasing the compliance current (a: 200, b: 400, c: 400 and d: 600 μA). After each SET, strong over-RESET was done to erase the filament. (e) Filament diameter increased with the compliance current. In addition, the filament position changed very much.

5.4. Summary of the switching schematics

Based on the results described above, SET/RESET operations are classified in **Figure 17**. There are two SET modes and two RESET modes.

When the MoO_x layer contains little Cu inclusions, a high SET voltage is required. The Cu of the anode moves quickly into MoO_x and generates deposits in a wide area, and they gather to form the filament (SET-1). When enough Cu has been dissolved in the initial state or during *I–V* cycles, the deposit appears on the TiN cathode and grows toward the Cu anode (SET-2). For enough resistance decrease, the filament connecting two electrodes is not necessarily required. The Cu^{z+} ions, oxygen vacancies and/or electrons are thought to contribute the total current. Connection of electrodes is achieved with sufficient over-SET.

There is a report on oxide CBRAMs with Ag [38]. When the Ag mobility in the oxide is low compared with the reduction rate, Ag ions are reduced to be metal before drifting for long distances, and the filament grows from the anode (Ag) to the cathode. SET-1 is categorized as this type as reported in ZrO_2 [27], SiO_2 [28] and WO_x [42]. On the other hand, when MoO_x contains sufficient Cu ions, the filament formation at the MoO_x–cathode interface can be discussed using the conventional electrochemical model [8, 10, 14, 22]. The Cu ions near the cathode can quickly reach the cathode and easily initiate the filament formation. At the same time, Cu ions are continuously generated by oxidation of the Cu electrode and supplied into MoO_x. As the result, the filament grows toward the anode (Cu). This is a plausible explanation for SET-2. A similar discussion was conducted in a previous report [53].

There are two RESET modes. The nonbridging filament tends to shrink toward the cathode (TiN). This is RESET-1. In this case, the filament acts as the anode. This transition is explained using the conventional model [8, 10, 14, 22]. The Cu filament is electrochemically dissolved in MoO_x

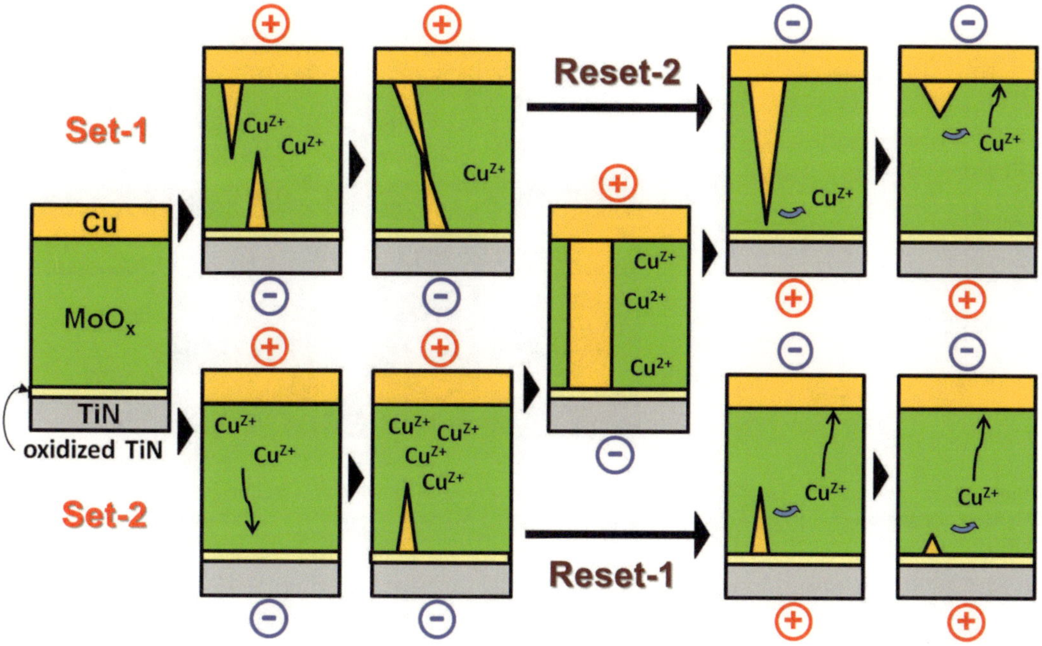

Figure 17. Switching schematics. There were two SET modes and two RESET modes.

and becomes thin overall due to widely spread current leakage. This tendency is thought to be enhanced with temperature increase during over-RESET with high current. In contrast, the filament bridging two electrodes ruptures in a region contacting with the anode (TiN); RESET-2. This is caused by the thin ox-TiN layer. The Joule heat is preferably generated near this area because of its high resistance, and Cu of the lower part of the filament is preferably dissolved in MoO_x. The dissolved ions move along the widely spread electric field. In both RESET modes, the heat generated in the filament must play an important role to the electrochemical processes.

Strictly speaking, the discussion here addresses filament formation/shrinkage during over-SET/over-RESET. Sharp resistance switching in stable *I–V* cycles can occur without such large changes. Even when the filament showed a remarkable change, this change did not occur at the moment of sharp SET/RESET switching. Stable switching occurs very locally.

5.5. Role of the interface region

As described above, large geometrical change of the filament (or deposit) was not identified at the switching moment. To check this phenomenon, the lower part of MoO_x layer was observed (**Figure 18**), where nonbridging deposit (area marked with "p" in **Figure 18(b-7)**) had been segregated at the MoO_x–ox-TiN/TiN interface. In the *I–V* measurement of **Figure 18(a)**, the switching current was less than 50 μA to prevent over-SET and over-RESET. While there was no change until **Figure 18(b2)**, the bottom edge of the Cu deposit swelled out downward into ox-TiN in state-3 after the SET switching (arrow in **Figure 18(b3)**). This faint contrast of the filament appeared to bridge the deposit and TiN as seen in **Figure 18(b4)–(b5)**. After the

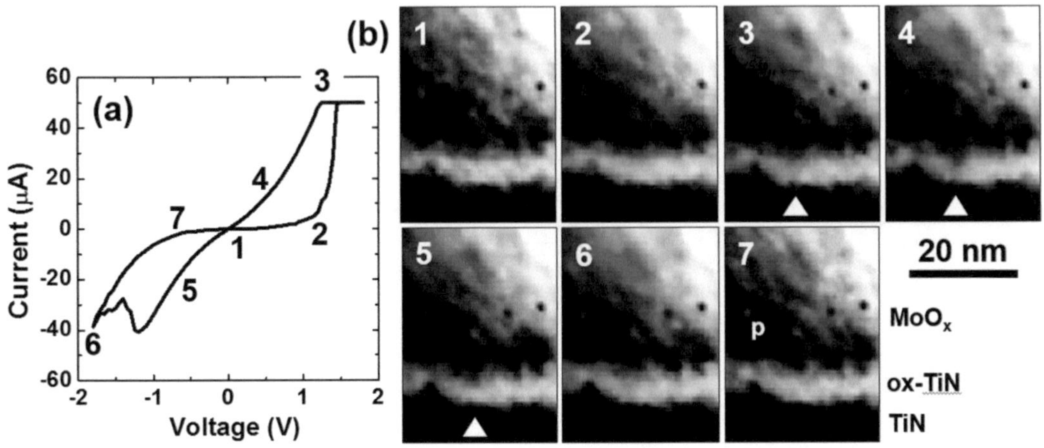

Figure 18. The SET/RESET operation showing formation/erasure of a nanofilament in thin ox-TiN at the MoO_x/TiN interface. The states 1–7 in (a) the *I–V* switching curve and (b) TEM images correspond to each other.

RESET switching around −1.5 V, this faint contrast disappeared (**Figure 18(b6)** and **(b7)**). This filament appearance/disappearance was observed at the same position also in another switching cycle. Its width was roughly 3–5 nm. Such a small filament contributes to ReRAM switching without over-SET and over-RESET. The filament in ox-TiN appeared from Cu to TiN and disappeared from TiN to Cu. The inconsistency of this phenomenon with the conventional model [8, 10, 14, 22] can be discussed with the reduction/oxidation of the Cu ions within the oxide layer [27, 28, 54] or the doping/dedoping effect [55].

This device structure is classified as a CBRAM with double switching layers like CuTe or Cu:MoO_x with GdO_x [56, 57] showing stable operation. The thick filament in the solid electrolyte may act as a narrow electrode limiting the switching region. Power control not to erase the thick filament in the solid electrolyte layer is important for stable switching repetition.

6. Device degradation

Majority of *in situ* TEM works has been done to study the switching mechanism (especially SET). They were low power switching because the slow operation makes easy observations. Considering realistic devices, studies of device reliability like data retention, endurance [58–60], and switching stability are required. For this purpose, multiple switching cycles with various currents should be performed. In this section, two device degradation tests will be demonstrated using Cu/MoO_x/TiN and Cu/WO_x/TiN. In both the examples, the operation was gradually strengthened in repetitive cycles to execute the accelerated aging tests [29, 42, 44].

6.1. Position instability of the filament after over-RESET

For an actual operation, a large resistance ratio HRS/LRS is needed. The high HRS resistance satisfies this demand. This can be achieved using over-RESET. However, the switching cycle was fatally damaged, while the stable cycle continued without it.

The reason can be discussed using **Figure 16** in Section 5.3. Five SET/RESET cycles were repeated using a Cu/MoO_x/TiN CBRAM until device destruction for I_{comp} = 1 mA. The filament formed in each SET was well erased using over-RESET. A filament appeared in the 1st SET of **Figure 16(a)**, and it was erased. In the 2nd cycle with larger I_{comp}, a thicker filament appeared at the position shifted along the left (**Figure 16(b)**). Its position changed again to the right in the 3rd SET (**Figure 16(c)**). In the 4th SET, it moved to the left (**Figure 16(d)**). In the example of Section 3.3 (without over-RESET), the filament kept the position, and the tiny filament nuclei were expected as residues. On the other hand, the nuclei must be removed after the strong over-RESET in **Figure 16**. Complete erasure of the filament can give a higher resistance value in HRS, and a large memory window can be achieved. However, at the same time, it possibly induces a position change of the filament and switching instability. Power control of RESET to maintain filament residuals is thought to be important for the stable switching operation.

6.2. HRS endurance failure

Strong over-RESET induces switching instability. Therefore, the SET/RESET switching cycles were investigated on Cu/WO_x/TiN without performing over-RESET for 10 times, where the voltage was back to 0 V after the RESET switching occurred. The I_{comp} was increased stepwise from 20 to 300 μA. A large current may increase temperature and induce widely spread leakage current. Therefore, these experiments are "accelerated aging tests" under severe conditions, which is usually done before practical use of electronic devices.

Typical *I–V* curves measured in TEM are shown in **Figure 19(a)–(d)**. The characteristics of these curves are quite similar to that of a conventional device (**Figure 1(b)**, 4 μm in diameter), both of which showed the sharp bipolar switching. The difference of the switching voltage from the conventional device is caused by the small device size of the TEM sample (~210 nm). The maximum SET current (I_{comp}) and the RESET currents ($|-I_{max}|$) are summarized in **Figure 19(e)**. The current $|-I_{max}|$ tended to increase with I_{comp} as pointed out in earlier reports

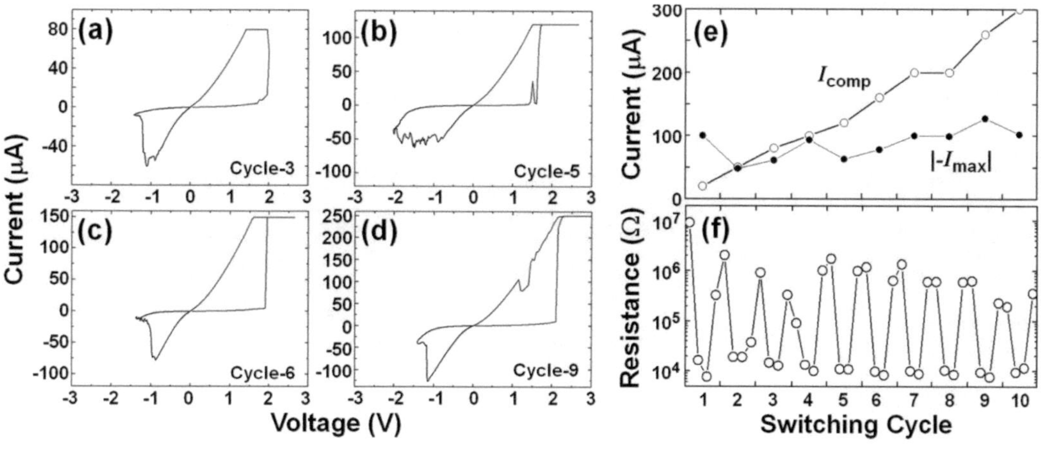

Figure 19. The SET/RESET operations of Cu/WO_x/TiN during *in situ* TEM observations. (a)–(d) Examples of *I–V* switching, (e) the relation between the compliance current I_{comp} and the maximum RESET current $|-I_{max}|$, and (f) the cyclic endurance graph where the resistances were evaluated using the *I–V* graphs both in the SET and RESET processes.

[61, 62]. The cyclic endurance is summarized in **Figure 19(f)**. The HRS/LRS resistance ratio was around 10^2. All of these properties satisfy switching fundamentals of the CBRAM devices. Thus, the *in situ* TEM results below can reflect the general ReRAM degradation property.

The resistance in the HRS gradually decreased in this graph, although the resistance ratio was still large. Here, the behavior of LRS could not be discussed because it was limited by the resistance of the serially connected substrate. Continuing the switching cycles, the device would reach HRS endurance failure as in conventional devices [58–60]. Corresponding TEM images in the initial state and after SET/RESET operations are listed in **Figure 20(a)** and **(b)–(h)**, respectively. After switching from the initial state, a filament was formed at the position marked with a triangle in **Figure 20(b)**. In the subsequent operations in **Figure 20(c)–(d)**, clear change of the filament was not identified. Afterward, small deposits grew on TiN as seen in **Figure 20(e)–(g)** with the increase of the SET current. When I_{comp} was 300 μA, a thick filament appeared at another position (**Figure 20(h)**). With the advancement of the cycles with increasing I_{comp}, the WO_x layer became thin. This indicates that current widely spread in WO_x when I_{comp} was high. The Cu moved along this current leakage and was deposited widely at the interface. Even after the filament formation, the switching layer other than the filament changes. This must be the origin of the HRS endurance failure. This failure that occurred in the operation with weak RESET was proposed to be caused by the ruptured filament tip [58, 60]. However, based on the result here, Cu tends to accumulate at the interface not only around the conductive filament.

6.3. Summary

The switching characteristics are influenced by the electric power injected into the device. High SET current enhances the filament growth and lowering of the LRS resistance as seen in **Figure 15**. Although the resistance decrease in this figure was hindered behind the substrate resistance, it will be clearly seen in **Figure 24(a)** in the next section. High HRS/LRS resistance ratio is expected in this condition. However, strong SET (or over-SET) induces unexpected Cu deposition around the filament due to Cu dissolution and movement along the widely spread current leakage. This makes the switching layer thin and the HRS endurance failure may occur. The strong RESET (or over-RESET) can recover this failure [58], which erases the filament (and deposits) and moves Cu inclusion back to the Cu electrode. However, the filament position tends to change in the next switching cycle.

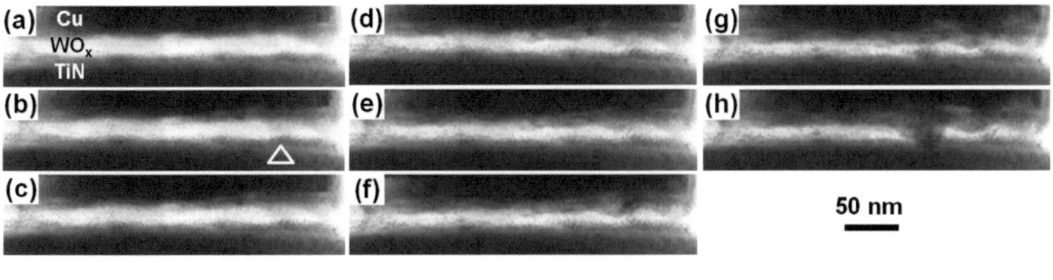

Figure 20. TEM images during device degradation of Cu/WO_x/TiN. The *I–V* switching cycles were performed with no over-RESET. (a) Initial, after SET/RESET of the (b) 1st (I_{comp} = 20 μA), (c) 2nd (50 μA), (d) 4th (100 μA), (e) 6th (150 μA), (f) 8th (200 μA), (g) 9th (250 μA), and (h) 10th (300 μA) cycles. The first filament was formed at the triangle in (b). The bright region corresponding to the WO_x became thin.

This may induce switching instability. The power balance of SET and RESET is important to avoid this degradation.

7. *In situ* TEM of nanofabricated CBRAM devices

Localization of the switching area may be effective to satisfy this requirement because the low power switching can be achieved without large change and easy power control of SET and RESET is expected. The nanofabricated multistacked device has a possibility to satisfy this requirement as used in the VCM [14, 63]. In this section, there is an example of *in situ* TEM of such devices [40, 41]. The evolution of the filament and Cu condensation are discussed in the nanometer range. Data retention and pulse endurance are also discussed.

Figure 21(a) is a schematic of the TEM sample. Nine devices were fabricated on a Si chip. Each CBRAM cell is composed of a Cu–Te-based solid electrolyte layer between the TE and the bottom insulator in the contact hole (30 or 70 nm). For *in situ* TEM, the device was processed by the focused ion beam technique (FIB). The current was measured between the biased TE and the grounded Si. Repetitive *I–V* cycles during *in situ* TEM are shown in **Figure 21(b)**, where 60 cycles were confirmed without degradation. The most important point is that the TEM sample reproduced the same characteristics as actual devices on memory chips.

7.1. *I–V* switching current and filament size

The *I–V* switching curves and TEM images of the 30-nm cell are tabulated in **Figure 22** where the data before and after SET and after RESET are compared for different I_{comp}. In all cases, the clear and sharp ReRAM switching was realized. In the main part of this table, the contact hole area was magnified with contrast enhancement. When I_{comp} was larger than 125 μA, contrast change due to filament formation/rupture is seen inside the insulator layer (triangle) while it could not be identified without the contrast enhancement. Other dark contrasts visible in the insulator, which did not show any change, are not related to the resistive switching and

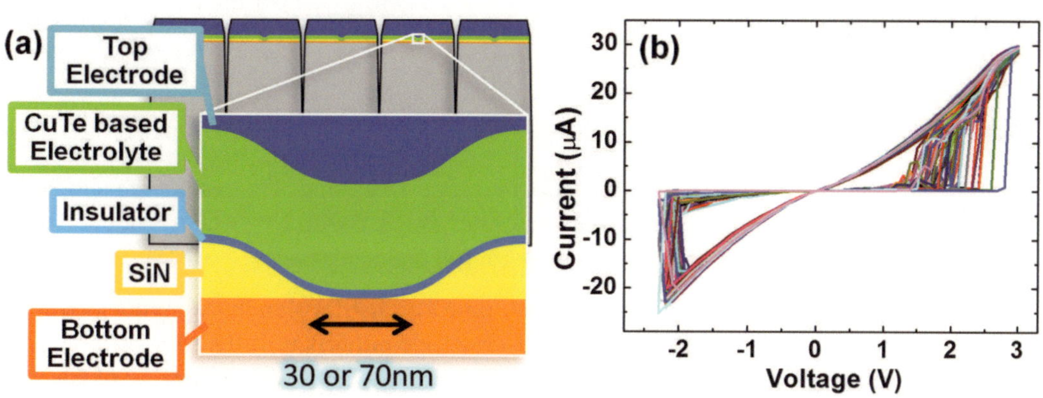

Figure 21. (a) Schematics of the nanofabricated device for *in situ* TEM, and (b) repetitive *I–V* switching (60 SET/RESET cycles) achieved in TEM.

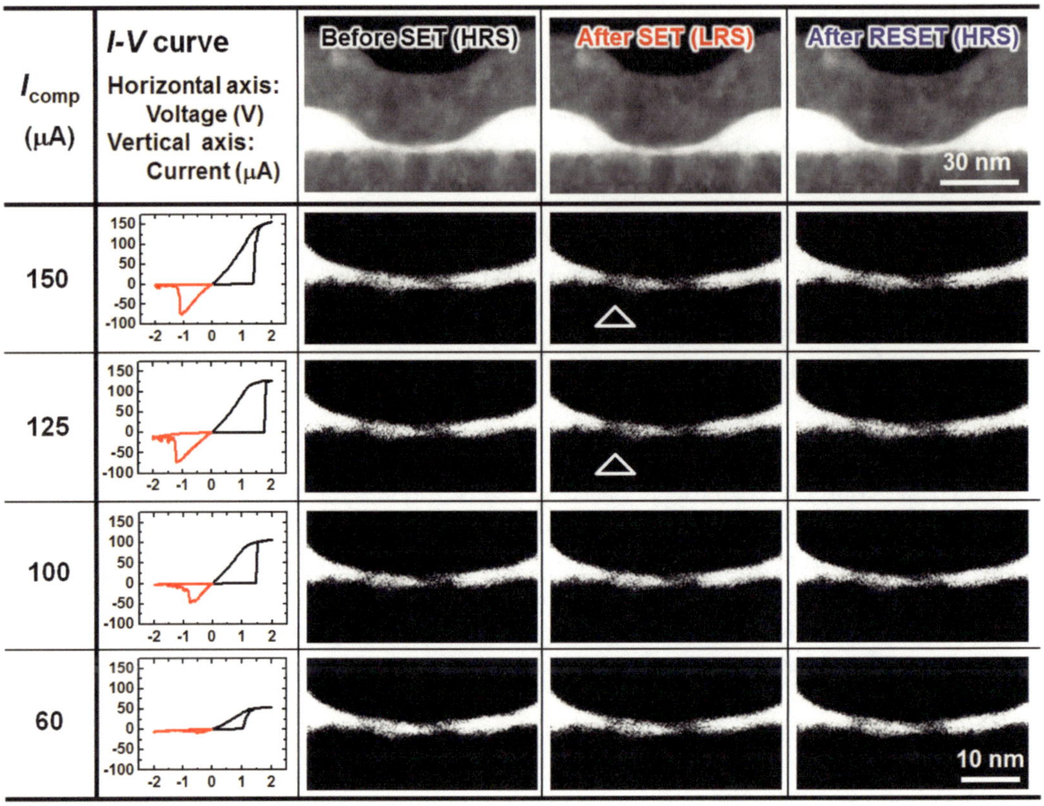

Figure 22. The *I–V* switching curve and TEM images of the 30-nm cell for various compliance current I_{comp}. The images in HRS before SET, LRS after SET, and HRS after RESET are compared. With large I_{comp}, the filament appeared and disappeared in the insulator layer (triangle).

thought to be wreckages of the solid electrolyte and/or electrodes appeared during the FIB process. The filament appeared and vanished at the same position near the edge of the contact hole. Electric field enhancement at the edge played an important role. On the other hand, no remarkable change was seen with low I_{comp}, while the SET/RESET switching was clearly seen. Very fine filaments must be formed in these cases.

7.2. Accumulation of Cu

To perform the elementary analyses, the EDX mapping was done. The results are shown in **Figure 23**, where the data in the initial state and after the SET with I_{comp} = 60 μA of the 70-nm cell, and after SET with I_{comp} = 450 μA of the 30-nm cell are compared.

In the initial state, both Cu and Te maps showed uniform distribution in the solid electrolyte layer. Little change in the distribution was observed for either Cu or Te after SET (60 μA) where a clear filament could not be seen in the TEM image. However, gathering of Cu was observed at the left end of the contact hole at SET with I_{comp} = 450 μA. In addition, the Cu moved and accumulated in the insulator layer. This was not seen in the Te map, where the insulator layer with a white contrast is still visible. This suggests that only Cu ions moved into

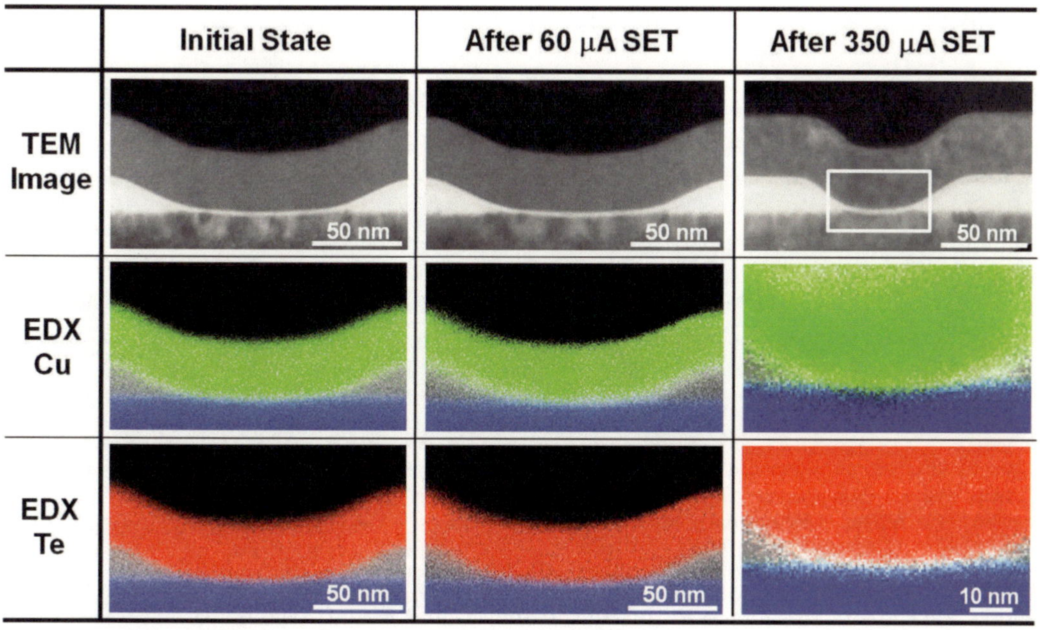

Figure 23. TEM images and EDX maps (Cu and Te) of three devices. Initial state and two SET processes with different I_{comp} are compared. In the right column, the square region in the TEM image was analyzed by EDX. When current was large, Cu movement into the insulator layer was identified. Note the magnification of the EDX maps are not constant..

the insulator by the electric field at SET. This is consistent with the filament formation shown in **Figure 22** and the model predicted in a previous report of the similar double-layer CBRAM device [56]. These results prove that resistive switching here was a result of a formation process of the Cu filament as discussed in the previous section.

7.3. Data retention and pulse endurance

Resistance variation after SET for various I_{comp} is shown in **Figure 24(a)**. The LRS formed with $I_{comp} \geq 40$ μA showed a good retention (more than 3×10^6 s = 3 months). Even with a small SET current generating very thin filament that was hard to be observed, a good retention could be achieved when the filament was localized in the thin insulator. The HRS retention capability was also confirmed to be more than 3 months because it is more stable than LRS. An additional issue can be discussed using **Figure 24(a)**. The resistance just after SET decreased with I_{comp}. This was caused by the thickened filament with large I_{comp} as shown in **Figure 22**.

Repeatable pulse-voltage operation is another issue to be investigated. A pulse endurance graph during *in situ* TEM is shown in **Figure 24(b)**. About 10^5 pulse switching cycles were achieved inside the TEM without any damage. These results clearly show that CBRAMs worked normally even during TEM experiments.

7.4. Summary

Considering the practical application, the switching operations of nanofabricated Cu-Te cells were explained in this section. Adopting the structure with double switching layers, the Cu

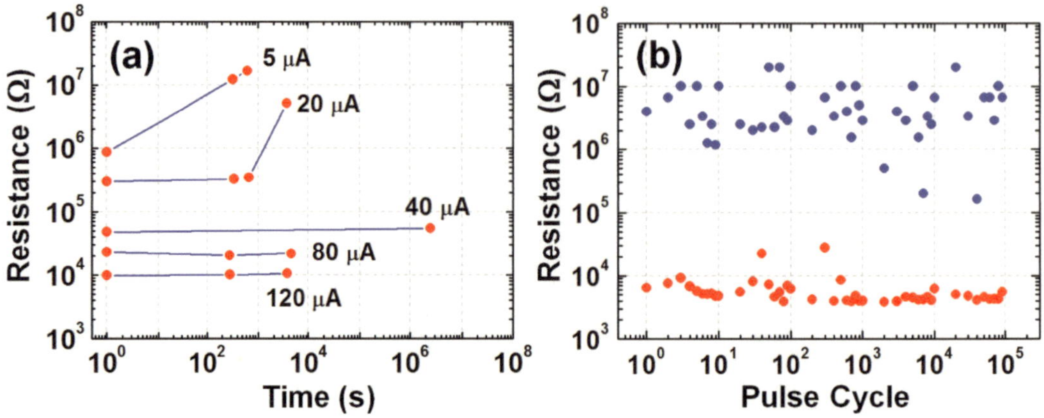

Figure 24. Reliability test performed during *in situ* TEM. (a) The LRS retention graph after SET with various compliance currents, where the read voltage was +0.2 V. (b) The pulse endurance graph. The pulse voltage and width were +3.0 V and 500 μs (for SET) or −1.5 V and 100 μs (for RESET).

nanofilament can be localized in the thin insulator, and a sharp switching can be achieved with a low current. The accumulation of Cu in the Cu-Te layer forms a thicker filament than the one in the insulator, and it acts as a miniaturized Cu electrode that limits the switching area. Increasing the switching current, the filament becomes thick for easy TEM observations, and the retention property improves. Selecting optimum operation condition, the 10^5 pulse switching and long retention over 3 months are possible during *in situ* TEM. The double-layer CBRAM can limit the switching area with short amount of Cu movement. This must be the key factor to realize stable and sharp switching properties.

8. Concluding remarks

In this contribution, we reviewed our recent *in situ* TEM works of various CBRAMs; uncovered Cu:GeS contacted with a needle-shaped electrode, stacked Cu/MoO_x/TiN or Cu/WO_x/TiN, and the nanofabricated Cu–Te-based ReRAM cell.

In all cases, the Cu conductive filament appeared in the SET process and shrank/vanished in the RESET process. There were two SET modes and two RESET modes. The growth/erasure direction of the filament depended on the switching history especially the amount of Cu dissolved in the switching layer. However, in the *I–V* switching cycles, the filament did not necessarily show remarkable change in geometry at the SET/RESET switching moment. The local area near the electrode is thought to contribute this switching. *In situ* TEM in nanometer or subnanometer scale is necessary for a detailed understanding of the filament evolution.

The Cu filament grew/shrank much during over-SET/over-RESET. For such a large change, the operation current (and accompanied temperature increase) seems to play an important role. With a current increase at SET, the filament became thick and the LRS resistance decreased. However, when strong RESET was not operated, influence of widely spread leakage current became conspicuous, and unexpected Cu deposits were formed widely at the interface. This reduced the effective thickness of the switching layer and lead to the HRS endurance failure. While strong RESET may prevent this degradation, the filament position changed under this condition, and the switching became unstable. The switching powers at SET and RESET should be balanced for clear and stable ReRAM switching.

This was realized by adopting miniaturized CBRAM cells with double switching layers. The thin filament in nm range was localized in a thin insulator layer, while thicker Cu condensation occurred in the solid electrolyte, which could act as a protrusion of the electrode. Sharp and stable switching was performed with low current, and less degree of Cu movement was expected. This sharp switching property is applicable for conventional binary memories. On the other hand, the sharp switching is not ideal for application of the artificial neural networks that require multilevel or analogue control of the resistance. Further device designing is needed to perform stable operation for this type of devices.

The operation failure is the critical issue to ensure the practical application of ReRAMs. It is indispensable to clarify main origins of the malfunction and to guarantee device reliability. We demonstrated many *in situ* TEM functions that are available for reliability tests: *I–V* characteristics, pulse switching, endurance, and data retention. While the time resolution is limited by the video frame rate (30 ms/frame in usual cases), other functions like TEM or scanning TEM (STEM) imaging as well as the elementary or chemical analyses using EDX or electron energy loss spectroscopy (EELS) are possible. *In situ* TEM is applicable to characterize nanometer-scale ReRAM cells expected for gigabit scale integration.

Acknowledgements

We acknowledge the financial support from the Japan Society for the Promotion of Science (JSPS, KAKENHI, 15H01706, 16H0433906, and 16K18073). This work was partly performed under the Nanotechnology Platform Program (Hokkaido Univ. and Kyushu Univ.) organized by the Ministry of Education, Culture, Sports, Science, and Technology (MEXT), Japan. Part of this work was carried out under the collaboration with the Semiconductor Technology Academic Research Center (STARC) as well as Sony Corp. We are grateful to Messer Kouichi Hamada and Yuji Mori for development of the experimental setup, especially piezo-TEM holders. Finally, we would like to emphasize that the works reviewed here could not be accomplished without the collaboration with our laboratory members.

Author details

Masashi Arita*, Atsushi Tsurumaki-Fukuchi and Yasuo Takahashi

*Address all correspondence to: arita@nano.ist.hokudai.ac.jp

Laboratory of Nanomaterial Engineering, Graduate School of Information Science and Technology, Hokkaido University, Sapporo, Japan

References

[1] Sacchetto D, Gaillardon PE, Zervas M, Carrara S, De Micheli G, Leblebici Y. Applications of multi-terminal memristive devices: A review. IEEE Circuits and Systems Magazine. 2013;**13**(2):23-41. DOI: 10.1109/MCAS.2013.2256258

[2] Seo K, Kim I, Jung S, Jo M, Park S, Park J, et al. Analog memory and spike-timing-dependent plasticity characteristics of a nanoscale titanium oxide bilayer resistive switching device. Nanotechnology. 2011;**22**(25):254023. DOI: 10.1088/0957-4484/22/25/254023

[3] Nayak A, Ohno T, Tsuruoka T, Terabe T, Hasegawa T, Gimzewski JK, Aono M. Controlling the synaptic plasticity of a Cu_2S gap-type atomic switch. Advanced Functional Materials. 2012;**22**(17):3606-3613. DOI: 10.1002/adfm.201200640

[4] Prezioso M, Merrikh-Bayat F, Hoskins BD, Adam GC, Likharev KK, Strukov DB. Training and operation of an integrated neuromorphic network based on metal-oxide memristors. Nature. 2015;**521**(7550):61-64. DOI: 10.1038/nature14441

[5] DeSalvo B, Vianello E, Garbin D, Bichler O, Perniola L. From memory in our brain to emerging resistive memories in neuromorphic systems. In: 2015 IEEE 7th International Memory Workshop; May 17-20, 2015; Monterey, CA, USA. Piscataway, NJ, USA: IEEE; 2015. pp. 9-12. DOI: 10.1109/IMW.2015.7150286

[6] Waser R, Aono M. Nanoionics-based resistive switching memories. Nature Materials. 2007;**6**(11):833-840. DOI: 10.1038/nmat2023

[7] Sawa A. Resistive switching in transition metal oxides. Materials Today. 2008;**11**(8):28-36. DOI: 10.1016/S1369-7021(08)70119-6

[8] Waser R, Dittmann R, Staikov G, Szot K. Redox-based resistive switching memories – Nanoionic mechanisms, prospects, and challenges. Advanced Materials. 2009;**21**(25-26): 2632-2663. DOI: 10.1002/adma.200900375

[9] Akinaga H, Shima H. Resistive random access memory (ReRAM) based on metal oxides. Proceedings of the IEEE. 2010;**98**(12):2237-2251. DOI: 10.1109/JPROC.2010.2070830

[10] Chen A. Ionic memory technology. In: Kharton VV, editor. Solid State Electrochemistry II: Electrodes, Interfaces and Ceramic. 1st ed. Weinheim, Germany: Wiley-VCH; 2011. pp. 1-30. DOI: 10.1002/9783527635566.ch1

[11] Kim KM, Jeong DS, Hwang CS. Nanofilamentary resistive switching in binary oxide system; a review on the present status and outlook. Nanotechnology. 2011;**22**(25):254002. DOI: 10.1088/0957-4484/22/25/254002

[12] Yang Y, Lu W. Nanoscale resistive switching devices: Mechanisms and modeling. Nanoscale. 2013;**5**:10076-10092. DOI: 10.1039/c3nr03472k

[13] Mickel PR, Lohn AJ, Marinella MJ. Memristive switching: Physical mechanisms and applications. Modern Physics Letters B. 2014;**28**(10):1430003

[14] Pan F, Gao S, Chen C, Song C, Zeng F. Recent progress in resistive random access memories: Materials, switching mechanisms, and performance. Materials Science and Engineering R. 2014;**83**:1-59. DOI: 10.1142/S0217984914300038

[15] Liu TY, Yan TH, Scheuerlein R, Chen Y, Lee JKY, Balakrishnan G, et al. A 130.7mm² 2-layer 32Gb ReRAM memory device in 24nm technology. In: Fujino LC, editor. 2013 IEEE Solid-State Circuits Conference (ISSCC): Digest of Technical Papers; Feb. 17-21, 2013; San Francisco, CA, USA. Piscataway, NJ, USA: IEEE; 2013. pp. 210-212. DOI: 10.1109/ISSCC.2013.6487703

[16] Fackenthal R, Kitagawa M, Otsuka W, Prall K, Mills D, Tsutsui K, et al. A 16Gb ReRAM with 200MB/s write and 1GB/s read in 27nm technology. In: Fujino LC, editor. 2014 IEEE International Solid-State Circuits Conference (ISSCC): Digest of Technical Papers; Feb. 9-13, 2014; San Francisco, CA, USA. Piscataway, NJ, USA: IEEE; 2014. pp. 338-340. DOI: 10.1109/ISSCC.2014.6757460

[17] Business Korea. Samsung Successfully Develops 3D Cross Point Memory [Internet]. Feb. 12, 2016. Available from: http://www.businesskorea.co.kr/english/news/ict/13818-chasing-intel-samsung-successfully-develops-3d-cross-point-memory [Accessed: Feb. 24, 2017]

[18] Sills S, Yasuda S, Calderoni A, Cardon C, Strand J, Aratani K, Ramaswamy N. Challenges for high-density 16Gb ReRAM with 27nm technology. In: 2015 Symposium on VLSI Technology: Digest of Technical Papers; 16-18 June 2015; Kyoto, Japan. Piscataway, NJ, USA: IEEE; 2015. pp. T106-T107. DOI: 10.1109/VLSIT.2015.7223639

[19] Nikkei Asian Review. Panasonic, UMC Join to Make Advanced Power-saving Memory [Internet]. Feb. 1, 2017. Available from: http://asia.nikkei.com/Tech-Science/Tech/Panasonic-UMC-join-to-make-advanced-power-saving-memory [Accessed: 23-02-2017]

[20] Hihara H, Tamagawa N, Imamura T, Sugaya H, Sugibayashi T, Miyamura M, et al. Programmable SpaceWire interface with atom switch. In: Parkes S, Carrie C, editors. 2016 International SpaceWire Conference Proceedings; Oct. 24-28, 2016; Yokohama, Japan. Piscataway, NJ, USA: IEEE; 2016. DOI: 10.1109/SpaceWire.2016.7771606

[21] Fujitsu Semiconductor. Fujitsu Semiconductor Launches World''s Largest Density 4 Mbit ReRAM Product for Mass Production [Internet]. Oct. 26, 2016. Available from: http://www.fujitsu.com/jp/group/fsl/en/resources/news/press-releases/2016/1026.html [Accessed: 23-02-2017]

[22] Goux L, Valov I. Electrochemical processes and device improvement in conductive bridge RAM cells. Physica Status Solidi A. 2016;**213**(2):274-288. DOI: 10.1002/pssa. 201532813

[23] Strobel J, Neelisetty KK, Chakravadhanula VSK, Kienle L. Transmission electron microscopy on memristive devices: An overview. Applied Microscopy. 2016;**46**(4):206-216. DOI: 10.9729/AM.2016.46.4.206

[24] Yang Y, Takahashi Y, Tsurumaki-Fukuchi A, Arita M, Moors M, Buckwell M, et al. Probing electrochemistry at the nanoscale: In situ TEM and STM characterizations of conducting filaments in memristive devices. Journal of Electroceramics (online Feb. 11, 2017) 2017;DOI: 10.1007/s10832-017-0069-y

[25] Fujii T, Arita M, Takahashi Y, Fujiwara I. In situ transmission electron microscopy analysis of conductive filament during solid electrolyte resistance switching. Applied Physics Letters. 2011;**98**(21):212104. DOI: 10.1063/1.3593494

[26] Choi SJ, Park GS, Kim K-H, Cho S, Yang WY, et al. In situ observation of voltage-induced multilevel resistive switching in solid electrolyte memory. Advanced Materials. 2011;**23**(29):3272-3277. DOI: 10.1002/adma.201100507

[27] Liu Q, Sun J, Lv H, Long S, Yin K, Wan N, et al. Real-time observation on dynamic growth/dissolution of conductive filaments in oxide-electrolyte-based ReRAM. Advanced Materials. 2012;**24**(14):1844-1849. DOI: 10.1002/adma.201104104

[28] Yang Y, Gao P, Gaba S, Chang T, Pan X, Lu W. Observation of conducting filament growth in nanoscale resistive memories. Nature Communications. 2012;**4**:732. DOI: 10.1038/ncomms1737

[29] Kudo M, Arita M, Ohno Y, Takahashi Y. Filament formation and erasure in molybdenum oxide during resistive switching cycles. Applied Physics Letters. 2014;**105**(17):173504. DOI: 10.1063/1.4898773

[30] Jooss Ch, Hoffmann J, Fladerer J, Ehrhardt M, Beetz T, Wu L, Zhu Y. Electric pulse induced resistance change effect in manganites due to polaron localization at the metal-oxide interfacial region. Physical Review B. 2008;**77**(13):132409. DOI: 10.1103/PhysRevB.77.132409

[31] Fujii T, Kaji H, Kondo H, Hamada K, Arita M, Takahashi Y. I-V hysteresis of $Pr_{0.7}Ca_{0.3}MnO_3$ during TEM observation. IOP Conference Series: Materials Science and Engineering. 2010;**8**:012033. DOI: 10.1088/1757-899X/8/1/012033

[32] Yang Y, Lu W, Yao Y, Sun J, Gu C, Gu L, et al. In situ TEM observation of resistance switching in titanate based device. Scientific Reports. 2014;**4**:3890. DOI: 10.1038/srep03890

[33] Kwon DH, Kim KM, Jang JH, Jeon JM, Lee MH, Kim GH, et al. Atomic structure of conducting nanofilaments in TiO_2 resistive switching memory. Nature Nanotechnology. 2010;**5**:148-153. DOI: 10.1038/NNANO.2009.456

[34] Fujii T, Arita M, Hamada K, Kondo H, Kaji H, Takahashi Y, et al. I-V measurement of NiO nanoregion during observation by transmission electron microscopy. Journal of Applied Physics. 2011;**109**(5):053702. DOI: 10.1063/1.3553868

[35] Chen JY, Hsin CL, Huang CW, Chiu CH, Huang YT, Lin SJ, et al. Dynamic evolution of conducting nanofilament in resistive switching memories. Nano Letters. 2013;**13**(8):3671-3677. DOI: 10.1021/nl4015638

[36] Park GS, Kim YB, Park SY, Li XS, Heo S, Lee MJ, et al. In situ observation of filamentary conducting channels in an asymmetric Ta_2O_{5-x}/TaO_{2-x} bilayer structure. Nature Communications. 2013;**4**:2382. DOI: 10.1038/ncomms3382

[37] Fujii T, Arita M, Hamada K, Takahashi Y, Sakaguchi N. In-situ transmission electron microscopy of conductive filaments in NiO resistance random access memory and its analysis. Journal of Applied Physics. 2013;**113**(8):083701. DOI: 10.1063/1.4792732

[38] Yang Y, Gao P, Li L, Pan X, Tappertzhofen S, Choi SH, et al. Electrochemical dynamics of nanoscale metallic inclusions in dielectrics. Nature Communications. 2014;**5**:4232. DOI: 10.1038/ncomms5232

[39] Fujii T, Arita M, Takahashi Y, Fujiwara I. Analysis of resistance switching and conductive filaments inside Cu-Ge-S using in situ transmission electron microscopy. Journal of Materials Research. 2012;**27**(6):886-896. DOI: 10.1557/jmr.2011.437

[40] Kudo M, Arita M, Takahashi Y, Ohba K, Shimuta M, Fujiwara I. Visualization of conductive filament during write and erase cycles on nanometer-scale ReRAM achieved by in-situ TEM. In: 2015 IEEE 7th International Memory Workshop; May 17-20, 2015; Monterey, CA, USA. Piscataway, NJ, USA: IEEE; 2015. pp. 85-88. DOI: 10.1109/IMW.2015.7150312

[41] Takahashi Y, Kudo M, Arita M. Visualization of conductive filament of ReRAM during resistive switching by in-situ TEM. ECS Transactions. 2015;**69**(10):299-309. DOI: 10.1149/06910.0299ecst

[42] Arita M, Takahashi A, Ohno Y, Nakane A, Tsurumaki-Fukuchi A, Takahashi Y. Switching operation and degradation of resistive random access memory composed of tungsten oxide and copper investigated using in-situ TEM. Scientific Reports. 2015;**5**:17103. DOI: 10.1038/srep17103

[43] Arita M, Ohno Y, Takahashi Y. Switching of Cu/MoO_x/TiN CBRAM at MoO_x/TiN interface. Physica Status Solidi A. 2016;**213**(2):306-310. DOI: 10.1002/pssa.201532414

[44] Arita M, Ohno Y, Murakami Y, Takamizawa K, Tsurumaki-Fukuchi A, Takahashi Y. Microstructural transitions in resistive random access memory composed of molybdenum oxide with copper during switching cycles. Nanoscale. 2016;**8**:14754-14766. DOI: 10.1039/c6nr02602h

[45] Arita M, Hamada K, Takahashi Y, Sueoka K, Shibayama T. In situ transmission electron microscopy for electronics. In: Khan M, editor. The Transmission Electron Microscope - Theory and Applications. Rijeka, Croatia: InTech; 2015. pp. 35-68. DOI: 10.5772/60651

[46] Kozicki MN, Park M, Mitkova M. Nanoscale memory elements based on solid-state electrolytes. IEEE Transactions on Nanotechnology. 2005;**4**(3):331-338. DOI: 10.1109/TNANO.2005.846936

[47] Sakamoto T, Lister K, Banno N, Hasegawa T, Terabe K, Aono M. Electronic transport in Ta_2O_5 resistive switch. Applied Physics Letters. 2007;**91**(9):092110. DOI: 10.1063/1. 2777170

[48] Kudo M, Arita M, Ohno Y, Fujii T, Hamada K, Takahashi Y. Preparation of resistance random access memory samples for in situ transmission electron microscopy experiments. Thin Solid Films. 2013;**533**:48-53. DOI: 10.1016/j.tsf.2012.10.102

[49] Thermadam SP, Bhagat SK, Alford TL, Sakaguchi Y, Kozicki MN, Mitkova M. Influence of Cu diffusion conditions on the switching of Cu–SiO_2-based resistive memory devices. Thin Solid Films. 2010;**518**:3293-3298. DOI: 10.1016/j.tsf.2009.09.021

[50] Tsuruoka T, Terabe K, Hasegawa T, Aono M. Forming and switching mechanisms of a cation-migration-based oxide resistive memory. Nanotechnology. 2010;**21**(42):425205. DOI: 10.1088/0957-4484/21/42/425205

[51] Bernard Y, Renard VT, Gonon P, Jousseaume V. Back-end-of-line compatible conductive bridging RAM based on Cu and SiO_2. Microelectronic Engineering. 2011;**88**(5):814-816. DOI: 10.1016/j.mee.2010.06.041

[52] Russo U, Kamalanathan D, Ielmini D, Lacaita AL, Kozicki MN. Study of multilevel programming in programmable metallization cell (PMC) memory. IEEE Transactions on Electron Devices. 2009;**56**(5):1040-1047. DOI: 10.1109/TED.2009.2016019

[53] Zhuge F, Li K, Fu B, Zhang H, Li J, Chen H, et al. Mechanism for resistive switching in chalcogenide-based electrochemical metallization memory cells. AIP Advances. 2015;**5**(5):057125. DOI: 10.1063/1.4921089

[54] Tian X, Yang S, Zeng M, Wang L, Wei J, Xu Z, et al. Bipolar electrochemical mechanism for mass transfer in nanoionic resistive memories. Advanced Materials. 2014;**26**(22):3649-3654. DOI: 10.1002/adma.201400127

[55] Valov I, Waser R. Comment on real-time observation on dynamic growth/dissolution of conductive filaments in oxide-electrolyte-based ReRAM. Advanced Materials. 2013;**25**(2):162-164. DOI: 10.1002/adma.201202592

[56] Aratani K, Ohba K, Mizuguchi T, Yasuda S, Shiimoto T, Tsushima T, et al. A novel resistance memory with high scalability and nanosecond switching. In: 2007 IEEE International Electron Devices Meeting (IEDM): Technical Digest; Dec. 10-12, 2007; Washington DC, USA. Piscataway, NJ, USA: IEEE; 2007. pp. 783-786. DOI: 10.1109/IEDM. 2007.4419064

[57] Yoon Y, Choi H, Lee D, Park JB, Lee J, Seong DJ, et al. Excellent switching uniformity of Cu-doped MoO_x/GdO_x bilayer for nonvolatile memory applications. IEEE Electron Device Letters. 2009;**30**(5):457-459. DOI: 10.1109/LED.2009.2015687

[58] Chen YY, Govoreanu B, Goux L, Degraeve R, Fantini A, Kar GS, et al. SET/RESET pulse for $>10^{10}$ endurance in HfO_2/Hf 1T1R bipolar RRAM. IEEE Transactions on Electron Devices. 2012;**59**(12):3243-3249. DOI: 10.1109/TED.2012.2218607

[59] Balatti S, Ambrogio S, Wang ZQ, Sills S, Calderoni A, Ramaswamy N, Ielmini D. Pulsed cycling operation and endurance failure of metal-oxide resistive (RRAM). In: 2014 IEEE International Electron Devices Meeting (IEDM): Technical Digest; Dec. 15-17, 2014; San Francisco, CA, USA. Piscataway, NJ, USA: IEEE; 2014. pp. 14.3.1-14.3.4. DOI: 10.1109/IEDM.2014.7047050

[60] Shenoy RS, Gopalakrishnan K, Jackson B, Virwani K, Burr GW, Rettner CT, et al. Endurance and scaling trends of novel access-devices for multi-layer crosspoint-memory based on mixed-ionic-electronic-conduction (MIEC) materials. In: 2011 Symposium on VLSI Technology: Digest of Technical Papers; June 14-16, 2011; Kyoto, Japan. Piscataway, NJ, USA: IEEE; 2011. pp. 94-95

[61] Kinoshita K, Tsunoda K, Sato Y, Noshiro H, Yagaki S, Aoki M, Sugiyama Y. Reduction in the reset current in a resistive random access memory consisting of NiO_x brought about by reducing a parasitic capacitance. Applied Physics Letters. 2008;**93**(3):033506. DOI: 10.1063/1.2959065

[62] Liu CY, Sung PW. Different resistive switching characteristics of a Cu/SiO_2/Pt structure. Japanese Journal of Applied Physics. 2011;**50**(9R):091101. DOI: 10.1143/JJAP.50.091101

[63] Wei Z, Kanzawa Y, Arita K, Katoh Y, Kawai K, Muraoka S, et al. Highly reliable TaO_x ReRAM and direct evidence of redox reaction mechanism. In: 2008 IEEE International Electron Devices Meeting (IEDM): Technical Digest; Dec. 15-17, 2008; San Francisco, CA, USA. Piscataway, NJ, USA: IEEE; 2008. pp. 1-4. DOI: 10.1109/IEDM.2008.4796676

Chapter 5

Resistive Switching in Metal Oxide/Organic Semiconductor Nonvolatile Memories

Henrique L. Gomes, Dago M. de Leeuw and
Stefan C.J. Meskers

Additional information is available at the end of the chapter

http://dx.doi.org/10.5772/intechopen.69023

Abstract

Diodes incorporating a bilayer of a metal oxide and an organic semiconductor can show unipolar, nonvolatile memory behavior after electroforming. Electroforming involves dielectric breakdown induced by prolonged bias voltage stress. When the power dissipated during breakdown is limited, electroforming is reversible and involves formation of defects at the organic-oxide interface that can heal spontaneously. When the power dissipation during breakdown exceeds a certain threshold, electroforming becomes irreversible. The fully electroformed diodes show electrical bistability, featuring (meta) stable states with low and high conduction that can be programmed by voltage pulses. The high conduction results from current flowing via filamentary paths. The bistability is explained by the coexistence of two thermodynamically stable phases at the interface between semiconductor and oxide. One phase contains mainly ionized defects and has a low work function, while the other phase has mainly neutral defects and a high work function. In the diodes, domains of the phase with low work function give rise to current filaments. In the filaments, Joule heating will raise temperature locally. When the temperature exceeds the critical temperature, the filament will switch off. The switching involves a collective recombination of charge carriers trapped at the defects as evidenced by bursts of electroluminescence.

Keywords: nonvolatile electronic memory, electroforming, unipolar resistive switching, phase transition, critical point

1. Introduction

Metal-insulator-metal (MIM) systems often show electrically induced resistive switching. Diodes of this type have therefore been proposed as replacement of standard NAND-flash nonvolatile electronic memory [1]. In their pristine state, the materials in the MIM diodes are usually high-resistivity insulators. Before the diodes show memory properties, they have to be electroformed by applying a high electric field in a current-voltage sweep with an appropriate current compliance. This induces a so-called soft breakdown. The electroformed device can be switched between a high conductance on-state and a low conductance off-state as shown in **Figure 1**. The resulting bistable current-voltage (I-V) characteristics can be applied as a nonvolatile memory. A surprisingly large variety of materials and material combinations can give rise to resistive switching [2–9], which indicates that the mechanism of the resistive switching may be very general.

The electric fields needed to induce the electroforming are usually close to the critical field for dielectric breakdown. In practice, the electroforming needs to be tightly controlled by, for example, programming a current compliance limit in the external circuit, in order to avoid permanent shorting and breakdown of the MIM diodes. The yield of active memory cells in the electroforming step is crucial for the success of memristors as a device technology. A detailed understanding of processes happening during electroforming is therefore of paramount importance.

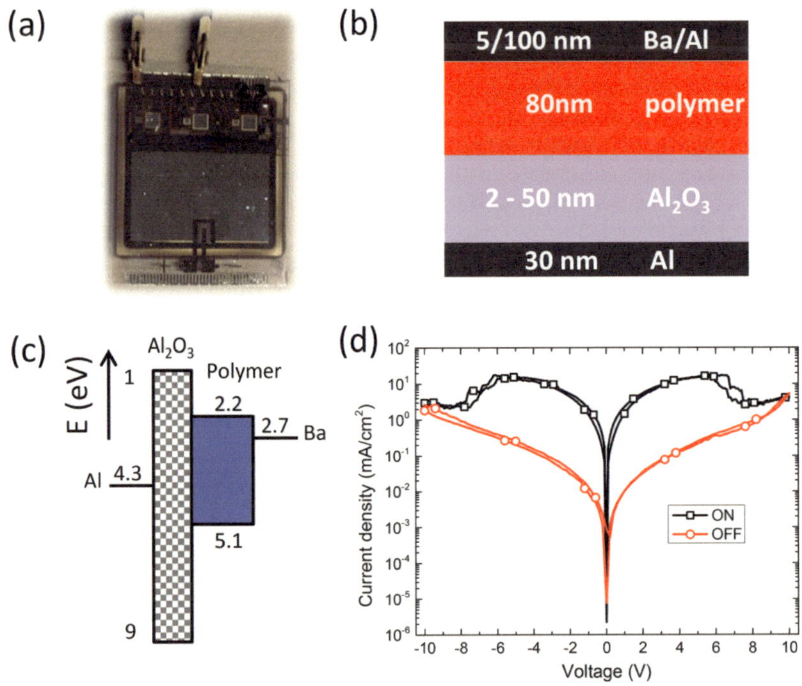

Figure 1. Diode layout. (a) Photograph of device containing several diodes. The devices with an active area of 9 mm^2 were encapsulated to exclude O_2 and H_2O. (b) Typical nominal e-only diode layout where the Al_2O_3 thickness is varied. (c) Flat band diagram where numbers are in eV. (d) J-V characteristics after forming showing a pronounced negative differential resistance.

Resistive switching was first reported in 1962 when Hickmott described a hysteretic I-V characteristic in thin anodic films [10]. A large negative resistance was observed for thin films of SiO_x, Al_2O_3, Ta_2O_5, ZrO_2, and TiO_2. Early research up to the 1980s has been thoroughly reviewed by Dearnaley et al. [11], by Oxley [12], and by Pagnia and Sotnik [13]. In the 1990s attention shifted from binary oxides to complex metal oxides and has been reviewed by Sawa [14] and by Waser and Aono [15].

The switching mechanism of electroformed diodes can be unipolar or bipolar depending on the type of oxide and the electroforming procedure applied [3]. In unipolar switching, the switching direction depends on the magnitude of applied bias but not on the polarity. The I-V curves of both the on-state and the off-state are symmetric, and the type of electrode is relatively unimportant. In contrast, the switching is called bipolar or antisymmetric when the set of voltage for the on-state occurs at one voltage polarity, while the reset to the off-state occurs at the reversed polarity. The I-V curves are asymmetric and depend on the type of electrode.

Here, we focus on unipolar switching in diodes containing a layer of Al_2O_3. In order to fabricate reproducible memories, a bilayer comprised of a thin insulating Al_2O_3 layer in series with a semiconducting layer is needed. The yield of active memories made with only an Al_2O_3 layer is extremely low. Electroforming then almost inevitably leads to hard shorts, irrespective of the set of current compliance or of the type of forming, for example, pulsed or voltage sweep. The electrodes melt or even evaporate. Already for the memories made in the 1960s and 1970s, it turned out that an unidentified layer of carbon enhances the reproducibility. Diodes made in high vacuum did not show switching. Oil vapor contamination from a rotary pump was needed to make reliable memories [13].

Reproducible memories with a yield of about unity could be fabricated by adding a well-defined, thin layer of a semiconducting polymer [16]. The devices therefore are often called polymer RRAMs. The type of electrodes turned out to be irrelevant. After electroforming, the I-V characteristics are symmetric. A narrow voltage region with a negative differential resistance (NDR) is observed in both polarities. The device can be switched between a high conductance on-state and a low conductance off-state at biases corresponding to the top and bottom of the NDR. The switching is unipolar and due to the Al_2O_3. The distributed series resistance of the polymer prevents thermal runaway when a local filament is turned on. Polymer/oxide diodes are then expected not only to exhibit a better control of the switching properties but also to have superior endurance as compared to oxide-only based memristors. In this feature we will show that the semiconducting polymer not only acts as a current-limiting series resistance but that the polymer also plays a crucial role by providing a charged layer of trapped electrons at the polymer/oxide interface. This charge layer enhances the tunneling across the oxide and tunes the formation of electrically bistable defects.

This contribution is an explanatory account of electroforming and unipolar switching in MIM diodes with an internal bilayer structure consisting of Al_2O_3 and a semiconducting polymer and is organized as follows. In Section 2 we describe investigations into the trapping of charges in pristine diodes and the dielectric breakdown and electroforming that occurs at high bias. In Section 3 we discuss the filamentary nature of the conduction in the diodes and the experimental evidence for this heterogeneous conduction from noise measurements. Finally, Section 4 is devoted to the switching process in the electroformed diodes.

2. Charge trapping and electroforming

Pristine diodes consisting of an Al/Al_2O_3/polyspirofluorene/Ba/Al stack have a large density of empty trap sites for electrons which are located at the interface between the semiconducting polymers. The trap sites can be studied by quasi-static capacitance-voltage (QSCV) measurements [17] and optical detrapping investigations. These measurements provide information on the position and number density of the trap sites.

The QSCV method is ideally suited to study traps that fill quickly but empty slowly. During the measurement, the bias voltage is swept over a certain voltage range and by integrating the current; one keeps track of the number of charges that enter the diode. From the voltage and charge, the capacitance is calculated. **Figure 2** shows the cyclic QSCV scans. First, the voltage is swept over the reverse bias range (V < 0). In this range a practically constant capacitance of 30 nF/cm^2 is recorded which we interpret as the geometrical capacitance, C_0. The minor hysteresis in the reverse bias range is due to a small leakage current. When subsequently

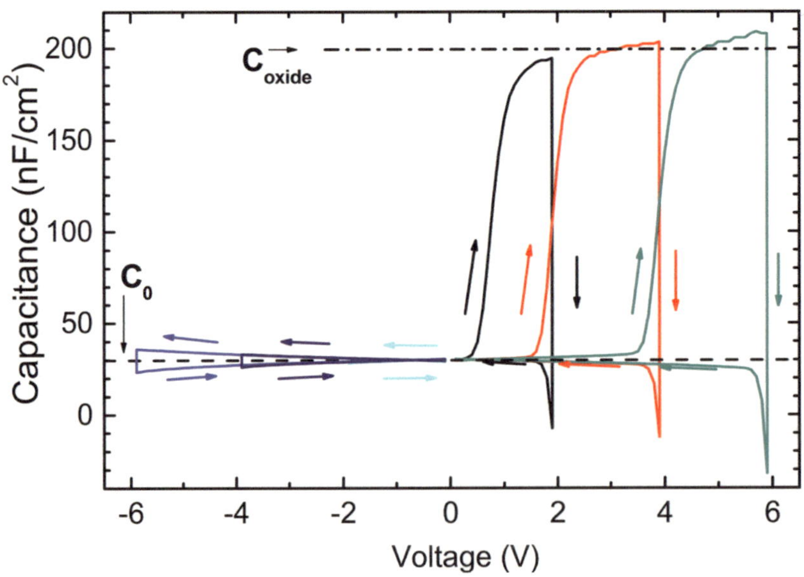

Figure 2. Sequential QSCV characteristics for a Al/Al_2O_3 (40 nm)/polymer(80 nm)/Ba/Al diode measured using an integration time of 4 s and a voltage step of 100 mV. For negative bias voltage V, no charge is injected into the polymer. Both oxide and polymer act as insulators. For positive bias, electrons are injected into the polymer and trapped near the polymer/oxide interface.

sweeping the bias voltage over the forward bias range, a much large hysteresis is observed. When the voltage is swept over a certain range for the first time, a very large capacitance is obtained, which we denote C_{oxide}. Scanning the voltage over the same range but now either in the reverse direction or for a second time in the same direction, the capacitance measured is low and practically equal to C_0. To account for the anomalously high capacitance values in the first scans, we note that under forward bias electrons can be injected into the semiconducting polymer. These electrons can migrate through the polymer layer under the influence of the applied bias and subsequently get trapped at the polymer/oxide interface. The trap sites are relatively deep, and spontaneous detrapping of the electrons is found to occur on the time scale of days. Detrapping of electrons can be accelerated by illumination with light of photon energy above the bandgap of the semiconducting polymer (3.1 eV).

By varying the thickness of the oxide layer, it can be shown that the anomalous capacitance is inversely proportional to the thickness of the oxide [18, 19]. From the QSCV and optical detrapping experiments [20], it follows that the density of trap sites at the interface exceeds 10^{17} m^{-2}.

Due to the accumulation of electrons at the polymer/oxide interface, the potential difference applied to the diodes as a whole mainly drops over the oxide layer. When increasing the bias voltage over the diode, one will eventually come to a point where the electric field in the oxide exceeds the critical field strength for electrical breakdown, which is estimated at 10^9 V/m for Al_2O_3 [21]. This could lead to catastrophic failure of the diode. In the case of the polymer/oxide diodes, however, the layer of semiconducting polymer acts as current-limiting element, preventing complete or "hard" breakdown of the diodes.

A subtle way of inducing "soft" electrical breakdown in the polymer/oxide diodes is to subject the structure to so-called constant current stress [22]. This is illustrated in **Figure 3**. In the particular example shown, the diode is subjected to a constant current of 1 μA/cm², and the voltage needed to maintain this current is monitored over time. As can be seen, the voltage that needs to be applied builds up rather quickly over the course of less than a second. This time scale corresponds to complete filling of the trap sites in the diode. When the voltage over the 10-nm-thick oxide reaches 10 V, the critical dielectric strength of the aluminum oxide exceeds, and a sudden, "soft" breakdown occurs. The dielectric breakdown allows the current through the diode to be maintained at much lower applied bias ($V < 1$ V).

An intriguing aspect of the "soft" dielectric breakdown shown in **Figure 3** is that the damaged insulator shows spontaneous repair. This "self-healing" is illustrated in **Figure 4**. When monitoring the leakage current through the damaged diode at a relative low applied bias voltage, one finds that the current decreases over time, following a power-law decay. Curiously, the self-healing can be temporarily inhibited, by first emptying the trap sites optically and then keeping the diode at short circuit. After 25 h, the self-healing process can be reactivated by refilling the traps and proceeds with the same kinetics as in the case without inhibition.

The dielectric breakdown under constant current stress has been investigated in more detail. We find that when the electrical power that is dissipated during the breakdown is limited to 0.1 mW/cm², the breakdown is fully reversible. In a tentative explanation, we attribute the breakdown and the subsequent self-healing to quasi-reversible formation of oxygen vacancy

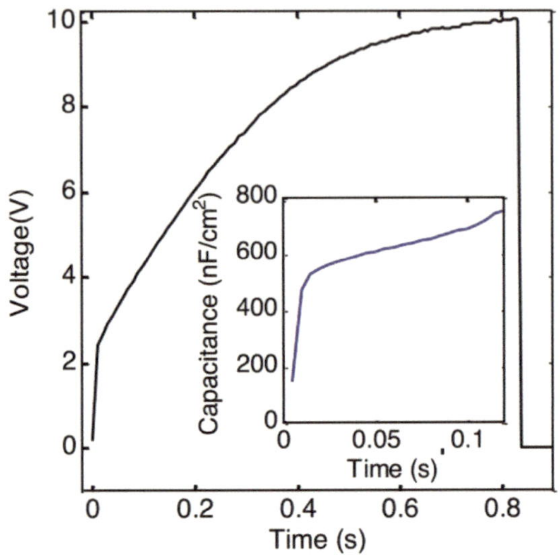

Figure 3. Breakdown under constant current stress. The voltage across the Al/Al_2O_3(20 nm)/polyspirofluorene(80 nm)Ba/Al capacitor as a function of time under a constant current stress of 1 μA/cm². An abrupt voltage drop is observed at 10 V. The inset shows the corresponding change in capacitance estimated from the change in slope of the voltage.

sites in the oxide near the polymer/oxide interface. This mechanism is described in **Figure 5**. Upon injection of positive charge carriers into the oxide, two oxygen ions dimerize into an O_2 molecule, whereby the electrons are annihilated by the trapped holes. The oxygen vacancies, also referred to as *F*-centers, can exist in a charge neutral state where an electron occupies the

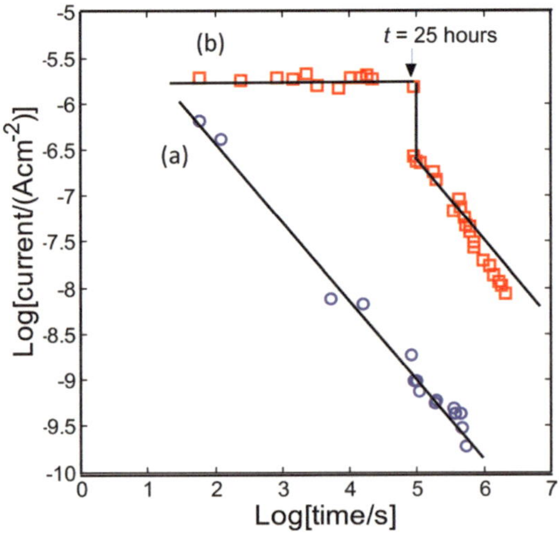

Figure 4. Inhibition of self-healing. Current-time plots for a capacitor electroformed with constant low current stress of 1 μA. (a) The post-breakdown current probed at 0.5 V bias. The current decays with a power-law dependence on time. (b) The current decay in the same electroformed but now after emptying electron traps with 1000 s illumination with a blue LED (350 ≤ λ ≤ 650 nm, λ_{max} = 440 nm). After t = 25 h triggers, the self-healing process can be reactivated by application of a brief 0–5V voltage ramp to refill the traps.

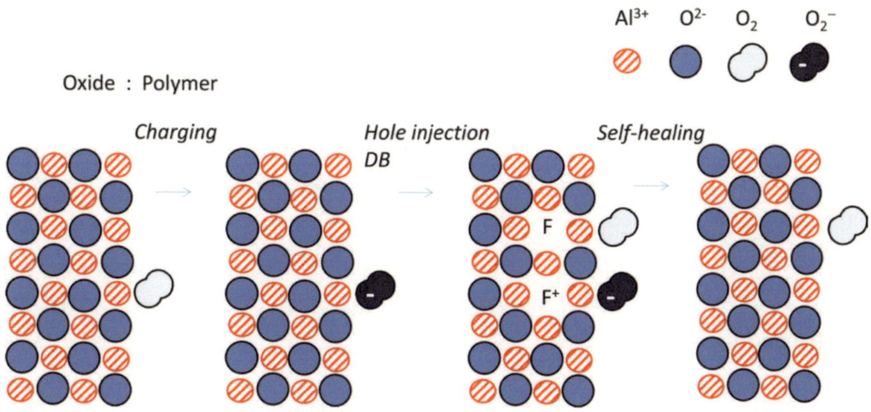

Figure 5. Self-healing mechanism. The hatched and filled spheres represent Al^{3+} and O^{2-} ions of the Al_2O_3 lattice. Neutral oxygen, O_2, and the superoxide ion, O^{2-} are presented by the lemniscates. The first electrons are trapped at the polymer/oxide interface. When the bias is larger than the flat band voltage, holes are injected into the oxide, and a highly polarized electric double layer is formed at the polymer/oxide interface. In dielectric breakdown oxygen vacancies, F-centers are formed. In self-healing, superoxide ions, O^{2-}, react with a neutral and charged oxygen vacancy to reform a defect-free Al_2O_3 lattice.

empty space left by the oxygen anion. When the electron leaves the vacancy, the *F*-center is ionized (*F*+). The ionized *F*+ center can be regarded as a trapped hole. The O_2 molecules may diffuse into the polymer layer, escape from the electroformed device, or even form oxygen interstitials, depending on the dissipated power used in the electroforming. As long as the O_2 molecules formed in the breakdown process remain close to the interface, we expect the breakdown to be reversible [23]. Due to their large electronegativity, the O_2 molecules trap electrons. The formed superoxide ions, O^{2-}, react with a neutral and charged oxygen vacancy to a defect-free Al_2O_3 lattice, indicated by the open square, as

$$F^{+} + F^{+} + O^{2-} \rightarrow \square \tag{1}$$

We note that binding of neutral molecular oxygen to *n*-type metal oxides is a process that occurs in mainly oxides [16, 24, 25], allowing one to monitor oxygen partial pressure through measurement of the electrical resistance. Reversible, electrically induced formation of anion vacancy sites (*F*-center) in ionic-wide bandgap semiconductors has also been demonstrated for alkali halide-polymer diodes [26–29].

As mentioned above, when the power dissipated during the electrical breakdown is high, the process becomes irreversible, and the diodes are electroformed. We find that the electrical resistance of the electroformed diodes can be switched reversibly by applying voltage pulses.

3. Filamentary conduction and noise measurements

The electrical current in memristor devices is not homogeneous but transported through localized paths or filaments. Evidences have been provided by scanning probe measurement which confirm the existence of conducting filaments in Al_2O_3 [30, 31] and by an IR-enhanced CCD camera [32]. The spatially resolved thermal images show, in the on-state, hot spots due to highly conductive paths. In the off-state, the spots disappear. However, the spots are not created and destroyed upon switching. Upon repeated switching between the on- and off-states, the same original hot spots were detected in the thermal image. From these observations it has been concluded that upon switching, filaments are neither generated nor destroyed but that individual filaments are turned on and off, like switches.

Relevant information about filament properties is obtained from a detailed electrical characterization. In oxide-/polymer-based memristors, three different behaviors are directly caused by filamentary conduction:

a. **Electrical noise**: Filaments cause discrete current fluctuations that generate random telegraph like noise and affect the memory reproducibility and scalability.

b. **Slow response upon repeating switching**: Filaments interact with nearby filaments, and this interaction may slow down the switching speed of a memory device.

c. **Anomalous temperature dependence of the current**: The mechanism to turn on filaments may lead to a counter-intuitive temperature dependence of the current.

In the next paragraphs, we discuss in detail all the electrical characteristics caused by filamentary conduction.

Electrical noise. Polymer/oxide memristor devices when operating in the on-state show different types of electrical noise depending on the bias point of the I-V curve where it is recorded [33]. For a bias of 0.5 V (ohmic region), the noise follows the $1/f$ dependence (see **Figure 6**). When the diode is biased at higher voltages, in a space-charge-limited (SCL) region, the noise follows a $1/f^{3/2}$ dependence. Hence, a new physical mechanism becomes active at high bias.

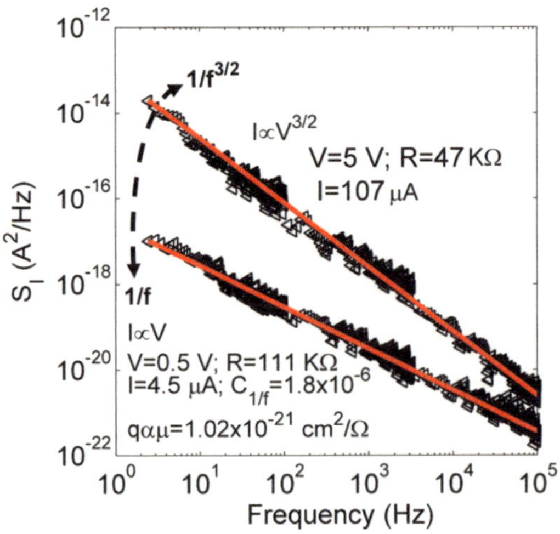

Figure 6. Current noise spectrum in the transition from ohmic to SCL region, indicating a diffusion mechanism at higher bias.

This mechanism is a switching-on and switching-off of conducting channels, at the Al_2O_3 contact. That process dominates the $1/f$ spectrum and the observed slope of the spectrum ($1/f^{3/2}$). Finally, very near to the onset of the NDR region, the noise shows discrete fluctuations like a random telegraph noise (RTN).

Typical time traces from a continuous measurement are presented in **Figure 7**. The time records show large discrete current fluctuations that can reach about 45 nA.

Discrete fluctuations in current-voltage or current-time characteristics appear when charge transport is controlled by the statistical capture/emission of electrons at electron trap sites. Especially when transport occurs through current-carrying filaments, large current fluctuations can occur.

The large discrete current fluctuations allow us to quantify the time that a filament is turned on, τ_{on}, and turned off, τ_{off}. The first and second traces in **Figure 7** exhibit a filamentary path that is most of the time active and only once in a while switches off, with τ_{off} ~ 0.7 ms. The third trace shows the filament being turned on and turned off at similar time scales of about 1.7 ms. The current fluctuations change their frequency in a random way.

Slow response upon repeating switching. When a memory device is in a high conductive state, there is a large ensemble of filaments. We will show here that when filaments are in relatively close proximity, the switching-on and switching-off of an individual filament not be a totally independent of a filament in the neighborhood. Filaments can interact with each other and contribute to turn on more filaments or even promote a cascade of switching-off events.

It is instructive at this point to investigate the changes in potential distribution and current flow patterns in the diode in the vicinity of a conducting filament. This was achieved using the COMSOL Multiphysics simulator.

In **Figure 8** the device is represented by a simple two-layer structure composed of a thin, high-resistivity oxide layer supporting a thicker, more conductive polymer layer. The color (online) maps represent the potential distributions (blue = −10 V, pink = 0 V) which are further emphasized by superimposed contour lines. In (a) the device is in the off-state; leakage current

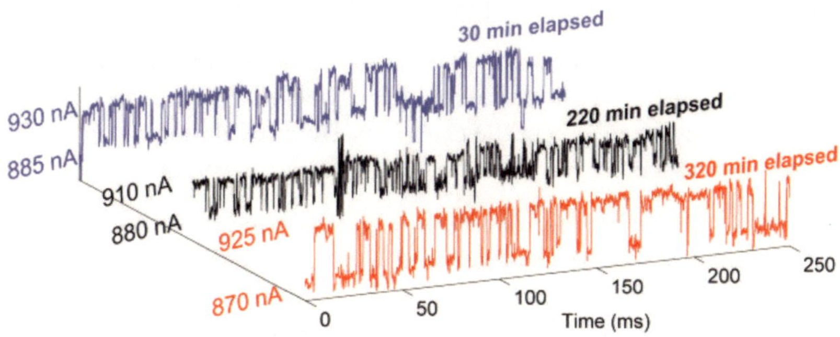

Figure 7. Electrical noise of a memristor programmed in the on-state at T= 220 K. The time traces show the current RTN fluctuations under an applied bias near the onset of the NDR region. The time traces were recorded at different times after the start of the measurements (elapsed time).

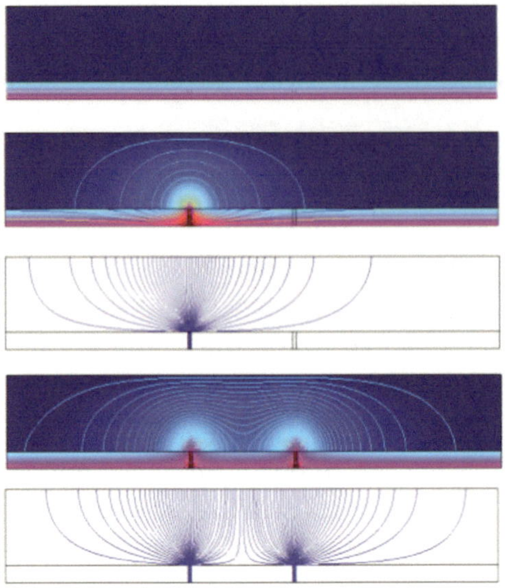

Figure 8. COMSOL simulations showing potential distributions represented both in color (blue = −10 V, pink = 0 V) and by superimposed contour lines (a), (b), (d), and current streamlines (c) and (e) in our two-layer capacitor model. The upper layer represents the polymer and the lower a thin oxide film. (a) Potential distribution in a device in the HRS. The corresponding current streamlines will be vertical and of low density. The changes in potential distribution and current streamlines arising from a single conducting filament in the oxide are shown in (b) and (c). The corresponding distributions for two adjacent filaments are given in (d) and (e).

through the oxide is minimal so that virtually all the applied voltage appears across the oxide layer owing to the higher conductivity of the polymer. Next, we include a conducting filament in the oxide. This results in significant changes in the local potential (b) and in the current density profile (c). We note two important changes:

(i) The potential at the polymer/oxide interface decreases giving rise to lateral electric fields and extensive distortion of the potential in both the polymer and oxide layers.

(ii) The current tunnels through the polymer into the filament from a circular area of the electrode whose radius exceeds the polymer film thickness.

In the case of low on-currents, conducting filaments are isolated and well separated. The non-uniform potential distribution (**Figure 8(b)** and **(c)**) allows electrons to be drawn through the polymer from a relatively large area of the electrode. The critical filament current required to effect efficient recombination and turn off the filaments is achieved at relatively low voltages.

For high on-currents, a large number of conducting paths are turned on, many in the neighborhood of an originating filament as discussed above. As seen in **Figure 8(d)** and **(e)**, the electrode area from which electrons are drawn does not increase in proportion to the number of neighboring filaments. Higher voltages will be required then to provide the critical electron current through the polymer for extinguishing these filaments. Consequently, within a volume extending out from the filament into the polymer, considerable Joule heating will occur. Significantly, it is well known that the electrical breakdown strength of most insulating materials decreases with increasing temperature: a relevant example is soft breakdown in SiO_2 films a few nanometers thick [34]. We postulate that as the applied bias increases, a combination of increasing oxide field and high temperature in the vicinity of the conducting filament triggers the switching of a nearby filament. **Figure 8(d)** and **(e)** shows that the region of disturbed potential and high current density now expands triggering further switching. This process is expected to continue until two local hot spots overlap or expansion becomes limited by the process(es) leading to the NDR. Even if further filamentary conduction is not initiated, additional thermally induced currents will flow in both the polymer and oxide leading to a similar expansion of the hot spot.

Anomalous temperature dependence of the current. The I-V characteristics for the on-state show a large increase in the magnitude of the current upon lowering the temperature of the diodes. This behavior is illustrated in **Figure 9**. The increase of current is more pronounced at higher bias voltages, in the voltage range below the sharp onset of the NDR.

To further explore this unusual temperature dependence, a diode was programmed into the on-state at room temperature and then cooled down until 120 K. Meanwhile, the current transient was recorded while applying a continuous bias voltage (2 V). The magnitude of the current increases more than double in a temperature range of 200°C, as illustrated in **Figure 10**. This observation corresponds to a positive temperature coefficient (PTC) [35–37] of the electrical resistivity, $\alpha \approx 0.01\ K^{-1}$, an anomalously large value when compared with typical values for metals ($\alpha = 0.0039\ K^{-1}$ for Cu). On the basis of the anomalously large PTC, it contradicts the explanations based on a metallic type of conduction.

The large and stepwise increase in current indicates that by lowering the temperature some filaments can be activated. In the next section, we provide a tentative explanation for this remarkable experimental observation.

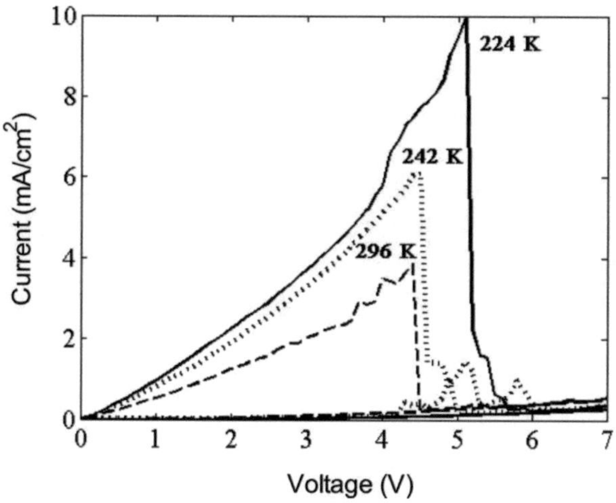

Figure 9. Temperature dependence of the I-V curve of a diode programmed into the on-state.

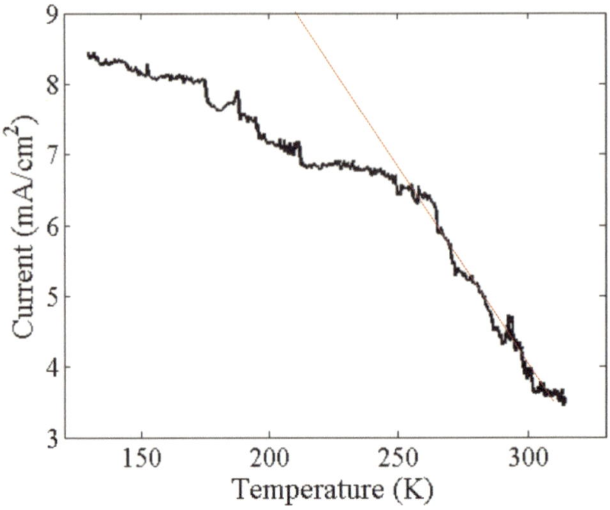

Figure 10. Temperature dependence of the I-V curve of a diode programmed into the on-state monitored at 2 V. The cooling speed is 1 K/min.

4. Electroluminescence and filament model

A key experimental observation in unraveling the mechanism of the nonvolatile electronic memory effects in aluminum oxide has been the occurrence of *electroluminescence* in the visible range of the spectrum during the switching [10, 38]. This observation provides direct experimental evidence that recombination of positive and negative charge carriers takes place at defects in the oxide. Furthermore, it has also been reported that electroformed oxide layers can emit electrons into the vacuum [11]. The latter observations show that an electroformed oxide layer on a metal can dramatically alter the work function of the underlying metal [39, 40].

In **Figure 11** we illustrate the occurrence of electroluminescence in electroformed Al_2O_3/polyfluorene diodes during switching. Starting at zero bias in the high conduction state, the current density rises rapidly with increasing bias. For voltages above 4 V, the diode shows negative differential resistance (NDR), and the current density actually decreases with increasing bias voltage. In the voltage range corresponding to the NDR behavior, the diode also shows irregular electroluminescence. Light is emitted during a series of short bursts. At high bias voltage ($V > 10$ V), the diodes show more steady light emission.

In order to account for the filamentary conduction and the electroluminescence, we propose that in the diode clusters of charged defects at the polymer/oxide interface are present. We propose a charged bilayer arrangement of charges with, for example, positively charged defects in the oxide compensated by trapped electrons on the polymer side of the interface. The double-layer arrangement locally changes the work function of the electrodes and

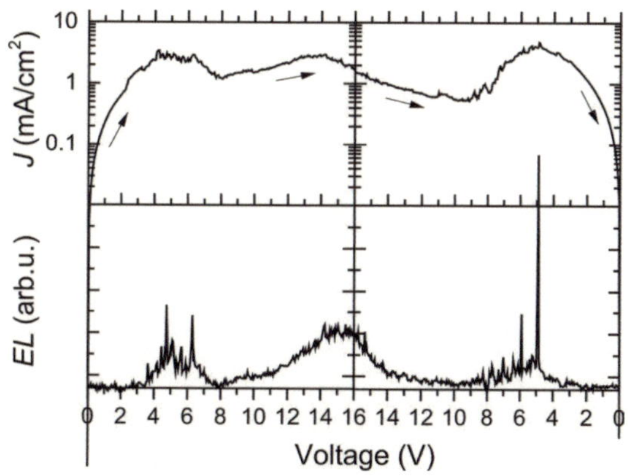

Figure 11. Electroluminescence. (Upper panel) current density (J) and (lower panel) electroluminescence (EL) intensity recorded simultaneously for an electroformed ITO/Al_2O_3 (10 nm)/polyfluorene (80 nm)/Ba/Al diode during a voltage sweep from 0 V→16 V→0 V.

allows current to flow at already low bias voltages. The local spots on the oxide layer where the effective work function has been altered give rise to current filamentary currents in the diode (see **Figure 12**). We note that formation of charged double layers near metal electrodes is well known in wet electrochemistry [41, 42].

To explain the electrical bistability of the nonvolatile memories, we propose the coexistence of two thermodynamically stable phases in the electroformed oxide layer [26]. The two phases occur in the quasi-two-dimensional double layer consisting of trapped electrons in the organic semiconductor and holes trapped at defects in the metal oxide. One phase containing mainly ionized defects has a low work function. The other phase comprises mainly defects in their neutral state and has a high work function. In the diodes, domains of the phase with low work function constitute current filaments.

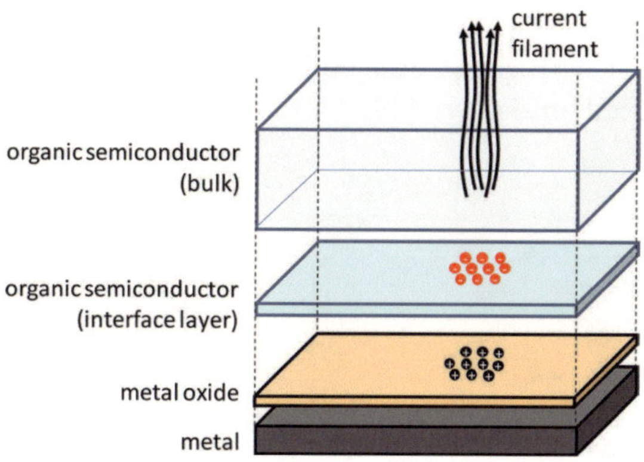

Figure 12. Schematic representation of current filament. In the electroformed diode, ionizable defects are present near the oxide/organic semiconductor interface with a number density above a critical limit. Due to cooperative interaction between the defects, the diode is electrically bistable. Arrays of mainly neutral defects have a high work function and constitute the off-state. Arrays of mainly ionized defects have a low work function and constitute the on-state.

In order to better explain the proposed thermodynamic bistability, we draw on an analogy with saturated salt solutions. Charged ions in such a system can be present in two phases, one where the ions are dispersed throughout the solutions and another phase where ions of opposite charge have condensed into a crystal. As is well, cooperative interactions between the oppositely charged ions give rise to crystallization of salt, for example, NaCl.

In rock salt, the positive and negative ions are packed in a cubic lattice (see **Figure 13**). If we however cut the crystal under an oblique angle, for example, parallel to the (1 1 1) plane, one sees that the crystal actually consists of layers of oppositely charged ions.

For the electroformed oxide layers, we argue that, provided neutral defect sites which are available with sufficient density, electrical charges that have been injected into the diode may condense spontaneously at the polymer/oxide interface due to their mutual electrostatic stabilization. By detailed consideration of the Coulomb interaction potentials of the charge defects, it can be shown that also the image charges in the nearby metal electrode contribute to the stabilization. The condensation of the charges can be mapped onto the 2D Ising model. Based on the 2D Ising model, one predicts that in analogy to ferromagnetism, a critical temperature T_c should exist. For temperatures lower than T_c, the coexistence of two thermodynamically stable phases is predicted. One of the phases should have mainly ionized defects and the other predominantly neutral defects. The magnitude of T_c depends on the strength of the interactions between the sites and should therefore be influenced by the density of defect states.

In order to explain the switching-off of current filaments, we argue that Joule heating associated with the current through the filaments in the oxide will cause the temperature in the oxide layer to rise locally. Once the temperature is above T_c, the mutual stabilization of charges is compromised, and sudden massive recombination of charges occurs. This recombination may account for the bursts of electroluminescence that can be observed during the switching process (see **Figure 11**). Furthermore, recombination of charges in the oxide layer will result in changes in the effective internal work function of the electrodes. This may account for the experimental observation of changes in the built-in potential of an electroluminescent diode during electrically induced breakdown [43].

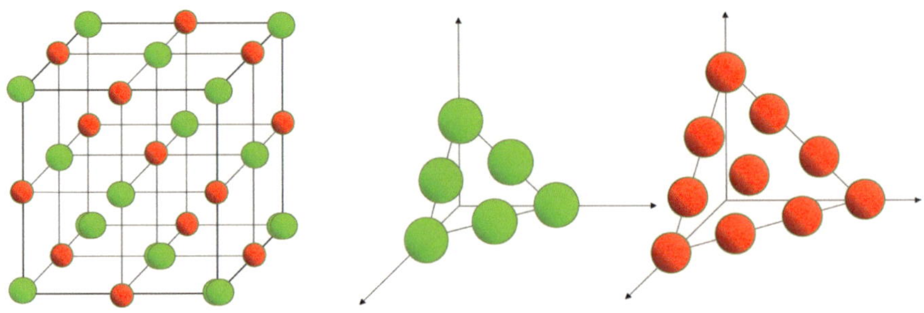

Figure 13. Crystal structure of rock salt (NaCl). Ions of the same charge are packed in layers that lie parallel to the (1 1 1) plane.

5. Conclusion

Unipolar switching in Al_2O_3 diodes involves defects that are created during the electroforming step. The density of defects is critical to the memory operation. Reproducible electroforming is possible by including in the device a well-defined thin layer of a semiconducting polymer. In their pristine state, the polymer/oxide diodes are insulating. The purpose of the polymer layer is threefold. Firstly, the polymer layer acts as a current-limiting series resistance that prevents thermal runaway during electroforming. Secondly, the presence of the polymer introduces an internal polymer/oxide interface, where electrons can accumulate. The trapped electrons stabilize positively charged defects that are generated during electroforming by electrostatic interactions. The trapped electrons promote injection of holes into the oxide, yielding a soft breakdown. Molecular oxygen is expelled and oxygen vacancies are formed. The third purpose of the polymer in the diode is to buffer the molecular oxygen formed.

The experimental evidence indicates that the density of defects in the metal-insulator-metal diodes is of crucial importance to obtain a memory diode with nonvolatile memory properties. If the defect density is too high, the diode will be low. If the density is too low, the critical temperature T_c for phase coexistence is also low. At temperatures $T > T_c$, phase coexistence is not possible, and the memory diode does not show electrical bistability. Upon cooling down, additional filaments should switch on as soon as the temperature drops below the T_c associated with the locale defect density near the filament. This prediction is supported by the experiments in Section 2. Noise measurements prove a unique tool to characterize the dynamics of the defect ionization and neutralization. The onset of discrete fluctuations and random telegraph signals may serve as a diagnostic to determine the difference between the actual defect density and the desired concentration for memory operation.

In summary, unipolar resistive switching poses a unique challenge to the materials that scientists design, deposit, and characterize with appropriate electronic structure, defect ordering, and internal charge carrier dynamics. This challenge seems parallel to development of, e.g., materials for high-temperature superconductivity. Fortunately, in the case of memristors, we have already the certainty from the present state of the art involving the electroforming that relatively simple materials exist with the required properties. The challenge is to gain control over the now largely random process of defect formation.

Author details

Henrique L. Gomes[1,2]*, Dago M. de Leeuw[3] and Stefan C.J. Meskers[4]

*Address all correspondence to: hgomes@ualg.pt

1 Instituto de Telecomunicações, Lisboa, Portugal

2 Universidade do Algarve, Faro, Portugal

3 Smart Materials, Delft University of Technology, The Netherlands

4 Molecular Materials and Nanosystems and Institute for Complex Molecular Systems, Eindhoven University of Technology, Eindhoven, The Netherlands

References

[1] Chen A, Hutchby J, Zhirnov VV, Bourianoff G, editors. Emerging Nanoelectronic Devices. 1st ed. New York: Wiley; 2015. 540 p. DOI: 10.1002/9781118958254

[2] Yang Y, Ouyang J, Ma L, Tseng RJ-H, Chu C-W. Electrical switching and bistability in organic/polymeric thin films and memory devices. Advanced Functional Materials. 2006;**16**(8):1001-1014. DOI: 10.1002/adfm.200500429

[3] Scott JC, Bozano LD. Nonvolatile memory elements based on organic materials. Advanced Materials. 2007;**19**(11):1452-1463. DOI: 10.1002/adma.200602564

[4] Cho B, Kim T-W, Song S, Ji Y, Jo M, Hwang H, Jung G-Y, Lee T. Rewritable switching of one diode–one resistor nonvolatile organic memory devices. Advanced Materials. 2010;**22**(11):1228-1232. DOI: 10.1002/adma.200903203

[5] Cho B, Song S, Ji Y, Kim T-W, Lee T. Organic resistive memory devices: Performance enhancement, integration, and advanced architectures. Advanced Functional Materials. 2011;**21**(15):2806-2829. DOI: 10.1002/adfm.201100686

[6] Lin WP, Liu SJ, Gong T, Zhao Q, Huang W. Polymer-based resistive memory materials and devices. Advanced Functional Materials. 2014;**26**(4):570-606. DOI: 10.1002/adma.201302637

[7] Heremans P, Gelinck GH, Müller R, Baeg K-J, Kim D-Y, Noh Y-Y. Polymer and organic nonvolatile memory devices. Chemistry of Materials. 2010;**23**(3):341-358. DOI: 10.1021/cm102006v

[8] Liaw D-J, Wang K-L, Huang Y-C, Lee K-R, Lai J-Y, Ha C-S. Advanced polyimide materials: Syntheses, physical properties and applications. Progress in Polymer Science. 2012;**37**(7):907-974. DOI: 10.1016/j.progpolymsci.2012.02.005

[9] Kurosawa T, Higashihara T, Ueda M. Polyimide memory: A pithy guideline for future applications. Polymer Chemistry. 2013;**4**(1):16-30. DOI: 10.1039/C2PY20632C

[10] Hickmott TW. Low-frequency negative resistance in thin anodic oxide films. Journal of Applied Physics. 1962;**33**(9):2669-2682. DOI: 10.1063/1.1702530

[11] Dearnaley G, Stoneham AM, Morgan DV. Electrical phenomena in amorphous oxide films. Reports on Progress in Physics. 1970;**33**(3):1129-1191. DOI: 10.1088/0034-4885/33/3/306

[12] Oxley DP. Electroforming, switching and memory effects in oxide thin films. Electrocomponent Science and Technology. 1977;**3**(4):217-224. DOI: 10.1155/APEC.3.217

[13] Pagnia H, Sotnik N. Bistable switching in electroformed metal–insulator–metal devices. Physica Status Solidi (a). 1988;**108**(1):11-65. DOI: 10.1002/pssa.2211080102

[14] Sawa A. Resistive switching in transition metal oxides. Materials Today. 2008;**11**(6):28-36. DOI: 10.1016/S1369-7021(08)70119-6

[15] Waser R, Aono M. Nanoionics-based resistive switching memories. Nature Materials. 2007;**6**(11):833-840. DOI: 10.1038/nmat2023

[16] Verbakel F, Meskers SCJ, Janssen RAJ, Gomes HL, Cölle M, Büchel M, De Leeuw DM. Reproducible resistive switching in nonvolatile organic memories. Applied Physics Letters. 2007;**91**(19):192103. DOI: 10.1063/1.2806275

[17] Ziegler K, Klausmann E. Static technique for precise measurements of surface potential and interface state density in MOS structures. Applied Physics Letters. 1975;**26**(7):400-402. DOI: 10.1063/1.88193

[18] Bory BF, Meskers SCJ, Janssen RAJ, Gomes HL, De Leeuw DM. Trapping of electrons in metal oxide-polymer memory diodes in the initial stage of electroforming. Applied Physics Letters. 2010;**97**(22):222106. DOI: 10.1063/1.3520517

[19] Gomes HL, Da Costa AMR, Moreira JA, De Leeuw DM, Meskers SCJ. The role of internal structure in the anomalous switching dynamics of metal-oxide/polymer resistive random access memories. Thin Solid Films. 2012;**522**:407-411. DOI: 10.1016/j.tsf.2012.08.041

[20] Chen Q, Bory BF, Kiazadeh A, Rocha PRF, De Leeuw DM, Meskers SCJ. Opto-electronic characterization of electron traps upon forming polymer oxide memory diodes. Applied Physics Letters. 2011;**99**(8):083305. DOI: 10.1063/1.3628301

[21] Verbakel F, Meskers SCJ, Janssen RAJ, Gomes HL, van den Biggelaar AJM, de Leeuw DM. Switching dynamics in non-volatile polymer memories. Organic Electronics: Physics, Materials, Applications. 2008;**9**(5):829-833. DOI: 10.1016/j.orgel.2008.05.022

[22] Chen Q, Gomes HL, Rocha PRF, De Leeuw DM, Meskers SCJ. Reversible post-breakdown conduction in aluminum oxide-polymer capacitors. Applied Physics Letters. 2013;**102**(15):153509. DOI: 10.1063/1.4802485

[23] Verbakel F, Meskers SCJ, Janssen RAJ. Electronic memory effects in diodes from a zinc oxide nanoparticle-polystyrene hybrid material. Applied Physics Letters. 2006;**89**(10):102103. DOI: 10.1063/1.2345612

[24] Verbakel F, Meskers SCJ, Janssen RAJ. Electronic memory effects in diodes of zinc oxide nanoparticles in a matrix of polystyrene or poly(3-hexylthiophene). Journal of Applied Physics. 2007;**102**(8):083701

[25] Verbakel F, Meskers SCJ, Janssen RAJ. Surface modification of zinc oxide nanoparticles influences the electronic memory effects in ZnO-polystyrene diodes. Journal of Physical Chemistry C. 2007;**111**(28):10150-10153. DOI: 10.1021/jp072999j

[26] Bory BF, Rocha PRF, Gomes HL, De Leeuw DM, Meskers SCJ. Unipolar resistive switching in metal oxide/organic semiconductor non-volatile memories as a critical phenomenon. Journal of Applied Physics. 2015;**118**(20):205503. DOI: 10.1063/1.4936349

[27] Rocha PRF, Gomes HL, Asadi K, Katsouras I, Bory B, Verbakel F, Van De Weijer P, De Leeuw DM, Meskers SCJ. Sudden death of organic light-emitting diodes. Organic Electronics: Physics, Materials, Applications. 2015;**20**:89-96. DOI: 10.1016/j.orgel. BF, Wang J, Gomes HL, Janssen RAJ, De Leeuw 2015.02.009

[28] Bory DM, Meskers SCJ. Relation between the electroforming voltage in alkali halide-polymer diodes and the bandgap of the alkali halide. Applied Physics Letters. 2014;**105**(23):233502. DOI: 10.1063/1.4903831

[29] Bory BF, Rocha PRF, Janssen RAJ, Gomes HL, De Leeuw DM, Meskers SCJ. Lithium fluoride injection layers can form quasi-Ohmic contacts for both holes and electrons. Applied Physics Letters. 2014;**105**(12):123302. DOI: 10.1063/1.4896636

[30] Kurnosikov O, De Nooij FC, LeClair P, Kohlhepp JT, Koopmans B, Swagten HJM, De Jonge WJM. STM-induced reversible switching of local conductivity in thin. Physical Review B. 2001;**64**(15):1534071-1534074. DOI: 10.1103/PhysRevB.64.153407

[31] Kim YS, Kim J-S, Choi JS, Hwang IR, Hong SH, Kang S-O, Park BH. Resistive switching behaviors of NiO films with controlled number of conducting filaments. Applied Physics Letters. 2011;**98**(19):192104. DOI: 10.1063/1.3589825

[32] Cölle M, Büchel M, de Leeuw DM. Switching and filamentary conduction in non-volatile organic memories. Organic Electronics: Physics, Materials, Applications. 2006;**7**(5):305-312. DOI: 10.1016/j.orgel.2006.03.014

[33] Rocha PRF, Gomes HL, Vandamme LKJ, Chen Q, Kiazadeh A, De Leeuw DM, Meskers SCJ. Low-frequency diffusion noise in resistive-switching memories based on metal-oxide polymer structure. IEEE Transactions on Electron Devices. 2012;**59**(9):2483-2487/6243198. DOI: 10.1109/TED.2012.2204059

[34] Lombardo S, Stathis JH, Linder BP, Pey KL, Palumbo F, Tung CH. Dielectric breakdown mechanisms in gate oxides. Journal of Applied Physics. 2005;**98**(12):121301. DOI: 10.1063/1.2147714

[35] Chen L, Xia Y, Liang X, Yin K, Yin J, Liu Z, Chen Y. Nonvolatile memory devices with Cu2S and Cu-Pc bilayered films. Applied Physics Letters. 2007;**91**(7):073511. DOI: 10.1063/1.2771064

[36] Joo W-J, Choi T-L, Lee K-H, Chung Y. Study on threshold behavior of operation voltage in metal filament-based polymer memory. Journal of Physical Chemistry B. 2007;**111**(27):7756-7760. DOI: 10.1021/jp0684933

[37] Gomes HL, Rocha PRF, Kiazadeh A, De Leeuw DM, Meskers SCJ. Anomalous temperature dependence of the current in a metal-oxide-polymer resistive switching diode. Journal of Physics D: Applied Physics. 2011;**44**(2):025103. DOI: 10.1088/0022-3727/44/2/025103

[38] Hickmott TW. Millimeter distance effects of surface plasmon polaritons in electroformed Al-Al2O3-Ag diodes. Journal of Applied Physics. 2017;**121**:083101. DOI: 10.1063/1.4976715

[39] Biederman H. Metal-insulator-metal sandwich structures with anomalous properties. Vacuum. 1976;**26**(11):513-523. DOI: 10.1016/S0042-207X(76)81130-X

[40] Eckertová L. Feldkathoden mit dünnen Isolatorschichten. Physica Status Solidi (B). 1966;**18**(1):3-40. DOI: 10.1002/pssb.19660180102

[41] Fedorov MV, Kornyshev AA. Ionic liquids at electrified interfaces. Chemical Reviews. 2014;**114**(5):2978-3036. DOI: 10.1021/cr400374x

[42] Healy TW, Scales PJ. The oxide water interface: How valid is the site dissociation surface equilibria model. Chemistry Letters. 2012;**41**(10):1020-1022. DOI: 10.1246/cl.2012.1020

[43] Bory BF, Gomes HL, Janssen RAJ, De Leeuw DM, Meskers SCJ. Electrical conduction of LiF interlayers in organic diodes. Journal of Applied Physics. 2015;**117**(15):155502. DOI: 10.1063/1.4917461

Section 2

Memristor Modelling

Chapter 6

Memristor Emulator Circuit Design and Applications

Carlos Sánchez-López, Illiani Carro-Pérez,
Victor Hugo Carbajal-Gómez,
Miguel Angel Carrasco-Aguilar and
Francisco Epimenio Morales-López

Additional information is available at the end of the chapter

http://dx.doi.org/10.5772/intechopen.69291

Abstract

This chapter introduces a design guide of memristor emulator circuits, from conceptual idea until experimental tests. Three topologies of memristor emulator circuits in their incremental and decremental versions are analysed and designed at low and high frequency. The behavioural model of each topology is derived and programmed at SIMULINK under the MATLAB environment. An offset compensation technique is also described in order to achieve the frequency-dependent pinched hysteresis loop that is on the origin and when the memristor emulator circuit is operating at high frequency. Furthermore, from these topologies, a technique to transform normal non-linear resistors to inverse non-linear resistors is also addressed. HSPICE numerical simulations for each topology are also shown. Finally, three real analogue applications based on memristors are analysed and explained at the behavioural level of abstraction.

Keywords: memristor, pinched hysteresis loop, current conveyor, non-linear resistor, behavioural modelling

1. Introduction

Memristors have turned out to be of considerable importance in several areas of research and application, such as analogue circuits, non-linear (chaotic) circuits, sensors, control systems, storage systems, cellular neural networks, logic circuits, power systems, neuromorphic circuits, etc. [1]. In order to research all those applications, the first step is understanding and modelling the behaviour of a memristor. In this scenario, there are, basically, three approaches:

behavioural modelling, SPICE type models and emulator circuits. In the former case, smooth continuous cubic non-linear functions [2], square non-linear functions [3], piecewise linear models [4] and hyperbolic sine models [5, 6] have been proposed to emulate the Hewlett-Packard (HP) memristor behaviour. Examples of this type of modelling are TEAM model [7], VTEM model [8] and Simmons tunnelling model [9]. Although these models are approaching the HP memristor behaviour with a level of error relatively low, a full custom software is required for solving the mathematical models [10]. Furthermore, this task becomes cumbersome when applications with several memristors are addressed, since a large set of equations must first be established according to the topology, and next, the system of equations must be numerically solved. In the second approach, SPICE models have also been developed in order to model the HP memristor, principally [11–16]. It is worth mentioning that the memristive effect is not limited to TiO_2, and this effect has also been glimpsed on nickel oxide [1], Ag-loaded Si films [17], TiO_2 sol-gel solutions [18], and other materials. Although this type of modelling is interesting, since the capabilities of commercially available tools are exploited, its major disadvantage is that numerical simulations of circuits based on memristors can only be done. In the latter, several emulator circuits have been proposed in the literature, which use different design methodologies and different topologies. In this way, grounded and floating memristor emulator circuits working at incremental or decremental mode and built with operational amplifiers and analogue multipliers have been proposed in [19–24]. Other interesting topologies were reported in [25, 26], where digital and analogue mixed circuits were used. More recently, other active devices such as current feedback operational amplifiers, positive second-generation current conveyors (CCII+) and differential difference current conveyor, see [27–33] and the references cited therein, have also been used to design a memristor emulator circuit. However, some of them not only become complex and bulky, requiring rigid conditions to operate, but also some emulators do not exhibit those fingerprints that are useful to affirm that the emulator circuit is a memristor or memristive device. With this in mind and depending on the application, any emulator circuit must accomplish some properties, some of them are: the frequency-dependent pinched hysteresis loop for any kind of flux- or charge-controlled incremental or decremental memristor/memductor, in its version grounded or floating, must pass through the origin for any periodic signal with any amplitude, operating frequency and initial conditions; the possibility for controlling the initial state of the emulator circuit, i.e. adjust of the initial conditions, non-volatility, memristive/memductive behaviour at high-frequency and without offset, etc. All in all, the design of memristor emulator circuits is also important in order to study and research real applications as those mentioned above. As a consequence, a lot of emulator circuits using off-the-shelf components have been developed to imitate not only the real behaviour of a memristor but also the real behaviour of meminductors and memcapacitors [1].

In this chapter, we discuss the design of three memristor emulator circuits. The aim is to show the conceptual idea on the design of an emulator, passing for numerical simulations and until experimental tests. Each behavioural model is derived and programmed at SIMULINK under MATLAB environment. From a circuit-design perspective and of the knowledge gained, a design guide is described in order to design a memristor emulator circuit in a systematic way. Then, we introduce a novel technique for achieving the frequency-dependent pinched hysteresis loop associated to a memristor emulator circuit that is operating at high frequency, and the crossing point does not deviate of the origin. Since a memristor is basically a charge- or flux-controlled resistor, we describe how to transform a non-linear resistor with its normal pinched hysteresis loop to an inverse behaviour. Therefore, the main difference of an inverse non-linear resistor with respect to normal resistors is that the behaviour of frequency-dependent pinched hysteresis loop becomes a straight line when the operating frequency of the signal source decreases. Finally, some real analogue applications are described.

2. Analogue memristor emulators

Unlike behavioural models and SPICE type models, an emulator circuit is very useful, since real applications based on memristors can be researched and built. In this section, we describe three memristor emulator circuits.

2.1. Floating memristor emulator circuit

The topology shown in **Figure 1(a)** was reported in [28]. By a straightforward analysis, the behaviour equation is given by:

$$\frac{v_{\mathrm{m}}(t)}{i_{\mathrm{m}}(t)} = M(\varphi_{\mathrm{m}}(t)) = R_1 \pm \frac{R_1 R_4}{10 R_2 R_3 C_z} \int_0^t v_{\mathrm{m}}(\tau) d\tau \tag{1}$$

From **Figure 1(a)**, the *S* switch is connected to ***I*** to obtain a memristor emulator circuit operating at incremental mode, whereas if ***S*** is connected to ***D***, then a decremental behaviour is obtained. These behaviours correspond to the signs + and − at Eq. (1), respectively. Assuming that

$v_{\mathrm{m}}(t) = A_{\mathrm{m}}\sin(\omega t)$, where A_{m} is the amplitude and $\omega = 2\pi f$ in rad/s, we obtain:

$$\frac{v_{\mathrm{m}}(t)}{i_{\mathrm{m}}(t)} = R_1 \pm \frac{R_1 R_4 A_{\mathrm{m}}}{10 R_2 R_3 C_z \omega} \cos(\omega t - \pi) \tag{2}$$

From Eq. (2), one can observe that the memristance is composed by a linear time-invariant resistor and a linear time-varying resistor. The relationship between both resistors is described by the ratio of their amplitudes, given as

$$k_{\mathrm{n}} = \frac{R_4 A_{\mathrm{m}}}{R_2 R_3 C_z \omega 10} = \frac{1}{\tau f} = \frac{T}{\tau} \tag{3}$$

where $\tau = \frac{20\pi R_2 R_3 C_z}{R_4 A_{\mathrm{m}}}$ is the time constant of the emulator circuit and $T = \frac{1}{f}$ is the period of $v_{\mathrm{m}}(t)$. In order to hold the pinched hysteresis loop in several operating frequencies, one can observe in Eq. (3) that τ must be updated according to f, since k_{n} will decrease as the frequency increases. Thus, the numeric value of τ can be updated by R_3 or C_z. On the other hand, Eq. (3) reveals that:

1. $k_{\mathrm{n}} \rightarrow 0$ when $f \rightarrow \infty$ or $A_{\mathrm{m}} \rightarrow 0$. Hence, Eq. (1) is dominated by its linear time-invariant part.

2. $k_n \to 1$ when $f \to 1/\tau$ or A_m is monotonically increased. Therefore, the maximum pinched hysteresis loop is obtained.

3. $k_n \to \geq 1$ when $f \leq 1/\tau$ or A_m increases too much. Here, the hysteresis loop is lost.

In order to ensure the behaviour of the frequency-dependent pinched hysteresis loop, the numerical value of k_n must be in the interval (0, 1). Once the behavioural model of the memristor has been deduced, numerical simulations can be realized. The numerical value of each element of **Figure 1(a)** used during numerical simulations and experimental tests can be found in [28]. Therefore, **Figure 2(a)** (solid line) shows only the incremental pinched hysteresis loop behaviour obtained of **Figure 1(b)** when a sinusoidal waveform operating to 16 Hz is applied. For this case and that follows, the direction of the hysteresis loop is clockwise, whereas for a decremental mode, the direction is counterclockwise. Therefore, a similar behaviour is obtained for the decremental case, as illustrated in **Figure 2(a)**.

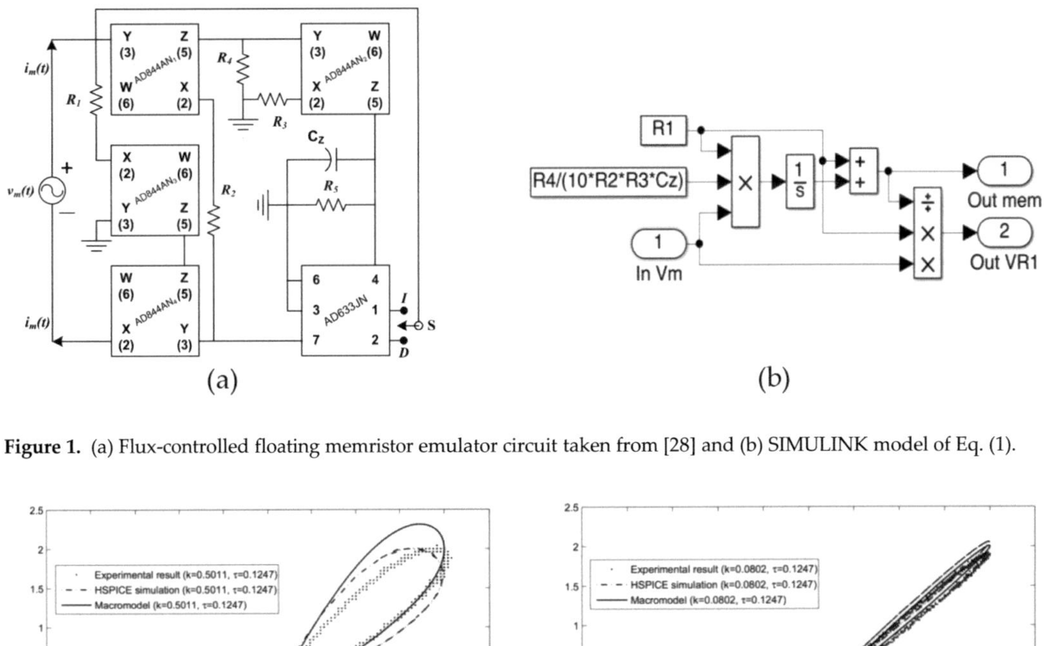

Figure 1. (a) Flux-controlled floating memristor emulator circuit taken from [28] and (b) SIMULINK model of Eq. (1).

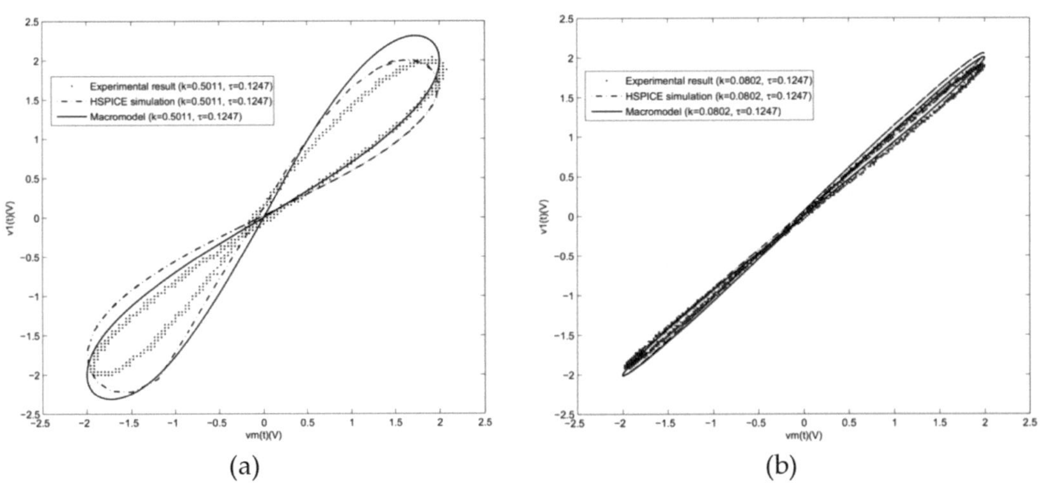

Figure 2. Numerical, HSPICE and experimental results of **Figure 1(a)** operating at: (a) 16 Hz and (b) 100 Hz.

Figure 1(a) was also simulated at HSPICE by using the macro-models associated to each active device and numerical results are shown in **Figure 2(a)** (dash-dot line). In order to validate the previous results, **Figure 1(a)** was experimentally tested, and the results are shown in **Figure 2(a)** (dot-dash line). On the other hand, when the operating frequency increases, the pinched hysteresis loop is gradually lost and the memristor behaviour becomes a straight line for all cases, as depicted in **Figure 2(b)**. Furthermore, the frequency-dependent pinched hysteresis loop is a necessary condition but not sufficient for claiming that the emulator circuit is emulating the real memristor behaviour. In this case, tests of non-volatility are necessary. Since capacitors and inductors are the solely elements that are storing energy, the non-volatility property is indirectly measured across C_z of **Figure 1(a)**. Thus, **Figure 3** shows experimental tests of non-volatility of **Figure 1(a)** when a narrow pulse train of 1.2 V of amplitude and 2.4 μs of pulse width (yellow line) is applied. According to **Figure 3**, one can observe that once programmed the incremental and decremental memristance, its value is keeping when the input signal is not applied. Note that during non-pulse period, the memristance is non-volatile, and its variation is negligible. For incremental topology, the memristance increases according to the amplitude and pulse width, as depicted in **Figure 3** (pink line), whereas for the decremental topology, the memristance decreases (blue line). It is important to point out that memristive behaviour in each operation mode can be reverted to its last value, when a negative pulse of the same size is applied.

2.2. Grounded memristor emulator circuit I

Recently in [28, 31, 32], floating and grounded memristor emulator circuits based on CCII+ were proposed. In this way, the behavioural model of the charge-controlled grounded memductor emulator circuit described in [32] and shown in **Figure 4(a)** is given by

$$\frac{i_{\mathrm{m}}(t)}{v_{\mathrm{m}}(t)} = W(q_{\mathrm{m}}(t)) = \frac{1}{R_1 + R_x} \pm \frac{A_v A_i}{10(R_{\mathrm{m}} + R_{\mathrm{x}})(C_{\mathrm{m}} + C_{\mathrm{a}})} \int_0^t i_{\mathrm{m}}(\tau) d\tau \tag{4}$$

where R_{x} and C_{a} are the parasitic resistance and capacitance connected in x- and z-terminal,

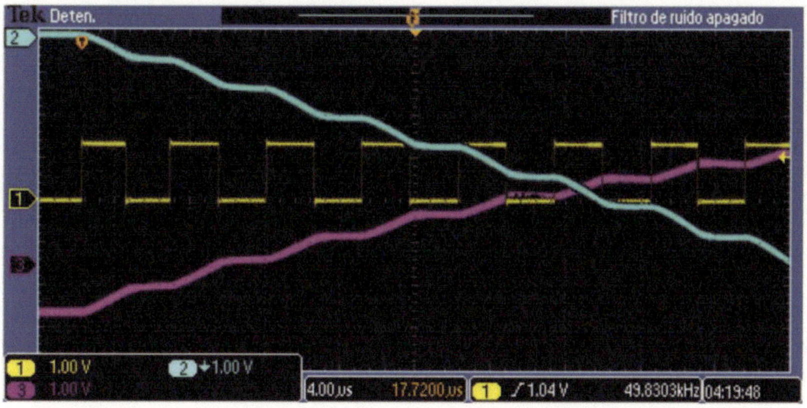

Figure 3. Experimental results of non-volatility property for incremental (pink line) and (blue line) decremental memristor. Pulse signal at yellow line.

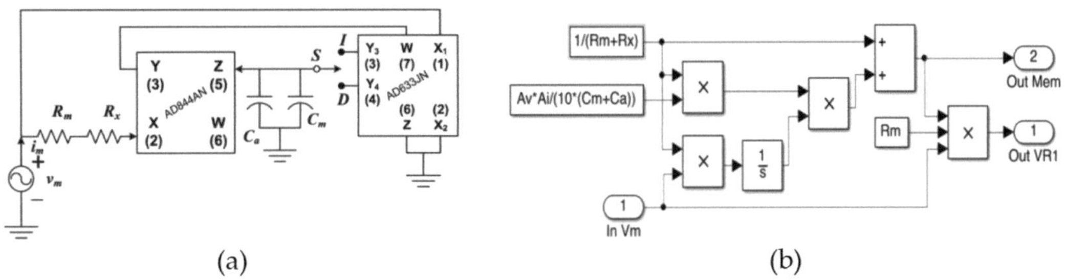

Figure 4. (a) Charge-controlled grounded memductor emulator circuit taken from [32] and (b) SIMULINK model of Eqs. (4) and (5).

respectively; A_v and A_i are the voltage and current gains between y- and x-terminal and x- and z-terminal of CCII+. Similarly as in Subsection 2.1, an incremental behaviour is obtained when the ***S*** switch is connected to ***I*** and a decremental behaviour is obtained if ***S*** is connected to ***D***. Each behaviour corresponds to the sign + and − at Eq. (4), respectively. According to the behaviour of the frequency-dependent pinched hysteresis loop, this is composed by two lobes with symmetric areas. Since the hysteresis loop is represented on the v-i plane, the average current occurs when the area of both lobes is zero, and hence, the hysteresis loop tends to be a straight line as $f \to \infty$. This last effect is achieved when the linear time-varying part of the memductor is zero, and hence, from Eq. (4), we get

$$i_m(t) = \frac{v_m(t)}{R_m + R_x} \tag{5}$$

From Eqs. (4) and (5), a SIMULINK model can be easily built, as shown in **Figure 4(b)**. Note that to obtain a decremental memductor, the input-terminal second of the block, shown in **Figure 4(b)**, must be negative. Considering $v_m(t) = A_m \sin(\omega t)$ and substituting Eq. (5) in Eq. (4), we get

$$\frac{i_m(t)}{v_m(t)} = \frac{1}{R_m + R_x} \pm \frac{A_v A_i A_m}{10\omega (R_m + R_x)^2 (C_m + C_a)} \cos(\omega t - \pi) \tag{6}$$

and the k_n parameter is given by

$$k_n = \frac{A_v A_i A_m}{10\omega (R_m + R_x)(C_m + C_a)} = \frac{1}{\tau f} = \frac{T}{\tau} \tag{7}$$

where $\tau = \frac{20\pi (R_m + R_x)(C_m + C_a)}{A_v A_i A_m}$. From Eq. (7), one can intuit that k_n will decrease as the frequency increases, but Eq. (7) also reveals that

1. $k_n \to 0$ when $f \to \infty$ or $A_m \to 0$. Therefore, Eq. (6) becomes dominated by its linear time-invariant admittance.

2. $k_n \to 1$ when $f \to 1/\tau$ or A_m is monotonically increased. Hence, the maximum frequency-dependent pinched hysteresis loop is obtained.

3. $k_n \to \geq 1$ when $f \leq 1/\tau$ or A_m increases too much. For this case, the hysteresis loop is lost.

In this manner, the behaviour of the frequency-dependent pinched hysteresis loop can be kept over a broad range of frequencies and amplitude A_m, when the numerical value of k_n is in the interval (0, 1) [32]. This means that τ must be updated according to f and A_m, respectively. The numerical value of each element of **Figure 4(a)** for different operating frequencies and amplitudes can be found in [32].

According to [32], **Figure 4(a)** was configured for working at 16 Hz in both operation modes. Henceforth, numerical results of the incremental topology will be shown below in the left side, whereas the decremental topology will be shown in the right side. From **Figure 4(b)**, numerical results for each topology are depicted in **Figure 5(a)** and **(b)** (solid lines). Let us now increase monotonically the operating frequency of $v_m(t)$ until $f = 500$ Hz. As depicted in **Figure 5(c)** and **(d)** (solid lines), the frequency-dependent pinched hysteresis loop for both topologies becomes dominated by the linear time-invariant admittance. In this stage, for widening the hysteresis loop of each topology and keeping $f = 500$ Hz, C_m or R_1 must be adjusted. Afterwards, each topology shown in **Figure 4(a)** was simulated at HSPICE and numerical results are illustrated in **Figure 5(a)** and **(b)** (dash-dot lines) operating at 16 Hz, respectively. Similarly as above, the operating

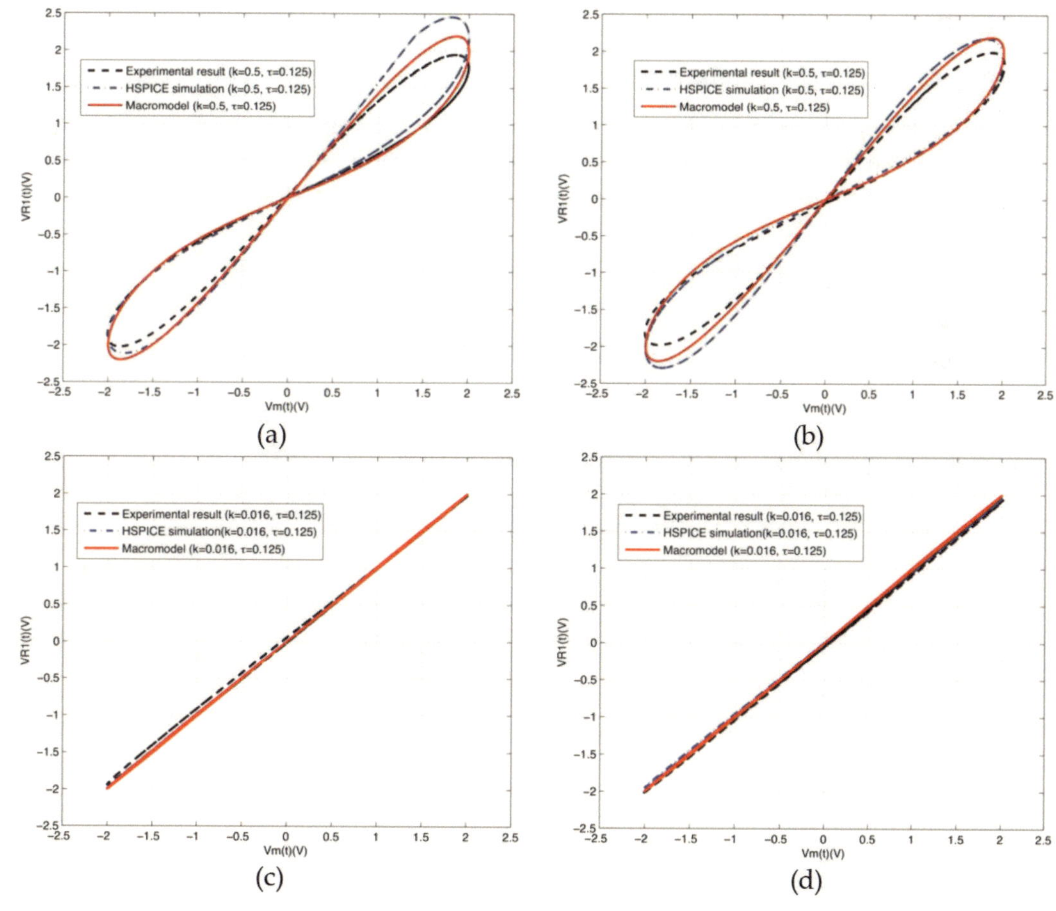

Figure 5. Numerical, HSPICE and experimental results of **Figure 4(a)** operating at: (a) 16 Hz and (c) 500 Hz, for incremental mode; (b) 16 Hz and (d) 500 Hz, for decremental mode.

frequency was increased until 500 Hz and, as a consequence, both pinched hysteresis loops become a straight line, as depicted in **Figure 5(c)** and **(d)** (dash-dot lines). In order to demonstrate the real behaviour of the memductor emulator circuit, **Figure 4(a)** was built with off-the-shelf devices.

In this way, **Figure 5(a)** and **(b)** (dashed lines) illustrate the pinched hysteresis loops for both operation modes and the upper and lower lobe area of both hysteresis loops becomes zero when the operating frequency increases and hence the hysteresis loop tends to be a straight line, as illustrated in **Figure 5(c)** and **(d)** (dashed lines), confirming the theory described before. To experimentally test the non-volatility of the memductor emulator circuit, the voltage across C_m of **Figure 4(a)** was measured for each incremental and decremental configuration. In both cases, a rectangular pulse train of 5 V of amplitude with 82 μs was applied in the input of **Figure 4(a)**. Therefore, **Figure 6(a)** shows the behaviour of $v_{Cm}(t)$ for the incremental case, whereas **Figure 6(b)** shows the decremental case. From **Figure 6**, one can observe that the variation of $v_{Cm}(t)$ is more pronounced for the decremental case. Observe, also, that the voltage is kept during non-pulse period. Again, the memductive behaviour in each operation mode can be reverted to its last value, whether a negative pulse of the same size is applied [32].

2.3. Grounded memristor emulator circuit II

As last example, we discuss the charge-controlled grounded memristor emulator circuit reported in [31] and illustrated in **Figure 7(a)**. Simple analysis of **Figure 7(a)** allows us to obtain the memristive behaviour given by

$$\frac{v_m(t)}{i_m(t)} = M(q_m(t)) = R_1 \pm \frac{R_2}{40C_1}\int_0^t i_m(\tau)d\tau \tag{8}$$

It is notable to point out that the positive sign in Eq. (8) correspond to the ***S*** switch connected to ***I*** in **Figure 7(a)** and hence, an incremental behaviour is obtained; whereas the negative sign is obtained when ***S*** is connected to ***D*** and hence a decremental behaviour. Again, following the idea described in previous subsections and reported in [28, 31], a frequency analysis can be

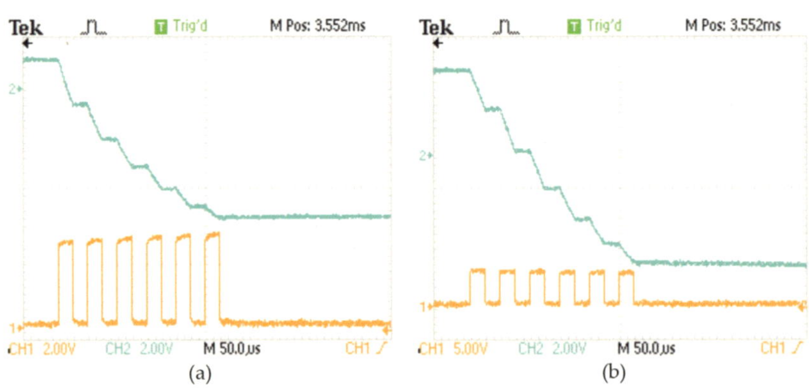

Figure 6. Experimental results of non-volatility property for: (a) incremental mode and (b) decremental mode.

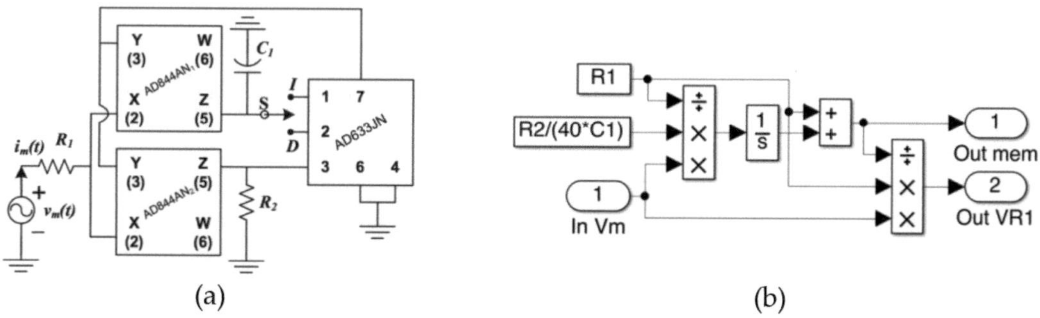

Figure 7. (a) Charge-controlled grounded memristor emulator circuit taken from [31] and (b) SIMULINK model of Eqs. (8) and (9).

done. According to Eq. (8), the average current will occur when the linear time-varying resistor is zero and hence from Eq. (8) we get:

$$i_m(t) = \frac{v_m(t)}{R_1} \tag{9}$$

By merging Eqs. (8) and (9), a SIMULINK model can be built, as depicted in **Figure 7(b)**. In this figure, the input-terminal second of the adder block must be negative to obtain a decremental behaviour. Assuming $v_m(t) = A_m\sin(\omega t)$ and substituting Eq. (9) in Eq. (8), we obtain

$$\frac{v_m(t)}{i_m(t)} = R_1 \pm \frac{R_2 A_m}{40 R_1 C_1 \omega} \cos(\omega t - \pi) \tag{10}$$

It follows from Eq. (10) that

$$k_n = \frac{R_2 A_m}{40 R_1^2 C_1 \omega} = \frac{1}{\tau f} = \frac{T}{\tau} \tag{11}$$

where $\tau = \frac{40\pi R_1^2 C_1}{R_2 A_m}$ is the time constant of the emulator circuit and $T = \frac{1}{f}$ is the period of $v_m(t)$. In the same way as in previous subsections, k_n will decrease as the operating frequency increases, and for holding the hysteresis loop at a particular frequency, the numeric value of τ must be updated by C_1. Analysing Eq. (11) for both configurations, we have

1. $k_n \to 0$ when $f \to \infty$ or $A_m \to 0$. Therefore, Eq. (10) becomes dominated by R_1.

2. $k_n \to 1$ when $f \to 1/\tau$ or A_m is monotonically increased. Thus, we see that the maximum pinched hysteresis loop is achieved.

3. $k_n \to \geq 1$ when $f \leq 1/\tau$ or A_m increases too much. For this case, the hysteresis loop is lost.

According to [31], the memristor emulator circuit was configured to operate at 16 Hz in both operation modes. By using **Figure 7(b)**, the hysteresis loop for each topology shown in **Figure 7(a)** is obtained, as depicted in **Figure 8(a)** and **(b)** (solid lines), respectively. By monotonically increasing the operating frequency of $v_m(t)$ until 100 Hz, both hysteresis loops become dominated by R_1,

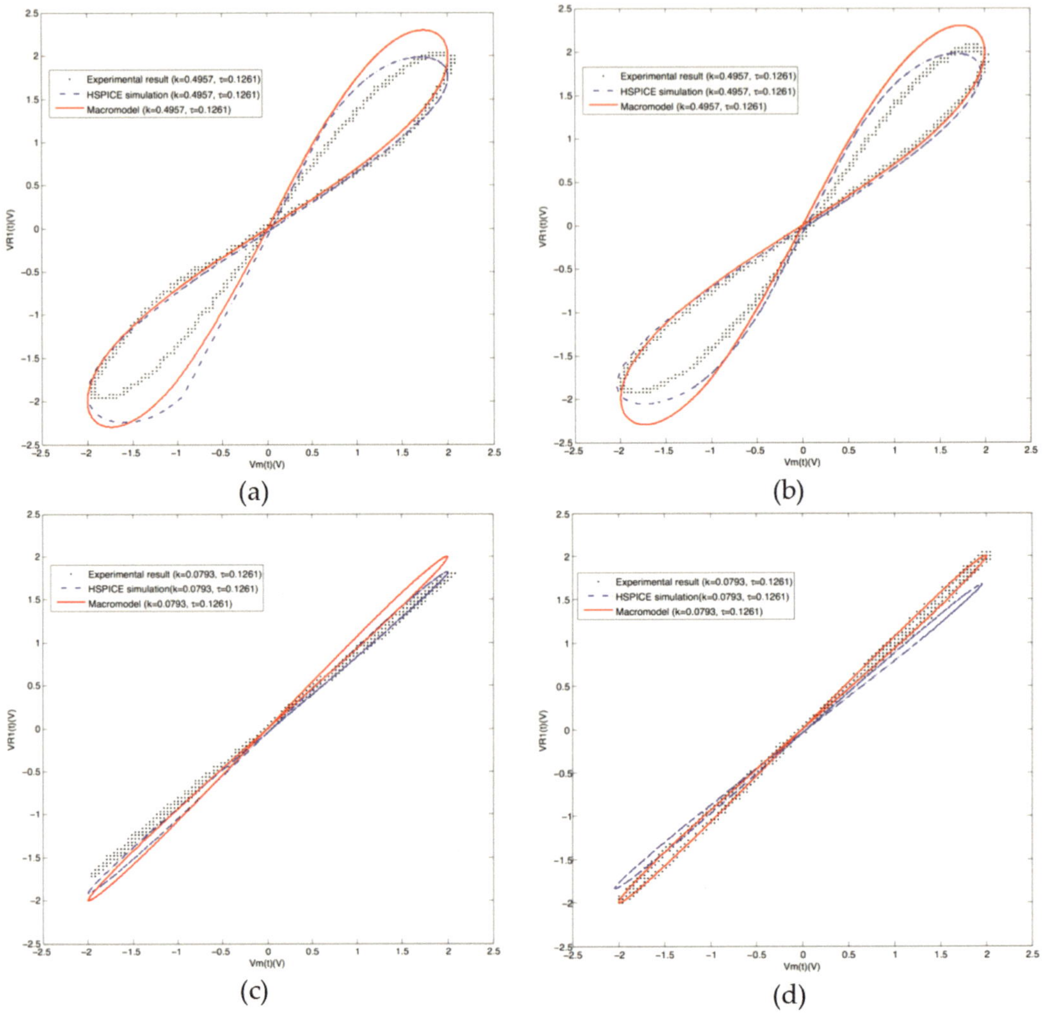

Figure 8. Numerical, HSPICE and experimental results of **Figure 7(a)** operating at: (a) 16 Hz and (c) 100 Hz, for incremental mode; (b) 16 Hz and (d) 100 Hz, for decremental mode.

as illustrated in **Figure 8(c)** and **(d)** (solid lines). It is worth stressing that to obtain the pinched hysteresis loops shown in **Figure 8(a)** and **(b)** (solid lines) but at $f = 100$ Hz, the numeric value of C_1 must be adjusted. Therefore, one can insight that by scaling down C_1, the hysteresis loop behaviour, for both topologies, can be pushed for operating at higher frequencies. On the other hand, **Figure 7(a)** was also simulated at HSPICE by using the numerical value of each element described in [31] and for both topologies. Simulation results are illustrated in **Figure 8(a)** and **(b)** (dash-dot lines), respectively; whereas the linear behaviours are depicted in **Figure 8(c)** and **(d)** (dash-dot lines).

To validate the results derived and demonstrate the real behaviour of the emulator circuit, **Figure 7(a)** was built and experimentally tested by using commercially available active devices. Therefore, **Figure 8(a)** and **(b)** (dot-square lines) show the experimental results for each topology and at each fundamental operating frequency; whereas **Figure 8(c)** and **(d)** (dot-square lines) show that the hysteresis loops become dominated by R_1, confirming the theory described above. A notable fingerprint of any memristor emulator circuit is the non-volatility of its memristance. This means that the memristance once programmed, its last value must be kept for a long time. In order to verify this property, the voltage across C_1 was first experimentally measured and next, by using Eq. (8), a post-processing was done for getting the memristance variation for each topology, as depicted in **Figure 9** (top figure). The memristance variations were obtained when a pulse train of 5 V of amplitude and 0.5 ms of pulse width was applied to **Figure 7(a)**, as illustrated in **Figure 9** (lower figure).

As one can observe in **Figure 9**, the memristance range for both emulator circuits is 7 kΩ, and although the pulse train is applied indefinitely, the maximum memristance achieved is 19 kΩ; whereas the minimum memristance for the decremental case is 5 kΩ. On the other hand, if the pulse train with −5 V of amplitude and same pulse width is applied, then the memristive behaviour is inverted for each topology shown in the top of **Figure 9** [31].

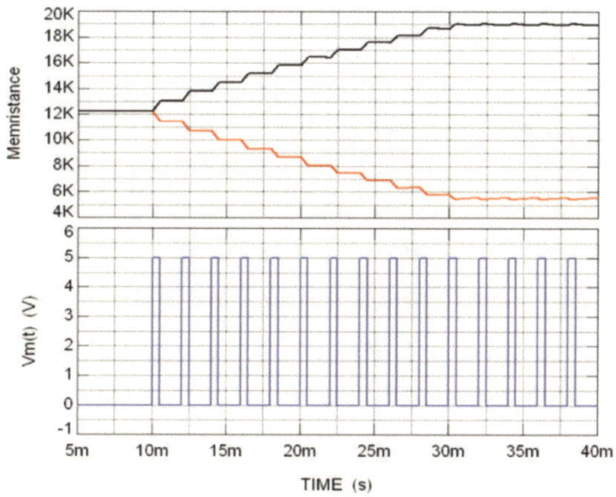

Figure 9. Experimental results of non-volatile memristance for incremental mode (black line) and decremental mode (red line). In the figure below, $v_m(t)$ as pulse train.

3. Design guide

According to Section 2, one can observe that Eqs. (1), (4) and (8) have the form

$$y_n(t) = x(t)\left(a_n \pm b_n \int_0^t z(\tau)d\tau\right) \tag{12}$$

where $y_n(t)$ is the current or voltage output signal, $x(t)$ is the voltage or current input signal and $z(t)$ is the voltage or current control signal; a_n represents the linear time-invariant gain and b_n represents the linear time-varying gain, which is associated with the time constant of the emulator circuit [28, 31, 32]. Assuming that $z(t) = A_m \sin(\omega t + \theta)$, where θ is the phase in degrees, we obtain

$$\int_0^t z(\tau)d\tau = -\frac{A_{\mathrm{m}}}{\omega}\cos(\omega t + \theta) = \mp\frac{1}{\omega}\sqrt{A_{\mathrm{m}}^2 - z^2(t)} \tag{13}$$

therefore, Eq. (12) becomes

$$y_{\mathrm{n}}(t) = x(t)\left(a_{\mathrm{n}} \mp \frac{b_n}{\omega}\sqrt{A_{\mathrm{m}}^2 - z^2(t)}\right) \tag{14}$$

According to [28, 31, 32], the linear time-varying gain can be computed in function of ω and A_{m} given by

$$b_{\mathrm{n}} = \frac{a_{\mathrm{n}}\omega k_{\mathrm{n}}}{A_{\mathrm{m}}} \tag{15}$$

where $k_{\mathrm{n}} \in (0, 1)$ is a parameter that is used to ensure the behaviour of the pinched hysteresis loop.

In order to design a memristor emulator circuit, the following four-step design procedure is proposed

Step 1. For all memristor emulator circuit that has the form given by Eq. (12) and to ensure the pinched hysteresis loop, we choose $k_{\mathrm{n}} = 0.5$.

Step 2. Given an operating frequency and A_{m}, use Eq. (15) to find the relation between b_{n} and a_{n}.

Step 3. Select the numeric value of a_{n}, which is associated to the linear time-invariant resistor/conductor. As a consequence, the numeric value of b_{n} is derived from Eq. (15).

Step 4. For each topology, b_{n} is related with those parameters of the emulator circuit and τ. Therefore, the numeric value of each resistor and capacitor can be deduced.

If the above procedure is followed, it is most likely that a memristor emulator circuit with good features will result and with a frequency-dependent hysteresis loop with relatively symmetrical lobes.

4. Offset compensation

Some properties that any emulator circuit must satisfy to be considered as memristor were described in Section 1. One of them is the frequency-dependent pinched hysteresis loop observed on the voltage-current plane, which must pass through the origin for any periodic signal with any amplitude, operating frequency and initial conditions [1]. Thus, whether a periodic signal is applied to the memristor emulator circuit, both the voltage and current are zero when any of them is zero. Therefore, any device is a memristor or a memristive device when it has a current-voltage hysteresis curve with identical zero crossing. However, until today, all the memristor emulator circuits reported in the literature [19–32] are operating in low-frequency and some of them present a deviation of the crossing point on the origin. This behaviour is more evident when the operating frequency of the stimulus signal increases, and hence, the emulator circuit does not only stop mimicking the behaviour of the memristor, but also reduces its application range. Note that below a certain critical frequency, the emulator circuit mimics well the behaviour of a memristor and beyond that of critical frequency, the circuit becomes a memristive device with an additional battery in series.

In order to overcome this shortcoming and achieve a pinched hysteresis loop operating at high frequency, an offset compensation technique must be applied. Such techniques have been reported in [33]. Basically, the technique involves adding two DC voltage sources in the analogue multiplier to vertically and horizontally control the offset of the hysteresis loop. However, as described in [33], this offset reduction technique is only applicable to floating and grounded memristor emulator circuits whose design is based on analogue multipliers. In this manner, let us consider the topologies shown in **Figure 1(a)** and **7(a)**, including the voltage sources, as depicted in **Figure 10(a)** and **(b)**, respectively. According to Eq. (1), **Figure 10(a)** and [28, 33], the controlled incremental and decremental memristance is modified as

$$M\left(\varphi_{\mathrm{m}}(t), V_{\mathrm{H}}, V_{\mathrm{V}}\right) = R_1 \pm \frac{R_4(R_1 - V_{\mathrm{V}})}{10R_2R_3C_{\mathrm{z}}}\int_0^t v_{\mathrm{m}}(\tau)d\tau - V_{\mathrm{H}} \tag{16}$$

Similarly for Eq. (8), **Figure 10(b)** and [31, 33], the memristance becomes:

$$M(q_{\mathrm{m}}(t), V_{\mathrm{H}}, V_{\mathrm{V}}) = R_1 \mp \frac{R_2}{20}V_{\mathrm{V}} \pm \frac{R_2}{40C_1}\int_0^t i_{\mathrm{m}}(\tau)d\tau \pm V_{\mathrm{H}} \tag{17}$$

where V_{H} is a DC voltage source to control the horizontally offset and V_{V} is other DC voltage source to control the vertical offset of the frequency-dependent pinched hysteresis loop on the voltage-current plane. Note that if $V_{\mathrm{H}} = V_{\mathrm{V}} = 0$, then Eqs. (16) and (17) are reduced to Eqs. (1) and (8), respectively. For both topologies shown in **Figure 10**, two switches, S_1 and S_2, are used to interchange the kind of memristor and to connect the V_{V} voltage source in each case. To validate the offset reduction method, **Figure 10(a)** was configured at decremental mode and operating to 14 kHz. In a first step, $V_{\mathrm{H}} = V_{\mathrm{V}} = 0$ were considered and simulation results are depicted in **Figure 11(a)** (solid line). Note that the pinched hysteresis loop deviates of the origin. In a second step, the DC voltage sources were monotonically decreased until $V_{\mathrm{H}} = -60.59$ mV and $V_{\mathrm{V}} = -160.3$ mV, and as a consequence, the offset was reduced, as shown

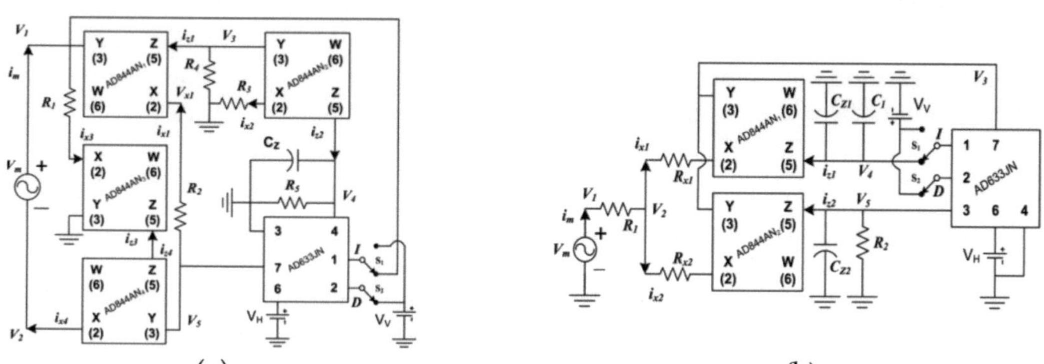

Figure 10. Offset compensated memristor emulator circuits: (a) **Figure 1(a)** and (b) **Figure 7(a)**.

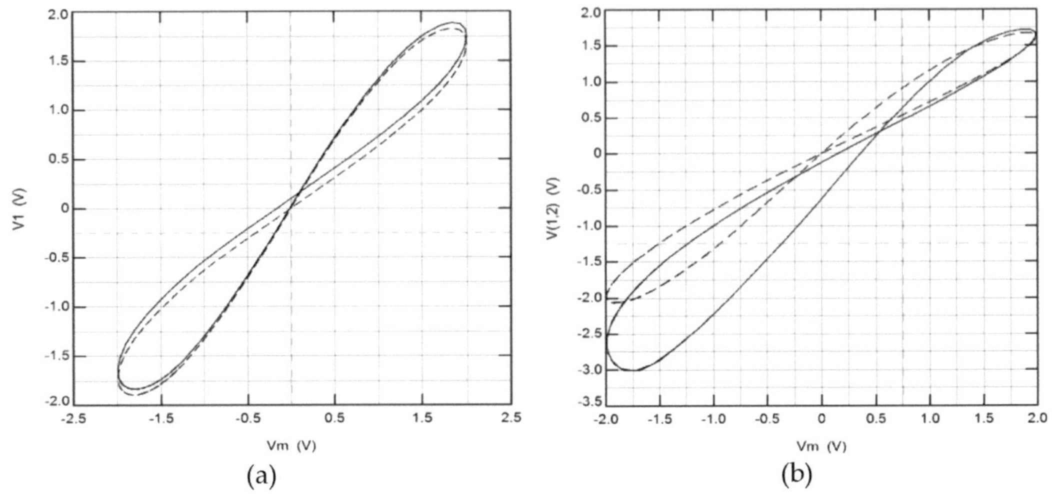

Figure 11. HSPICE results for: (a) decremental topology of **Figure 10(a)** and (b) incremental topology of **Figure 10(b)**. For both figures: offset uncompensated (solid lines) and compensated (dashed lines).

in **Figure 11(a)** (dashed line). A similar analysis procedure was realized to the topology depicted in **Figure 10(b)** but operating to 160 kHz. In this manner, the grounded memristor emulator circuit was connected as incremental mode and considering $V_H = V_V = 0$. HSPICE simulations were obtained and shown in **Figure 11(b)** (solid line). In order to reduce the offset in **Figure 11(b)** (solid line), the DC voltage sources were updated to $V_H = -195.5$ mV and $V_V = 1.568$ V, and hence, the crossing point was pulled towards the origin, as shown in **Figure 11(b)** (dashed line). It is worth to stress that the value of each DC voltage source associated to each topology was derived to trial and error, and it should slightly be updated for each operating frequency. Hence, an open question is how to automatically compute the numeric value of each DC voltage source associated to each topology and operation mode. Moreover, in **Figure 11(b)** (solid lines), one can observe that each frequency-dependent pinched hysteresis loop becomes slightly deformed, resulting at an asymmetrical behaviour with regards to the origin, and hence, the hysteresis lobe area is not equal. Nonetheless, after of the offset compensation, the hysteresis lobe area for all frequency-dependent pinched hysteresis loops become relatively equal as depicted in **Figure 11(b)** (dashed lines). As a result, it is predicted that the frequency behaviour of the pinched hysteresis loops for both memristor emulator circuits can be pushed for operating in higher frequencies and holding a symmetrical behaviour, since the offset voltage glimpsed can again be reduced by updating the DC voltage sources.

5. Transformation of normal non-linear resistors to inverse

A memristor/memductor is basically a resistor/conductor whose resistance/conductance can be changed by applying a voltage across its terminals or by applying a flow of current. The type of control signal depends on the type of memristor/memductor, i.e. flux- or charge-controlled. In any case, the frequency-dependent pinched hysteresis loop of a normal non-linear resistor/conductor will become a straight line if the operating frequency increases. This effect is because a normal non-linear resistor/conductor uses an integrator block and, in general, its behaviour can be modelled by Eq. (12). Since the inverse operation of an integral is the derivate, the hysteresis loop behaviour of a normal non-linear resistor can be inverted whether a differentiator block is used instead of an integrator block. Under this assumption and following the idea presented in Section 3, we have modified Eq. (12) as

$$y_{\mathrm{i}}(t) = x(t)\left(a_{\mathrm{i}} \pm b_{\mathrm{i}}\frac{dz(t)}{dt}\right) \tag{18}$$

where $y_{\mathrm{i}}(t)$ is the inverse current or voltage output signal, $x(t)$ is the voltage or current input signal and $z(t)$ is the voltage or current control signal; a_{i} represents the linear time-invariant gain and b_{i} is the linear time-varying gain. Assuming $z(t) = A_{\mathrm{m}} \sin(\omega t + \theta)$, we obtain

$$\frac{dz(\tau)}{dt} = A_{\mathrm{m}}\omega\cos(\omega t + \theta) = \pm\omega\sqrt{A_m^2 - z^2(t)} \tag{19}$$

and Eq. (18) becomes

$$y_{\mathrm{i}}(t) = x(t)\left(a_{\mathrm{i}} \pm b_{\mathrm{i}}\omega\sqrt{A_m^2 - z^2(t)}\right) \tag{20}$$

Comparing Eqs. (14) and (20), one can observe that the sole difference is the position of ω. According to Section 3 [28, 31, 32], the linear time-varying gain can be computed in function of ω and A_{m} given by

$$b_{\mathrm{i}} = \frac{a_{\mathrm{i}}\omega k_{\mathrm{i}}}{A_{\mathrm{m}}} \tag{21}$$

where $k_{\mathrm{i}} \in (0, 1)$. In Section 2, the behavioural model of normal flux- or charge-controlled resistors was derived and one can observe that each model has an integrative part. As first approximation and for obtaining an inverse flux- or charge-controlled resistor from a normal resistor, the integrator circuit of the latter must be replaced by a differentiator circuit in the former. This task can be done by simply interchanging C_1 by R_2 in **Figure 1(a)**, as depicted in **Figure 12(a)**, and analysing this figure we obtain

$$\frac{v_{\mathrm{m}}(t)}{i_{\mathrm{m}}(t)} = R_1 \pm \frac{R_1R_3R_4C_{\mathrm{z}}}{10R_2}\frac{dv_{\mathrm{m}}(t)}{dt} \tag{22}$$

Considering $v_{\mathrm{m}}(t) = A_{\mathrm{m}}\sin(\omega t + \phi)$, where ϕ is the phase in degrees and by using Eqs. (14) and (20), Eqs. (1) and (22) are rewritten as

$$\frac{v_{\mathrm{m}}(t)}{i_{\mathrm{m}}(t)} = R_1 \pm \frac{R_1R_4}{10R_2R_3C_{\mathrm{z}}\omega}\sqrt{A_{\mathrm{m}}^2 - v_{\mathrm{m}}^2(t)} \tag{23}$$

$$\frac{v_{\mathrm{m}}(t)}{i_{\mathrm{m}}(t)} = R_1 \pm \frac{R_1R_3R_4C_{\mathrm{z}}\omega}{10R_2}\sqrt{A_{\mathrm{m}}^2 - v_{\mathrm{m}}^2(t)} \tag{24}$$

Comparing Eqs. (23) and (24) with Eqs. (14) and (20), respectively, one obtains

$$a_n = a_i = R_1, b_n = \frac{R_1 R_4}{10 R_2 R_3 C_z}, b_i = \frac{R_1 R_3 R_4 C_z}{10 R_2} \quad (25)$$

At this point, our results indicate that by selecting adequately the numerical values of each element of Eq. (25) for a particular operating frequency, the emulator circuits of **Figures 1(a)** and **12(a)** are able to generate normal and inverse pinched hysteresis loops, respectively. It is worth to stress that the transformation methodology is only applicable for those topologies where the integrator circuit is clearly defined, and when it is replaced by a differentiator circuit, the behaviour of the resulting emulator circuit, in general, is not modified. However, floating and grounded non-linear resistor emulator circuits without this requirement have also been reported in the literature [27–33]. One example of them was shown in **Figure 7(a)**. However, whether C_1 is replaced by an inductor L_1 as shown in **Figure 12(b)**, we get

$$\frac{v_m(t)}{i_m(t)} = R_1 \pm \frac{R_2 L_1}{40} \frac{di_m(t)}{dt} \quad (26)$$

Afterwards assuming that $i_m(t) = A_m \sin(\omega t + \phi)$ and by considering Eqs. (14) and (20), Eqs. (8) and (26) take the form

$$\frac{v_m(t)}{i_m(t)} = R_1 \pm \frac{R_2}{40 C_1 \omega} \sqrt{A_m^2 - i_m^2(t)} \quad (27)$$

$$\frac{v_m(t)}{i_m(t)} = R_1 \pm \frac{R_2 L_1 \omega}{40} \sqrt{A_m^2 - i_m^2(t)} \quad (28)$$

Comparing Eqs. (27) and (28) again with Eqs. (14) and (20), respectively, one obtains

$$a_n = a_i = R_1, b_n = \frac{R_2}{40 C_1}, b_i = \frac{R_2 L_1}{40} \quad (29)$$

Note that although the behaviour of the inductor can be emulated by using gyrators, the resulting circuit becomes bulky and complex. Hence, this transformation technique does not

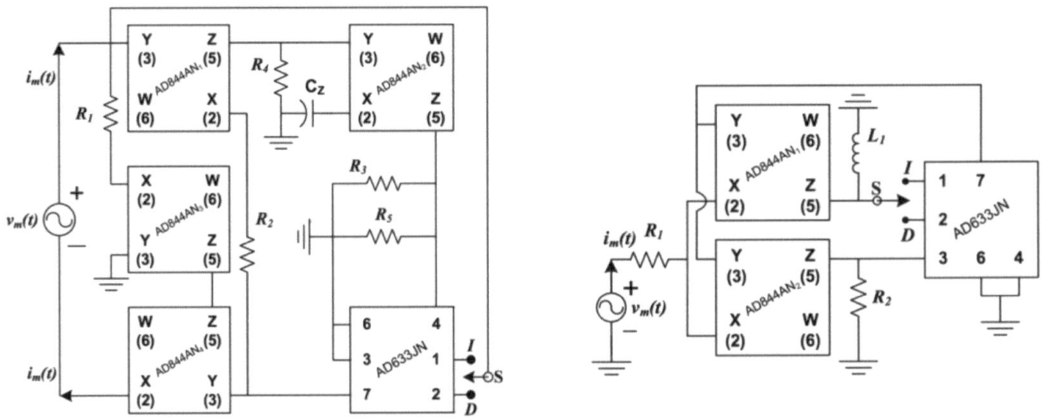

Figure 12. Inverse versions of: (a) **Figure 1(a)** and (b) **Figure 7(a)**.

http://dx.doi.org/10.5772/intechopen.69291

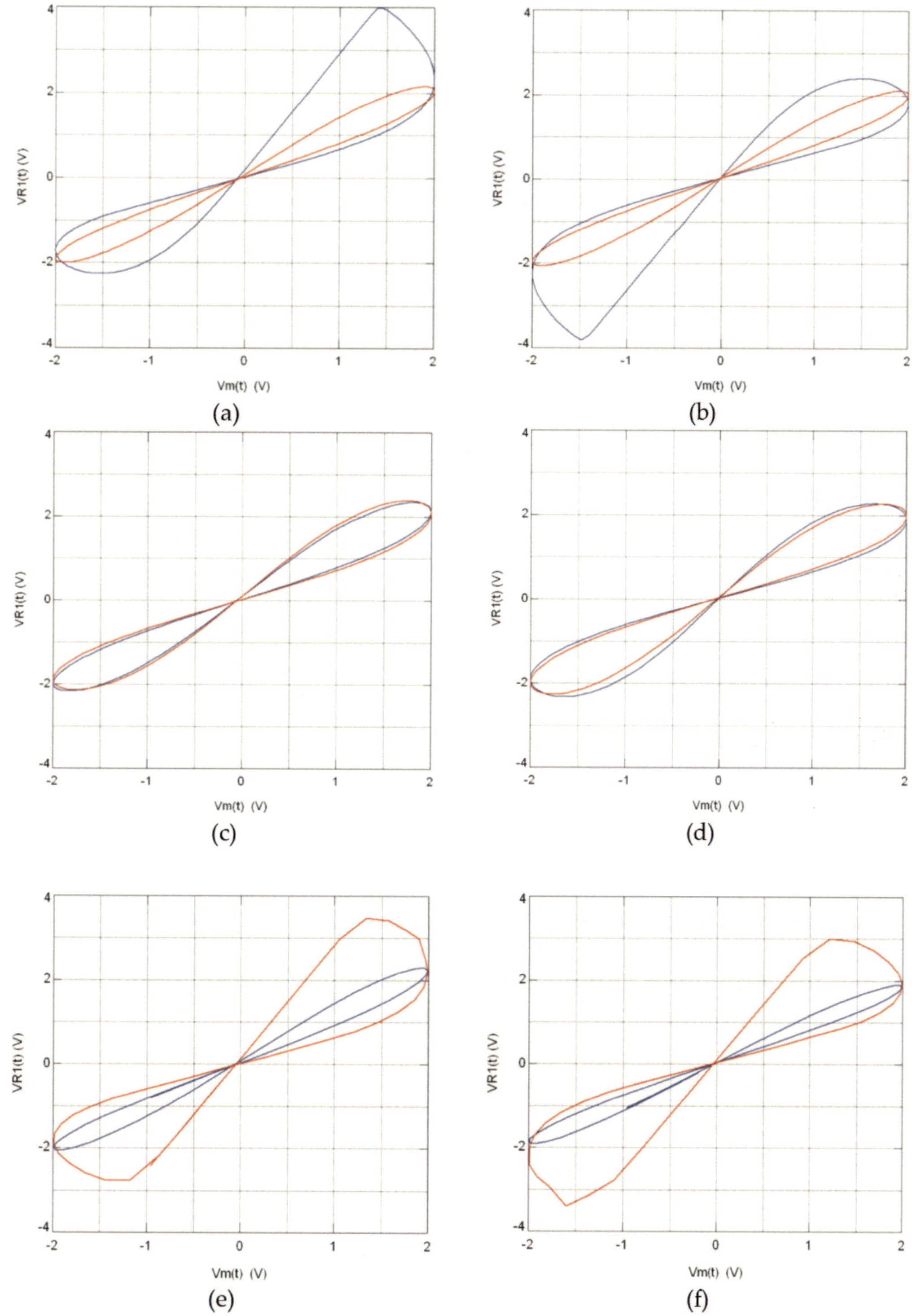

Figure 13. Frequency-dependent hysteresis loop of **Figure 1(a)** (blue line) and **Figure 12(a)** (red line) operating to: 1 kHz for (a) incremental and (b) decremental mode; 2 kHz for (c) incremental and (d) decremental mode; 4 kHz for (e) incremental and (f) decremental mode.

show any advantage with respect to the methodology mentioned above. Without loss of generality, only HSPICE results of **Figures 1(a)** and **12(a)** configured at incremental mode will be shown on the left side of **Figure 13**, whereas that for the decremental configuration will be shown on the right side. In a first step, both emulator circuits were configured to $f = 2$ kHz. HSPICE results are illustrated in **Figure 13(c)** and **(d)** and it is evident that these hysteresis loops are almost similar. Later, the operating frequency was decreased to $f = 1$ kHz, and as one can observe in **Figure 13(a)** and **(b)**, the hysteresis loops present the behaviour forecasted. Finally, the operating frequency of $v_m(t)$ was increased to $f = 4$ kHz, and hence, the behaviour of the hysteresis loops was inverted, as depicted in **Figure 13(e)** and **(f)**. From all these figures, we can observe that for inverse non-linear resistors, the hysteresis loop becomes a straight line when the operating frequency decreases, whereas for normal non-linear resistors, this behaviour is achieved when the operating frequency increases. Note that although the topology of an inverse non-linear resistor shows a frequency-dependent pinched hysteresis loop, this cannot be considered as memristor emulator circuit, since the property of non-volatility is not satisfied. **Table 1** gives the numerical value for each passive element.

Variable	A_m	$a_n = a_i$	b_n	b_i	k_n	k_i
$F = 1$ kHz	2	10e3	3.14e7	0.19	0.99	025
$F = 2$ kHz					0.5	0.5
$F = 4$ kHz					0.25	0.99
Element	R_1	R_3	R_2	R_4	R_5	C_z
Figure 1(a)	10 kΩ	3.18 kΩ	100 kΩ			10 nF
Figure 12(a)		20 kΩ				

Table 1. Numerical variables of Eq. (25) and component list of **Figures 1(a)** and **12(a)**.

6. Analogue applications based on memristor emulator circuits

This section discusses three examples at the behavioural level of abstraction on the use of memristor emulator circuits in real analogue applications.

6.1. Frequency-shift keying (FSK) modulator

Modulator circuits are important blocks in digital communications since they are used to convert a unipolar bit sequence in an appropriate form for modulation and transmission [34]. Among the modulator circuits, frequency-shift keying (FSK) modulation is a frequency modulation scheme in which digital information is transmitted through discrete frequency changes of a carrier wave. Thus, the higher frequency of the modulator is assigned to signal **1** and the lower frequency is assigned to signal **0** [35]. This behaviour can be achieved by using a single-memductor controlled sinusoidal oscillator (SMCO), as shown in **Figure 14(a)**. Through routine analysis, we get

http://dx.doi.org/10.5772/intechopen.69291

$$s^2 + \frac{1}{C_1}\left(\frac{1}{R_1} - \frac{1}{R_3}\right)s + \frac{W_2}{R_3C_1C_2} \tag{30}$$

From Eq. (30), the condition of oscillation (CO) is: $R_3 = R_1$ and the frequency of oscillation (FO) is: $f_0 = \frac{1}{2\pi}\sqrt{\frac{W_2}{R_3C_1C_2}}$. It is seen that CO and FO can independently be controlled by R_1 and W_2, respectively. By merging **Figure 4(b)** with Eq. (30), a SIMULINK model can be built. Such model is depicted in **Figure 14(b)** where the voltage and current gains are unitary (i.e. $A_v = A_i = 1$). Note that the SMCO along with an incremental memductor is depicted in the upper part of **Figure 14(b)**, whereas the SMCO along with a decremental memductor is illustrated in the bottom. More detailed analysis of Eq. (30) is found in [36]. For this application, the SMCO was designed with an oscillation centre frequency of $f_0 = 577$ kHz and hence, $R_1 = 1$ kΩ, $R_3 = 942$ Ω, $C_1 = C_2 = 140$ pF and $W_2 = 0.33$ mS. In order to vary the incremental memductance, a pulse train with 2 V of amplitude and pulse width of 3 μs is used to increase W_2; whereas for the decremental memductance, a pulse of 0.3 V of amplitude and with the same pulse width mentioned before is used to decrease W_2. For both cases, when negative pulses with the same amplitudes mentioned before are applied, both memductances return to their last state [32]. By applying these control signals in **Figure 14(b)**, one obtains an FSK signal, as shown in **Figure 15 (a)** and **(b)**. On these last figures and into the interval [0, 2 ms], the operating frequency of the FSK modulator is the same as SMCO. Next, when a positive digital signal is applied to the incremental and decremental memductor, the memductance increases or decreases, respectively. As a consequence, the FO of the SMCO also increases or decreases, as shown in **Figure 15(a)** and **(b)** into the interval [2 ms, 4 ms], approximately. Afterwards, by applying a negative digital signal to the memductors, the FSK modulator returns to its original FO.

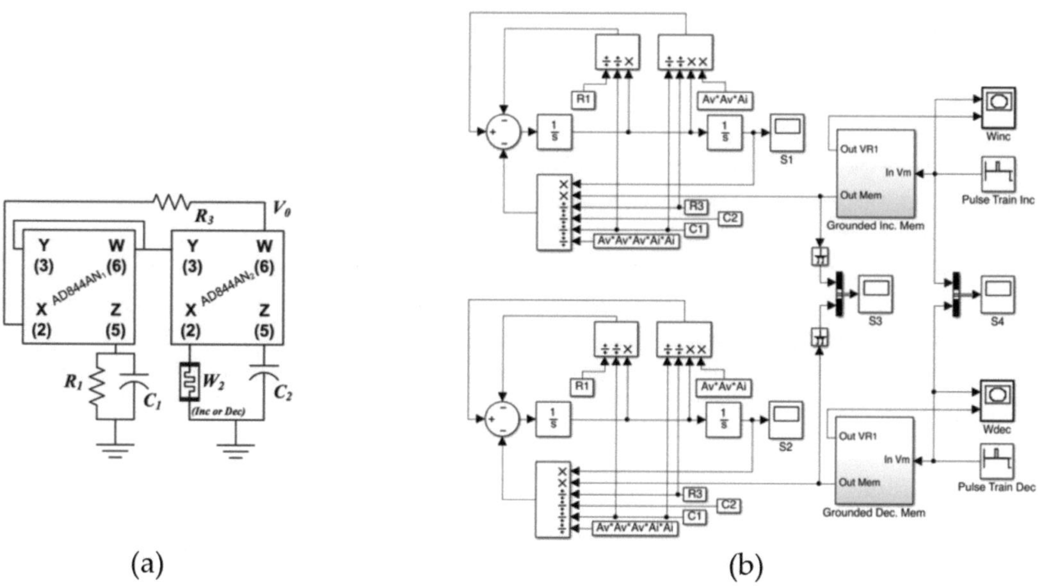

Figure 14. (a) FSK modulator based on SMCO by using **Figure 4(a)**; and (b) SIMULINK model of Eq. (30).

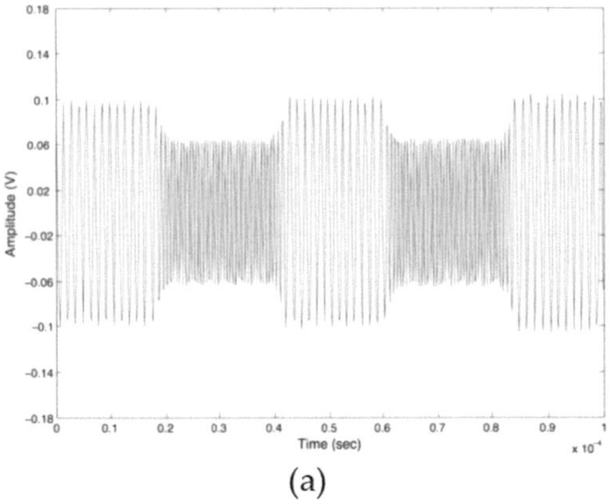

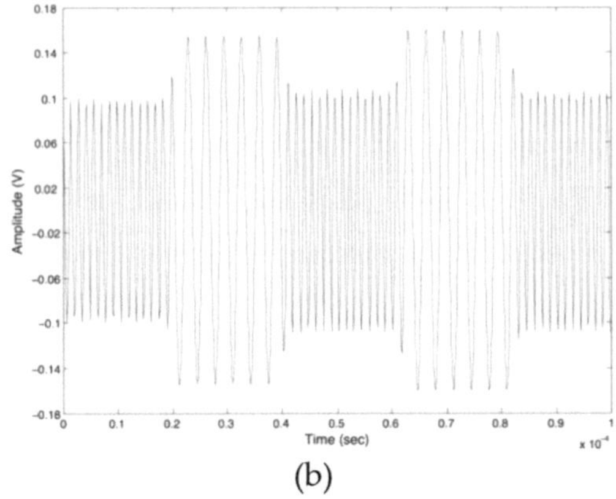

Figure 15. Time response of the FSK modulator using: (a) incremental memductor and (b) decremental memductor.

Therefore, we can observe that a memductor (or memristor) device is useful for controlling the FO of a SMCO and they can be used to design an FSK modulator.

6.2. Proportional-integral-derivative (PID) controller

Proportional-integral-derivative (PID) control has been used successfully for regulating processes in industry for more than 60 years, due to its simple and easy design, low cost and wide range of applications. A PID controller involves three parts: proportional part, integral part and derivative part, and its target is to minimize the error between the set point and the measured output. It is worth mentioning that for a complex or non-linear process, sometimes it is very difficult to find the optimal parameters of the PID controller.

In this sense, the oldest and simplest method was proposed by Ziegler and Nichols [37]. However, this tuning method provides a large overshoot and settling time, and hence, the PID parameters must subsequently be refined. Other methods that can also be used for choosing the parameters of PID controller were reported in [38]. However, this method presents drawbacks when applied to certain types of plants. Furthermore, the PID parameters are always constant and almost without knowledge of the process to control. Therefore, an efficient and effective online tuning mechanism is widely demanded. This last task can be achieved by using a memristor/memductor, since its memristance/memductance can be kept even when the current flow in the memristor/memductor is stopped [1, 28–33, 35]. This property asserts that it is possible to update the parameters of a continuous PID controller online, i.e. the proportional gain (k_p), integral gain[1] (k_i) and derivative gain (k_d). In order to illustrate this idea, the transient response of a second-order low-pass filter is controlled by a PID controller [39]. The transfer function of the filter is given by

$$H(s) = \frac{\frac{1}{LC}}{s^2 + \frac{s}{RC} + \frac{1}{LC}} \tag{31}$$

The numeric value of each element of Eq. (31) is $R = 100\ \Omega$, $L = 0.475$ mH, and $C = 1\ \mu$F. At this point, the PID controller parameters, $k_p = 80$, $k_i = 1e5$ and $k_d = 2e\text{-}3$, were obtained according to [37].

[1]This parameter should not be confused with k_i parameter associated to the inverse nonlinear resistor.

Since the integral and derivative parts of the continuous PID controller are, in practice, designed with R-C elements and active devices [27], one can obtain $R_i = R_d = 2\ \text{k}\Omega$, $C_i = 5$ nF and $C_d = 1$ μF. Under this assumption, **Figure 4(b)**, the PID controller and Eq. (31) are merged to build a SIMULINK model. It is worth mentioning that the memductor shown in **Figure 4(b)** was configured to operate at 300 Hz. Thus, **Figure 16** shows all feedback systems to be simulated [39]. In the upper part of **Figure 16**, the plant with feedback is illustrated. In the second block, the PID controller with fixed parameters along with the plant is depicted. The third block is the PID controller based on incremental memductor along with the plant; and finally, the fourth block depicts the PID controller based on decremental memductor along with the plant. For the last two cases, the memductance is varied by applying a pulse train, and a square signal with 5 V of amplitude and $f = 200$ Hz is applied to all feedback systems. **Figure 17** shows all the transient responses of **Figure 16**. As a first step, the square signal (magenta line) is applied to the feedback plant, and its transient response is underdamped (green line), as shown in **Figure 17(a)**. Hence, the plant needs to be controlled. In a second step, the transient response of the second block is obtained and shown in **Figure 17(a)** (black line). Here, the rise- and fall-time are symmetric and cannot be modified online. In order to get that effect, the incremental and decremental memductor is used [39]. For both memductances, the pulse train was adjusted to get the following cases:

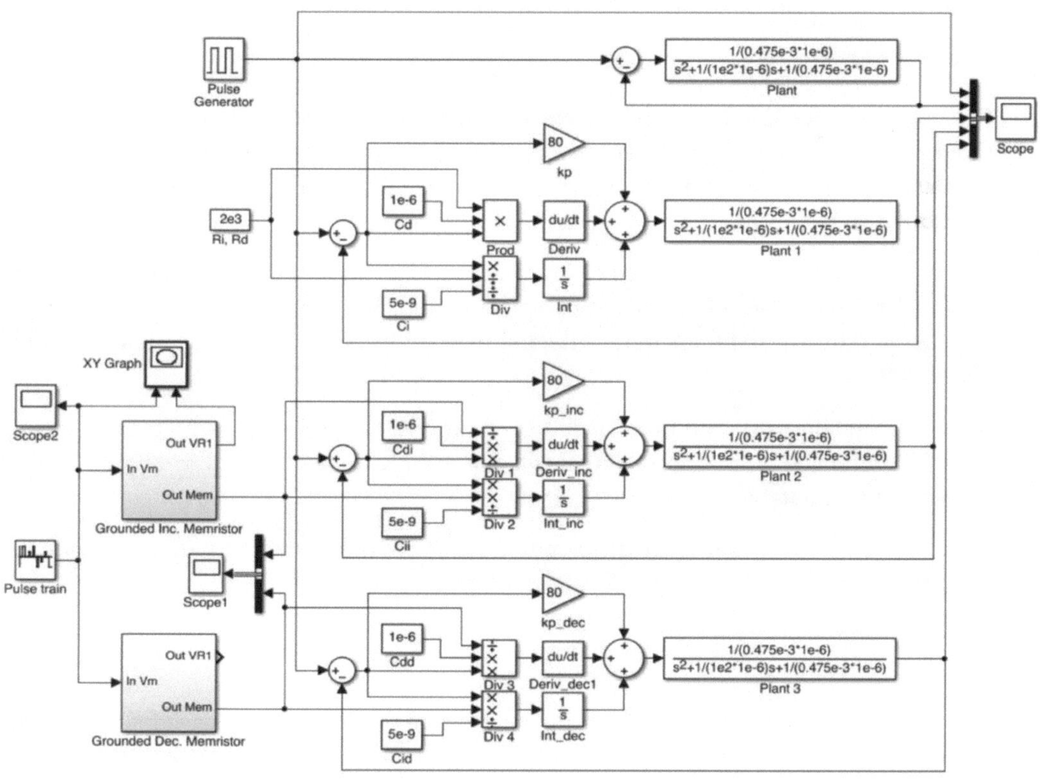

Figure 16. PID controller based on memductors.

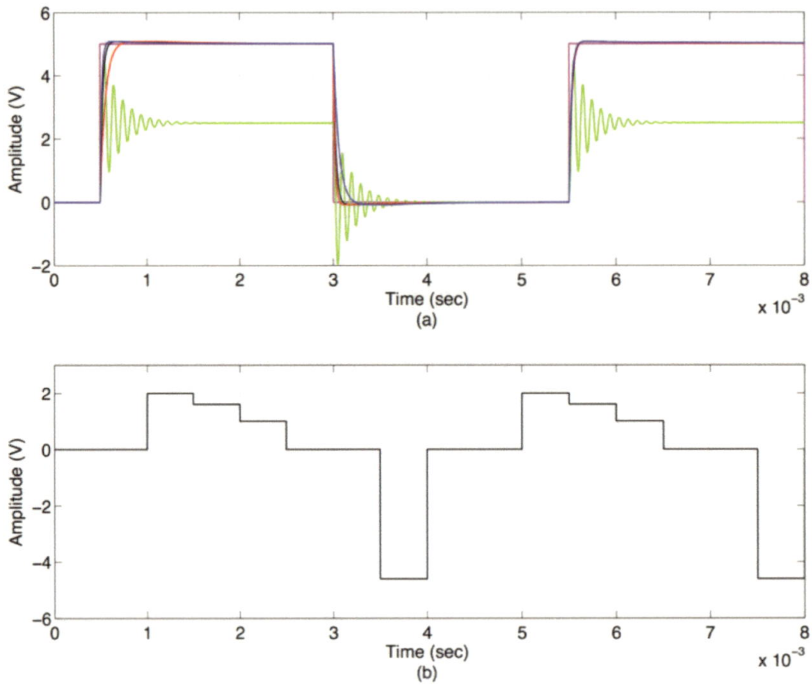

Figure 17. (a) Transient response of the plant and PID controllers. (b) Pulse train for controlling the incremental and decremental memductance.

1. By using an incremental memductor, the rise-time (red line) of the system is largest than the rise-time gotten with fixed parameters (black line) and those obtained with the decremental memductor (blue line). In fact, the rise-time of the latter is the shortest, as depicted in **Figure 17(a)**.

2. By using a decremental memductor, the fall-time (blue line) of the system is largest than the fall-time gotten with fixed parameters (black line) and those obtained with the incremental memductor (red line). In fact, the fall-time of the latter is the shortest, as shown in **Figure 17(a)**.

3. In order to get the same rise-time in all cases, both memductances were adjusted by using the pulse train shown in **Figure 17(b)**, and the result can be observed in **Figure 17(a)** at 5.5 ms, approximately.

Therefore, we can observe that memristors/memductors are useful for controlling the rise- and fall-time of the transient response of a feedback system.

6.3. Memristive synapses

As a last example, but not the least important, we describe the analysis and design of a synaptic circuit based on memristors. Basically, synapses are specialized sites where several neurons are connected, which receive and send information from other cells; this junction is the foundation of complex brain tasks and functions related to learning and memory. Emulation of biological synapses is the basis to build large-scale brain-inspired systems [40]. A key property of the brain is its ability to learn, this process lies in the plasticity of the synapses that allows the nervous system to adapt. Memristor is a candidate suitable to emulate a synapse, due to its non-volatility property and programmable device. But a single memristor cannot accomplish this task; in fact, there are several topologies that enable this behaviour, depending on the approach used for artificial neural network, i.e. cellular neural networks (CNN) [41], spiking neural networks (SNN) [42, 43], feed-forward neural networks (FFNN) [44] and recurrent neural networks (RNN) [45]. Few architectures based on memristors are focused on feed-forward artificial neural networks, which completely satisfies the requirements of an artificial synapse. On the other hand, there are several requirements that must be met for a synaptic learning [46]:

1. The weight must be stored always in the absence of learning.
2. The synapse must be computed as an output, i.e. the product of the input signal with the synaptic weight also called synaptic weighting.
3. Each synapse must occupy a reduced area.
4. Each synapse must operate with low power dissipation.
5. Each synapse must be capable of implementing a learning rule such as Hebbian or Back propagation [1, 40, 46].

Table 2 shows a comparison among the most recent memristive neural networks. Thus, the third column of the table shows whether design meets the five rules mentioned before, such that the synapse can be considered as *learning synapse*. Design of [41] does not meet rule 5, since to change a negative weight to positive not only additional circuitries is required, but on line training is not also possible; [43] meets some of the properties of [46], because it is implemented through an ideal memristor model whose applications are limited to simulations; [44] uses a high number of active components (i.e. 64) for building a synapse, considering the memristor emulator reported in [49]. The fourth column is the frequency of the spikes for SNN approach and for the case of MCNN and ANN the time for weight setting from its lowest to the highest value is described. If weight setting time is too long, then weight processing will take longer which affects its performance. Thus, only [44] simulates and fully implements a synapse based on a memristor emulator. Unlike [41, 42, 47], its hardware applications are not limited to HP memristor fabrication, but the number of elements and the operating frequency are parameters that restrict its performance. However, frequency is limited and the number of active components is high. On the other hand, the proposed synaptic memristive bridge circuit begins with the analysis of memristance of the flux-controlled memristor of **Figure 1(a)**. First, memristance variation of **Figure 1(a)** is analysed, where Eq. (1) can be rewritten as

$$M(\varphi_{\mathrm{m}}(t)) = R_1 \pm R_1 \alpha \varphi_{\mathrm{m}}(t) \tag{32}$$

The maximum value of memristance for an incremental memristor is: $M_{\mathrm{inc}} = R_1 + R_1 k_{\mathrm{n}}$ and the minimum is $M_{\mathrm{inc}} = R_1 - R_1 k_{\mathrm{n}}$, as shown in **Figure 18(a)**.

Reference	Approach	Learning synapse	Frequency (Hz)	Memristor	Active devices	
					Synapse	Neuron
[44]	FFNN	Yes	142	Emulator	69	5
[47]	SNN		5		2	3
[43]			30	HP model	2	13
[42]			300		2	8
[48]			100		–	–
[41]	MCNN	No	0.71		1	1
[45]	RNN	Yes	1		–	1

Table 2. Comparison among memristive neural networks.

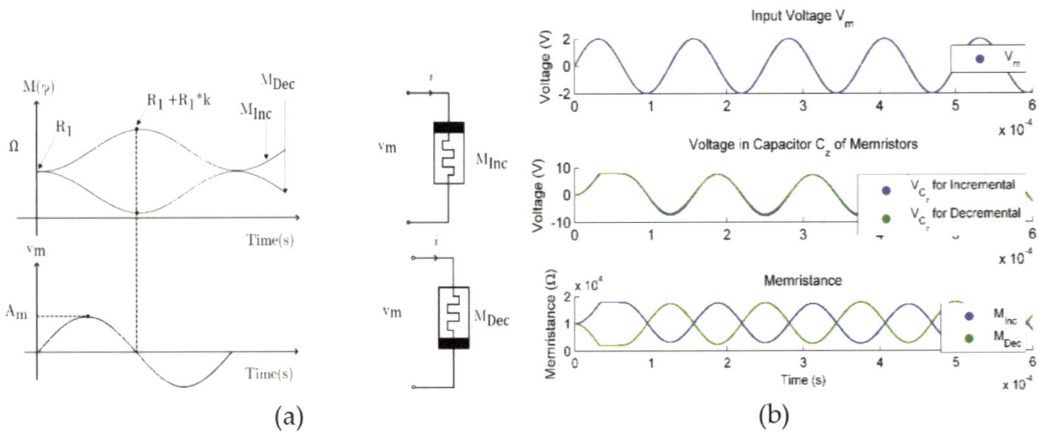

Figure 18. (a) Incremental and decremental memristance when $v_m = A_m \sin(\omega t,)$. (b) Simulation results of memristance for $A_m = 2$ V, $f = 8$ kHz and $k_n = 0.8$.

Considering that $k_n \in (0, 1)$, it is preferable to use $k_n \to 1$ to assure more range of variation; however, it is necessary to recall that memristance value is limited. In this frame of reference, several tests varying k_n were performed in HSPICE with incremental and decremental memristors tested separately and in different operating frequencies, as shown in **Figure 18(b)**. Nevertheless, secondary effects are observed when varying $k_n \to 0.8$, and therefore, the memristors have a different behaviour compared with **Figure 18(a)**, since in this case, the incremental and decremental memristance vary within the same range of memristance. In order to obtain the same behaviour of memristance from **Figure 1(a)** and for several operating frequencies, each discrete element must be updated according to **Table 3**. Note that the proposed topology takes advantage of memristance behaviour and uses only two flux-controlled floating memristor emulators, $M_1(\phi_m(t))$, configured as decremental and $M_2(\phi_m(t))$ as an incremental memristor, along with two passive resistors $R_a = R_b = 10$ kΩ, as shown in **Figure 19(a)** [50]. The analysis of **Figure 19(a)** is as follows: when a positive pulse is applied, $M_1(\varphi_m(t))$ decreases and $M_2(\varphi_m(t))$ increases. As a consequence, v_B decreases and v_A increases. Moreover, when a

Element	R_1	$R_2 = R_4$	R_3	C_z
$F = 8$ kHz	10 kΩ	100 kΩ	1.97 kΩ	2.5 nF
$f = 10$kHz				2 nF
$f = 5$kHz			3 kΩ	2.652 nF

Table 3. Component list of **Figure 1(a)** configured in several operating frequencies.

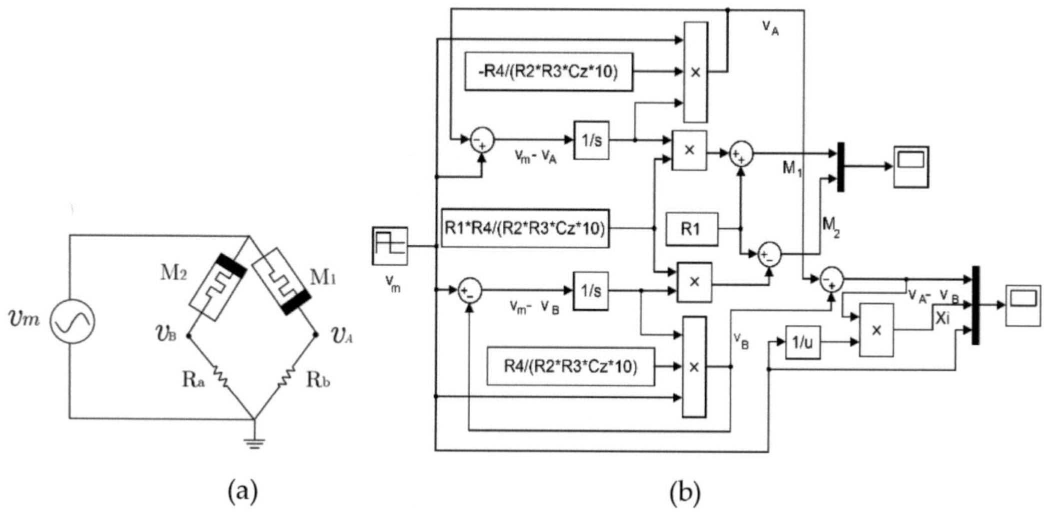

Figure 19. (a) Synaptic memristive bridge and (b) SIMULINK model of Eqs. (34)–(38).

negative pulse is applied, an inverted behaviour is glimpsed. Whether the pulse width is wide enough, the output voltage $v_{AB} = v_A - v_B$ varies gradually from negative to positive voltages and vice versa. Therefore, the memristances $M_1(\phi_m(t))$ and $M_2(\phi_m(t))$ are varied within $v_m - v_A$ and $v_m - v_B$ voltages, respectively. For synapse design, first the voltage v_2 was considered and it is described by

$$v_2 = \pm v_1 \alpha \int_0^t v_m(\tau) d\tau \tag{33}$$

Hence, considering Eq. (33), v_A and v_B are redefined as

$$v_A = -v_m(t)\alpha\varphi_{M_2}(t), \; \nu_A = \nu_m(t)\alpha\varphi_{M_1}(t) \tag{34}$$

where the magnetic flux of each memristor is

$$\phi_{M_1} = \int_0^t v_m(\tau) - v(\tau)_A d\tau, \; \phi_{M_2} = \int_0^t v_m(\tau)v(\tau)_B d\tau \tag{35}$$

Hence, v_{AB} and ξ, the weight, are obtained as

$$v_{\mathrm{AB}} = \alpha v_{\mathrm{m}}\left(\phi_{M_1}(\mathrm{t}) + \phi_{M_2}(\mathrm{t})\right),\ \xi = \frac{v_{\mathrm{AB}}}{v_{\mathrm{m}}} = \alpha\left(\phi_{M_1}(\mathrm{t}) + \phi_{M_2}(\mathrm{t})\right) \tag{36}$$

Memristance variation for $M_2(\phi_{\mathrm{m}}(t))$ is

$$M_2\left(\phi_{M_2}(\mathrm{t})\right) = R_1 + R_1\alpha\phi_{M_2}(t) \tag{37}$$

Similarly, memristance variation for $M_1(\phi_{\mathrm{m}}(t))$ is:

$$M_1\left(\phi_{M_1}(\mathrm{t})\right) = R_1 + R_1\alpha\phi_{M_1}(t) \tag{38}$$

As observed in Eqs. (37) and (38), the memristances depend on Eq. (35) and each memristor in the synapse is designed with the same parameters, so their memristances vary at same rate. From Eqs. (34)–(38), a SIMULINK model is built and depicted in **Figure 19(b)**. The synaptic memristive bridge was simulated in HSPICE and numerical simulations of **Figure 19(b)** were obtained at MATLAB. Thus, the memristance variation $M_1(\phi_{M_1}(t))$ and $M_2(\phi_{M_2}(t)$ are shown in **Figure 20**, respectively. The v_{AB} voltage for k_{n} = 0.8 behave as sawtooth wave, as seen in **Figure 21**, and ξ is approximated by

$$\xi = \begin{cases} 49077t - 1.5338 & 0 \geq t \geq T/2 \\ -48567 + 4.5373 & T/2 \geq t \geq T \end{cases} \tag{39}$$

whose confidence level is $Q^2 = 0.996$. This value represents the linearity of ξ, if $Q^2 \rightarrow 1$ means that there is a linear relation between input pulses and ξ. To verify the behaviour of the synaptic memristive bridge, three basic steps are performed [44, 46].

1. ***Sign setting***. This stage refers to configure a positive sing or negative weight, and assures that ξ is within the desired range. Therefore, a bi-pulse signal with $v_{\mathrm{m}} = \pm 2$ V of amplitude configured at several frequencies is applied, as depicted in **Figure 22**. To configure a positive sign, it is necessary to apply a falling edge pulse, when a rising edge pulse is applied, a negative ξ is configured.

2. ***Weight setting***. Once the sign is established, it is necessary to apply a pulse width to set weight of the synapse. For the case 8 kHz, the allowed maximum pulse width is 62.5 μs, in the general case it is $T/2$. Therefore, pulse signal v_{m} with pulse width of range (0, $T/2$) is applied to set the weight to a desired ξ. In **Figure 22** a pulse v_{m} is shown whose pulse width is 2.5 μs which sets $\xi = -0.8495$.

3. ***Synaptic weight processing***. This operation refers to perform $v_s = \xi v_{\mathrm{p}}$, which is the multiplication of a narrow input pulse v_p and the pre-established ξ weight. The pulse width of v_{p} is narrow due to an effect called *memristance drifting* which is drifting of flux accumulation φ_{M_1} and φ_{M_1} caused by v_{p} [1, 40]. However, the response to that narrow pulse is governed by the settling time (*st*) and slew rate (*SR*) of multiplier AD633 used in the memristor emulator circuit, whose *st* = 2 μs at output voltage V_0 = 20 V and *SR* of 20 V/μs. The AD633 can be replaced by AD734 multiplier whose *SR* = 450 V/μs at V_0 = 20 V and *st* = 200 ns.

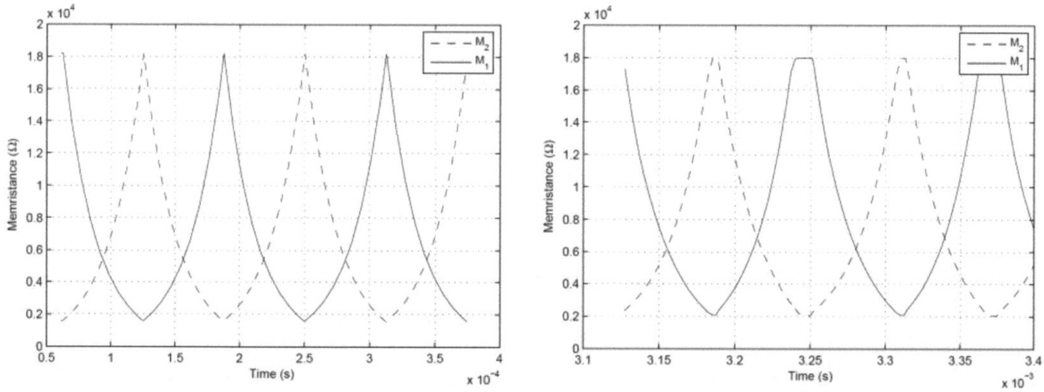

(a) (b)

Figure 20. Memristance variations of **Figure 19(a)** when the bi-pulse signal $v_m = \pm 2$ V at 8 kHz is applied: (a) MATLAB® and (b) HSPICE®.

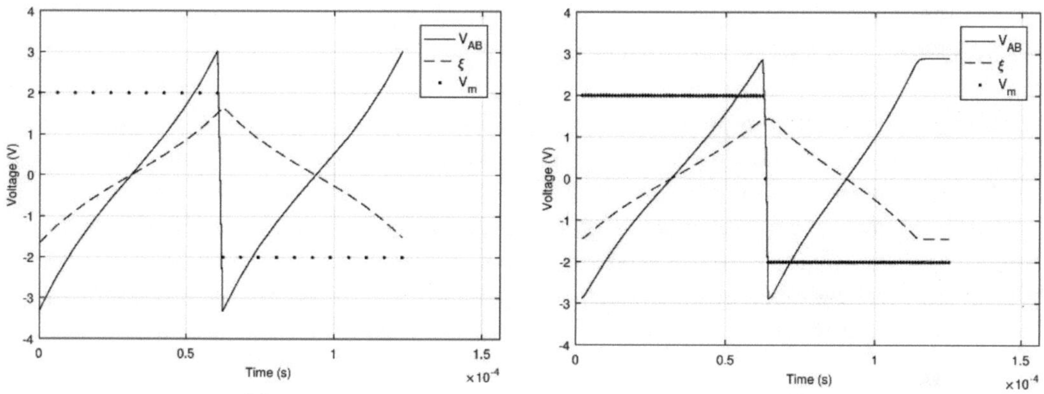

(a) (b)

Figure 21. ξ variations of **Figure 19(a)** when the bi-pulse signal $v_m = \pm 2$ V at 8 kHz in (a) MATLAB® and (b) HSPICE®.

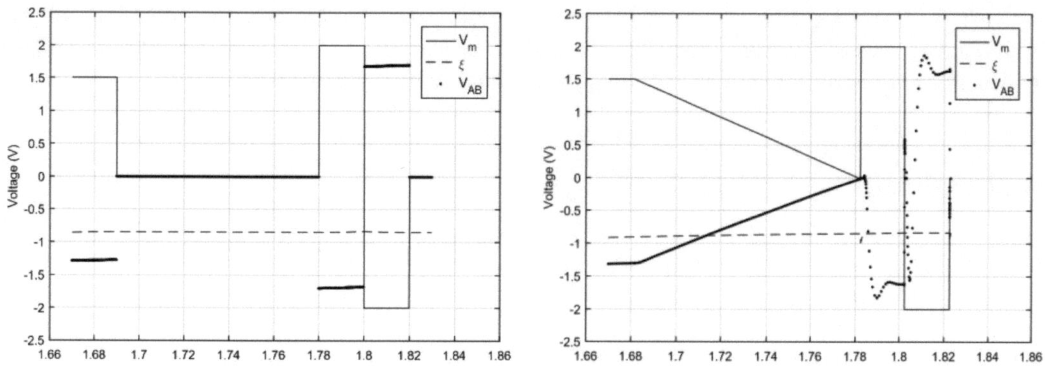

(a) (b)

Figure 22. Synaptic multiplication when $\xi = 0.8495$ and a pulse signal $v_p = 1.5$ V of amplitude with pulse width of 200 ns is applied: (a) MATLAB results and (b) HSPICE simulations.

Finally, **Figure 22(a)** presents a MATLAB simulation of a pulse v_P = 2 V whose pulse width is 200 ns. This pulse is multiplied by ξ, obtaining $v_s = -1.699$. On the other hand, the synaptic weight processing at HSPICE shown in **Figure 22(b)** is done following the same methodology [50].

7. Conclusion

Memristor emulator circuits are useful for developing real memristor-based application circuits as well as for educational purposes. In this chapter, we have studied three memristor/memductor emulator circuits whose behaviour can be configured as incremental or decremental. Two of them are grounded versions whereas the latter is floated. The behavioural model for each topology was derived and its SIMULINK model was also programmed. The design guide suggested in this chapter provides a systematic way for designing memristor/memductor emulator circuits with good features. Further, an offset compensation technique was also described in order to achieve the frequency-dependent pinched hysteresis loop that does not deviate of the origin when the operating frequency of the input signal increases. As a result, it is predicted that the frequency behaviour of the pinched hysteresis loops of memristor/memductor emulator circuits can be pushed for operating in higher frequencies and holding a symmetrical behaviour, since the offset voltage glimpsed can again be reduced by updating the DC voltage sources. Moreover, a transformation methodology for obtaining the behaviour of inverse non-linear resistors from normal non-linear resistors has also been described, and as it was observed in Section 5, the methodology consists in replacing the integrator circuit, clearly defined in the normal topologies by a differentiator circuit, so that not only an inverse behaviour is obtained, but also the resulting topology is not drastically modified with respect to the original topology. Finally, three real analogue applications based on memristors/memductors were addressed.

Acknowledgements

This work was supported in part by the National Council for Science and Technology (CONACyT), Mexico, under Grant 222843 and in part by the Program to Strengthen Quality in Educational Institutions, under Grant C/PFCE-2016-29MSU0013Y-07-23.

Author details

Carlos Sánchez-López[1]*, Illiani Carro-Pérez[2], Victor Hugo Carbajal-Gómez[1], Miguel Angel Carrasco-Aguilar[1] and Francisco Epimenio Morales-López[1]

*Address all correspondence to: carlsanmx@yahoo.com.mx

1 Department of Electronics, Autonomous University of Tlaxcala, Tlaxcala, Mexico

2 Department of Mechatronics, Technological Institute of Monterrey, Puebla Campus, Mexico

References

[1] Adamatzky A, Chua LO. Memristor Networks. Switzerland: Springer International Publishing; 2014

[2] Wang X, Li C, Huang T, Duan S. Predicting chaos in memristive oscillator via harmonic balance method. Chaos. 2012;**22**(4):043119-1-043107-1

[3] Donato C, Giuseppe G. On the simplest fractional-order memristor-based chaotic system. Nonlinear Dynamic. 2012;**70**(2):1185-1197

[4] Itoh M, Chua LO. Memristor oscillators. International Journal of Bifurcation and Chaos. 2008;**18**(11):3183-3206

[5] Yang JJ, Pickett MD, Li X, Ohlberg DAA, Stewart DR, Williams RS. Memristive switching mechanism for metal/oxide/metal nanodevices. Nature Nanotechnology. 2008;**3**(7):429-433

[6] Chang T, Jo SH, Kim KH, Sheridan P, Gaba S, Lu W. Synaptic behaviors and modeling of a metal oxide memristor device. Applied Physics A. 2011;**102**(4):857-863

[7] Kvatinsky S, Friedman EG, Kolodny A, Weiser UC. TEAM: Threshold adaptive memristor model. IEEE Transactions on Circuits and Systems I Regular Papers. 2013;**60**(1):211-221

[8] Kvatinsky S, Ramadan M, Friedman EG, Kolodny A. VTEAM: A general model for voltage controlled memristors. IEEE Transactions on Circuits and Systems II Express Briefs. 2015;**62**(8):786-790

[9] Pickett MD, Strukov DB, Borghetti JL, Yang JJ, Snider GS, Stewart DR, Williams RS. Switching dynamics in titanium dioxide memristive devices. Journal of Applied Physics. 2009;**106**(7):074508

[10] Prodromakis T, Pin-Peh B, Papavassiliou C, Toumazou C. A versatile memristor model with nonlinear dopant kinetics. IEEE Transactions on Electron Devices. 2011;**58**(9):3099-3105

[11] Yakopcic C, Taha TM, Subramanyam G, Pino RE. Chapter 12: Memristor SPICE modeling. Advances in Neuromorphic Memristor Science and Applications. Springer Series in Cognitive and Neural Systems. 2012;**4**:211-244

[12] Benderli S, Wey TA. On SPICE macromodelling of TiO_2 memristors. Electronics Letters. 2009;**45**(7):337-379

[13] Sharifi MJ, Banadaki YM. General SPICE models for memristor and application to circuit simulation of memristor-based synapses and memory cells. Journal of Circuits Systems and Computers. 2010;**19**(2):407-424

[14] Shin S, Kim K, Kang SM. Compact models for memristors based on charge-flux constitutive relationships. IEEE Transactions on Computer-Aided Design of Integrated Circuits and Systems. 2010;**29**(4):590-598

[15] Rak A, Cserey G. Macromodeling of the memristor in SPICE. IEEE Transactions on Computer-Aided Design of Integrated Circuits and Systems. 2010;**29**(4):632-636

[16] Yakopcic C, Taha TM, Subramanyam G, Pino RE. Generalized memristive device SPICE model and its application in circuit design. IEEE Transactions on Computer-Aided Design of Integrated Circuits and Systems. 2013;**32**(8):1201-1214

[17] Jo SH, Chang T, Ebong I, Bhadviya BB, Mazumder P, Lu W. Nanoscale memristor device as synapse in neuromorphic systems. Nano Letters. 2010;**10**(4):1297-1301

[18] Gergel-Hackett N, Hamadani B, Dunlap B, Suehle J, Richter C, Hacker C, Gundlach D. A flexible solution-processed memristor. IEEE Electron Device Letters. 2009;**30**(7):706-708

[19] Bo-Cheng B, Jian-Ping X, Gua-Hua Z, Zheng-Hua M, Ling Z. Chaotic memristive circuit: Equivalent circuit realization and dynamical analysis. Chinese Physics B. 2011;**20**(12):120502-1-120502-6

[20] Muthuswamy B, Kokate PP. Memristor-based chaotic circuits. IEEE Technical Review. 2009;**26**(6):417-429

[21] Muthuswamy B. Implementing memristor based chaotic circuits. International Journal of Bifurcation and Chaos. 2010;**20**(5):1335-1350

[22] Muthuswamy B, Chua LO. Simplest chaotic circuit. International Journal of Bifurcation and Chaos. 2010;**20**(5):1567-1580

[23] Iu HHC, Yu DS, Fitch AL, Sreeram V, Chen H. Controlling chaos in a memristor based circuit using a twin-T notch filter. IEEE Transactions on Circuits and Systems I Regular Papers. 2011;**58**(6):1337-1344

[24] Zhi-Jun L, Yi-Cheng Z. A memristor oscillator based on a twin-T network. Chinese Physics B. 2013;**22**(4):040502-1-040502-6

[25] Pershin YV, Di Ventra M. Practical approach to programmable analog circuits with memristors. IEEE Transactions on Circuits and Systems I Regular Papers. 2010;**57**(8):1857-1864

[26] Bao B, Ma Z, Xu J, Lu Z, Xu Q. A simple memristor chaotic circuit with complex dynamics. International Journal of Bifurcation and Chaos. 2011;**21**(9):2629-2645

[27] Sánchez-López C. Pathological equivalents of fully-differential active devices for symbolic nodal analysis. IEEE Transactions on Circuits and Systems I Regular Papers. 2013;**60**(3):603-615

[28] Sánchez-López C, Mendoza-López J, Carrasco-Aguilar MA, Muñiz-Montero C. A floating analog memristor emulator circuit. IEEE Transactions on Circuits and Systems II Express Briefs. 2014;**61**(5):309-313

[29] Yesil A, Babacan Y, Kacar F. A new DDCC based memristor emulator circuit and its applications. Microelectronics Journal. 2014;**45**(3):282-287

[30] Abuelma'atti MT, Khalifa ZJ. A continuous-level memristor emulator and its application in a multivibrator circuit. International Journal of Electronics and Communication. 2015;**69**(4):771-775

[31] Sánchez-López C, Carrasco-Aguilar MA, Muñiz-Montero C. A 16 Hz-160 kHz memristor emulator circuit. International Journal of Electronics and Communication. 2015;**69**(9):1208-1219

[32] Sánchez-López C, Aguila Cuapio LE. A 860 kHz grounded memristor emulator circuit. International Journal of Electronics and Communication. 2017;**73**(1):23-33

[33] Sánchez-López C, Carrasco-Aguilar MA, Morales-López FE. Offset reduction on memristor emulator circuits. Proceedings of the IEEE International Conference on Electronics and Circuits Systems. 2015;**1**(1):296-299

[34] Lau FCM, Tse CK. Chaos-based Digital Communication Systems. Berlin: Springer-Verlag, Germany; 2003

[35] Göknar IC, Öncül F, Minayi E. New memristor applications: AM, ASK, FSK and BPSK modulators. IEEE Antennas and Propagation Magazine. 2013;**5**(2):304-313

[36] Sánchez-López C, Aguila-Cuapio LE, Carro-Pérez I, González-Hernández HG. High-level simulation of an FSK modulator based on memconductor. Proceedings of the IEEE International Conference on Micro-Nanoelectronics, Technology and Applications. 2016;**1**(1):1-5

[37] Ziegler JG, Nichols NB. Optimum settings for automatic controllers. Transactions on American Society of Mechanical Engineers. 1942;**64**(1):759-768

[38] Cohen GH, Coon GA. Theoretical consideration of retarded control. Transactions on American Society of Mechanical Engineers. 1953;**75**(1):827-834

[39] Sánchez-López C, Morales-López FE, Carrasco-Aguilar MA. High-level simulation of a PID controller based on memristor. Proceedings of the IEEE International Conference on New Circuits Systems. 2016;**1**(1):1-4

[40] Tetzlaff R. Memristors and Memristive Systems. New York: Springer Science Business Media; 2014

[41] Hu X, Duan S, Wang L. A novel chaotic neural network using memristive synapse with applications in associative memory. Abstract and Applied Analysis. 2012;**2012**(1):19

[42] Cantley KD, Subramaniam A, Stiegler HJ, Chapman RA, Vogel EM. Hebbian learning in spiking neural networks with nanocrystalline silicon TFTs and memristive synapses. IEEE Transactions on Nanotechnology. 2011;**10**(5):1066-1073

[43] Zhang Y, Zeng Z, Wen S. Implementation of memristive neural networks with spike-rate-dependent plasticity synapses. Proceedings of International Joint Conference on Neural Networks. 2014;**1**(1):2226-2233

[44] Adhikari SP, Yang C, Kim H, Chua LO. Memristor bridge synapse-based neural network and its learning. IEEE Transactions on Neural Networks and Learning Systems. 2012;**23**(9):1426-1435

[45] Yang J, Wang L, Wang Y, Guo T. A novel memristive Hopfield neural network with application in associative memory. Neurocomputing. 2017;**227**(1):142-148

[46] Hasler P, Diorio C, Minch BA, Mead C. Single transistor learning synapse with long term storage. Proceedings IEEE International Symposium on Circuits and Systems. 1995;**1**(1): 1660-1663

[47] Pershin YV, Di Ventra M. Experimental demonstration of associative memory with memristive neural networks. Neural Networks. 2010;**23**(7):881-886

[48] Wang L, Li H, Duan S, Huang T, Wang H. Pavlov associative memory in a memristive neural network and its circuit implementation. Neurocomputing. 2016;**171**(1):23-29

[49] Kim H, Sah MP, Yang C, Cho S, Chua LO. Memristor emulator for memristor circuit applications. IEEE Transactions on Circuits and Systems I Regular Papers. 2012;**59**(10): 2422-2431

[50] Carro-Pérez I, González-Hernández HG, Sánchez-López C. High-frequency memristive synapses. Proceeding IEEE Latin American Symposium on Circuits & Systems. 2017;**1**(1):1-4

Chapter 7

Simulating Memristive Networks in SystemC-AMS

Dietmar Fey, Lukas Riedersberger and
Marc Reichenbach

Additional information is available at the end of the chapter

http://dx.doi.org/10.5772/intechopen.69662

Abstract

This chapter presents a solution for the simulation of large memristive networks with SystemC-AMS. SystemC-AMS allows simulating memristors both on analogue level and on digital level to link analogue memristive devices to digital circuits and system level specifications. We investigate the benefits and drawbacks of a SystemC-AMS simulation compared to a simulation in SPICE. We show for the example of a two-layer memristive network emulating an optical flow algorithm by the detection of moving edges that large memristive networks can be simulated with a free available SystemC-AMS simulation environment, whereas free available SPICE simulation environment fails. However, it is also shown that commercial SPICE simulators are superior against current SystemC-AMS implementations concerning the size of simulated memristive networks. However, SystemC-AMS simulations of memristive networks offer both still more flexibility and similar run times compared to commercial SPICE simulators for small-sized memristive networks. The flexibility and the powerfulness of a SystemC-AMS solution is demonstrated for a complex network that solves edge detection, filtering and detecting of moving objects. The possible run times of the memristive network are determined in the SystemC-AMS simulation environment and are compared with an optical flow algorithm on classical hardware like a CPU and a GPU.

Keywords: memristive networks, SystemC-AMS, memristor modelling, optical flow, SPICE memristor simulation

1. Introduction

One of the missing things in the research on modelling and simulation of large memristor networks is the availability of an adequate simulation system, which is both fast and flexible. Available SPICE models offer for commercial products, for example, Spectre Circuit Simulator, fast simulation times but don't offer flexibility. To establish links to higher abstraction levels, for example, to the system level, in order to combine memristive circuits with extensive digital circuits, or even the integration in processor architecture descriptions to execute software in virtual environments is very cumbersome.

Therefore, we established a model for memristors in SystemC-AMS. A SystemC simulation can be carried as fast as SPICE simulations but allows a better linking to higher system levels as it is possible, for example, with Verilog-A, for which already memristor models exist [1]. SystemC-AMS allows also a detailed investigation of the analogue behaviour in the same way as one it is used it in SPICE.

For the modelling of single memristor behaviour in SystemC-AMS, we used the possibility to model variable resistors in SystemC-AMS with electrical linear networks (ELNs) as starting point. The resistance values of such elements can be controlled and modified by a discrete event input signal. We start to demonstrate this possibility with the well-known SPICE memristor model from Biolek et al. [2], which is based on an electronic equivalent circuit of the simple memristor behaviour description from Hewlett-Packard.

However, we do not mimic the electronic equivalent circuit in SystemC-AMS. The memristor model is realized in SystemC-AMS as an own object-orientated class. Using object-orientated programming principles allows simply exchanging the model for the memristive behaviour by another one. In principle, it is possible to use any other model as long as it is specified by a C/C++ code snippet. We have implemented in SystemC-AMS two memristor models, the HP model that is also used in Biolek's SPICE model [2] and a statistic description for a commercial memristor coming from Knowm Inc. [3].

We demonstrate the usefulness and the strength of a SystemC-AMS-based simulation system for a three-dimensional (3D) memristive circuit that implements a detection based on an optical flow. For this application, a memristive network was proposed in Ref. [4]. We adapt this solution and modelled the complete network in SystemC-AMS. We compare the achieved results with an implementation on a GPU to evaluate possibilities and limits of the compute capability of memristive circuits. The chapter is organized as follows. In Section 2, we present our solution for the modelling of memristors in SystemC-AMS. Section 3 gives a brief insight in the optical flow algorithm we used for an implementation on a GPU and a multi-core CPU serving as reference architecture for the simulated memristive network. The corresponding memristor network calculates optical flow gradients as moving edges with a memristive network. We selected exactly this network as a representative complex example for a SystemC-AMS specification of memristive networks. Section 4 specifies the achieved results for the simulation and compares it with a GPU/CPU implementation concerning the run time. Furthermore, the simulation time of a SystemC-AMS specification and a SPICE simulation of the specific memristive network are compared. Finally, the chapter ends with a conclusion.

2. Modelling memristors in systemC-AMS

SystemC-AMS is an extension of the modelling language SystemC about analogue-mixed signals. It allows not only the modelling of digital hardware and corresponding software in one homogeneous environment but also the combination of discrete and continuous analogue systems. SystemC-AMS contains a solver for the Kirchhoff equations which are used for the computation of the behaviour of electrical networks. SystemC as well SystemC-AMS is not a new language but an extension of C++ about a corresponding library. Therefore, it allows the modelling of analogue and digital systems using a class-orientated structure. This feature is very beneficial for designing complex memristor networks using different models. Just by instantiating another memristor model in the SystemC-AMS program, a whole network can be simulated with another memristor model in a very convenient way. A modification of the electronic network is not necessary.

SystemC-AMS offers three main options for the modelling of discrete and continuous systems on different abstraction levels. Furthermore, these models can also be coupled via matched interfaces. An example scenario for such a coupling of components modelled in different domains consists of, for example, a binary module that is connected to a linear electronic circuit. In this case, the binary module could differ between two states which are used to control a voltage source. According to a state transfer of the binary output, the polarization of the continuous output voltage signal is reversed. For the work presented in this chapter, we used a proof-of-concept implementation of SystemC-AMS from Accellera and Coseda Technologies [5], which is freely available under an Apache 2.0 licence. Since this implementation was developed primarily with respect to its correct implementation of the IEEE standard 1666.1, the main focus was not laid on the simulation speed. Therefore, it is to investigate how other possible SystemC-AMS simulators could offer an alternative in future, resp. a re-evaluation has to be done when the current version of Coseda leaves its current proof-of-concept state.

2.1. SystemC-AMS modelling options

In the following, we briefly present the above-mentioned three modelling options offered by SystemC-AMS and evaluate them for their appropriateness to model memristors.

The *timed data flow* (TDF) model allows the modelling of discrete time steps. Each TDF module has a couple of inputs and outputs, which consume an event at discrete time steps. As result of this occurred event, the module can change its internal state. However, processing at discrete time steps does not help us to model the analogue behaviour of memristors. The *linear signal flow* (LSF) allows solving continuous equations. For that purpose, different basic blocks like adders, multipliers and integrators are offered, which can be connected and are processed by a built-in solver for differential equations. Also, this option does not meet our intention of memristor modelling since LSF is more orientated to model signal-processing algorithms based on pre-built blocks. The third main modelling method is thought to model analogue systems as *electrical linear networks* (ELNs). It allows the set-up and solving of electrical networks by applying the Kirchhoff circuit laws for electronic meshes and nodes. An electrical network consists of modules which are connected via nodes. Using these laws, increasing and decreasing currents and voltages can be determined for the devices. Since memristors are part of electronic circuits, we use this modelling technique primarily for the memristor modelling.

In the following, we describe in detail the SystemC-AMS specification we selected for the memristor modelling. **Figure 1** shows a block diagram of the corresponding model. The basic idea is to model the memristor with a SystemC-AMS built-in data type *variable resistor* which allows changing dynamically its resistance by a discrete value. For each memristor in the simulated network, the voltage, which drops down at its ports *p* and *n*, is read out via *get_voltage*() in each simulation step. Depending on the used memristor model, the new memristor's memristance is calculated. Subsequently, the new value is assigned to the variable resistance via assigning a discrete signal by the method *set_resistance*().

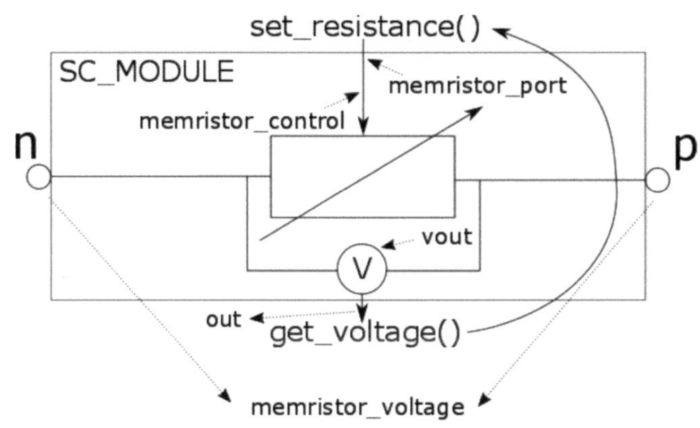

Figure 1. Block diagram for the selected SystemC-AMS model for a memristor.

The code fragment shown below is the corresponding SystemC-AMS specification:

1. The memristor is modelled as an object-orientated *class Memristor* in SystemC-AMS. The memristance is calculated and stored as discrete variable in *R*.

2. The memristor has two ports *p* and *n*.

3. The memristor device, denoted as *memristor_resistor,* is modelled as variable resistor. It inherits its characteristics from the SystemC-AMS built-in type ***sca_eln::sca_de::sca_r***. This variable is used in the circuit to which an instanced memristor element of the *class Memristor* is connected to via the ports *p* and *n*.

4. The voltage drop at the memristor can be measured by a kind of display variable *out,* this is the readable voltage value, that is given out via the virtual voltage metre *vout*. The corresponding voltage value is stored at *memristor_voltage*.

5. SystemC uses a discrete-event simulation, for that it is necessary to define a so-called control port parameter that checks if a signal change occurs at its input. This is the variable *memristor_control*. To this port, a signal has to be attached which is *memristor_port*.

6. The functional behaviour of a memristor, defined by its specific model, is specified by a later instanced virtual function *solve*(), which can be implemented in C/C++ code for each specific memristor model:

```
//Base class
class Memristor {
public:
double R;
//ports of the memristor
sca_eln::sca_terminal p,n;
//resistor controlled by discrete-event input signal, needs input
sca_eln::sca_de::sca_r memristor_resistor;
//converter and voltage meter
sca_tdf::sca_out<double> out;
sca_eln::sca_tdf::sca_vsink vout;
//systemc ams interface to read voltage over the resistor
sca_tdf::sca_signal<double> memristor_voltage;
//control port of controlled resistor
sc_core::sc_in<double> memristor_control;
//systemc ams interface to set the new resistance
sc_core::sc_signal<double> memristor_port;
//solve must be implemented by the specific model
virtual void solve(const double dt) = 0;
};
```

A specific memristor is modelled by an inheritance from the *class Memristor*. This is shown in the following for the specification of a *class MemristorBiolek,* which is inherited by the generic *public class Memristor*. The functional behaviour of the inherited memristor is orientated to the SPICE equivalent model from Biolek given in Ref. [2]. Some physical features for the memristor are defined as constants at the beginning like the *DRIFT_MOBILITY* of the ions and the *LENGTH* of the channel of the modelled memristor. Furthermore, variables for the maximum and the minimum resistance, *R_ON* and *R_OFF*, and the width of the doped region, *w*, are declared. Furthermore, the class constructor and some parameters

(*R_ON, R_OFF, R_INIT*) are defined, which can be passed to the class element when it is instanced to initialize these memristor parameters. The functionality of the memristor type is defined by the method ***solve***. A discrete solution of a differential equation for the memristance change is used; the step width for the integration is defined by *dt*. The method *solve* is the central key of the flexibility in the simulation. It can be changed by another function to implement another model.

The following SystemC-AMS code sequence shows the specification of a class that models a memristor's behaviour specification according to the Biolek model

```
class MemristorBiolek: public Memristor {
private:
  const double DRIFT_MOBILITY = 440000.0 * pow(10.0, -18.0);
  const double LENGTH = 41.0 * pow(10.0, -9.0);
  double R_ON, R_OFF, w;
public:
MemristorBiolek(const double R_ON, const double R_OFF,
const double R_INIT);
void solve(const double dt, std::function<double(double)>
voltage_function = [](const double val) -> double
{
return val;
}
);
std::string name() const { return "Biolek"; }
};
```

The following code snippet specifies the constructor for the inherited class *MemristorBiolek*:

```
Memristor::Memristor(const double R_INIT): R(R_INIT) {} ;
MemristorBiolek::MemristorBiolek(const double R_ON, const double R_
OFF, const double R_INIT): R_ON(R_ON), R_OFF(R_OFF), Memristor(R_INIT)
{
double x = (R_INIT - R_OFF)/(R_ON - R_OFF);
if (x > 1.0) x = 1.0;
```

```
if (x < 0.0) x = 0.0;

w = x * LENGTH;

}
```

The next code sections show the implementation of the method *solve*() to calculate the memristance of the memristor. The nonlinear behaviour of the memristor is modelled by the window function *windowBiolek*() that was set up by Biolek in Ref. [2] in order to modify the changing of the width of the memristor's doped region *w* at the edges of the device

```
inline long double windowBiolek(double x, double I,

double const P_WINDOW) const

{

if (-I >= 0)

return 1 - pow(x - 1, 2 * P_WINDOW);

return 1 - pow(x, 2 * P_WINDOW);

}

void MemristorBiolek::solve(const double dt, std::function<double(dou
ble)> voltage_function) {

double U = memristor_voltage.read(0);

double I = U/R;

R = R_ON * (w/LENGTH) + R_OFF * (1 - w/LENGTH);

double vD = ((DRIFT_MOBILITY * R_ON)/LENGTH) *

I * windowBiolek(w/LENGTH, I, 7.0);

w += vD * dt;

write_resistance();

}

} ;//end of definition of class Memristor
```

Figure 2 shows multiple overlaid hysteresis curves for the I-U relation at the memristor's poles. Throughout, the memristor was simulated with a minimum resistance R_{OFF} = 200 Ω, a maximum resistance R_{ON} = 28 Ω and an initial resistance R_{INIT} = 100 Ω. A sinusoidal voltage source is attached serially to the memristor. The voltage source is oscillating with 1 kHz between −1 and 1 V. The simulated time was set to 1 s with a time resolution of 1 μs. It is to observe that with each oscillation, the hysteresis curve becomes more flat until it ends in a more or less straight line, that is, the non-linear behaviour disappears.

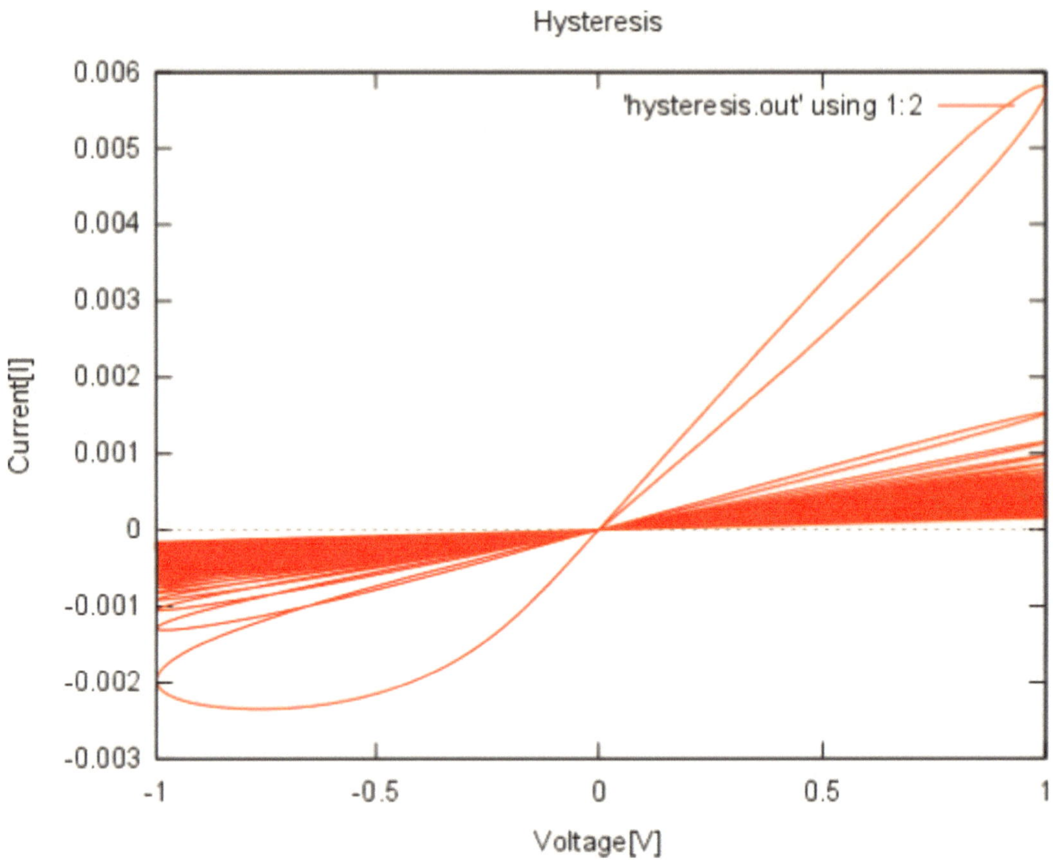

Figure 2. Result of SystemC-AMS simulation of a memristor excited by a sinusoidal voltage signal.

3. Simulation of an optical flow algorithm with a memristor network in SystemC-AMS

In the last chapter, we have shown how to simulate the analogue behaviour of a single memristor element. The next step is to demonstrate the possibility to simulate a much more complex example, namely the simulation of optical flow as detection of moving edges in a grid of memristors. The network mimics the functional behaviour of an artificial retina with a network consisting of resistors and memristors. The network was presented in Ref. [4]. In the following, we describe the set-up of the memristive network and the necessary functions to realize the detection of moving edges. We compare in the following the solution with an optical flow implementation on classical hardware. The optical flow follows the procedure according to Horn and Schunk [6]. For reasons of completeness, we briefly describe this algorithm first and the corresponding memristive network later as well as its SystemC-AMS specification developed by us.

3.1. Procedure of the optical flow

The procedure of Horn and Schunk was one of the first optical flow methods. It provides a dense and smooth global result. Global in this sense means that the whole image is considered and not only a local region around a pixel in order to solve the equation motion for pixels in two subsequent images. In an optical flow procedure, a vector field h is computed according to Eq. (1) that describes the translation of pixel *(x,y)* in a two-dimensional (2D) image over time $\frac{dx}{dt}$ and $\frac{dy}{dt}$.

$$h = (u, v) = \left(\frac{dx}{dt'}\frac{dy}{dt}\right) \tag{1}$$

For the calculation of translating pixels, it is assumed that their intensities remain constant after the translation. That means, a pixel, which is moved between two images *I(x,y,t)* and *I(x,y,t+dt)*, has to maintain its brightness

$$I(x, y, t) = I(x + u \cdot dt, y + v \cdot dt, t + dt) \tag{2}$$

As a consequence, each algorithm, which is based on this equation, has to calculate with scalar, that is, grey values, and not with colour values. This has to occur also later in the memristive network. Finally, after applying the chain rule, Eq. (2) can be transformed to the central Eq. (3) that is solved in a similar way by detecting moving edges by the corresponding memristive network presented in Ref. [3]. This network is simulated here with SystemC-AMS to demonstrate that complex memristive networks can be simulated with our approach of modelling the dynamic of memristors with variable resistors

$$I(x, y, t) = I(x, y, t) + u \cdot dt\frac{\partial I}{\partial x} + v \cdot \frac{\partial I}{\partial y} + dt\frac{I}{\partial t} \tag{3}$$

$$I_x(x, y) \cdot u + I_y(x, y) \cdot v + I_t(x, y) = 0 \tag{4}$$

3.2. Memristive network and SystemC-AMS specification

In the following, we exemplarily consider the details only for the derivatives in the space to x and y dimension for a corresponding 2D memristor network. The extension to the time domain would be an additional layer in the third direction between corresponding pixels in neighboured images. As mentioned, the algorithm works on grey-scaled images; therefore, the scales have to be inverted in corresponding voltages. For the simulation, it is enough to restrict to an 8-bit resolution. Since the voltage of a photo-sensitive cell is in the range of 0–40 mV, we get the following scaling of the input voltage for each pixel Eq. (4)

$$V_p(x) = x \cdot \left(\frac{40}{255}\right)\mathrm{mV} \tag{5}$$

This scaling has to be carried out for each pixel in the image. In our SystemC-AMS specification, this is done per instruction code, which calculates Eq. (4) and uses the result to instantiate a DC voltage source. **Figure 3** shows a scheme for a memristive circuit that handles each pixel in the image.

The voltage *V*, representing a changed grey value, is attached to the network via a resistance R_C, which influences the time behaviour of the network for solving the optical flow. Since the optical flow changes dynamically in the network, the flow is modelled by current flowing through dynamically adapting resistances for which memristors are required. A memristor R_M, which stores the result of the optical flow, again as an encoded grey value, and two further memristors, denoted as outer plexiform layer (OPL) in **Figure 3**, complete the circuit handling a pixel.

A corresponding description of the header file for the pixel (without the OPL) in SystemC-AMS is shown below. Firstly, the parameters are specified for the constructor of a pixel class called *PixelNode*. Since an instance of *PixelNode* is one pixel within a 2D array, it receives two identifiers. The first one is *image_id*. It identifies in which image the pixel is, remember the optical flow requires two subsequent layers connected with each other. The second identifier, *idx*, addresses uniquely the pixel within the image. Then, four resistance values are as follows: R_CONST, the starting value for the top resistor R_C, R_ON, R_OFF and R_INIT for the initial setting of the memristor denoted as *A* in the class, which corresponds to the bottom memristor R_M in **Figure 3**. The parameters *initial_pixel* and *vsource* correspond to the input grey value of the pixel and the input voltage *V*, which has to be calculated elsewhere in the code according to Eq. (4). The further specifications *eln_pixel* and *neighbours* refer to the virtual electronic network to make a connection to a virtual potentiometer to measure current running through the pixel and the voltage applied at that pixel, respectively, to the connection to the neighboured pixels via the OPL. Both specifications and the ground connection, *gnd*, also require unique identifiers which are passed as strings, *eln_pixel* and *gnd*, in the parentheses to the instances of *A*. Finally, the instructions given within the brackets provide the connections to the memristor as variable resistor analogue to the example given in the previous chapter for a memristor of the class *MemristorBiolek*. The result voltage will adjust at R_C. It is calculated in the method *PixelNode::pixel_value*. This voltage can be used in order to calculate the resulting grey value

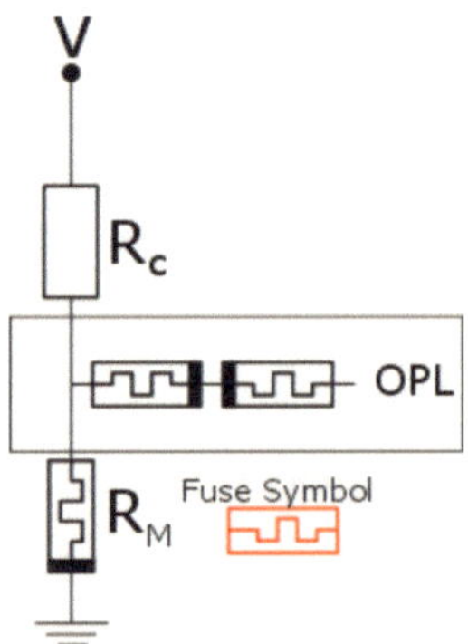

Figure 3. Electrical network for one pixel. The memristive fuse OPL realizes the connection to the neighbour pixel. All pixels correspond to the mid-layer. The resistance R_C controls the speed of the adaption of the memristive network, the voltage over resistance R_M corresponds to the result, that is, if a moving pixel was detected according to a detected optical flow.

```
PixelNode::PixelNode(const size_t image_id, const size_t idx,
const double R_CONST, const double R_ON,
const double R_OFF, const double R_INIT,
const unsigned char initial_pixel_value,
const double vsource):
R_CONST(R_CONST),
initial_pixel_value(initial_pixel_value),
vsource(vsource),
A(R_ON,R_OFF,R_INIT),
eln_pixel(("eln_pixel_"+std::to_string(image_id)+"_"
+std::to_string(idx)).c_str(,vsource,R_CONST),
neighbours(("eln_pixel_neighbour_node_"+std::to_string(image_id)+"_"
+std::to_string(idx).c_str()),
gnd(new              sca_eln::sca_node_ref(std::string("gnd"+std::to_
string(image_id)+"_"
+std::to_string(idx).c_str())) {
eln_pixel.memristor_controll(A.get_control_port());
eln_pixel.out(A.get_voltage_port());
eln_pixel.neighbours(neighbours);
A.write_resistance();
}
double PixelNode::pixel_value() const {
double mapped_voltage = A.read_voltage() *
((R_CONST+A.resistance())/A.resistance());
return mapped_voltage;
}
```

If a low-resistance value is assigned to R_C, the voltage drop at the resistance will occur slowly, and due to the higher voltage that is applied to the subsequently attached memristors, in this case, their memristances are changing faster. In opposite, a higher resistance produces a more time-lag reaction in the network since now the memristors need more time to adapt their internal states. This new generated voltage via R_C is now the input for the main layer of the network. The function of this main layer is adapted to the outer plexiform layer of the retina. This main layer mimics horizontal cells in the retina. Therefore, a connection to the neighbour pixels has to be realized via the so-called *memristive fuses*. These fuses provide an automatic averaging of the voltages connected to neighboured pixels. If there is a high potential difference between two neighboured pixels, then the memristive fuse adjusts faster a higher memristance. This leads to an edge-preserving property of the filter since the influence of the pixel decreases by the time. However, this idea would not work with a single memristor because the potential difference on that memristor could be either positive or negative. In the case of a negative potential, the memristance would decrease. This is the reason why two memristors, which are connected with reversed poles, are seen as depicted in **Figure 3**. Doing this, it does not play a role if the applied voltages are either negative or positive. In case an edge is detected, one of the memristors behaves always different to the other one and we receive as output the voltage that can be detected at resistor R_C.

The following specification in SystemC-AMS shows the code for a memristive fuse. Such a fuse has also a positive and a negative port like a single memristor. Therefore, it can be attached to an electrical network. Furthermore, as already shown in the example for a memristor, we need control signals, *memristor_control_one* and *memristor_control_two*, as discrete input signals to change the resistances of the variable resistors, *memristor_resistor_one* and *memristor_resistor_two*. These memristors are connected via an electrical node called *node*, which is defined in the constructor as well as the binding of their control signals *memristor_control_one/two* to their ports *memristor_resistor_one/two.inp*. Furthermore, the virtual circuit points *memristor_resistor_vout_one/two.n/p* are defined to measure the voltage at these memristors via the signals *memristor_resistor_vout_one/two.outp*. These signals allow displaying the voltages at both memristors

```
SC_MODULE(memristive_fuse)
{
 //negative and positive terminal
 sca_eln::sca_terminal n, p;
 sc_core::sc_in<double> memristor_control_one, memristor_control_two;
 sca_tdf::sca_out<double> memristor_resistor_voltage_one;
 sca_tdf::sca_out<double> memristor_resistor_voltage_two;
private:
 sca_eln::sca_node node;
 sca_eln::sca_tdf::sca_vsink memristor_resistor_vout_one;
 sca_eln::sca_tdf::sca_vsink memristor_resistor_vout_two;
 //two memristors
 sca_eln::sca_de::sca_r memristor_resistor_one;
```

http://dx.doi.org/10.5772/intechopen.69662

```
sca_eln::sca_de::sca_r memristor_resistor_two;
SC_CTOR(memristive_fuse) :
memristor_resistor_one("memristor_resistor_one",1.0),
memristor_resistor_two("memristor_resistor_two",1.0),
node("node"),
memristor_resistor_voltage_one("memristor_resistor_voltage_one"),
memristor_resistor_voltage_two("memristor_resistor_voltage_two"),
memristor_resistor_vout_one("memristor_resistor_vout_one")
memristor_resistor_vout_two("memristor_resistor_vout_two")
{
//setup memristors
memristor_resistor_one.n(node);
memristor_resistor_one.p(p);
memristor_resistor_one.inp(memristor_control_one);
memristor_resistor_two.n(node);
memristor_resistor_two.p(p);
memristor_resistor_two.inp(memristor_control_two);
//setup voltage measurements for memristor one and two
memristor_resistor_vout_one.p(n);
memristor_resistor_vout_one.n(p);
memristor_resistor_vout_one.outp(memristor_resistor_voltage_one);
memristor_resistor_vout_two.n(node);
memristor_resistor_vout_two.p(p);
memristor_resistor_vout_two.outp(memristor_resistor_voltage_two);
}
};
```

After the definition for a pixel and a memristive_fuse, both these devices can be connected to construct the circuit shown in **Figure 3** by attaching one of the ports *p* or *n* of the memristive fuse to the port *neighbor* of a pixel node. The connection scheme for one pixel detecting the derivatives I_x and I_y in a 2D grid for a direct hexagonal neighbour connection is shown in **Figure 4**.

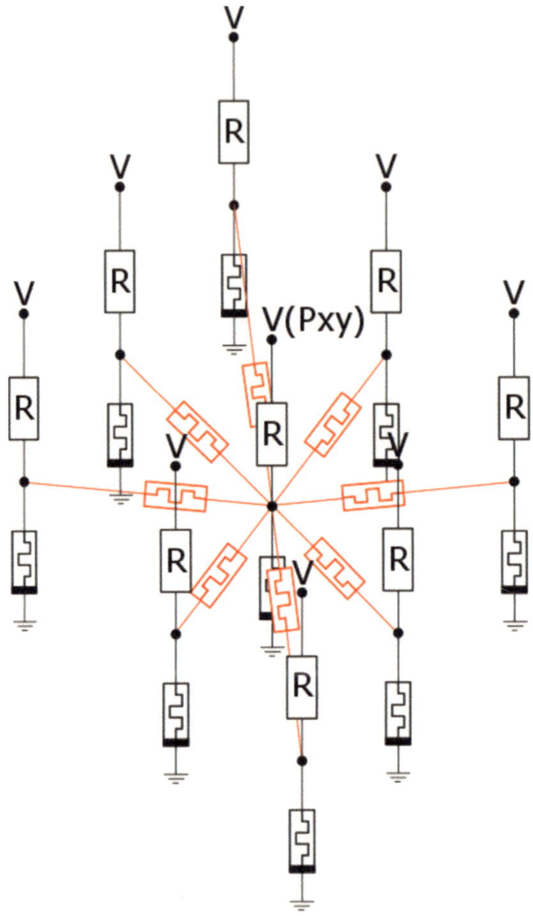

Figure 4. Scheme for the 2D memristive grid with X connection, that is, each pixel has eight connections to four neighbours in rectangular direction (left, right, top, bottom) and to the four diagonals.

This can also be specified in SystemC-AMS which we are unable to present in this paper due to reasons of clarity since the corresponding code is larger. Before we can move to the achieved simulation results, some things concerning the functionality of the network have to be explained before.

The electrical network constructed in this way fulfils several tasks. For example, before the optical flow processing takes place, a Gaussian filtering is carried out on the pixels, which is done by the OPL imitating memristive fuses, too.

An important thing that has to be avoided is that both memristors of a fuse have the same initial mid resistance $= \frac{R_{ON} + R_{OFF}}{2}$. In this case, the changes of memristances in both memristors countermand themselves. If the memristance of one memristors increases, the memristance of the other one decreases. A possible solution for this problem is that both memristors are initialized with a low resistance. In case of a given potential difference between two neighboured pixels, independent of its direction, only one memristor increases, whereas the other one's memristance stays low and we can detect a corresponding voltage change at R_C corresponding to a given edge pixel.

The result voltage U_G is given to, it can be converted to a grey value x according to Eq. (5):

$$U_G = I_M \cdot (R_C + R_M) \; x = U_G \cdot \left(\frac{255}{40 \text{ mV}}\right) \tag{6}$$

Both things, initializing the memristors as described earlier and the grey scale conversion, are performed in our SystemC-AMS specification by appropriate instruction codes, for example, the calculation of the result voltage is carried out with the method *PixelNode::pixel_value* shown above in the class description of *PixelNode*. Besides the automatic filtering of neighboured input voltages, the network as described above allows the detection of edges, too, because edges are nothing else than potential differences. **Figure 5** shows the scheme for a potential propagation if the input voltage is applied left and the ground is applied right. Since this happens also for small differences very fast due to the memristive fuses, a threshold has to be introduced in order to detect real edges. The detection assigns a pixel only then as edge pixel if at least three of the neighbour pixels are above the threshold. This is directly programmed in the SystemC-AMS code which is not shown here. We have not seen a possibility to carry out such thresholding directly in the original analogue network published in Ref. [4].

So far, we have described a solution for determining the derivatives I_x and I_y within the 2D network and its SystemC-AMS equivalent. However, the optical flow requires the input and analysis of input data from two subsequent images in order to detect also the derivative I_t. Therefore, the network has to be extended in the third dimension and we have done that also in our SystemC-AMS specification. This is shown in **Figure 6** in a lateral view for two neighboured pixels located at the same coordinate in two subsequent layers which are connected in the same way as the lateral connections by an additional memristive fuse.

That means we connected together in SystemC-AMS two grids of the size 16 × 12 as shown for one pixel in **Figure 4**. The first gird hosted an image *I(x,y,t)* and the second one the timely

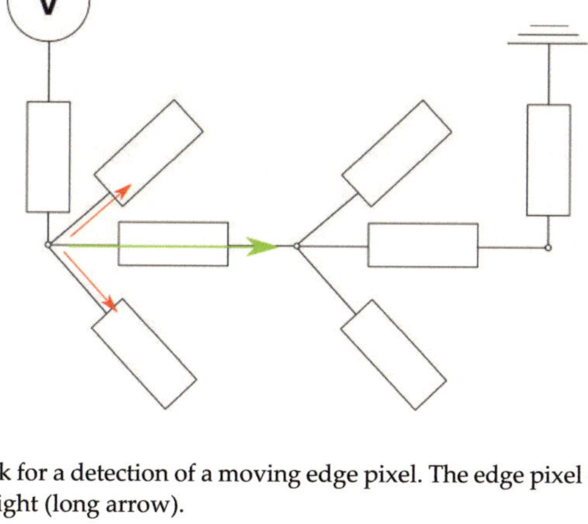

Figure 5. SystemC-AMS network for a detection of a moving edge pixel. The edge pixel disappears on the left (two short arrows) side and moves to the right (long arrow).

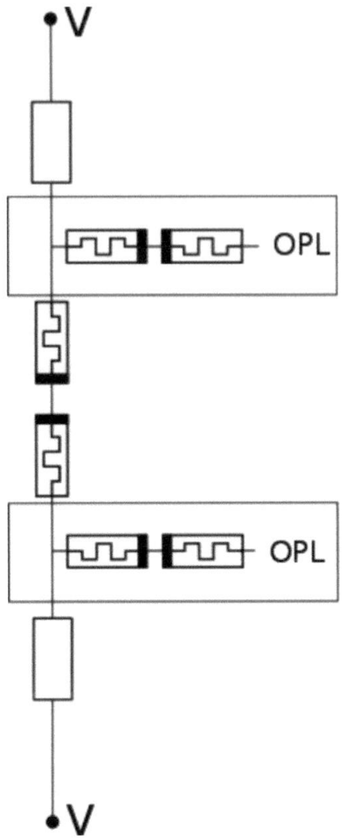

Figure 6. 3D connection of a pixel between two pixels neighboured in subsequent images.

displaced image *I(x,y,t+dt)*. A larger size could not be selected because the free SystemC-AMS version of Coseda did not allow generating more active elements. The SystemC-AMS code we tested extends more than 3000 memristors in all fuses and pixels for two images of size 16 × 12.

4. Results

Figure 7 shows the achieved functional results of the SystemC-AMS simulation for a traffic scene with the memristive network that works on the detection of moving edges with the memristive 2D network compared to a classical solution calculated according to Horn and Schunk on an Inteli5-6600 CPU. It is to recognize that the Horn and Schunk procedure algorithm works much better on a higher resolution, (a) versus (b), whereas the lower resolution is sufficient for the SystemC-AMS detection of moving edges (c). The low resolution was selected since this was the limit for the SystemC-AMS simulation with the proof-of-concept software solution. These moving edges are combined in one object. The grey edges are the disappearing edges, whereas the dark square corresponds to an appearing edge. The assignment

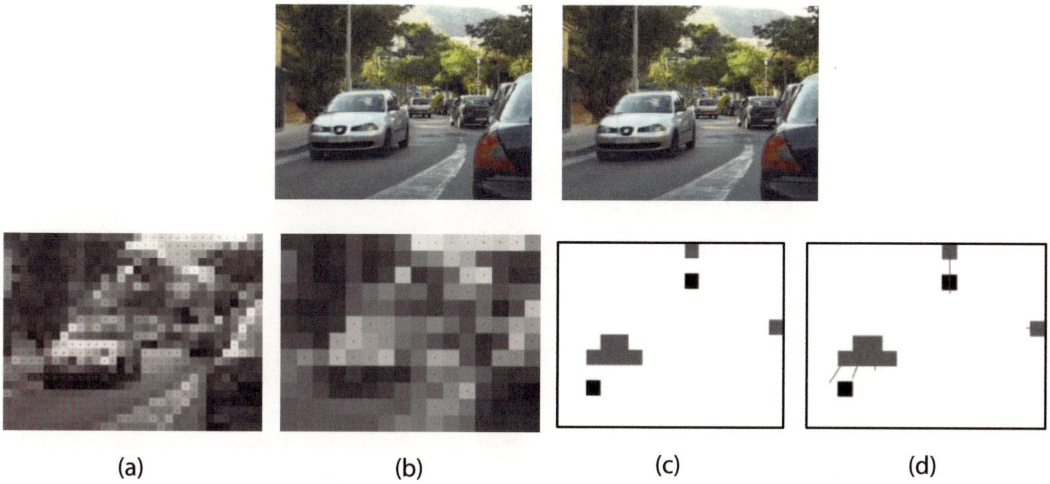

Figure 7. Used test input images (top), the two scenes are slightly displaced. On the bottom left side, (a) solution based on Horn and Schunck procedure calculated on CPU with 32 × 24 image size; (b) solution for 16 × 24 image size. On the bottom right side, the solution for the same scenes determined with the simulated memristive network in SystemC-AMS. Firstly, the detected edges (c), afterwards the detected directions of the moving edges (d).

between the two edges (see arrows in **Figure 7(d)**) can be identified and by this also the moving of the cars shown in front and of the smaller one shown behind in the image.

The results of **Figure 7** demonstrate that it is possible to detect moving objects with the memristive network and its SystemC-AMS model. We are now interested on how fast the network and the SystemC-AMS simulation work. The simulation of the detected moving edges in **Figure 7(c)** shows simulation results for a simulated memristive network for a time interval of 3000 ms. In this case, Biolek model was not used for the memristors but the model from Knowm which produced a significantly higher contrast. At the beginning, only a wave can be observed. After a simulated real time of 3000 ms, a higher contrast is given with that model compared to the input image and the moving objects can be detected. As comparison with existing hardware, we have determined the run times of the detection with the optical flow based on Horn and Schunk on a CPU (corei5-6600 corresponds to Intel's Skylake microarchitecture) and a Jetson TX1-embedded GPU board from Nvidia. The CPU could compute in 3000-ms image sizes of 160×120. It is to expect that the memristive network works also on higher resolution since it is a highly local parallel-processing scheme.

Therefore, the memristive network lies in the same range as the CPU concerning the compute performance. The situation is different compared to the GPU. We measured a time of about 100 ms for an image size of 640 × 480. Hence, the GPU has clear advantages versus the memristive network concerning the run time.

However, the actual interesting point in this paper is the simulation time of the SystemC-AMS specification. In order to get significant values we have carried out a series of possible optimization measures concerning the network topology and the monitoring, resp., the virtual voltage measuring during the simulation. **Figure 8** shows the simulation time

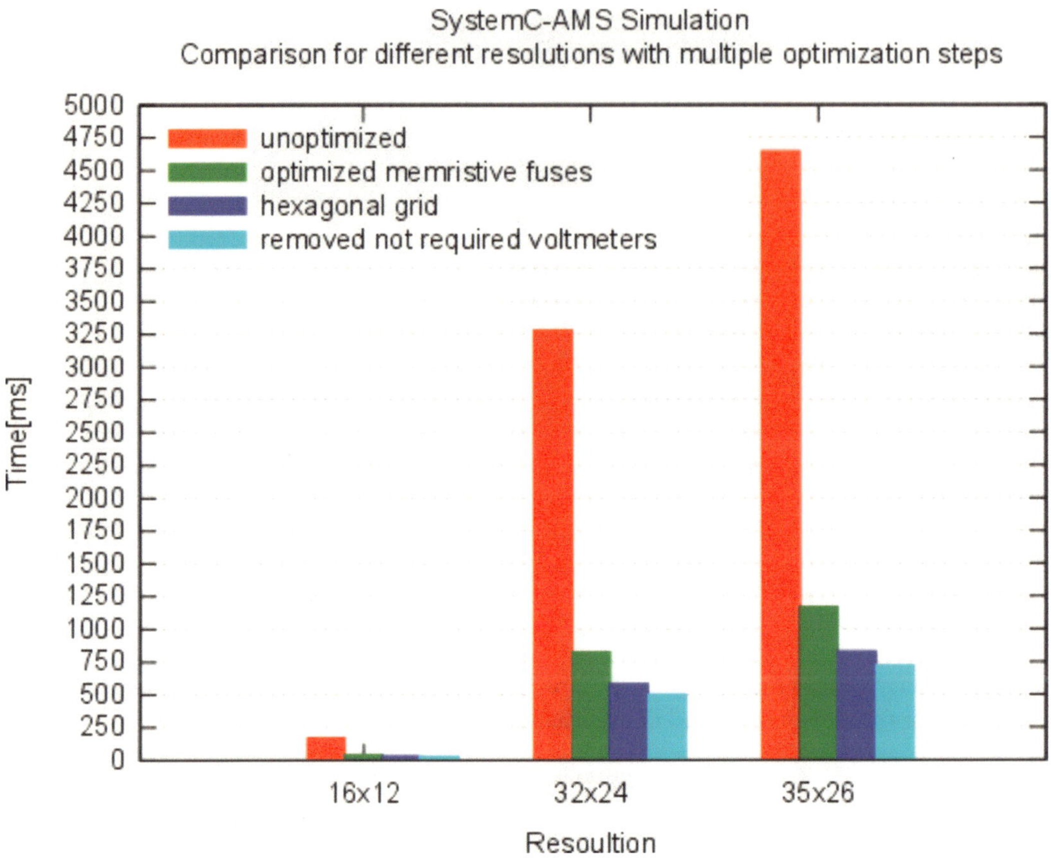

Figure 8. Measuring the simulation time in SystemC-AMS for different options.

for filtering and edge detection in one image for the following different sizes 16 × 12, 32 × 24 and 35 × 26 for a not optimized version (most-left bars—non-optimized), a version, which uses only one memristor in the fuses which is sufficient for edge detection as we found out (second left bar—optimized memristive fuses), using a hexagonal grid instead a 3 × 3 grid as local neighbourhood for a pixel (second right bar—hexagonal grid), and removing the voltage potentiometers for each memristor in the SystemC-AMS code (most right bar—removed not required potentiometers). It is to detect that simulation time can be drastically reduced, for example, for a 35 × 26 image from 4500 ms down to about 750 ms for the largest resolution of 35 × 26 if all optimization steps are applied subsequently.

Our efforts to carry out an equivalent SPICE simulation with LT Spice have been in vain. The LT Spice simulator ended in an endless loop by the trial to simulate this large memristive network. With the PSpice A/D Lite version, the simulation aborted orderly with the message that the symbol table entry is out of bounds. May be the commercial version of Pspice allows to simulate such a large amount of devices. In all, in the 32 × 24-sized grid 768 voltage sources, 1536 resistors and 5461 memristor subcircuits have to be simulated. Further work has been done using Cadence Virtuoso. While Virtuoso was able to read the network and create a schematic view, it was not possible to start the Spectre simulation due to incompatibilities using the memristor Spice description.

In an older work [7], a similar 32 × 32 array of memristors was simulated in SPICE. Recently, Biolek et al. published a work [8] in which they used a parallel version of a commercial HSPICE simulator which allowed them to simulate extremely large memristor networks. They managed it to simulate a 100 × 100 memristive grid network containing 20,200 memristors in 5.5 s and a 1500 × 1500-sized memristive network containing 4.5 million memristors in 76 min by applying a modified version of the so-called S-model for memristors on a current Intel core i7 architecture.

5. Conclusion

Exploiting the flexibility of a high-level language like SystemC-AMS, the presented simulation environment enables designers to carry out extensive investigations on large memristive circuits to estimate latency and energy consumption just by simple C++ code modifications. Furthermore, such a system allows the simulation of thousands of connected memristors at acceptable simulation times, which is shown by a direct comparison to an equivalent SPICE simulation. A SystemC-AMS description allows faster simulation, but currently the investigated SystemC-AMS implementations do not allow the simulation for networks concerning more than 10 k memristors. Therefore, there seems to be a need for action concerning an extension of SystemC-AMS environments in the future. On the other side, free available SPICE versions failed to simulate memristor networks in the size of 1000 s, whereas the presented SPICE-AMS implementation could handle it in acceptable simulation time of 4–5 s and around 1 s for an optimized version. However, compared to commercial HSPICE simulators only smaller-sized networks of memristors can be investigated. On the other side, a SystemC-AMS solution simplifies a coupling to digital system layers to realize mixed-signal simulations. We demonstrated this flexibility in principle in this paper for the optical flow algorithm.

For the optical flow example, a comparison of a memristive network with real processor architecture like a GPU was carried out. It could be shown by simulations that using a GPU architecture is more efficient for the optical flow problem than a 2D grid memristive network solving the problem by detecting moving edges. The performance of a current CPU solution on the other side offers not more compute power than the memristive network which probably requires less energy consumption than the CPU. At all, we think that mixed-signal solutions are to favour, which combine analogue memristive circuits with digital processors, to unite computational flexibility and the benefits of energy-saving neuromorphic analogue memristor networks. A SystemC-AMS-based simulation environment is generally well suited for the design of such architectures and to estimate the required power and processing time. Our solution laid the foundation for such work in the future.

Author details

Dietmar Fey*, Lukas Riedersberger and Marc Reichenbach

*Address all correspondence to: dietmar.fey@fau.de

Friedrich-Alexander-University Erlangen-Nürnberg (FAU), Computer Architecture, Department of Computer Science, Erlangen, Germany

References

[1] Kvatinsky S, Friedman EG, Kolodny A, Weiser UC. TEAM: ThrEshold adaptive memristor model. IEEE Transactions on Circuits and Systems. 2013;**60-I**(1):211-221

[2] Biolek Z, Biolek D, Biolkov V. SPICE model of memristor with nonlinear dopant drift. Radioengineering. 2009;**18**(2):210-214

[3] Nugent MA, Molter TW. AHaH computing–From metastable switches to attractors to machine learning. PLoS ONE. 2014;**9**(2):e85175. DOI: doi:10.1371/journal.pone.0085175

[4] Lim CKK, Gelencser A, Prodromakis T. Computing image and motion with 3-D memristive grids. In: Adamatzky A, Chua L, editors. Memristor Networks. Cham: Springer International Publishing; 2014. pp. 553-583

[5] Coseda Technologies GmbH. SystemC AMS Proof-of-Concept Download [Internet]. Available from: http://www.coseda-tech.com/systemc-ams-proof-of-concept [Accessed: 20-March-2016]

[6] Horn BKP, Schunck BG. Determining optical flow. Artificial Intelligence. 1981;**17**

[7] Wang Y, Fei W, Yu H. SPICE simulator for hybrid CMOS memristor circuit and system. In: 13th International Workshop on Cellular Nanoscale Networks and their Applications (CNNA 2012); August 29-31, 2012; Turin, Italy: IEEE; 2012. pp. 1-6

[8] Biolek D, Kolka Z, Biolkova V, Biolek Z. Memristor models for spice simulation of extremely large memristive networks. In: IEEE International Symposium on Circuits and Systems (ISCAS); May 22-25, 2016, Montreal, QC: IEEE; 2016. pp. 389-392

Modeling of Coupled Memristive-Based Architectures Applicable to Neural Network Models

Jason Kamran Jr Eshraghian, Herbert H.C. Iu and
Kamran Eshraghian

Additional information is available at the end of the chapter

http://dx.doi.org/10.5772/intechopen.69327

Abstract

This chapter explores the dynamic behavior of dual flux coupled memristor circuits in order to explore the uncharted territory of the fundamental theory of memristor circuits. Neuromorphic computing anticipates highly dense systems of memristive networks, and with nanoscale devices within such close proximity to one another, it is anticipated that flux and charge coupling between adjacent memristors will have a bearing upon their operation. Using the constitutive relations of memristors, various cases of flux coupling are mathematically modeled. This involves analyzing two memristors connected in composite, both serially and in parallel in various polarity configurations. The new behavior of two coupled memristors is characterized based on memristive state equations, and memductance variation represented in terms of voltage, current, charge and flux. The rigorous mathematical analysis based on the fundamental circuit equations of ideal memristors affirms the memristor closure theorem, where coupled memristor circuits behave as different types of memristors with higher complexity.

Keywords: memristor, memductance, coupling, flux, charge, series, parallel

1. Introduction

In 1969, Leon Chua became the first person to publish non-linear circuit theory against a mathematical foundation [1]. In doing so, it became apparent that there was a hole in the circuit equations at the time. Shortly after, in 1971 he postulated that symmetry implies the existence of a fourth fundamental circuit element to link the missing relationship between charge and flux —that circuit element being the memristor [2]. This research resurfaced and was popularized in 2008, when Hewlett-Packard fabricated the first functional nanoscale memristor [3]. This particular brand of memristor was based on a bi-level titanium dioxide thin film containing dopants which migrate across the width of the memristor when a current is applied to it.

Each fundamental circuit element holds a relationship between any two of either voltage, current, charge, or flux. The memristor thus becomes a fundamental circuit element as it fills the missing gap of the charge-flux relationship. It is important to note that even though q and ϕ are referred to as charge and flux, they do not have to be associated with a physical charge or real flux as is the case with classical conductors and inductors [4]. The integrating relationship between voltage and flux results in memristors being able to retain history, and exhibiting potentially different current values when the same voltage is applied to it. By definition, this enables the memristor to have different resistance values regardless of identical voltage excitation, stemming from memristance being a function of historical voltage. This gives rise to the nomenclature surrounding the memristor, a portmanteau of 'memory resistor'.

The inherent characteristics of this revolutionary device have enabled its application in a diverse field of areas, including neuromorphic circuits [5] and non-volatile memory applications [6]. These applications often see arrays of memristors behaving compositely with one another. In addition to the functionality of single discrete memristors, the behaviors of multiple memristors in structures of connectivity have also been analyzed.

Memristors are polarity dependant—while this complicates circuit analysis, it allows for many more configuration permutations than the other fundamental circuits: the resistor, capacitor and inductor. The behavior of two memristor emulators in both serial and parallel connections are experimentally evaluated in Ref. [7], however, only identical polarity directions are considered. Two charge controlled memristors are connected in series and in parallel in Ref. [8], with their responses evaluated when polarity is varied. The composite behavior is analyzed by probing the relationships between flux, charge and memristance. The results show novel *I-V* characteristics which will prove to be useful applications in neural networks and logic circuits. The magnetic coupling of memristors are also considered in terms of mutual induction and capacitive connections in Ref. [9].

Many researchers have sought to use memristors to represent the synapses between neurons in artificial networks, and more recently, a memristive crossbar array has been successfully fabricated which implements a neural network, and is successfully capable of performing limited classifications and simple pattern recognition [10]. By training such networks on sets of known example patterns and tuning the weights of the 'synaptic' connections, unknown patterns and images can be recognized. Ultimately, researchers anticipate that networks with a density of 100 billion synapses per square centimeter in each layer should soon be possible by shrinking memristors down to 30 nm across. This indicates highly dense 3D structures with a very large number of memristors within very close proximity of one another will be the norm, and coupling memristor theory is of fundamental significance to this field. The use of memristive crossbar architectures has been gaining much traction in computing large sets of data [11–14], and the theory behind memristive coupling is absolutely essential in ensuring information is not lost due to undesirable coupling, or by manufacturing more efficient modes of information storage by utilizing coupling theory.

The coupling effects of capacitors and inductors via electric and magnetic fields are well known. The mutual capacitances and inductances of circuits comprised of multiple TiO_2 memristors are dependent upon the physical features of each memristor cell [14], such as size and position.

Therefore, coupling is to be expected between adjacent memristors, and must be taken into account when analyzing highly concentrated circuits. In addition to series and parallel connections, coupling has thus been established as a third unique relation in memristive systems [15].

The behavior of coupled memristors was rigorously analyzed in a systematic manner for the first time in Ref. [16] with consideration given to all polarity combinations. The theoretical analysis is confirmed in the same paper by use of a separately presented memristor emulator circuit from Ref. [17]. However, the results in the analysis is based on a memristor which exhibits a linear relationship between memductance and flux. This is obviously not the case for many memristors, such as the simplest case of a flux-controlled switching memristor presented in Ref. [18] where flux is controlled independent of memductance. As such, there is only a very narrow scope of memristors which the research in Ref. [16] applies to. The results in Ref. [18] served to broaden this assumption to ideal switching memristors which operate in two states, and obtain new results based on the same constitutive relation equations. This chapter dissects the results in Ref. [18] and presents them in a more comprehensive format, with the use of fundamental memristor theory to form the basis of the analysis to produce valid results. As such, the findings in this chapter can be applied more broadly and yet maintain the complex behavior which makes the memristor so attractive. The theoretical analysis and analytical solutions provide for novel memductance behavior in terms of flux, charge, voltage and current of ideal memristors. In the process, it is proven that the memristor closure theorem continues to stand for coupled memristors [19].

2. Coupled memristors

The two types of ideal memristors considered are charge controlled or flux controlled [2]. The relationship between current and voltage of a charge controlled memristor is expressed by

$$V(t) = M(q)i(t), \tag{1}$$

where t is time, $v(t)$ is voltage, $q(t)$ is charge and $M(q)$ is memristance. In its derivative form, memristance can be defined as

$$M(q) = {d\varphi(q)}\Big/{dq}, \tag{2}$$

where $\phi(q)$ is flux (the time integral of voltage $v(t)$). Contrastingly, the current of a flux controlled memristor is

$$i(t) = W(\varphi)v(t), \tag{3}$$

where $W(\phi)$ denotes the memductance and

$$W(\varphi) = {dq(\varphi)}\Big/{d\varphi}. \tag{4}$$

The memductance W is the slope of the q-ϕ curve, which is a characteristic embedded into the memristor at the time of fabrication.

Flux ϕ and charge q are two intrinsic state variables which affect memductance. Two memristors can be coupled by either flux or charge as shown in **Figures 1** and **2**.

If two flux controlled memristors are considered, the ideal coupled memristive systems can be defined by the following set of equations,

$$i_1(t) = W_1(\varphi_1, \varphi_2)v_1(t), \tag{5a}$$

$$i_2(t) = W_2(\varphi_1, \varphi_2)v_2(t), \tag{5b}$$

$$d\varphi_1 \big/ dt = v_1(t), d\varphi_2 \big/ dt = v_2(t). \tag{5c}$$

While a general rule cannot be ascertained which would be applicable for all ideal memristors, the most appropriate manner in approaching the task of modeling a pair of coupled memristors is to provide a procedural methodology instead. This is done by way of example with use of a particular type of switching memristor, complete with a known q-ϕ relationship.

Instead of assuming a linear relationship between memductance and flux as in Ref. [15], it is more appropriate to consider the ideal memristor proposed in Ref. [4], and derive the associated relationship between flux and memductance from a given q-ϕ relationship. An example of an ideal switching memristor is shown below in **Figure 3**, and the response of the memristor can be completely described by the q-ϕ curve displayed.

For the purposes of this paper, this example of an ideal switching memristor is completely characterized by the following equations:

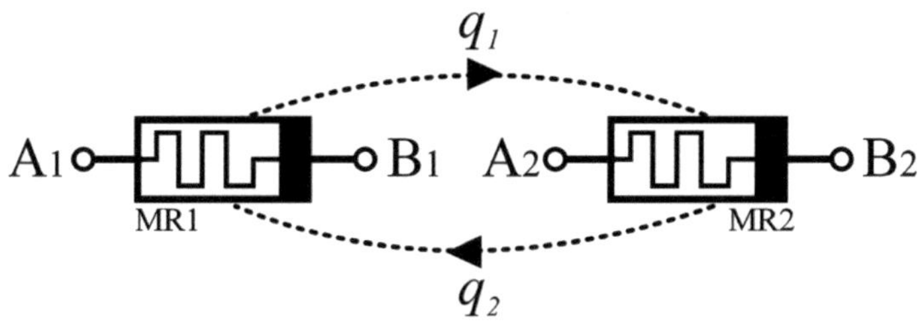

Figure 1. Dual charge coupled memristors.

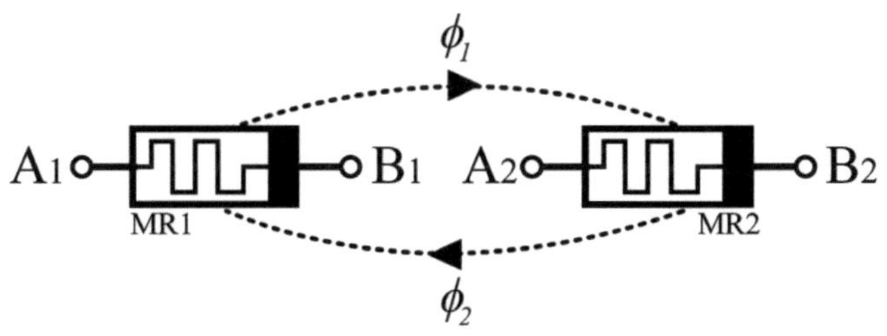

Figure 2. Dual flux coupled memristors.

$$\varphi(t) = 0.8(1 - \cos t) - 0.4, \tag{6a}$$

$$q(t) = 0.01\varphi(t) + 0.04\,|\varphi(t) + 0.25| - 0.04\,|\varphi(t) - 0.25|. \tag{6b}$$

Given Eqs. (6a) and (6b), the memductance value can be derived from Eq. (4) and is graphed below in **Figure 4**.

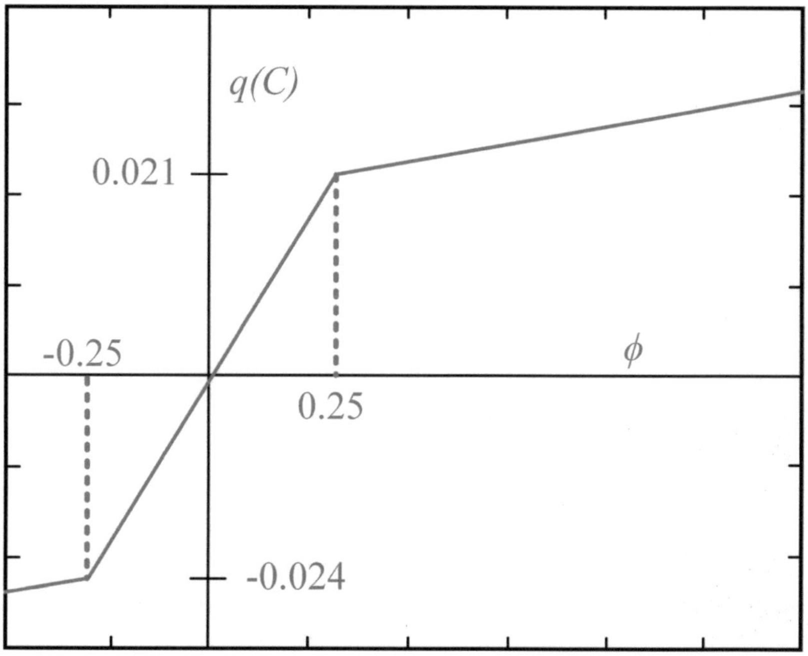

Figure 3. The q-ϕ relationship for an ideal switching memristor proposed in Ref. [4].

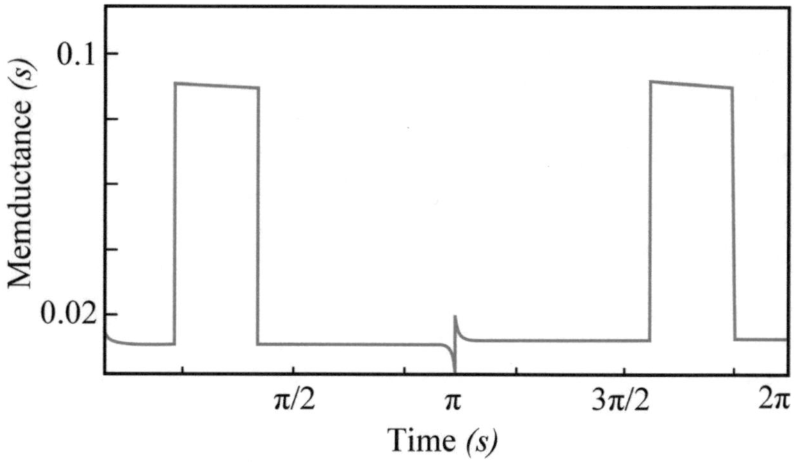

Figure 4. The memductance curve as a function of time derived from Eqs. (4), (6a), and (6b) displays how a memristor with a three part piecewise linear relationship between flux can switch between high and low current states.

The memductance can be approximated by

$$W = \begin{cases} \alpha, & |\varphi| < |\varphi_t| \\ \beta, & |\varphi_t| < |\varphi| < |\varphi_{max}| \end{cases} \tag{7}$$

where α is a constant representing the high memductance state, β is the low memductance state, ϕ_{max} is the maximum value of flux for a given sinusoidal voltage input (which in this particular case can be calculated by substituting $t = \pi$ rads into Eq. (6a) where $\phi_{max} = 1.2$), and ϕ_t is a certain threshold of flux where both current and memductance become discontinuous (in this case $\phi_t = 0.4$). Once again, it is reiterated that even though q and ϕ are referred to as charge and flux, they are not necessarily associated with real physical charge and flux in the way they are in classical conductors and inductors.

If this specific type of memristor is purely flux coupled with an identical memristor (without any other composite connections), and assuming the simple case of a first order mathematical model of coupling, the individual memductance of each device can be ascertained from Eqs. (5) and (7) as

$$W_1(\varphi_1, \varphi_2) = \begin{cases} \alpha_1 + \kappa_2\varphi_2, & |\varphi_1| < |\varphi_t| \\ \beta_1 + \kappa_2\varphi_2, & |\varphi_t| < |\varphi_1| < |\varphi_{max}| \end{cases} \tag{8a}$$

$$W_2(\varphi_2, \varphi_1) = \begin{cases} \alpha_2 + \kappa_1\varphi_1, & |\varphi_1| < |\varphi_t| \\ \beta_2 + \kappa_1\varphi_1, & |\varphi_t| < |\varphi_1| < |\varphi_{max}| \end{cases} \tag{8b}$$

The coupling strength between these two memristors is reflected by the coupling coefficients κ_1 and κ_2 which can be tuned based on physical factors in fabrication. Therefore, the two memristors can be tightly or loosely coupled depending on the values of κ_1 and κ_2.

A solvable equation with physical meaning requires assumptions about the physical behavior of the memristors. By considering the special case of identical excitations and voltage history (alternatively, the same initial conditions), and allowing for $\alpha_1 = \alpha_2 = \alpha$, $\beta_1 = \beta_2 = \beta$, and $\kappa_1 = \kappa_2 = 0.1$ (which can be precisely achieved by fabrication) the constitutive relations are used to identify behavior unachievable by the lone memristor. Memductance after coupling effects in Eq. (8) can be attained by summing flux from Eq. (6a) with memductance from Eq. (7). Current is recalculated to take into account the effect from coupling due to the composite memristor. This can be done by taking the time derivative of Eq. (6a) which is the driving voltage source, and substituting it into Eq. (3).

The *I-V* characteristic plane can be mapped by considering the two purely coupled memristors (without any other connections) as a single device. This procedure is carried out with two identical ideal flux-coupled memristors represented by **Figure 3** and configured as in **Figure 2**, to provide the *I-V* characteristics below.

When compared to the original hysteresis loop of just one of the two memristors, there are two notable differences: (i) the current spans a larger range of values due to the additive effect of ϕ_2 on i_1 (conversely, ϕ_1 has an identical effect on i_2), and (ii) the single memristor has two different

http://dx.doi.org/10.5772/intechopen.69327

slope values which correlate to two different states, whereas in the coupled case, there are infinite states.

Despite this being the result of a specific type of switching memristor, it is reasonable to conclude these two changes will occur in all cases of purely coupled switching memristors.

This result can be exploited in neural circuits where synaptic spikes have more complexity than mere 'ON-OFF states'. On the other hand, it may have an undesirable effect on memristive logic gates where having two states is essential for functionality. Necessary physical precautions must be taken in order to minimize the values of κ_1 and κ_2 for such processes, and to additionally account for excessive current passage through the memristor due to coupling. But if logic gates were to be extended beyond high and low states, then the multiple states of the memristor could be harnessed into a multi-level logic gate on a nanometer scale.

3. Coupled memristors in serial connections

Two different configurations of serially connected memristors exist according to polarity combinations. The same approximation of the ideal memristors will apply to this section in the same form as in Eq. (7).

3.1. Serial connection with identical polarities

Connecting terminal B_1 to A_2 allows for a serial circuit structure for two memristors in identical polarities as shown in **Figure 5**.

Applying Kirchhoff's voltage Law (KVL) and equating the current through both memristors, the voltage across and current through A_1 and B_2 can be written as

$$v_{12}(t) = v_1 + v_2, \tag{9a}$$

$$i(t) = W_1(\varphi_1, \varphi_2)v_1(t) = W_2(\varphi_2, \varphi_1)v_2(t). \tag{9b}$$

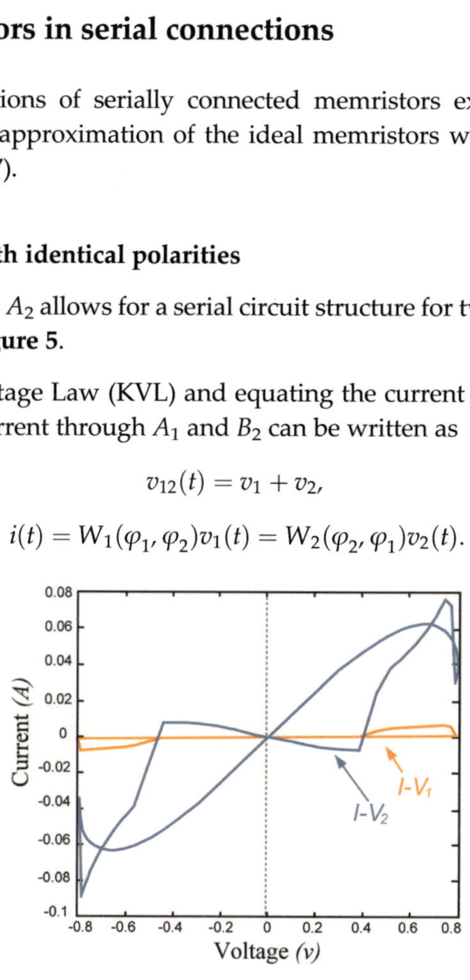

Figure 5. Memristors serially coupled with identical polarity configuration.

Integrating both sides of Eq. (9a) leads to Eq. (10a), and substituting Eq. (8) into Eq. (9b) leads to Eq. (10b),

$$\varphi_{12}(t) = \varphi_1 + \varphi_2 \tag{10a}$$

$$\begin{aligned} i &= v_1\left(\begin{cases} \alpha_1 + \kappa_2\varphi_2, & |\varphi_1| < |\varphi_t| \\ \beta_1 + \kappa_2\varphi_2, & |\varphi_t| < |\varphi_1| < |\varphi_{max}| \end{cases}\right) \\ &= v_2\left(\begin{cases} -\alpha_2 + \kappa_1\varphi_1, & |\varphi_1| < |\varphi_t| \\ -\beta_2 + \kappa_1\varphi_1, & |\varphi_t| < |\varphi_1| < |\varphi_{max}| \end{cases}\right) \end{aligned} \tag{10b}$$

From Eqs. (5), (9a) and (10), and by considering the special case of $\alpha_1 = \alpha_2 = \alpha$, $\beta_1 = \beta_2 = \beta$, $\kappa_1 = \kappa_2 = \alpha$, the following set of differential equations are obtained:

$$d\varphi_1/dt = v_{12}(1 + \varphi_1)/(2 + \varphi_{12}) \tag{11a}$$

$$d\varphi_2/dt = v_{12}(1 + \varphi_2)/(2 + \varphi_{12}) \tag{11b}$$

Eq. (11) reflects the complexity of memristive coupling: the derivatives of ϕ_1 and ϕ_2 are both functions of themselves and one another. If ϕ_1 changes due to an excitation voltage, a change in ϕ_2 is observed based on Eq. (11b). The change in ϕ_2 will affect ϕ_1 (independently of the initial excitation change), which goes back around to affect ϕ_2 and so on. The complex behaviors of memristive coupling are reflected in the way the flux variables are entangled in the solution of one another. Time dependence can therefore be eliminated in order to produce a solvable equation by substituting Eqs. (9a) and (10a) into Eq. (11), and dividing Eq. (11a) by Eq. (11b) (resp. Eq. (11b) by Eq. (11a)), which results in

$$d\varphi_1/d\varphi_2 = (1 + \varphi_2)/(1 + \varphi_1). \tag{12}$$

This can be analytically solved to give

$$\varphi_1(\varphi_2) = c_1\varphi_2 + c_1 - 1 \tag{13a}$$

$$\varphi_2(\varphi_1) = c_2\varphi_1 + c_2 - 1, \tag{13b}$$

where c_1 and c_2 are both constants calculable based on pre-determined initial conditions of ϕ_1 and ϕ_2. A number of cases are considered in order to ascertain a general rule for the values of c_1 and c_2 in terms of initial conditions. All of these cases can easily be created by simply biasing the relevant memristor with a rectangular voltage pulse over a given time in order to adjust the initial flux conditions. It is also worth noting that constants c_1 and c_2 can be changed at any time by switching off the driving voltage and re-biasing the memristor values. If it is assumed the flux

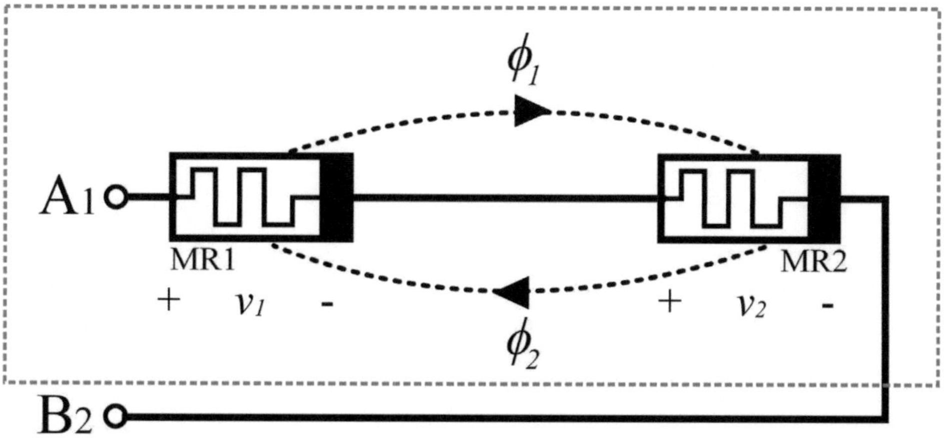

Figure 6. As initial condition u changes, c_1 produces a reciprocal curve and c_2 displays linear behavior.

state of MR1 from **Figure 5** is initially at $\phi_1 = 0$ while the flux in MR2 ϕ_2 is varied, a general rule regarding the relationship between c_1 and c_2 with initial condition of MR2 $\phi_2(\phi_1 = 0) = u$ is developed and graphed in **Figure 6**:

$$c_1 = {}^1\!/(1 + u) \tag{14a}$$

$$c_2 = u + 1 \tag{14b}$$

3.1.1. *Serial Case 1: parity at* $u = 0$, $u = -2$

Substituting $u = 0$ into Eq. (13b) results in the simple solution of $c_1 = c_2 = 1$, or $\phi_1(\phi_2) = \phi_2$ and $\phi_2(\phi_1) = \phi_1$. Substituting this into Eq. (10a) results in parity between the flux value of each memristor: $\phi_1 = \phi_2 = ½\phi_{12}$. Where $u = -2$, $c_1 = c_2 = -1$, $\phi_1(\phi_2) = \phi_2 - 2$ and $\phi_2(\phi_1) = \phi_1 - 2$.

3.1.2. *Serial Case 2:* $u = 0 \rightarrow \infty$, $u = -1 \rightarrow -\infty$

As u increases from 0, c_2 linearly approaches ∞, and $c_1 \rightarrow 1/\infty$. As an example, if $u = 1$, then the constants $c_1 = ½$, $c_2 = 2$, and $\phi_1(\phi_2) = ½\phi_2 - ½$, $\phi_2(\phi_1) = 2\phi_1 + 1$. By assuming the excitation voltage is a sinusoidal input, the peak-to-peak amplitude of flux across ϕ_1 is half of that in Serial Case 1, whereas ϕ_2 has quadrupled. A tug-of-war of sorts occurs between ϕ_1 and ϕ_2: as ϕ_2 increases, ϕ_1 decreases. Conversely, as u decreases from -2, $c_2 \rightarrow -\infty$, and $c_1 \rightarrow -1/\infty$.

3.1.3. *Serial Case 3:* $u = 0 \rightarrow -1$, $u = -2 \rightarrow -1$

This case behaves similarly to Case 2, but reversed. As u decreases from 0 towards -1, $c_1 \rightarrow \infty$. As u increases from -2 towards -1, $c_1 \rightarrow -\infty$. It is asymptotical at $u = -1$, while c_2 behaves linearly and passes through 0 at $u = -1$. The advantage of this case over Case 2 is that much less power is required to bias a memristor between these values in order to attain a flux value that approaches infinity. In other words, given a memristor without state boundary conditions, one can control it to behave like a regular resistor instead if so desired.

3.1.4. Serial Case 4: $u = -1$

Mathematically, there is no solution for c_1 as it approaches $\pm\infty$ (depending on which side it approaches in accordance with **Figure 6**). Hence, in theory, MR1 is never in equilibrium when the two memristors are serially flux coupled with identical polarities, where the initial flux value of MR2 is -1 and MR1 is 0. Eq. (13a) shows that as $c_1 \to \infty$, $\phi_1 \to \infty$. If this behavior is mapped against the given charge-flux relationship of the memristor characterized by **Figure 3**, the top segment of the memristor is a straight line. Therefore, after a sufficiently long time interval, ϕ_1 tends to the breakpoint and the memristor becomes equivalent to a resistor with a resistance of the inverse slope of the final segment (resp. where $c_1 \to -\infty$, $\phi_1 \to -\infty$ and the memristor becomes equivalent to a resister with the value of the inverse slope of the first segment of the q–ϕ curve).

The effect seen here with flux approaching an infinite value is identical to an ideal memristor being connected to a DC source. A constant non-periodic voltage source will also result in flux tending indefinitely towards $\pm\infty$, due to the integral relationship implied by Eq. (5c).

This result will not hold true for all ideal memristors [4]. If the memristor was defined by a polynomial $q - \phi$ curve, while $\phi \to \pm\infty$, $\frac{dq}{dt} = i(t) \to \pm\infty$. This implies that the memristor in question does not have a dc *V-I* curve, and in practice, the memristor would burn out long before the current became too large. This must also be considered in both Case 2 and Case 3, where current values can potentially go beyond the memristors capacity.

Given a sinusoidal voltage for v_{12} from Eq. (9a) in the general form of

$$v_{12} = A\sin(2\pi f t), \tag{15}$$

where A is the amplitude of v_{12}, both ϕ_1 and ϕ_2 will take on a sinusoidal form as well, and functions for memductance, voltage and flux can be found in terms of time, initial conditions and amplitude A—all of which can easily be predetermined.

For the sake of both attaining a meaningful solution and demonstration, flux is first determined as a function of time where the term from Eq. (15) ($2\pi f$) is assumed to be 1 rad. This simplification yields

$$\varphi_2(t) = -\gamma\cos(t) + u, \tag{16a}$$

where γ is the amplitude of ϕ_2, and if Eq. (16a) is substituted into Eq. (13a) results in

$$\varphi_1(t) = -c_1\gamma\cos(t) + (c_1 u + c_1 - 1). \tag{16b}$$

Substituting Eq. (16) into Eqs. (9a) and (5c) results in

http://dx.doi.org/10.5772/intechopen.69327

$$v_{12} = v_1 + v_2 = (\gamma + c_1\gamma)\sin(t) \tag{17}$$

Alternatively,

$$\gamma + c_1\gamma = A \tag{18}$$

And substituting Eqs. (14) and (18) into Eq. (16) gives

$$\varphi_1(t) = -A/(2+u)\cos(t) \tag{19a}$$

$$\varphi_2(t) = -A(1+u)/(2+u)\cos(t) + u \tag{19b}$$

The assumption used in deriving Eq. (14) was that the initial condition of MR1 was $\phi_1 = 0$, at which time $\phi_2 = u$. Consider when $t = \pi/2$ *s*: ϕ_1 is indeed 0, and ϕ_2 is reduced to the initial condition u.

To find memductances W_1 and W_2 after serial coupling Eq. (19) is substituted into Eq. (8) to give

$$W_1 = \begin{cases} \alpha_1 - \kappa_1\left((A(1+u))/(2+u)\cos(t) + u\right), & |\varphi_1| < |\varphi_t| \\ \beta_1 - \kappa_1\left((A(1+u))/(2+u)\cos(t) + u\right), & |\varphi_t| < |\varphi_1| < |\varphi_{max}| \end{cases} \tag{20a}$$

$$W_2 = \begin{cases} \alpha_2 - \kappa_2\left(A/(2+u)\cos(t)\right), & |\varphi_1| < |\varphi_t| \\ \beta_2 - \kappa_2\left(A/(2+u)\cos(t)\right), & |\varphi_t| < |\varphi_1| < |\varphi_{max}| \end{cases} \tag{20b}$$

The memductance (and by extension, current) can therefore be adjusted based on u. Biasing the initial state of MR2's flux for a desired value allows the two memristors to behave harmoniously like a pair of complementary variable switching resistors (while still maintaining the high-low voltage states of the single memristor represented in **Figure 4**).

When $u = 0$, and in the special case of $\alpha_1 = \alpha_2$, $\beta_1 = \beta_2$, and $\kappa_1 = \kappa_2$, Eq. (20) shows that $W_1 = W_2$ and $v_1 = v_2 = ½v_{12}$. As u increases from 0, W_1 increases and W_2 decreases. This is agreeable with Serial Case 2 of **Figure 6**: ϕ_2 increases and is the cause for coupling with MR1 which results in the increase of W_1 (resp. the decrease of ϕ_1 as u increases is the cause of the decrease in W_2). The same methodology applies for the other cases too.

While a memristor has a variable resistance by its very definition, this variation is limited by the value of $d\phi/dq$ according to the charge-flux curve. However, when two memristors have an additional parameter u which contributes to this variation, the two serially flux coupled memristors behave as variable memristors which can be adjusted based on Eq. (20).

Figure 7 represents memductances derived from Eq. (18) at $\kappa_1 = \kappa_2 = 0.02$, $\alpha_1 = \alpha_2 = 0.1$, $\beta_1 = \beta_2 = 0.01$, and as shown in Serial Case 1, when $u = 0$ the two memristors operate with identical flux values which leads to identical memductance values $W_1 = W_2 = W$. When the

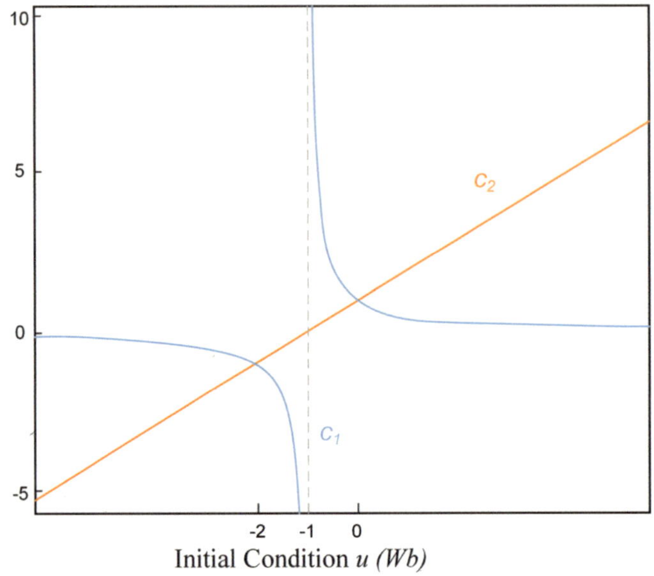

Figure 7. The memductance curve of serially coupled memristors, $u = 0$ for W, and $u = 0.02$ for W_1 and W_2.

initial condition of MR2 is changed to $u = 0.02$, the memductance of MR1 shifts upwards while the memductance of MR2 is approximately the same as W.

3.2. Serial connection with opposite polarities

Following a similar procedure to above where one of two memristors in **Figure 8** are flipped such that either terminals A_1 and A_2, or B_1 and B_2 are connected, as shown in **Figure 9**, applying KVL to Eqs. (5) and (8) yields

$$\begin{aligned} i = v_1 &\begin{cases} \alpha_1 - \kappa_2\varphi_2, & |\varphi_1| < |\varphi_t| \\ \beta_1 - \kappa_2\varphi_2, & |\varphi_t| < |\varphi_1| < |\varphi_{max}| \end{cases} \\ = v_2 &\begin{cases} -\alpha_2 + \kappa_1\varphi_1, & |\varphi_1| < |\varphi_t| \\ -\beta_2 + \kappa_1\varphi_1, & |\varphi_t| < |\varphi_1| < |\varphi_{max}| \end{cases} \end{aligned} \tag{21}$$

and substituting Eq. (5c) along with the same assumptions $\beta_1 = \beta_2 = \beta$, $\alpha_1 = \alpha_2 = \kappa_1 = \kappa_2 = \alpha$ into Eq. (21) results in the following differential equations

$$d\varphi_1/dt = -(1+\varphi_1)/(1-\varphi_2) \tag{22a}$$

$$d\varphi_2/dt = -(1-\varphi_2)/(1+\varphi_1), \tag{22b}$$

which solving simultaneously assuming initial conditions $\phi_1(t) = \phi_2(t) = \phi(0)$ results Eqs. (23a) and (23b), pictorially represented in **Figure 10**.

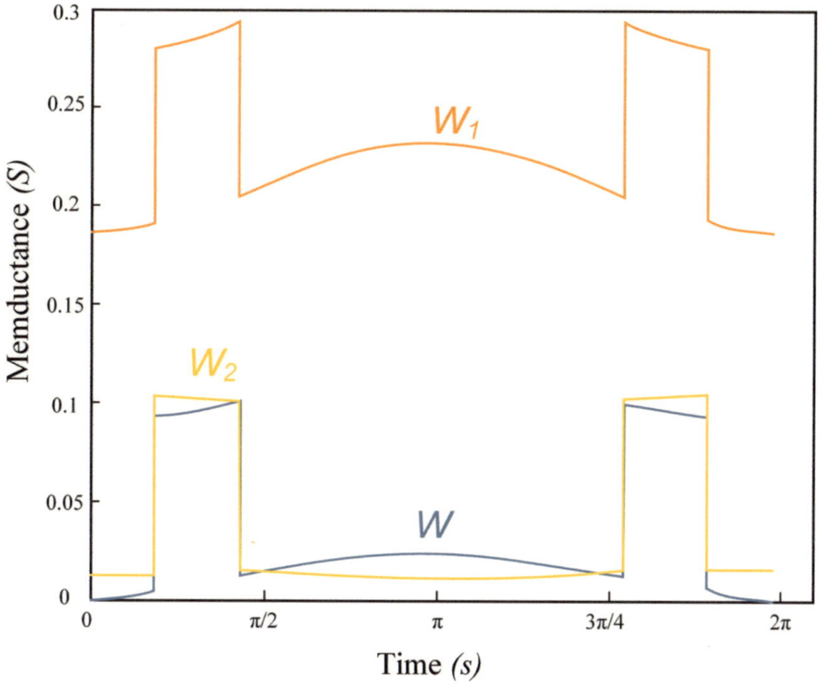

Figure 8. The *I-V* characteristic of two identical flux-coupled memristors shown in **Figure 2** denoted $I\text{-}V_2$ compared to the *I-V* characteristic of just one memristor $I\text{-}V_1$.

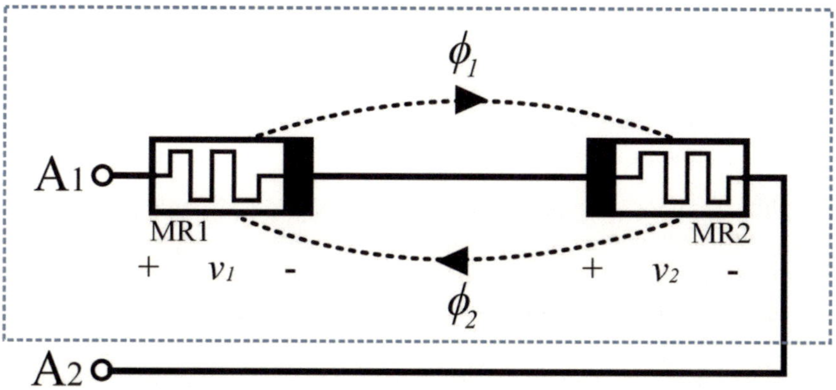

Figure 9. Memristors serially coupled with opposite polarity configuration.

$$\varphi_1 = \frac{1}{2}(-1 + e^{2t}), \tag{23a}$$

$$\varphi_2 = 1/2 - (e^{-2t})/2 \tag{23b}$$

Therefore, memductance of the individual memristor can be obtained by substituting Eq. (23) into Eq. (8), and assuming $\beta_1 = \beta_2 = \beta$, $\alpha_1 = \alpha_2 = \alpha$, $\kappa_1 = \kappa_2 = \kappa$.

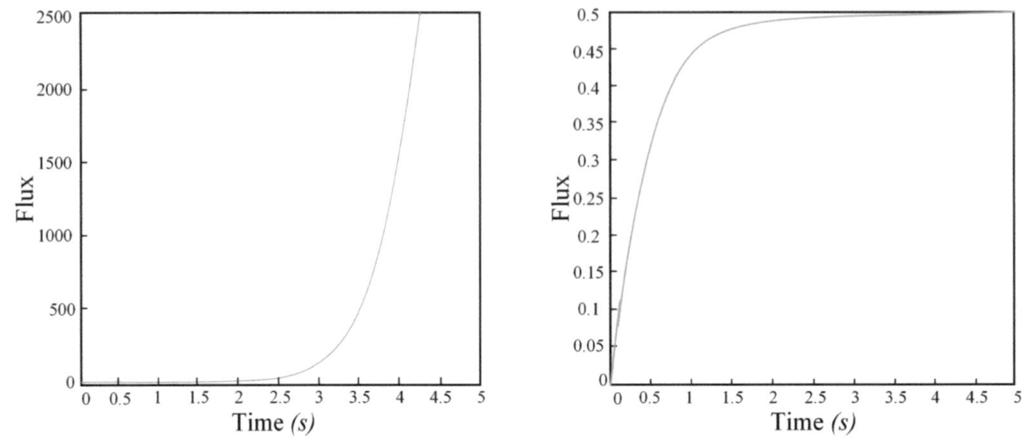

Figure 10. Flux variation with time in anti-serial connection: figure on left displaying $\phi_1(t)$ from Eq. (23a); figure on right figure showing $\phi_2(t)$ from Eq. (23b).

$$W_1(\varphi_1, t) = \begin{cases} \alpha + \kappa\left(\frac{1}{2} - \frac{e^{-2t}}{2}\right), & |\varphi_1| < |\varphi_t| \\ \beta + \kappa\left(\frac{1}{2} - \frac{e^{-2t}}{2}\right), & |\varphi_t| < |\varphi_1| < |\varphi_{max}| \end{cases} \tag{24a}$$

$$W_2(\varphi_2, t) = \begin{cases} \alpha + \frac{\kappa}{2}(-1 + e^{2t}), & |\varphi_2| < |\varphi_t| \\ \beta + \frac{\kappa}{2}(-1 + e^{2t}), & |\varphi_t| < |\varphi_2| < |\varphi_{max}|. \end{cases} \tag{24b}$$

In **Figure 10**, $\phi_1(t)$ never stops, but increases to $+\infty$. Hence, just as calculated in Serial Case 4 of 'Serial Connection with Identical Polarities', one of two ideal memristors can never be in equilibrium when coupled in anti-serial connection.

Once again, this behavior is mapped against the given charge-flux relationship of the switching memristor characterized by the shape of the curve in **Figure 3**. The first and final segments of the curve are theoretically non-ending straight lines, and thus, after a voltage pulse is applied for a sufficiently long time interval to increase flux far beyond the upper breakpoint $\phi_1 = 0.25$ (resp. a negative voltage pulse to decrease flux beyond the lower breakpoint $\phi_1 = -0.25$), the memristor becomes the equivalent of a resistor with the resistance value of the inverse slope of the final segment.

This behavior is considered comparatively against a single ideal memristor excited by a DC voltage. Suppose a battery with voltage *E volts* is connected across this memristor at $t = 0$. Where $E > 0$, $\phi(t)$ tends towards $+\infty$. Just as in the case of MR1 of the two anti-serially flux-coupled memristors, the DC-excited memristor is equivalent to a resistor with value of the inverse of the charge-flux slope.

Ignoring threshold switching effects, the memductance of MR1 reaches a steady state value while MR2 never achieves stability and instead tends towards a perfect conductor. However, these memristors will not display this behavior independently and so it is more practical to consider the two memristors as a single black box device. Equivalent memductance across A_1 and A_2 can be numerically obtained as $W_1W_2/(W_1+W_2)$ based on values of α, β and κ.

4. Coupled memristors in parallel connections

Two different configurations of parallel connected memristors exist according to polarity combinations, just as is the case with serially connected memristors. The same approximation of the ideal memristors will apply to this section in the same form as in Eq. (7). The first case to consider where memristors are configured with identical polarities is depicted in **Figure 11**.

4.1. Parallel connection with identical polarities

The current passing through A_1 and B_2 as well as flux ϕ_{12} can be derived from Kirchhoff's Current Law (KCL) and Eq. (8),

$$i = i_1 + i_2,\ \varphi_{12} = \varphi_1 + \varphi_2, \tag{25}$$

$$i = \begin{cases} v_1(\alpha_1 + \kappa_2\varphi_2) + v_2(\alpha_2 + \kappa_1\varphi_1),\ |\varphi_{12}| < |2\varphi_t| \\ v_1(\beta_1 + \kappa_2\varphi_2) + v_2(\beta_2 + \kappa_1\varphi_1), |2\varphi_t| < |\varphi_{12}| < |2\varphi_{max}| \end{cases} \tag{26}$$

Integration both sides of Eq. (24) yields

$$q = \begin{cases} (\alpha_1 + \alpha_2)\varphi_{12} + \frac{1}{2}(\kappa_1 + \kappa_2)\varphi_{12}^2,\ |\varphi_{12}| < |2\varphi_t| \\ (\beta_1 + \beta_2)\varphi_{12} + \frac{1}{2}(\kappa_1 + \kappa_2)\varphi_{12}^2,\ |2\varphi_t| < |\varphi_{12}| < |2\varphi_{max}| \end{cases} \tag{27}$$

Memductance can accordingly be calculated,

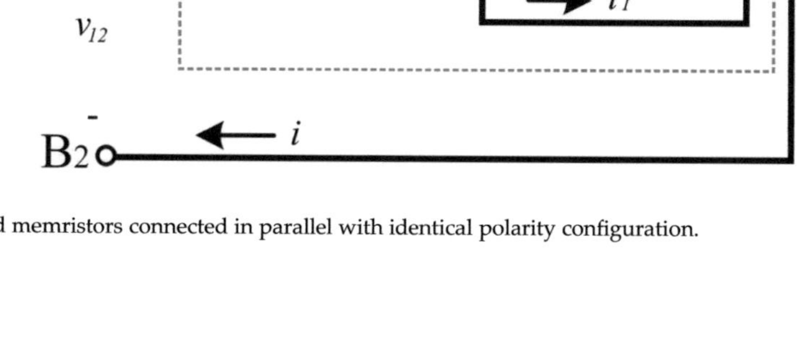

Figure 11. Coupled memristors connected in parallel with identical polarity configuration.

$$W_{12}(\varphi_{12}) = \frac{dq(\varphi_{12})}{d\varphi_{12}} = \begin{cases} (\kappa_1 + \kappa_2)\varphi_{12} + \alpha_1 + \alpha_2, & |\varphi_{12}| < |2\varphi_t| \\ (\kappa_1 + \kappa_2)\varphi_{12} + \beta_1 + \beta_2, & |2\varphi_t| < |\varphi_{12}| < |2\varphi_{max}| \end{cases} \quad (28)$$

In this case the variation between the memductance and flux ϕ_{12} is dependent on the total of the coupling coefficient values, $\kappa_1 + \kappa_2$. While the total coupling coefficient is positive, memductance is in positive proportion to the excitation flux: a higher flux will result in higher memductance. Conversely, when the total coupling coefficient is negative, the memductance will linearly decrease with the increase of flux. It can be clearly observed from Eq. (28) that flux coupled memristors in parallel connection behave as a new flux controlled memristor, with the equivalent memductance equivalent to the sum of the individual memductances.

4.2. Parallel connection with opposite polarities

A similar procedure can be used in order to ascertain the behavior of anti-parallel connected flux coupled memristors.

In the case shown in **Figure 12**, the current and flux across terminals A_1 and A_2 are also derived from KCL with the same relationship as in Eq. (25). When considered with respect to Eqs. (3) and (8), and using similar mathematical derivations to the previous sections the following result is obtained:

$$i(t) = \begin{cases} v_1(\alpha_1 - \kappa_2\varphi_2) + v_2(\alpha_2 + \kappa_1\varphi_1), & |\varphi_{12}| < |2\varphi_t| \\ v_1(\beta_1 - \kappa_2\varphi_2) + v_2(\beta_2 + \kappa_1\varphi_1), & |2\varphi_t| < |\varphi_{12}| < |2\varphi_{max}| \end{cases} \quad (29)$$

Integrating both sides of Eq. (29) results in a coupled charge-flux relationship as shown below,

$$q = \begin{cases} (\alpha_1 + \alpha_2)\varphi_{12} + \frac{1}{2}(\kappa_1 - \kappa_2)\varphi_{12}^2, & |\varphi_{12}| < |2\varphi_t| \\ (\beta_1 + \beta_2)\varphi_{12} + \frac{1}{2}(\kappa_1 - \kappa_2)\varphi_{12}^2, & |2\varphi_t| < |\varphi_{12}| < |2\varphi_{max}| \end{cases} \quad (30)$$

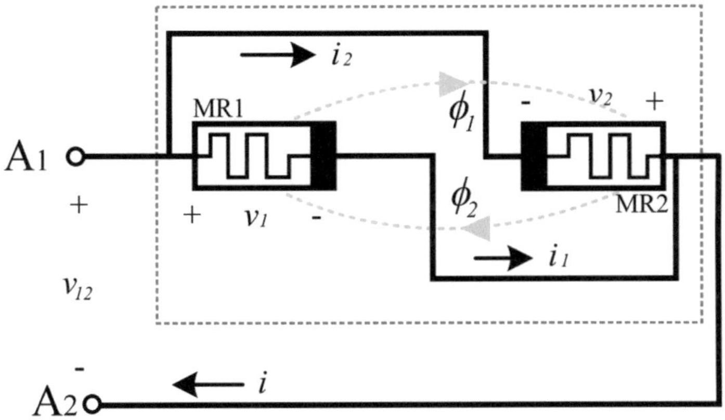

Figure 12. Coupled memristors connected in parallel with opposite polarity configuration.

Finally, substituting Eq. (30) into Eq. (4) gives the total memductance of the coupled memristors in parallel connection:

$$W_{12}(\varphi_{12}) = \frac{dq(\varphi_{12})}{d\varphi_{12}} = \begin{cases} (\kappa_1 - \kappa_2)\varphi_{12} + \alpha_1 + \alpha_2, & |\varphi_{12}| < |2\varphi_t| \\ (\kappa_1 - \kappa_2)\varphi_{12} + \beta_1 + \beta_2, & |2\varphi_t| < |\varphi_{12}| < |2\varphi_{max}| \end{cases} \tag{31}$$

For the uncoupled case of $\kappa_1 = \kappa_2 = 0$, the parallel memristors operate as a new memristor where the memductance states (α_1, α_2, β_1, β_2) are additive, and all contribute towards the total coupled memductance. This particular aspect of the relationship is common to both parallel connection combinations when polarity is changed. The difference between the two cases is in the effect of the coupling coefficient.

5. Conclusion

A comprehensive theoretical analysis of flux coupled memristors displays various kinds of new behaviour which are otherwise unattainable from a single memristor. The simplest case of coupling between two switching memristors is shown to have a diverse range of properties when memristors are acting in composite with each other. The results presented only consider bi-state memristors, and as such, we can expect different types of memristors with different charge-flux relationships to expand the types of dynamic behaviors exhibited, with the ability to modify the states attainable by tuning the variables associated with the coupling coefficient (such as physical proximity and device material just to name a couple of examples).

In summary, two serially connected memristors with identical polarities are shown to produce a pair of variable memristors determinable from initial conditions; two serially connected memristors with opposite polarities display behavior often displayed by memristors connected to DC sources, or otherwise resistive behavior. Parallel memristive systems are shown to produce a variation rate in terms of the coupling coefficients. This is a feature that can be determined at the time of fabrication.

Further, what has been considered in this paper is the simplest case of identical memristors with identical initial conditions. The potential application of coupled memristors, in addition to the undoubtedly interesting characteristics of arrays of coupled memristors will serve to open up new avenues of applications, and also provide for guidelines on avoiding undesirable behaviors by having fabrication plants devise methods to reduce the coupling coefficient as low as practicable where design specifications see it fit. In particular, where neural networks will see densely populated circuits which depend on memristors behaving functionally, the effects of coupling must either be mitigated to avoid unexpected and fallible outcomes. The alternative view is that memristive coupling makes it possible to have more than two states between a pair of memristors which would otherwise only be capable of being switched either on or off, and as such, if these intermediary states are quantized, then a large system of many varying states can be produced out of a mere two memristors connected compositely.

Acknowledgements

This work was supported by the Australia-Korea Foundation—Department of Foreign Affairs and Trade under the AKF00640 grant.

Author details

Jason Kamran Jr Eshraghian[1]*, Herbert H.C. Iu[2] and Kamran Eshraghian[3]

*Address all correspondence to: jeshraghian@gmail.com

1 Chungbuk National University, Cheongju, South Korea

2 University of Western Australia, Perth, Australia

3 iDataMap Corporation Pty Ltd, Adelaide, Australia

References

[1] Chua LO. Introduction to Nonlinear Network Theory. New York: McGraw-Hill; 1969

[2] Chua LO. Memristor: The missing circuit element. IEEE Transactions on Circuit Theory. 1971;**18**(5):507-519

[3] Strukov DB, Snider GS, Stewart DR and Williams RS. The missing memristor found. Nature. 2008;**453**:80-83. DOI: 10.1038/nature06932

[4] Chua LO. If it's pinched it's a memristor. Semiconductor Science and Technology. 2014;**29**(10):104001-1040042

[5] Sharifi MJ and Banadaki YM. General SPICE models for memristor and application to circuit simulation of memristor-based synapses and memory cells. Journal of Circuits, Systems and Computers. 2010;**19**(2):407-424

[6] Ho Y, Huang GM and Li P. Nonvolatile memristor memory: Device characteristics and design implications. In: IEEE/ACM International Conference on Computer-Aided Design, 2009; 2-5 Nov. 2009; 2009. pp. 485-490

[7] Yu DS, Iu HHC, Fitch AL and Liang Y. A floating memristor emulator based relaxation oscillator. IEEE Transactions on Circuits and Systems I: Regular Papers. 2014;**61**(10):2888-2896

[8] Budhathoki RK, Sah MP, Adhikari SP, Kim H and Chua LO. Composite behavior of multiple memristor circuits. IEEE Transactions on Circuits and Systems I: Regular Papers. 2013;**60**(10):2688-2700

[9] Mladenov V and Kirilov S. Analysis of the mutual inductive and capacitive connections and tolerances of memristors parameters of a memristor memory matrix. In: 2013 European Conference on Circuit Theory and Design (ECCTD); 8-12 Sept. 2013; 2013. pp. 1-4

[10] Prezioso M, Merrikh-Bayat F, Hoskins BD, Adam GC, Likharev KK, Strukov DB. Training and operation of an integrated neuromorphic network based on metal-oxide memristors. Nature. 2015;**521**:61-64. DOI: 10.1038/nature14441

[11] James AP, Fedorova I, Ibrayev T, Kudithipudi D. HTM spatial pooler with memristor crossbar circuits for sparse biometric recognition. IEEE Transactions on Biomedical Circuits and Systems. 2017;**11**(99):1-12. DOI: 10.1109/TBCAS.2016.2641983

[12] Adam GC, Hoskins BD, Prezioso M, Merrikh-Bayat F, Charkrabarti B, Strukov DB. 3-D memristor crossbars for analog and neuromorphic computing applications. IEEE Transactions on Electron Devices. 2017;**64**(1):312-318. DOI: 10.1109/TED.2016.2630925

[13] Truong SN, Pham KV, Yang W and Min KS. Sequential memristor crossbar for neuromorphic pattern recognition. IEEE Transactions on Nanotechnology. 2016;**15**(6): 922-930. DOI: 10.1109/TNANO.2016.2611008

[14] Yakopcic C, Alom MZ and Taha TM. Memristor crossbar deep network implementation based on a Convolutional neural network. In: 2016 International Joint Conference on Neural Networks (IJCNN); 24-29 July 2016; Vancouver, BC, Canada. IEEE; 2016. DOI: 10.1109/IJCNN.2016.7727302

[15] Cai W and Tetzlaff R. Beyond series and parallel: Coupling as a third relation in memristive systems. In: 2014 IEEE International Symposium on Circuits and Systems (ISCAS); 1-5 June 2014; 2014. pp. 1259-1262

[16] Yu DS, Iu HHC, Liang Y, Fernando T and Chua LO. Dynamic behavior of coupled memristor circuits. IEEE Transactions on Circuits and Systems I: Regular Papers. 2015;**62** (6):1607-1616

[17] Yu DS, Liang Y, Iu HHC, Chua LO. A universal mutator for transformations among memristor, memcapacitor and meminductor. IEEE Transactions on Circuits and Systems II: Express Briefs. 2014;**61**(10):758-762

[18] Eshraghian JK, Iu HHC, Fernando T, Yu DS, Li Z. Modelling and characterization of dynamic behavior of coupled memristor circuits. In: 2016 IEEE International Symposium on Circuits and Systems (ISCAS); 22-25 May 2016; 2016. pp. 690-693. DOI: 10.1109/ISCAS.2016.7527334

[19] Chua LO. Resistance switching memories are memristors. Applied Physics A. 2011;**102** (4):765-783. DOI: 10.1007/s00339-011-6264-9

Chapter 9

Mathematical Modeling of Memristors

Yasin Oğuz

Additional information is available at the end of the chapter

http://dx.doi.org/10.5772/intechopen.73921

Abstract

The memristor has quite a reputation as a missing circuit element. It is a powerful candidate for next-generation applications after being first implemented in HP's laboratories. At this point, mathematical models were needed for the analysis of the memristor, and a lot of studies were done on this subject. In this chapter, mathematical modeling and simulations of the memristor device have been emphasized. Firstly, linear drift and nonlinear drift models have been described on the basic HP model. The window functions used in the nonlinear drift model have been widely examined. Different from HP model, the Simmons tunnel barrier and the threshold adaptive memristor model (TEAM) have been also mentioned. As a result, the most widely used modeling techniques have been described in detail.

Keywords: memristor modeling, HP model, linear drift model, nonlinear drift model, window functions, exponential model, Simmons tunnel barrier model, TEAM

1. Introduction

In the circuit theory, it refers to the existence of three basic circuit elements that define connections between basic circuit parameters such as current (i), voltage (v), charge (q), and magnetic flux (φ). These are resistor, inductor, and capacitor. However, a circuit element that determines the relationship between the charge and the magnetic flux is not defined. The fourth fundamental circuit element representing this relation was firstly presented by Chua in mathematical terms in 1971 with the name of the memristor (memory + resistor) [1]. In 2008, a group of researcher from HP laboratories announced that they were physically producing memristor [2]. In **Figure 1**, the relationship between fundamental circuit elements and basic circuit parameters is shown.

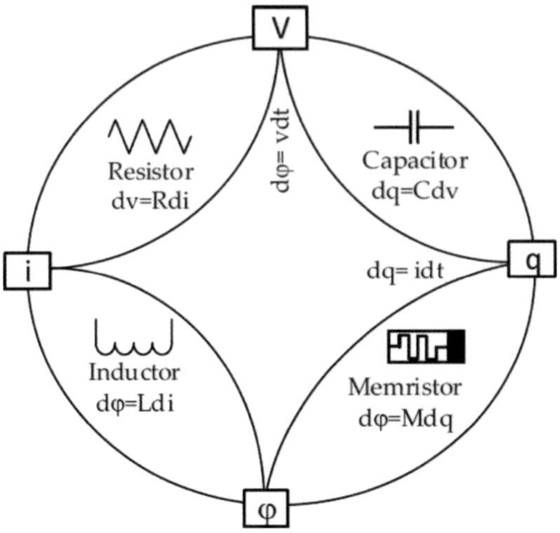

Figure 1. Linkage between four fundamental circuit elements and basic circuit parameters such as current (i), voltage (v), charge (q), and magnetic flux (φ).

The relationship between current, voltage, charge, and flux for the memristor is given by:

$$v(t) = M\big(q(t)\big)\, i(t) \tag{1}$$

$$M(q) = d\varphi(q)/dq \tag{2}$$

$$i(t) = W(\varphi(t))\, v(t) \tag{3}$$

$$W(\varphi) = dq(\varphi)/d\varphi \tag{4}$$

where M(q) has the unity of resistance and W(φ) has the unity of conductance [1].

Memristor has properties that are different from other fundamental circuit elements and can only be seen in a memristor such as nonvolatile memory effect, passivity, and pinched hysteresis loop.

When Eqs. (1) and (2) are opened, Eqs. (5) and (6) can be written as follows:

$$v(t) = M\left(\int_{-\infty}^{t} i(t)dt\right) i(t) \tag{5}$$

$$i(t) = W\left(\int_{-\infty}^{t} v(t)dt\right) v(t) \tag{6}$$

Eqs. (5) and (6) show that the memristance value is related to the history of the current passing through the memristor. That is, when the current passing through the memristor is cut off, it remains at the value of the memristance value. The memristance value starts to change from the last value when it provides the current again to memristor. In other words, the memristor has a nonvolatile memory effect. On the other hand, memristor is not an element that stores energy [3, 4].

Memristor is similar to resistor with memory. It shows a nonlinear resistance characteristic that the charge parameter is state variable [5].

Another distinguishing feature of the memristor is that the I-V change shows the pinched hysteresis loop characteristic. A memristor fed by a bipolar periodic signal always exhibits a pinched hysteresis I-V characteristic that passes through the origin. As the frequency of the excitation signal increases, the hysteresis lobe area decreases monotonically. When the frequency tends to infinity, the pinched hysteresis loop shrinks toward a single-valued function [6, 7].

The memristor, with being a passive circuit element, has a unique ability to remember the state of resistance that it possesses by maintaining the relationship between voltage and current time integrals. Due to these features, they are being nominated for many different applications such as resistive memories, soft computing, neurocomputing, etc.

Different materials and techniques are used at the point of producing the memristor. The memristor structures produced from different materials can be given as example, such as titanium dioxide (TiO_2) memristor [2], zinc oxide memristor [8, 9], silicon oxide memristor [10], and GST ($Ge_2Sb_2Te_5$) memristor [11].

2. Modeling of memristor

2.1. HP memristor model

Memristor-based applications require a suitable model for analysis and simulation of the system. When looking at the literature, the HP memristor model where the memristor mechanism based on the drift of oxygen vacancies is widely used. The memristor model developed by HP Lab is composed of $Pt/TiO_2/Pt$ structure as shown in **Figure 2**. Here, the TiO_2 layer in which the one side doped with positive charged-rich oxygen vacancies (TiO_{2-x}) is placed between two platinum layers [2].

The doped part of the TiO_2 layer exhibits a low resistance behavior, while the undoped part exhibits a high resistance behavior. As a result of the appropriate excitation on this structure,

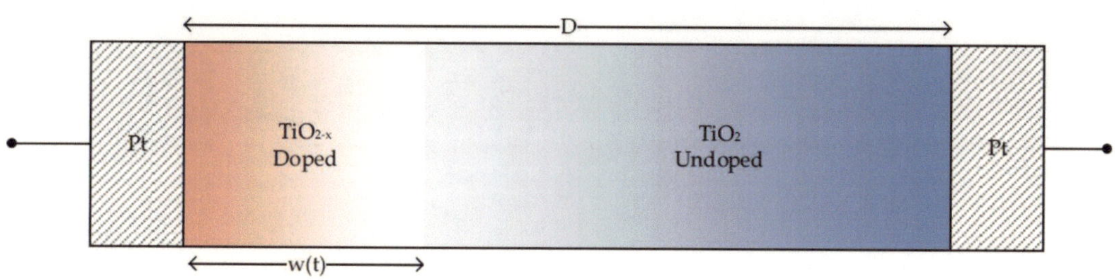

Figure 2. Structure of memristor reported by HP Lab [2].

the ionic drift between the doped part and the undoped part results in a dynamic change in the width of the doped region. That is, the width of the doped region is taken as a state variable. As the width of the doped region approaches zero ($w \rightarrow 0$), the memristor goes to a high resistance state (HRS), and as the width of the doped region approaches D ($w \rightarrow D$), the memristor goes to a low resistance state (LRS) as shown in **Figure 3** [3].

Since the memristor's dimensions are very small (in few nm), it causes a change in the doped region even with a small stimulation applied. Thus the resistance of the memristor varies between HRS and LRS [3].

2.2. Linear drift model

In the model known as the linear drift model, the relation between the current and the voltage of the memristor is defined by the following equation:

$$v(t) = [R_{on}x(t) + R_{off}(1 - x(t))]\,i(t) \tag{7}$$

$$x(t) = \frac{w(t)}{D} \qquad \in (0,1) \tag{8}$$

where R_{on} and R_{off} are the values of the resistance for $w(t) = D$ and $w(t) = 0$, respectively [2, 8, 9].

From Eq. (7), the value of memristance can be expressed by

$$M(q(t)) = \frac{v(t)}{i(t)} = R_{on}x(t) + R_{off}(1 - x(t)) \tag{9}$$

As shown in **Figure 3**, the state of change of the memristor resistance is represented by x(t) value in Eq. (8). The speed of movement of the boundary between the doped layer and undoped layer is expressed as dx/dt with Eq. (10) [12, 13]:

$$\frac{dx(t)}{dt} = \mu_v \frac{R_{on}}{D^2} i(t) \tag{10}$$

where μ_v is the average drift mobility of the charges. If Eq. (10) is taken integral for time, the following expression is derived:

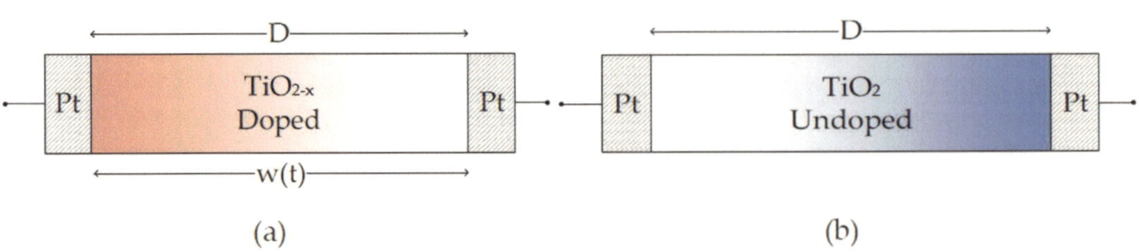

Figure 3. Representation of the HRS and LRS states of the memristor. (a) LRS and (b) HRS.

$$x(t) = \mu_v \frac{R_{on}}{D^2} q(t) \tag{11}$$

If Eq. (11) is put in its place in Eq. (9), the following memristance expression is achieved:

$$M(q(t)) = R_{on}\mu_v \frac{R_{on}}{D^2} q(t) + R_{off}\left(1 - \mu_v \frac{R_{on}}{D^2} q(t)\right) \tag{12}$$

This expression can be written as

$$M(q(t)) = R_{off}\left(1 - \mu_v \frac{R_{on}}{D^2} q(t)\right) \tag{13}$$

if the left side of the total expression is neglected because $R_{on} << R_{off}$ [2].

Through this model, the characteristics of the memristor can be observed by the simulations as shown in the ongoing part. The following values are used for the simulations performed in this section. $\mu_v = 10^{-14}\ m^2 s^{-1}\ V^{-1}$, D = 10 nm, initial value of w is 3 nm, input signal $V_{input} = V_o.\sin(\omega t)$ where $V_o = 1$ V and f = 1 Hz ($\omega = 2\pi f$), $R_{on} = 100\ \Omega$, and $R_{off} = 160\ k\Omega$. **Figure 4** shows the change of the current and voltage of the memristor with time for the given parameter values. The pinched hysteresis loop in the I-V plane shown in **Figure 5** is one of the fingerprint characteristics of the memristor. **Figure 6** shows the relationship between state variable and memristance. This indicates that the memristance depends on the state variable x. This figure also shows that the state variable is limited between 0 and 1. In **Figure 7**, the change of memristance with applied voltage is seen.

As shown in **Figure 8**, as the frequency increases, the I-V pinched hysteresis loops become narrower. As the frequency increases toward infinity, the I-V characteristic seems to be a linear resistance characteristic. **Figure 9** shows the variation of the I-V characteristic for different amplitude values of the excitation signal.

2.3. Nonlinear drift model and window functions

The linear drift model supposes that the state variable (x) of the memristor is proportional to the charge flowing through the memristor. This proportion is acceptable to the interface between the electrodes and the interface between the doped and undoped parts of the memristor. The position of the doped part changes with the applied input signal. Furthermore, the linear drift model assumes that the vacancies have the freedom to move along the all length of the memristor. These assumptions made in the HP model have been greatly simplified, neglecting some basic laws. The reported literature shows that the drift of vacancies is not linear in the region near the boundary interfaces. The reason is that even a small excitation signal can create a large electric field causing nonlinear drift of the vacancies near the boundary interfaces in the memristor. Another problematic situation related to the linear drift model is that the state variable (x) never reaches zero, indicating that oxygen vacancies are not

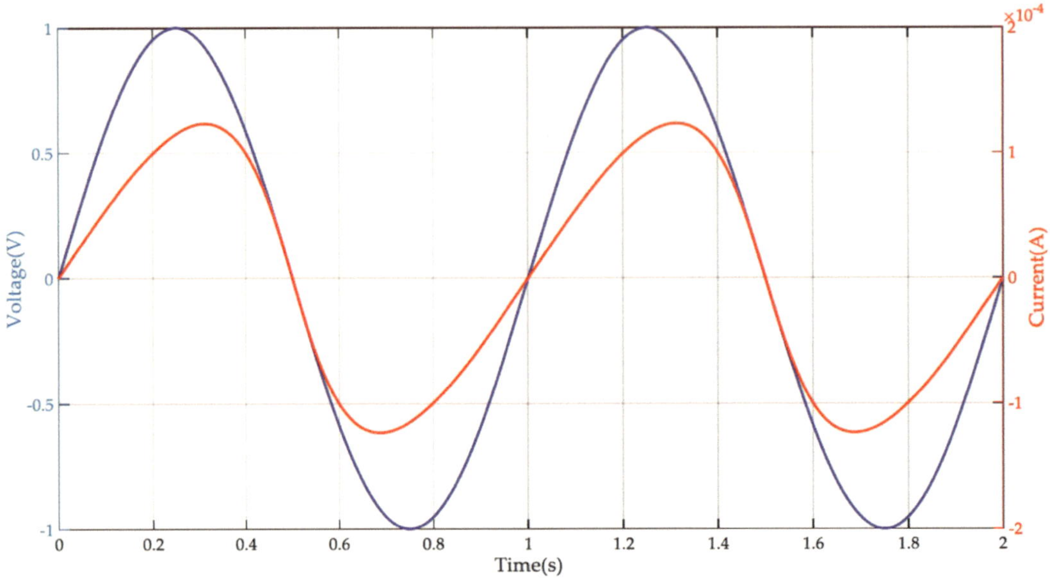

Figure 4. Change of the current and voltage of the memristor with respect to time.

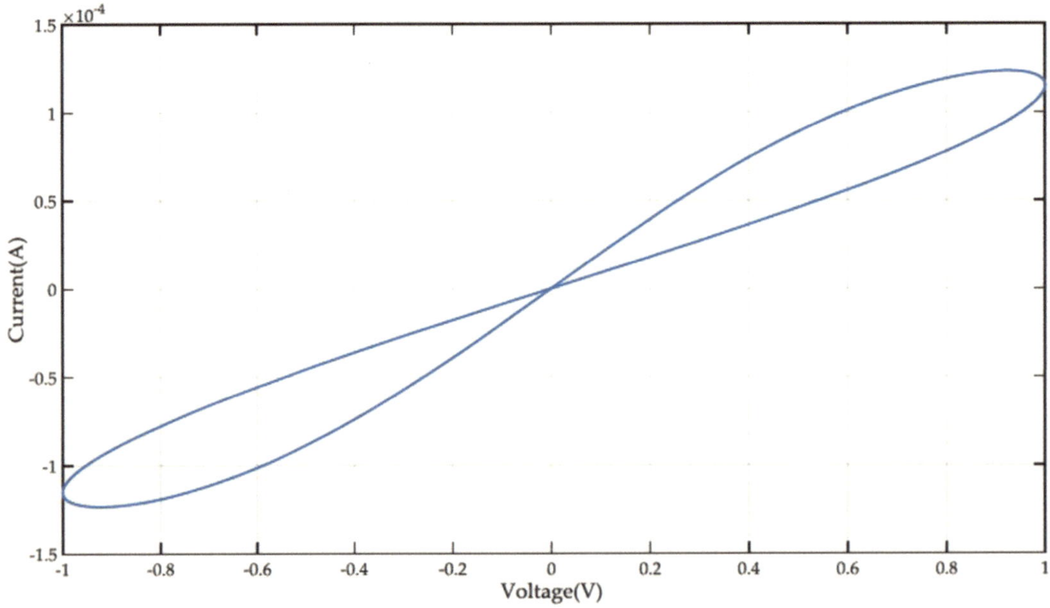

Figure 5. I-V pinched hysteresis loop of the memristor.

present in the memristor. Similarly, the doped region cannot cover the entire length of the memristor, because there will be no undoped part and the memristor will not work in this way [3, 14, 15].

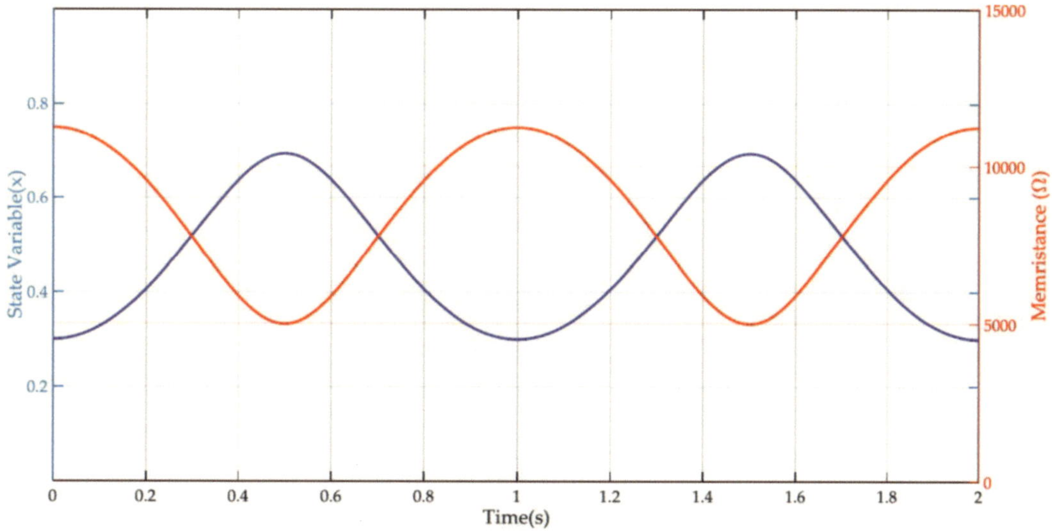

Figure 6. Change of the state variable and memristance of the memristor with respect to time.

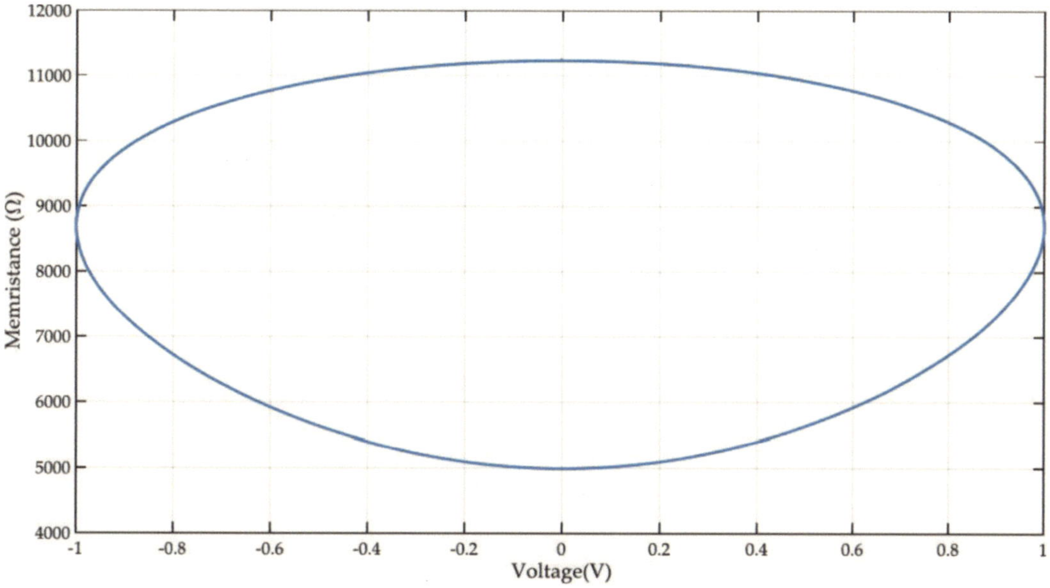

Figure 7. Change of the memristance of the memristor with respect to voltage.

In order to provide nonlinearity for the boundary problems mentioned above, functions called window function are introduced. This function is implemented by rearranging the expression Eq. (10) as

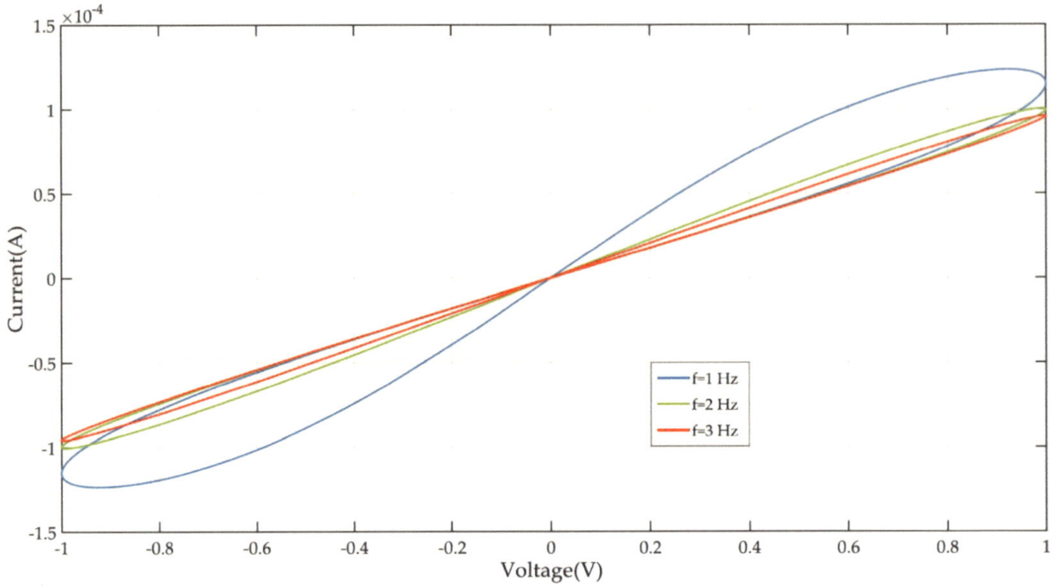

Figure 8. I-V pinched hysteresis loops of the memristor for Vo = 1 V and different frequency values.

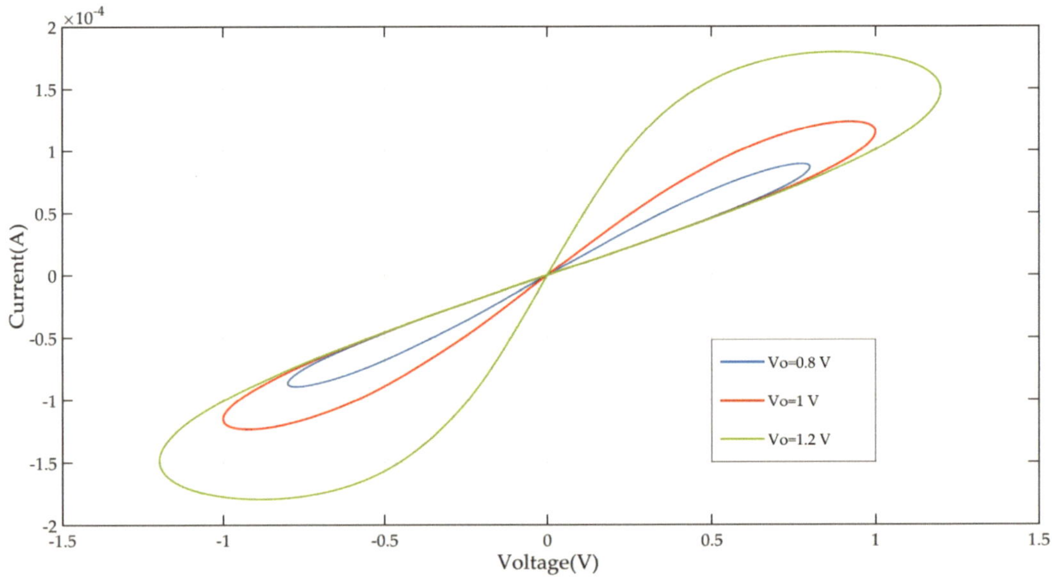

Figure 9. I-V pinched hysteresis loops of the memristor for f = 1 Hz and different V_o values.

$$\frac{dx(t)}{dt} = \mu_v \frac{R_{on}}{D^2} i(t) f(x(t)) \tag{14}$$

The function f(x) should have zero at the limits of the memristor (x = 0 and x = 1) and maximum value at the middle of the memristor (x = 0.5) [11]. An effective window function should satisfy the following conditions for modeling of nonlinearity [16]:

- The function should take account of the boundary situation at the top and bottom electrodes of the memristor.
- The function should provide nonlinear drift across the entire active area of the memristor.
- The function should ensure linkage between the linear and nonlinear drift models.
- The function should be scalable in the interval of $f_{max}(x)$ can be obtained such that $0 \leq f_{max}(x) \leq 1$.
- The function should include the control parameter to set the model.

Many different window functions are proposed as a result of the studies carried out in order to provide these criteria.

2.3.1. *Joglekar's window function*

Joglekar's window function can be given as

$$f(x) = 1 - (2x - 1)^{2p} \tag{15}$$

where p is the control parameter which changes the flatness of the *f(x)* curve around its maximum value at $x = 0.5$ and is a positive integer [17].

In **Figure 10**, the change of window function proposed by Joglekar for different p values is shown. The characteristic of this function is similar to the rectangular window function by increasing p value, and the nonlinear drift effect is reduced. The disadvantage of Joglekar's window function is the cling situation of the state variable at the boundaries, and it is difficult to change the window function due to the zero value at both boundaries. That is, the nonlinear drift problem is solved, but the boundary lock is not taken into account. When memristor arrives in R_{on} or R_{off} terminal condition, this state will be maintained forever due to zero value taken from the window function [13, 14].

2.3.2. *Biolek's window function*

Biolek has introduced a window function that provides a solution for model errors (the cling situation of the state variable at the boundaries) of Joglekar's window function. Biolek's window function is expressed as follows:

$$f(x) = 1 - \left(x - stp(-i)\right)^{2p} \tag{16}$$

$$stp(i) = \begin{cases} 1, & i \geq 0 \\ 0, & i < 0 \end{cases} \tag{17}$$

where p is positive integer and i is the memristor current [18].

Figure 11 shows the variation of the window function proposed by Biolek for different p values. The proposed window function by Biolek depends not only on the state variable but

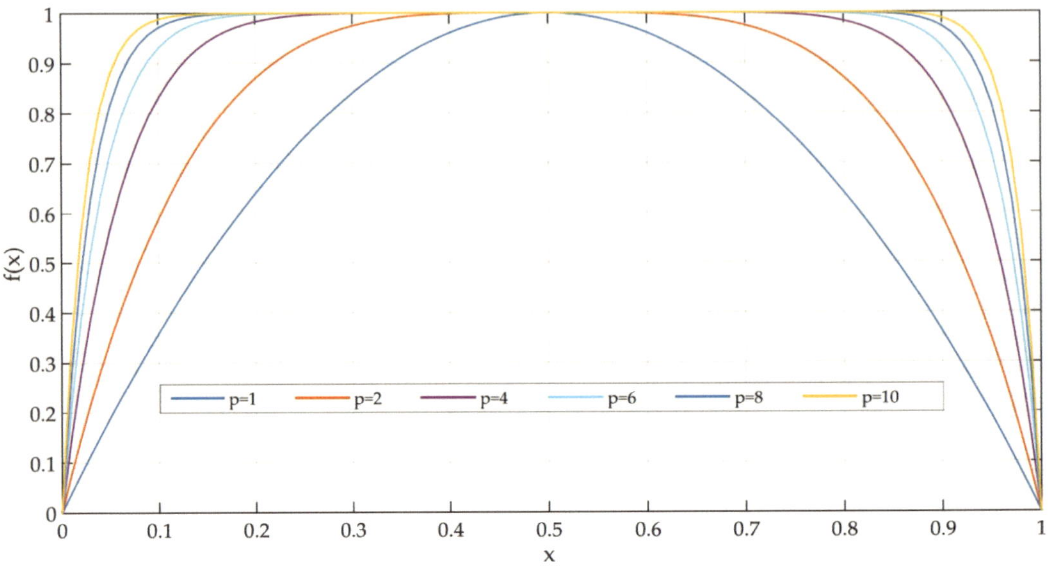

Figure 10. Joglekar window function for different p values.

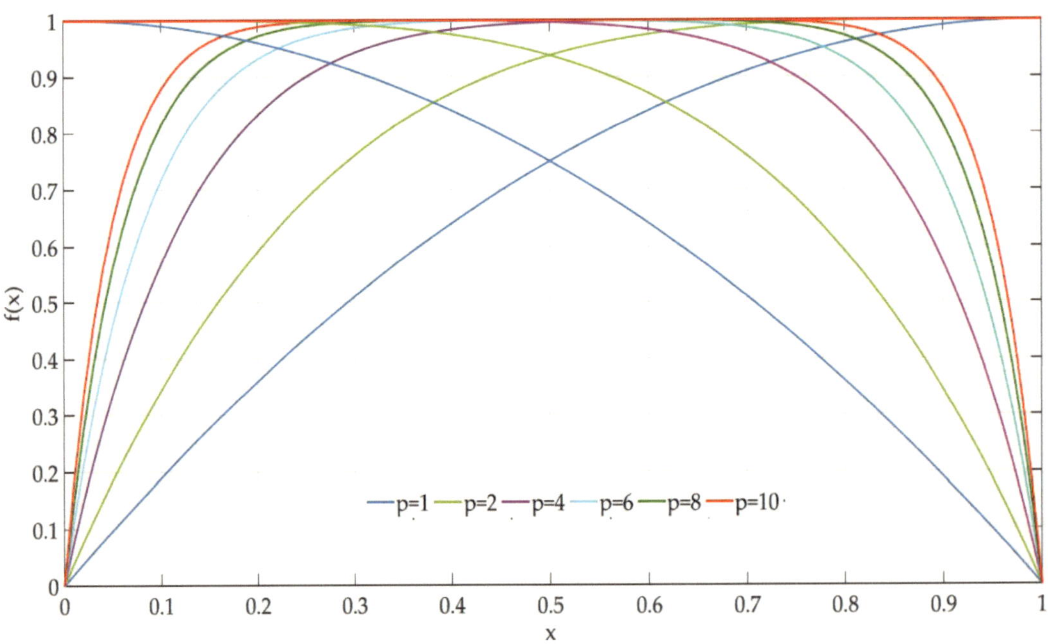

Figure 11. Biolek's window function for different p values.

also on the current flow through the memristor. Thus, the problem of boundary lock is resolved. However, this window function does not include the scalability factor, so the maximum value of the window function cannot be set to a lower or greater value [13].

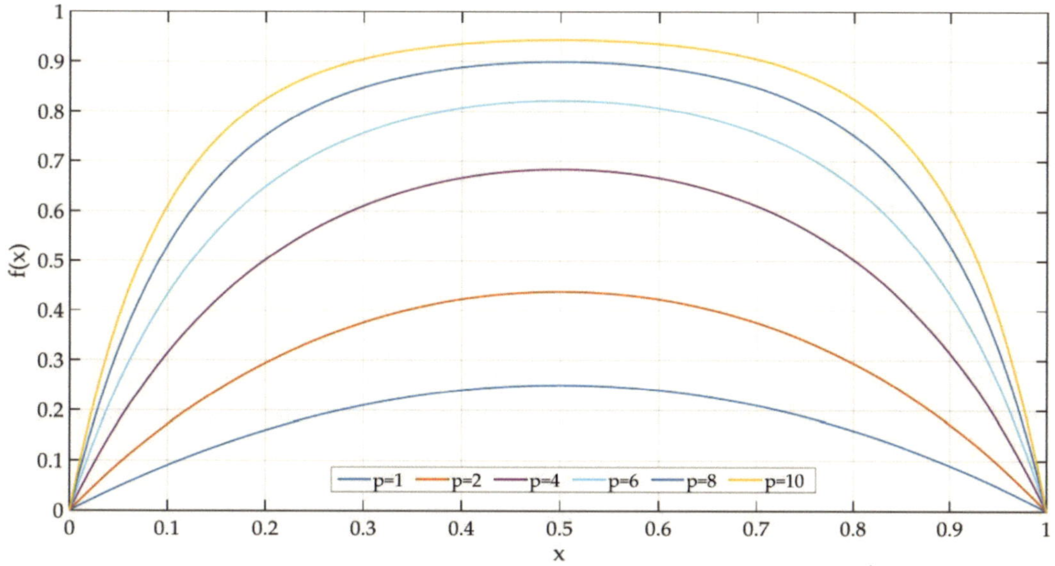

Figure 12. Prodromakis' window function for j = 1 and different p values.

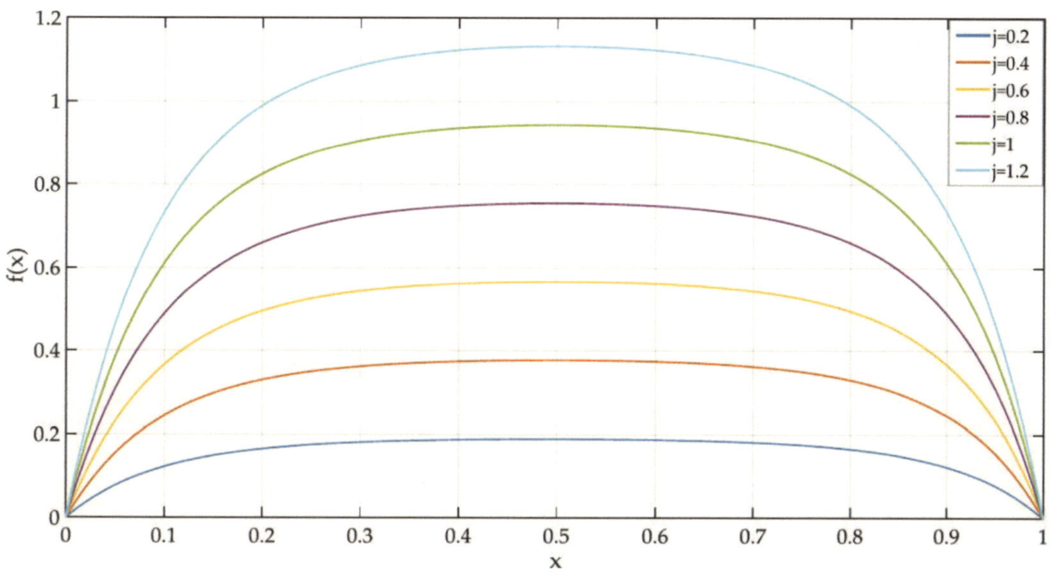

Figure 13. Prodromakis' window function for p = 10 and different j values.

2.3.3. Prodromakis' window function

Prodromakis' window function is

$$f(x) = j\left(1 - \left[(x - 0.5)^2 + 0.75\right]^p\right) \tag{18}$$

where p and j are a positive real number [16]. In **Figure 12**, the change of Prodromakis' window function for j = 1 and different p values is shown. **Figure 13** shows the variation of the Prodromakis' window function for p = 10 and different j values.

Prodromakis proposes a solution for the scalability problem in the aforementioned by the presented window function. Prodromakis' window function provides a connection to the linear dopant drift model for sufficiently large values of p. However, the model built by Prodromakis still contains the problem of boundary lock [13].

2.3.4. *Zha's window function*

This function has been introduced by Zha as a new window model so that boundary lock, scalability, and nonlinear effects can be met at the same time. Zha's window function is expressed as follows:

$$f(x) = j\left(1 - \left[0.25\left(x - stp(-i)\right)^2 + 0.75\right]^p\right) \tag{19}$$

where stp(*i*) is given in Eq. (17) and p and j are positive real numbers [13]. Zha's window function for j = 1 and different p values in **Figure 14** is shown. **Figure 15** shows the Zha's window function for p = 10 and different j values.

2.3.5. *Comparison of window functions*

In this section, the simulation results have been given over the nonlinear drift model of the window functions given in the previous sections. **Figure 16** shows the change of window

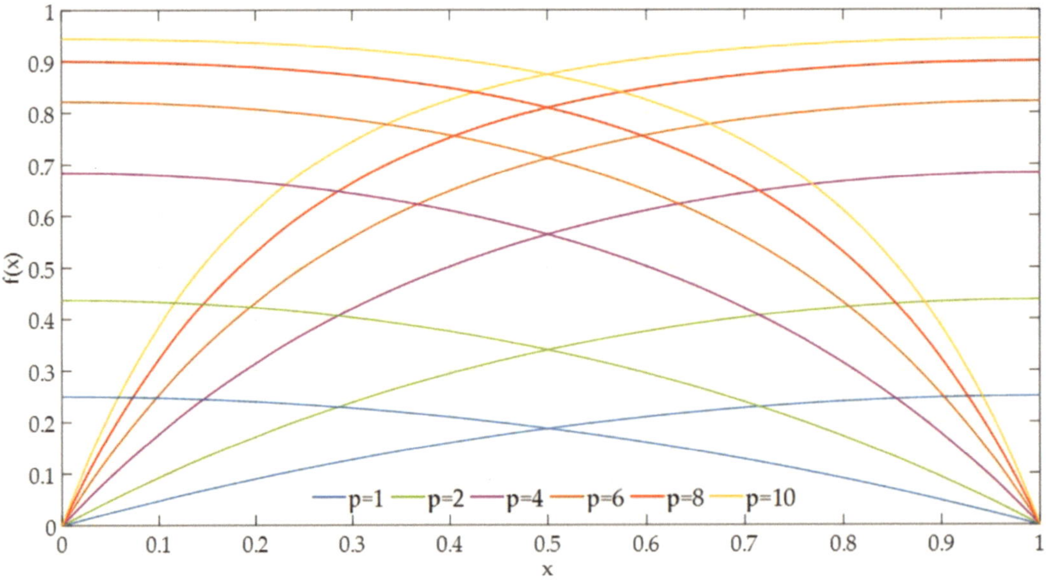

Figure 14. Zha's window function for j = 1 and different p values.

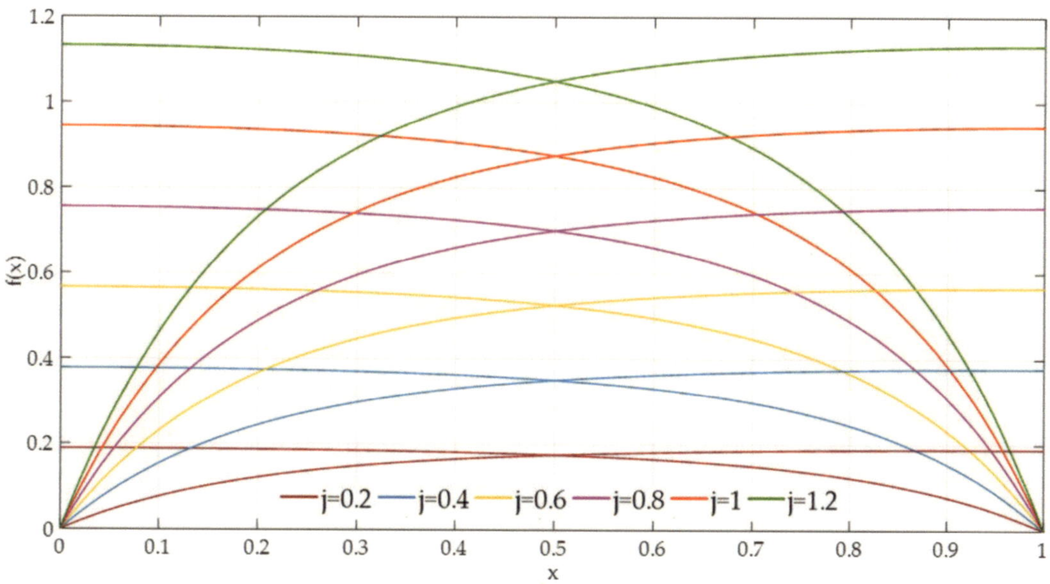

Figure 15. Zha's window function for p = 10 and different j values.

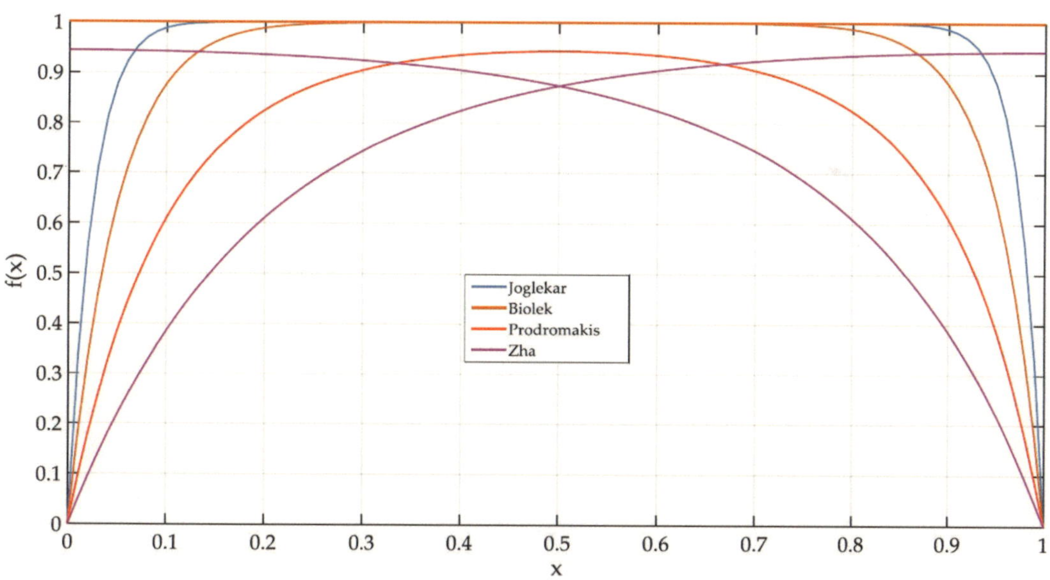

Figure 16. Different window functions for p = 10 and j = 1.

functions according to state variable x for p = 10 and j = 1 values. In **Figure 17**, I-V characteristics have been plotted for the window functions in **Figure 16**. In **Figure 18**, the change of the memristance of the memristor with the applied voltage for the window functions of **Figure 16** has been presented. For simulations using these window functions, $\mu_v = 10^{-14}$ m^2s^{-1} V^{-1}, D = 10 nm, initial value of w is 3.145 nm, input signal $V_{input} = V_o.\sin(\omega t)$ where V_o = 1.2 V and f = 1 Hz ($\omega = 2\pi f$), R_{on} = 100 Ω, and R_{off} = 160 kΩ.

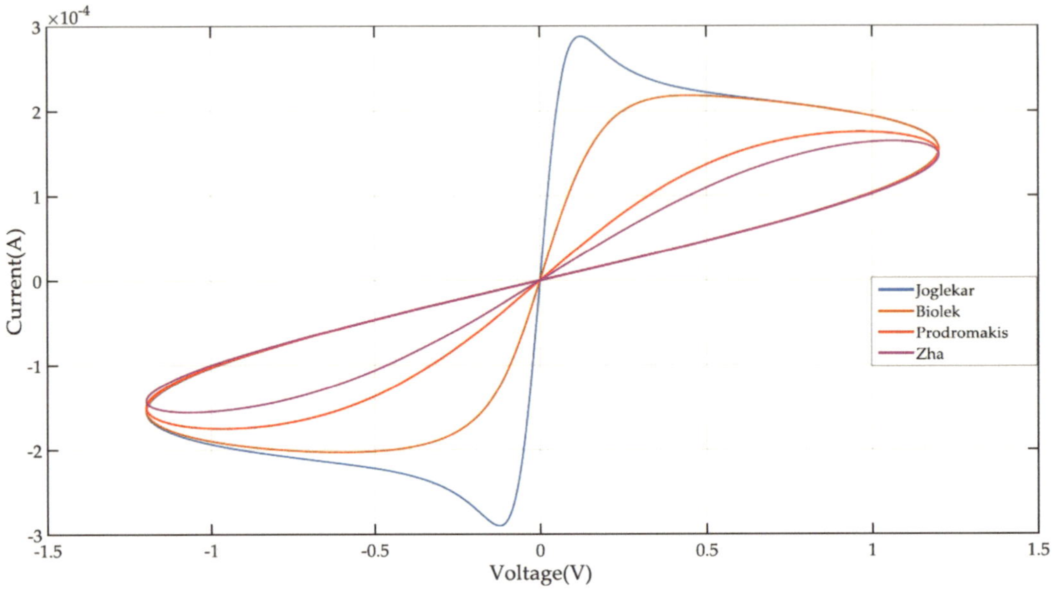

Figure 17. Change of I-V pinched hysteresis loops of the memristor for different window functions.

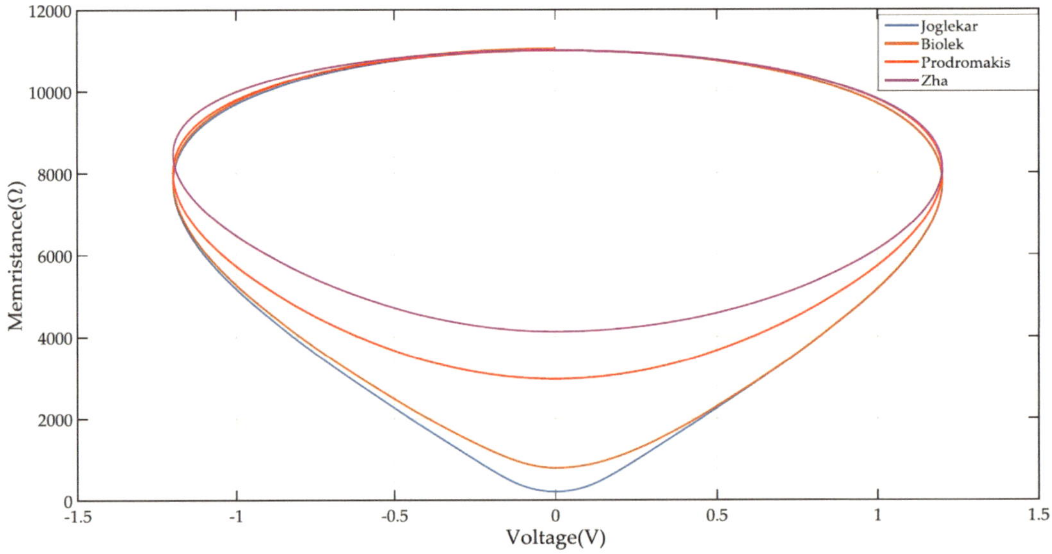

Figure 18. Change of the memristance of the memristor with respect to voltage for different window functions.

2.4. Exponential model

Even in the models described so far, the nonlinearity of the large electric field in the memristor is still not taken into consideration. In [19], an exponential model that accounts the effect has been presented. In this model, the relation between the current of the memristor and the voltage is defined as follows:

$$i = x(t)^n \beta \sinh(\alpha\, v(t)) + \chi\left(\exp(\gamma\, v(t)) - 1\right) \tag{20}$$

where β, α, χ, and γ are experimental fitting parameters. How the state variable can influence the current is determined by the n parameter [12, 19]. According to Eq. (20), when the model is ON state, asymmetrical switching behavior is shown (sinh part). When the OFF state, the exponential part of the Eq. (20) has the dominant part of the current, which is similar to an ideal PN junction [12, 14].

In this model, the differential equation of state variable is written as

$$\frac{dx(t)}{dt} = a \cdot v(t)^m f(x) \tag{21}$$

where a and m are fitting parameters. f(x) can be any window function [14].

2.5. Simmons tunnel barrier model

The models described so far were based on the HP model, which consisted of two regions, each of which was modeled as resistance. But Pickett presented another physical model of the memristor as an alternative to the HP model, consisting of a resistor and an electron tunnel barrier in series [20].

Figure 19 shows the memristor structure of the Simmons tunnel barrier model where w is the tunneling barrier and R_s is the channel resistance.

w is the state variable of the model and can be written as

$$\frac{dw(t)}{dt} = \begin{cases} f_{off}\sinh\left(\frac{i}{i_{off}}\right)\exp\left[-\exp\left(\frac{w - a_{off}}{w_c} - \frac{|i|}{b}\right) - \frac{w}{w_c}\right], & i > 0 \\ f_{on}\sinh\left(\frac{i}{i_{on}}\right)\exp\left[-\exp\left(\frac{w - a_{on}}{w_c} - \frac{|i|}{b}\right) - \frac{w}{w_c}\right], & i < 0 \end{cases} \tag{22}$$

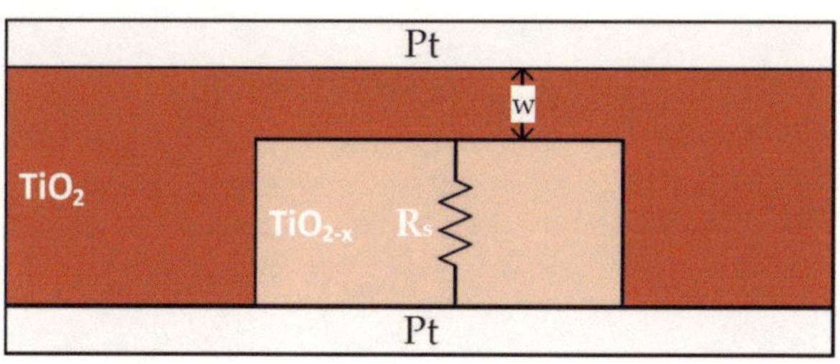

Figure 19. Memristor structure of Simmons tunnel barrier model.

where f_{off}, f_{on}, a_{off}, a_{on}, i_{off}, i_{on}, and b are fitting parameters [20]. The f_{on} value has an amplitude order greater than f_{off}. It is also effective in changing w in both parameters. The i_{on} and i_{off} parameters effectively limit the current threshold. In this model, a window function is not required, because a_{off} and a_{on} values force upper and lower bounds of x, respectively. Although this model is the most accurate model for a memristor, it is a nongeneric model that is defined for a particular type of memristor, which has a nonobvious relationship between current and voltage [14].

2.6. ThrEshold Adaptive Memristor (TEAM) model

TEAM model is a memristor model with several assumptions for analysis simplification and computational efficiency. These assumptions are as follows:

1. There is no change in the status variable for values below a certain threshold value.
2. A polynomial relationship is established between the current of memristor and the internal state drift derivative instead of the exponential dependence.

Taking these assumptions into account, the derivation of the state variable is written as

$$\frac{dw(t)}{dt} = \begin{cases} k_{off} \cdot \left(\frac{i(t)}{i_{off}} - 1\right)^{\alpha_{off}} \cdot f_{off}(w), & 0 < i_{off} < i \\ 0 & , i_{on} < i < i_{off} \\ k_{on} \cdot \left(\frac{i(t)}{i_{on}} - 1\right)^{\alpha_{on}} \cdot f_{on}(w), & i < i_{on} < 0 \end{cases} \tag{23}$$

where k_{off} ($k_{off} > 0$,) k_{on} ($k_{on} < 0$),α_{off}, and α_{on} are constants, i_{off} and i_{on} are current thresholds, and w is the effective electric tunnel width. Dependency on state variable w by $f_{off}(w)$ and $f_{on}(w)$ functions is provided. These functions can be thought of as window functions to limit the state variable between w_{on} and w_{off}. If we assume that the memristance changes linearly with w as in Eq. (7), the relationship between current and voltage can be written as

$$v(t) = \left[R_{on} + \frac{R_{off} - R_{on}}{w_{off} - w_{on}}(w - w_{on})\right] i(t) \tag{24}$$

If we assume that the memristance changes exponentially with w, the relationship between current and voltage can be written as

$$v(t) = R_{on} e^{\left(\frac{\lambda}{w_{off} - w_{on}}(w - w_{on})\right)} \cdot i(t) \tag{25}$$

where λ is fitting parameter [21]:

$$\lambda = \ln\left(\frac{R_{off}}{R_{on}}\right) \tag{26}$$

3. Conclusion

This chapter describes the mathematical modeling and simulation of the memristor device. Firstly, brief information about the historical development of the memristor has been given. The emergence of the memristor idea and the formation of mathematical theory have been mentioned. Then, information about the realization of the memristor as a physical element and the HP memristor model has been given.

In the memristor applications, the memristor device must be mathematically modeled correctly for analysis and simulation studies. For this reason, mathematical modeling and modeling methods of the memristor have been emphasized.

We mainly focus on five different models such as linear drift model, nonlinear drift model, exponential model, Simmons tunnel barrier model, and TEAM model. In addition, the different window functions proposed for the nonlinear drift model have been examined. We provided simulation results for some of the models reviewed. The effects on the I-V characteristics of the window functions have been shown graphically with simulation results.

Author details

Yasin Oğuz

Address all correspondence to: yasin.oguz@gumushane.edu.tr

Gümüşhane University, Gümüşhane, Turkey

References

[1] Chua LO. Memristor-the missing circuit element. IEEE Transaction Circuit Theory. 1971; **18**(5):507-519. DOI: 10.1109/TCT.1971.1083337

[2] Strukov DB, Snider GS, Stewart DR, Williams RS. The missing memristor found. Nature Letter. 2008;**453**:80-83. DOI: 10.1038/nature06932

[3] Dongale TD. Development of High Performance Memristor for Resistive Random Access Memory Application [Thesis]. Kolhapur Maharashtra, India: Shivaji University; 2015

[4] Georgiou PS. A Mathematical Framework for the Analysis and Modelling of Memristor Nanodevices [Thesis]. London: Chemistry of Imperial College London; 2013

[5] Kavehei O. Memristive Devices and Circuits for Computing, Memory, and Neuromorphic Applications [Thesis]. Australia: The University of Adelaide; 2011

[6] Adhikari S, Sah M, Kim H, Chua L. Three fingerprints of memristor. IEEE Transactions on Circuits and Systems I: Regular Papers. 2013;**60**(11):3008-3021. DOI: 10.1109/TCSI.2013.2256171

[7] Chua LO. Resistance switching memories are memristors. Applied Physics A. 2011;**102**: 765-783. DOI: 10.1007/s00339-011-6264-9

[8] Gul F, Efeoglu H. ZnO and ZnO 1-x based thin film memristors: The effects of oxygen deficiency and thickness in resistive switching behavior. Ceramics International. 2017; **43**(14):10770-10775. DOI: 10.1016/j.ceramint.2017.05.090

[9] Gul FE, Efeoglu H. Bipolar resistive switching and conduction mechanism of an Al/ZnO/Al-based memristor. Superlattices and Microstructures. 2017;**101**:172-179. DOI: 10.1016/j.spmi.2016.11.043

[10] Mehonic A, Cueff S, Wojdak M, Hudziak S, Jambois O, Labbé C, Garrido B, Rizk R, Kenyon AJ. Resistive switching in silicon suboxide films. Journal of Applied Physics. 2012;**111**(7):074507. DOI: 10.1063/1.3701581

[11] Wang Q, Sun HJ, Zhang JJ, Xu XH, And Miao XS. Electrode materials for $Ge_2Sb_2Te_5$-based memristors. Journal of Electronic Materials. 2012;**41**(12):3417-3422. DOI: 10.1007/s11664-012-2256-6

[12] Elgabra H, Farhat IAH, Al Hosani AS, Homouz D, Mohammad B. Mathematical modeling of a memristor device. In: 2012 International Conference On Innovations in Information Technology (IIT); 18-20 mar 2012; Abu Dhabi, United Arab Emirates: IEEE; 2012. pp. 156-161

[13] Zha J, Huang H, Liu Y. A novel window function for memristor model with application in programming analog circuits. IEEE Transactions On Circuits and Systems—II: Express Briefs. 2016;**63**(5):423-427. DOI:0.1109/TCSII.2015.2505959

[14] Radwan AG, Fouda ME. On the Mathematical Modeling of Memristor, Memcapacitor, and Meminductor. Springer; 2015. p. 244. DOI: 10.1007/978-3-319-17491-4

[15] McDonald NR, Pino RE, Rozwood PJ, Bryant TW. Analysis of dynamic linear and non-linear memristor device models for emerging neuromorphic computing hardware design. In: 2010 IEEE International Joint Conference on Neural Networks (IJCNN); 18-23 July 2010; Barcelona, Spain: IEEE; 2010. pp. 1-5

[16] Prodromakis T, Peh BP, Papavassiliou C, Toumazou C. A versatile memristor model with non-linear dopant kinetics. IEEE Transactions on Electron Devices. 2011;**58**(9):3099-3105. DOI: 10.1109/TED.2011.2158004

[17] Joglekar YN, Wolf SJ. The elusive memristor: Properties of basic electrical circuits. European Journal of Physics. 2009;**30**(4):661-675. DOI: 10.1088/0143-0807/30/4/001

[18] Biolek Z, Biolek D, Biolkova V. SPICE model of memristor with nonlinear dopant drift. Radioengineering. 2009;**18**(2):210-214

[19] Yang JJ, Pickett MD, Li X, Ohlberg DAA, Stewart DR, Williams RS. Memristive switching mechanism for metal/oxide/metal nanodevices. Nature Nanotechnology. 2008;**3**(7):429-433. DOI: 10.1038/nnano.2008.160

[20] Pickett MD, Strukov DB, Borghetti JL, Yang JJ, Snider GS, Stewart DR, Williams RS. Switching dynamics in titanium dioxide memristive devices. Journal of Applied Physics. 2009;**106**(7):074508-6-074508-1. DOI: 10.1063/1.3236506

[21] Kvatinsky S, Friedman EG, Kolodny A, Weiser UC. TEAM: ThrEshold Adaptive Memristor Model. IEEE Transactions on Circuits and Systems I: Regular Papers. 2013;**60**(1):211-221. DOI: 10.1109/TCSI.2012.2215714

Section 3

Memristor Neuromorphic Applications

Chapter 10

Introduction to Memristive HTM Circuits

Alex James, Timur Ibrayev, Olga Krestinskaya and
Irina Dolzhikova

Additional information is available at the end of the chapter

http://dx.doi.org/10.5772/intechopen.70123

Abstract

Hierarchical temporal memory (HTM) is a cognitive learning algorithm intended to mimic the working principles of neocortex, part of the human brain said to be responsible for data classification, learning, and making predictions. Based on the combination of various concepts of neuroscience, it has already been shown that the software realization of HTM is effective on different recognition, detection, and prediction making tasks. However, its distinctive features, expressed in terms of hierarchy, modularity, and sparsity, suggest that hardware realization of HTM can be attractive in terms of providing faster processing speed as well as small memory requirements, on-chip area, and total power consumption. Despite there are few works done on hardware realization for HTM, there are promising results which illustrate effectiveness of incorporating an emerging memristor device technology to solve this open-research problem. Hence, this chapter reviews hardware designs for HTM with specific focus on memristive HTM circuits.

Keywords: hierarchical temporal memory, spatial pooler, temporal memory, memristor, non-volatile memory, memristive crossbars

1. Introduction

The ideas that created a basis for development of hierarchical temporal memory (HTM), a type of machine learning algorithm that emerged from the consideration of the Bayesian neural network (BNN) and spatial-temporal algorithm, was first introduced by Jeff Hawkins in 2004 in his book *On Intelligence* [1] written in collaboration with Sandra Blakeslee. One year later, in 2005, Hawkins launched Numenta company that worked on the implementation of HTM technology. The first version of the HTM algorithm implementation was developed in

2006 and is now known as HTM-Zeta1 [2]. Three more years of work on the improvement of the HTM-Zeta1 produced a new version of HTM algorithm that is based on the cortical learning algorithm (CLA) and is now presented in the updated white paper of Numenta [3].

The aim of this chapter is to familiarize the reader with one of the latest versions of the machine learning algorithms in the face of hierarchical temporal memory (HTM). The focus of the chapter is utilization of the nanoscale memristive devices for hardware implementations of the HTM. However, due to the complex background of the novel learning algorithm the authors purposefully start from the general descriptions and useful explanations of the major concepts. A variety of concrete examples of HTM realizations in both software and hardware is presented in this chapter. This is done to give the reader comprehensive understanding of the current situation in the HTM research area.

The chapter is organized as follows. We discuss the structure and main concepts of the HTM algorithm in Section 2. The description of the concepts closely follows the white paper documents of Numenta company. In addition to that, a high level overview of the mathematical formulation of HTM phases is given based on the framework that has been demonstrated by Mnatzaganian et al. [4]. Section 3 summarizes the existing implementations of the HTM in both software and hardware. This is followed by the short Section 5 that is dedicated to the memristive device, which is currently widely used for different application. Most importantly, memristor demonstrated a great potential to be especially useful for neuromorphic applications. One of such application is realization of the synaptic behavior in the circuits. This is what Section 5 is about. Finally, Section 6 summarizes the works that demonstrated the application of memristive devices for implementation of hardware designs of HTM.

2. Structure and basic concepts of HTM

For the timely varying set of data to be analyzed the regular horizontal organization that is being utilized in the most of the conventional computer memories will not work. There should be a hierarchy notion that needs to be implemented. This is what the major idea of HTM is based on. As the name suggests the HTM memory utilizes the hierarchical structure with the cells being the primary elements [3]. **Figure 1** depicts an example of hierarchical structure of HTM consisting of three levels. The primary element of the HTM is a cell. These cells perform the function of artificial neurons that resembles the functionalities of the biological neuron. Several cells are grouped to form a node, which is also known as column. The set of columns are combined to form a region, and several regions are interconnected in a hierarchical manner, where the higher level in the hierarchy utilizes the patterns that were learned from the lower levels. The connectivity of the neurons in biology is established by synapses. Being inspired from this concept, HTM cells are interconnected using synapses. In the framework of HTM, the strength of the synapse is known as permanence [3]. The permanence value determines which of the synapses are strong enough to establish the connection for further communication that enables the learning from other cells and lower levels.

http://dx.doi.org/10.5772/intechopen.70123

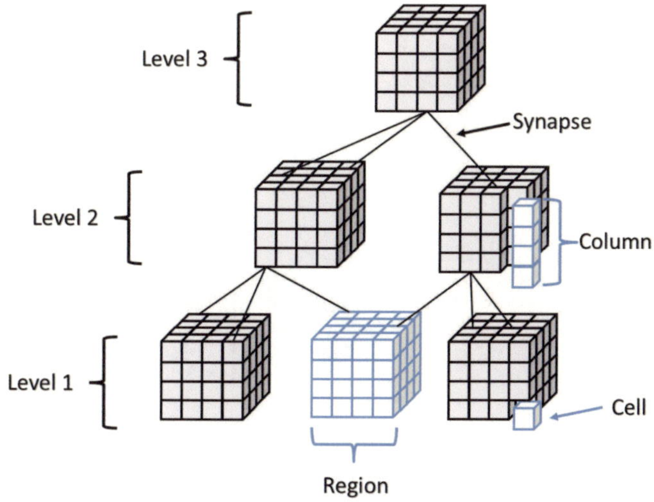

Figure 1. Detailed demonstration of the HTM structure consisting of 3 levels, each composed of certain number of regions with 16 columns each having 4 cells.

Figure 2 demonstrates how the concept of hierarchy could be used in the image recognition application. Here the single level is represented by the single region that composed of several nodes, where the number of nodes is reduced as we go from the bottom level to the top level. Reduced number of the nodes in the higher levels could be explained by the fact that as we go up, we combine certain elements to form the features. As an example let consider an input image that illustrates the face of the human. By looking at the image and using the top-down approach, we realize that the given image represents the human face that in turn has several apparent features, such as nose, eyes, and lips. We then can go deeper and consider the visible features of the eye that incorporate the iris and pupil. Finally, we might zoom in the image and realize that features of the images are formed by certain pixels. Thus, it could be seen that at different HTM levels we have access to different levels of details of the input information.

Two mechanisms that allow the HTM to operate by searching for the common patterns in the spatial domain and determining the common temporal patterns are represented by the spatial pooler (SP) and temporal memory (TM), respectively [3]. Here the term spatial pattern means that there is the combination of the input bits, which is represented by the activation of certain cells in the column, often appearing together. Temporal patterns in turn consider how the sequence of the spatial patterns changes over time [3].

For the realization of HTM, first of all, the SP is required to convert the binary form of the input data into sparse distributed representation (SDR). This type of representation is formed by activating only very small number of bits to illustrate a particular input. SDR in contrast to the dense representation reduces the requirements for the storage capacity because the input data is presented by highly distributed cells. In addition to that, the sparsity of the active bits leads to the improved robustness of the system to the noise.

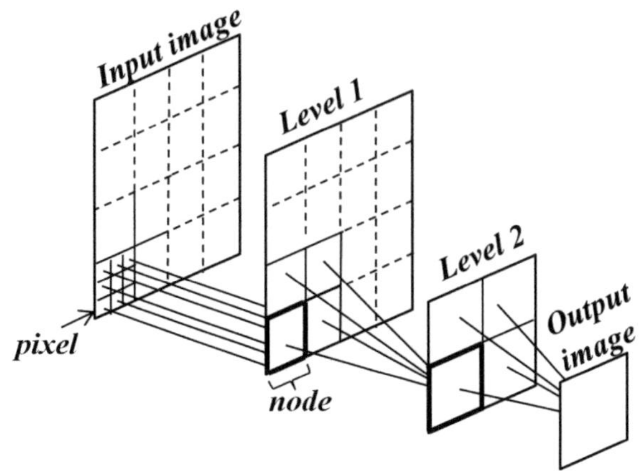

Figure 2. Illustration of the HTM hierarchy based on the image recognition example.

Before talking about the advantage of SDR based systems in terms of storage capacity itself, let first clearly understand the difference between the dense representations and SDRs, the two methods that are utilized for information storage and processing by the traditional computers and brain, respectively.

An example of storing the information in the traditional computer is as follows. The computer uses 8, 32 or 64, bit word with all different combinations of 1's and 0's. By taking any individual bit from the word, one will not get any useful information. The combination of bits itself and position of the active and inactive bits (1's and 0's) with respect to each other, this is what plays an important role. As an example 11010101 is the dense representation of the letter "j" in the ASCII code. The problem might occur even if only single bit of the word is corrupted, such as the third bit from the left swept to the 1 and as a result the dense representation 1101110 will demonstrate a totally different letter in ASCII code, which is "n."

Contrary to this, the functionality of the brain is based on the SDR. This means that for the input consisting of the thousands of bits, at every instant only small portion of these bits is active (represented by 1), while others being 0. In contrast to dense representation, in SDR every bit has its meaning that defines some attribute that describes the information (for example in case of the letter the attribute could define upper-case or lower-case letter, whether it is vowel or consonant). **Figure 3a** demonstrates SDR of the 1000 bits with very small number of bits being 1. These representation can be stored by considering the positions of the 1's in the stream of bits, i.e. the indexes of active bits. Thus, the SDR on **Figure 3a** will be stored as [1, 11, 998] which requires very little space. The comprehensive description of the SDR in the HTM could be found in the technical report of Hawkins and George [2].

This idea of SDR is used in the HTM algorithm. **Figure 3b** shows an example how the input information representing the set of geometrical figures could be stored in the HTM hierarchy in the distributed way with very few of the cells in the region being activated. The realization of the SP requires consideration of the following three phases: overlap phase, inhibition phase and learning phase.

http://dx.doi.org/10.5772/intechopen.70123

Figure 3. Example of (a) how SDR can be used to represent a bit stream and (b) how SDR is formed within HTM hierarchy to represent different geometrical figures.

A purely mathematical formalization of HTM SP was presented by Mnatzaganian et al. [4]. This mathematical framework was established to optimize the development of the HTM designs on hardware. Bellow we discuss the three phases of SP based on pseudocode that was presented in the white paper of Numenta and the work of the Mnatzaganian.

Before the first phase of SP occurs, the initialization should be performed. During the initialization, the initial synapses are established for each column and their permanence value, which is analogous to the synapse weight concept in the neuroscience, is randomly chosen. The first phase of overlap is responsible for determination of the number of active connected synapses. The activity of the synapse is determined by the input to which it is connected, i.e. the high input would make a synapse active, while low input would result in inactive synapse. The connectivity of the synapse in turn is based on the weight of the synapse: only the weights higher than the threshold would make the synapse connected. The optimum threshold depends on the distribution of the data and application of HTM. The optimized threshold can be selected empirically. The example of the empirical selection of the threshold value for pattern recognition application, where the threshold depends on the intensity of the data features, is shown in Ref. [15]. The threshold is selected by testing the HTM method with various threshold values for different databases. The overlap of the individual synapse α is represented by Eq. (1). The value of α would be 1 only if two conditions are satisfied, namely input bit u_i is 1 and weight of the weight of the synapse is higher than the threshold.

$$\alpha_i = \begin{cases} 1 & \text{if } u_i \times w_i \geq \text{threshold} \\ 0 & \text{otherwise} \end{cases} \tag{1}$$

The total overlap of the column that consists of N synapses is given by Eq. (2).

$$\text{Overlap} = \sum_1^N \alpha_i \tag{2}$$

Based on the calculated overlap values the second stage determines the columns that will still be winners after the inhibition. The number of desired winning columns could be controlled with help of parameter k such that the winner is considered that column whose overlap value is greater than the k-th highest overlap value within the inhibition region that is represented in Eq. (3) by γ.

$$\gamma = \text{kmax}(\alpha, k) \tag{3}$$

In the phase of learning the weight values that were higher than γ value are increased by the specified amount, while the other weight decreases its value [3]. Such an update of the weights allows the consideration of the previous state when treating a new input.

TM deals with the time variable of the learning process and could be used to predict what patterns will be followed the given pattern based on the previous observations. Ideally, the learning process occurs in both SP and TM. However, in the SP the learning is based on the connections between the input bits and columns, while in TM learning considers the establishment of the synapses (connections) between the cells of the same region. The TM learns the sequences by considering an active cell and the connection that it formed to the cells that were active in the previous time instant.

The input to the TM are the winning columns from the SP. Like SP, TM consists of three phases. In the first phase, the state of each cell of the columns is checked and the certain cells of the columns are activated. The second phase is responsible for the setting the cells of the columns in predictive state, while the last phase updates the permanence of the synapses [3].

3. Software and hardware realizations of HTM

Despite HTM is classified as a type of cognitive learning algorithm, its fundamental concepts related to neuroscience and, particularly, to the working principles of neocortex make it like deep neural networks, which, in turn, have already shown significant results on a variety of real world problems. Combined with the distinctive features of the algorithm, expressed by its sparsity, hierarchy, and modularity, HTM algorithm attracted interest of various research groups. There is now several research works, which illustrate effectiveness of the algorithm on various recognition tasks. For example, work in Ref. [5] verifies HTM capability on abnormality detection, Refs. [6, 7] present results for pattern and object recognitions, in Ref. [8] HTM was used for object categorizations. Similarly, works in Refs. [9, 10] illustrate suitability of the algorithm for robotics and movement detection, respectively. However, these works were focused on the software realizations of HTM.

http://dx.doi.org/10.5772/intechopen.70123

Despite it was originally developed as the software algorithm, promising results reported in the works listed above resulted in the rise of interest in a hardware realization of HTM. Limited number of works proposes various designs for the hardware realization of HTM within digital, analog, and mixed-signal domains. The work in Ref. [11] proposed conceptual application-specific integrated circuit (ASIC) design for HTM. The work in Ref. [12] proposed reconfigurable field-programmable gate array (FPGA) implementation. The work in Ref. [13] proposed non-volatile HTM spatial pooler design using flash memories. The work in Ref. [14] proposed mixed-signal design for HTM based on the combination of spin-neuron devices and memristor crossbars. The work in Ref. [15] proposed analog design for HTM utilizing memristor crossbar circuits.

The works in Refs. [13–15] are based on the implementation of HTM using non-volatile memories. This is driven by the fact that, in order to compute large amount of data, HTM should have dense neuronal structures with considerations on area and power efficiency. Based on these parameters, the work in Ref. [16] provides data illustrating superior potential of memristor devices over flash memories conventionally used to implement brain-inspired architectures.

4. Memristor for HTM

Memristor (memory resistor) is a non-linear device firstly proposed by Leon Chua in 1972 and firstly fabricated only in 2003 by HP Labs [17]. The main distinctive feature of the device is its ability to change its state not only according to the current input value, but also according to the history of the inputs. Moreover, additional advantages of memristors include low on-chip area, resulting from fabrication methods differing from methods used for silicon devices, and low power consumption, resulting from absence of leakage currents associated with high power dissipation in CMOS technology [17]. These properties of the device resulted in its applications in brain-inspired architectures. Single memristor may be used to represent synaptic connection (or, simply synapse) with its memristance value representing strength of the connection between pre- and post-synaptic neurons. Possibility to combine synaptic processing as well as memory storage within single device made memristors invaluable in the design of synapses, critical building blocks in architectures based on neuroscientific concepts. Nanoscale devices allow compact storage of many synapses as well as enable parallel processing within architecture.

5. Single synapse circuit realizations using memristor devices

Single synapse is said to be a connection between two communicating neurons. In biology, in simple terms communication occurs when transmitting neuron, i.e. pre-synaptic neuron, sends information via signals to receive neuron, i.e. post-synaptic neuron, through synaptic connection. Because there are a huge number of neuronal interconnections, the receiving signal importance is said to be dependent on the strength (also called as the weight) of synaptic connection. It means that neuronal cell, receiving various signals from the number of pre-synaptic neurons, selects and processes important signal according to the weight of synapse.

It is usually assumed that learning appears when the weight of the synapse increases or decreases, according to the importance of the information received through that particular synaptic connection. Hence, it is also crucial to consider effect of time-variance of the incoming data stream on the strength of synapse.

Based on the neuroscientific concepts, synapse, hence, is required not only to be able to process input value but also to store the weight value, determining its importance. Because the latter attribute is dependent on the time variance of the input data, memristor is attractive device, which can combine neuronal functions, such as memorization and data processing, within single unit. Depending on the input signal type, i.e. either current or voltage mode design, there are various possibilities of establishing synapse circuits using memristor devices and CMOS transistors. In particular, work in Ref. [16] presents basic synapse circuits.

The work in Ref. [18] proposed single synapse circuit with specific intentions to precisely model synapse as it is explained and used within HTM framework. **Figure 4** illustrates the circuit design of the single synapse, which can be divided into four parts: input current mirror, memristor, buffer, and voltage-to-current converting NMOS. First part is responsible for establishment of the pre-synaptic signal. The second part is responsible for storing the weight of the synapse, expressed by the memristance value of the memristor. These two parts are responsible for implementation of overlap phase of HTM, such that the voltage across memristor represents the product of the input signal (expressed by current value) and the weight of the synapse (expressed by the memristance value). The third part of the circuit is buffer and is responsible for activation function establishment. It means that buffer outputs voltage value of 1 V if the overlap value is higher than the threshold and outputs 0 V if it is not. Hence, if the input to that synapse is active connected, then the buffer will output high value, and if it is

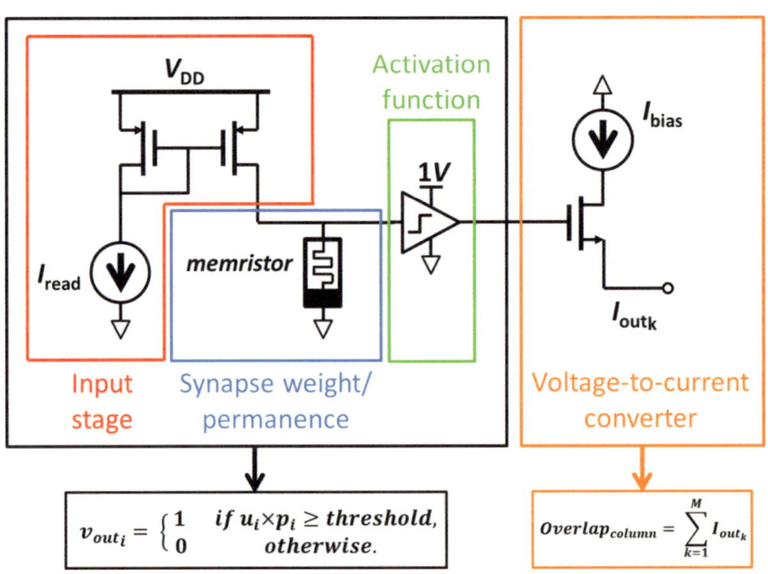

Figure 4. Single synapse circuit design proposed in Ref. [18] designed specifically for HTM architecture.

either not active (input bit value is low) or not connected (weight value is low), then the buffer will output low value. Finally, NMOS transistor is required to convert voltage signal into current signal to sum up all overlap values of individual synapses within single HTM column.

6. HTM circuit realizations using memristor devices

As HTM is a nascent area in brain inspired machine learning algorithms and architectures, a very small number of the HTM circuit configurations have been proposed. There are two major architectures proposed for the HTM hardware implementation with memristive circuits. These are memristor crossbar array-based HTM implementation integrated with CMOS circuits [15] and the HTM implementation using memristive arrays and spin-neuron devices [14]. Both hardware configurations were tested for pattern recognition application.

The memristor-CMOS circuit implementation of HTM has been proposed in Ref. [15]. In this work, the hardware implementation of the HTM SP, applied for face and speech recognition tasks, is presented. The main role of the HTM SP in the proposed system is to extract the most relevant spatial features from the images and remove irrelevant ones for further application for face and speech recognition using template matching method. The feature extraction relies on SDR of the features. The selection of the most relevant features from the sparse data depends on the threshold value shown in Eq. (1). The sparse features greater than

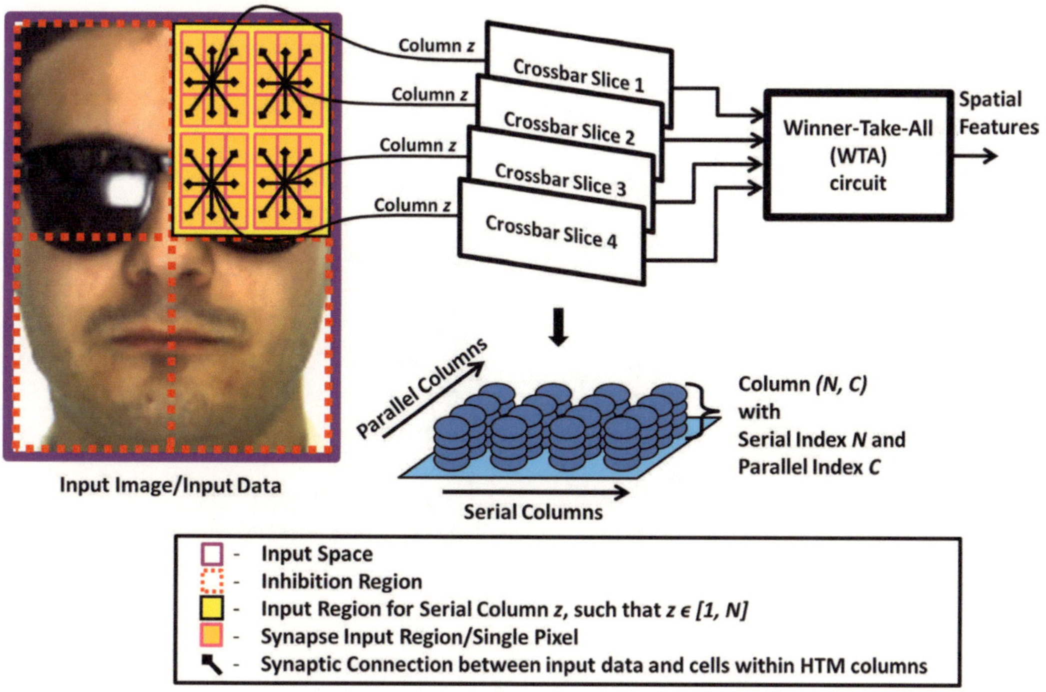

Figure 5. HTM image processing method proposed in Ref. [15].

the threshold are stored in the memory. The example of the input image is shown in **Figure 5**. The image is divided into blocks with a certain number of pixels, which are the inputs to the crossbar slice circuits.

The number of crossbar slices corresponds to the number of the image blocks. Each crossbar slice refers to a single column in the set of serial columns in HTM. The number of synapses in the column corresponds to the number of synapses or pixels in the image blocks. Several image blocks form a single inhibition block. The number of inhibition blocks equals to the number of parallel columns in the HTM. Each inhibition region consists of several serial columns. The set of pixels in the serial column correspond to a single crossbar slice. The sum of the pixels within each crossbar slice is calculated. The outputs from the crossbar slices are fetched to the winner take all (WTA) circuit to produce the final set of the sparse image features. The highest value of crossbar slice outputs is selected by the WTA. Then, the inhibition region is binarized. The inhibition region component corresponding to the highest value of the crossbar slices is represented as 1, and the other components are set to 0. This binarized inhibition regions represent the final set of the sparse image features.

The overall architecture of the HTM crossbar slice circuit consists of the memristor crossbar, read and write circuits, synapse overlap calculation circuit and column overlap calculation circuit, shown in **Figure 6**. The memristors in the memristive crossbar array are used to represent the synapse weight and strength of the synaptic connection. The memristors in read/write part of the circuit implement the expected ideal permanence and determine the final connection of the column, which is either active or inactive. The memristors in the crossbar array are preprogramed

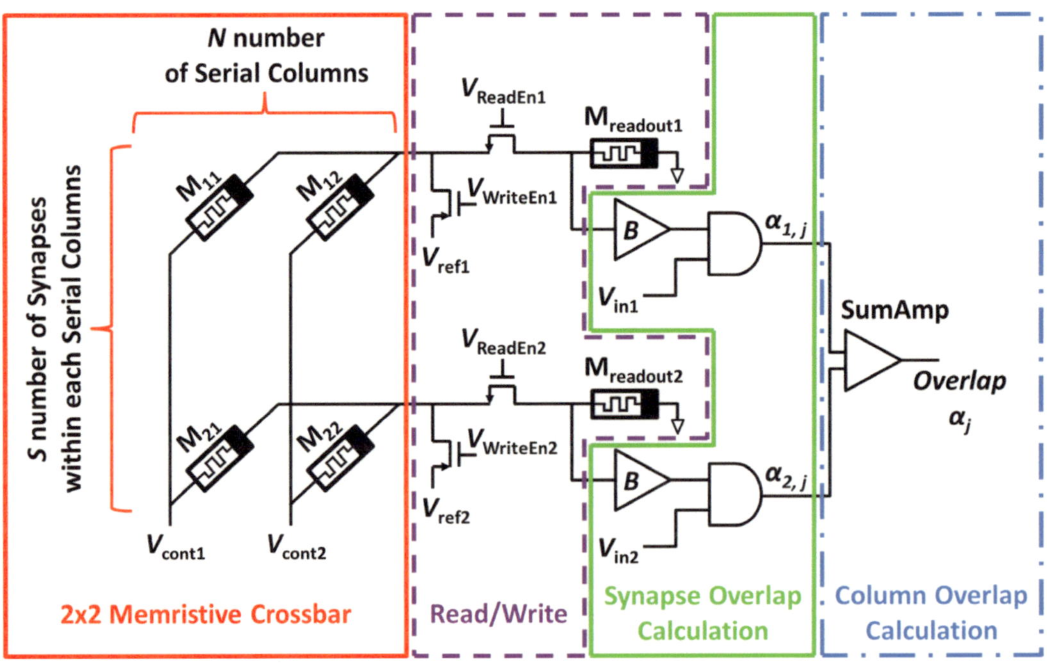

Figure 6. HTM circuit implementation [15].

in the initial stage and later are updated only during the learning phase. When the synaptic connection is determined, the connection value (output from the read/write circuit) is fetched to the AND gate through the buffer, which performs thresholding operation, shown in synapse overlap calculation stage in **Figure 6**. The buffer converts the signal from read/write stage to the binary connectivity value, which is either 0 or 1. The single synapse overlap calculation is made by the AND gate, where one input is the binary synapse connectivity value and the other is the input signal from the processed pattern. The column overlap calculation is made by the summing amplifier that is used for the summation of all single synapses.

After the overlap phase, the inhibition phase is executed, where the overlaps of the parallel columns are compared using WTA circuit, illustrated in **Figure 7**. The overlap values obtained from the summing amplifier are fetched to the WTA circuit and the highest value is selected and set to 1 with the help of bias current source and the comparators. The other values from the inhibition region are set to 0. The output of the WTA circuit is index of the winning columns, which are used for classification process. The circuit implementation results show the power consumption of 31.567 uW and on-chip area of 2.735 um^2 to process 2 column block with 2 synapses. The area and power required to process an individual synapse overlap are 1.37 um^2 and 31.56 uW, respectively. For the column overlap calculation the area of 4.325 um^2 and the power of 160 uW are required.

After the HTM SP processing, the features are compared with the stored training patterns, and the classification of the input pattern is executed using a memristive pattern matcher shown in **Figure 8**. Memristive pattern matcher is based on memristive the XOR gate, which, in turn, consists of the memristive NOR gate and the CMOS inverter. The output of the memristive pattern matcher is either 1 for the detected match or 0 for the mismatch.

The other research work representing memristive circuits-based HTM implementation is presented in Ref. [14]. In this work, memristive crossbar arrays are combined with spin-neuron devices. The system is tested on object and handwritten text recognition. It is assumed that

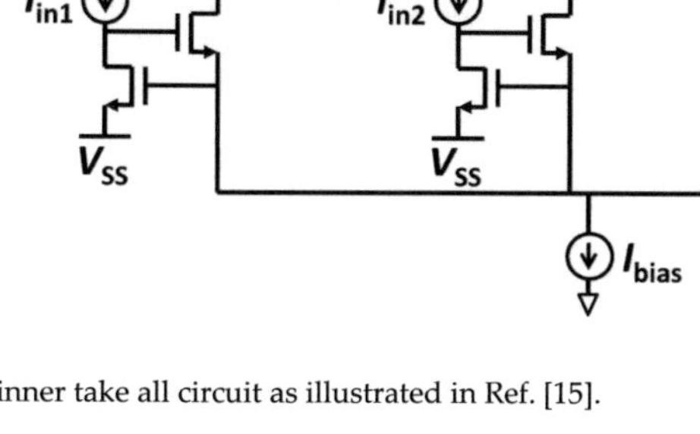

Figure 7. Winner take all circuit as illustrated in Ref. [15].

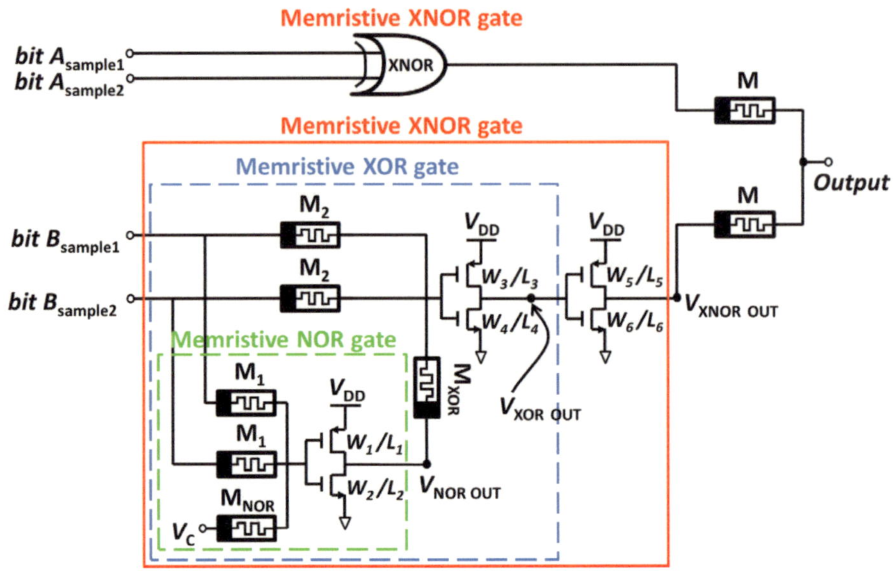

Figure 8. Memristive pattern matcher presented in Ref. [15].

the training of the system is executed by the software and the hardware part of HTM is used for inference (testing) stage, where pattern classification is performed.

The overall HTM hardware configuration is illustrated in **Figure 9**. Image processing is performed in a hierarchical manner. The processed image is divided into 16 patches of the same size, which are fetched into separate HTM nodes in Level 1. Therefore, there are 16 HTM nodes in Level 1. The number of inputs to each Level 1 HTM node equals to the number of pixels in the patch. Level 1 nodes produce 16 outputs, which are divided into 4 groups of 4 Level 1 outputs. Each group of these outputs is fetched into particular Level 2 HTM node. Level 2 contains 4 HTM nodes producing 4 separate outputs. Level 2 outputs are input to Level 3 HTM node, which calculates the final output value.

The overall architecture of the implemented HTM node consists of resistive crossbar network (RCN), successive approximation register analog to digital converter (SAR ADC) and winner take all (WTA) circuit. RCN is used to calculate dot products (DP) in the HTM SP part and the HTM TM part. RCN enables a parallel processing of all image pixels from a single image patch. The digital input pattern from the image patch is fetched into the HTM SP, where it is converted to analog form for the RCN processing. The RCN circuit performs the DP calculation producing an analog output vector. This vector is detected and converted to the digital form with the spin-neuron-based SAR ADC, which forms the output vector of the HTM SP. This output vector is sent to the HTM TM circuit, where it is converted into the analog form again followed by the DP calculation and SAR ADC processing, which forms the output vector of the HTM TM. The HTM TM output vector is fetched to WTA circuit, which identifies the index of the winner from temporal group.

The circuit example of RCN with a single digital input and three spin-neurons is shown in **Figure 10**. To convert digital RCN inputs to the analog form, a deep triode current source

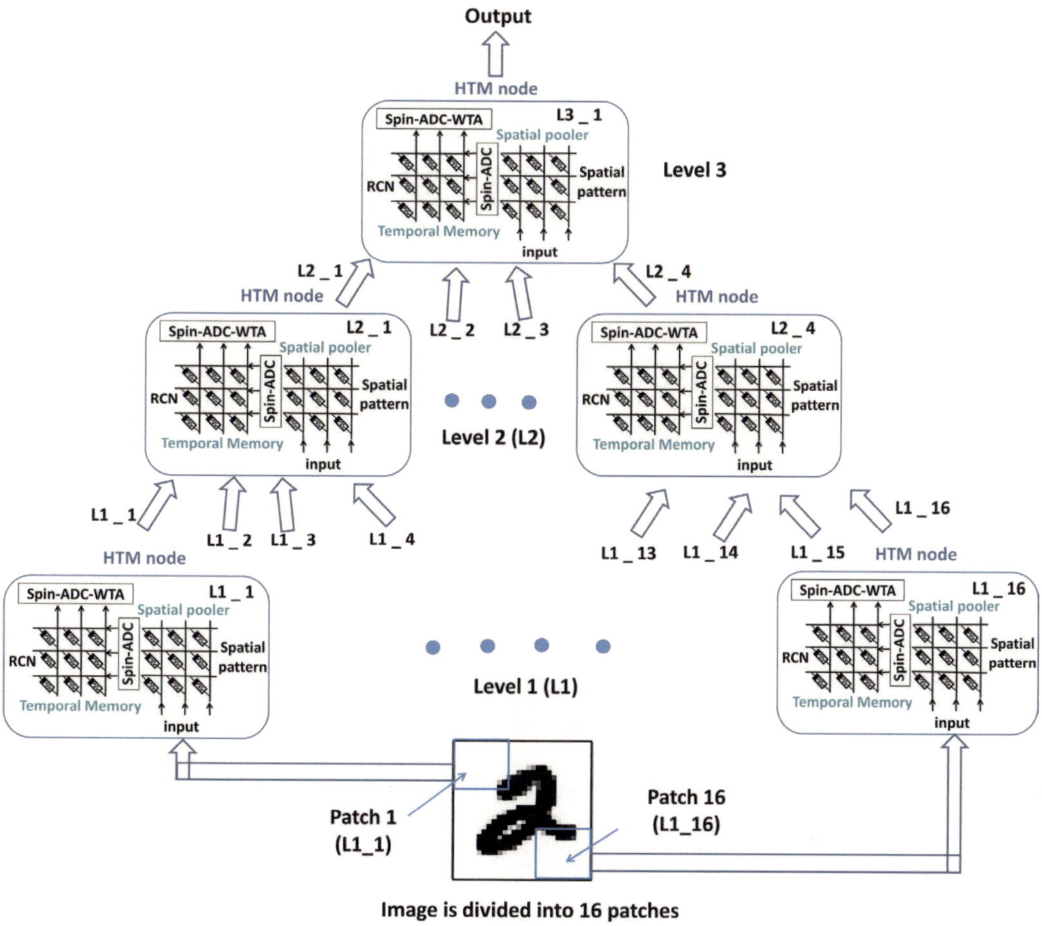

Figure 9. HTM hardware configuration proposed in Ref. [14].

digital to analog converter (DTCS DAC) based on the switching circuit is used. Next, the analog DTCS ADC outputs are fetched to RCN circuit.

The example of 3 × 3 RCN circuit is shown in **Figure 11**. The RCN has a configuration of the memristive array. Such configuration enables calculation of the DP required for the SP as well as for the TM. Therefore, the pixels of the input image matrix are processed in parallel. The input voltage V_i in a horizontal upper row is multiplied by each preprogramed memristor conductance value within the raw g_{ij}. Then, the correlation between the stored patterns and the input signals is calculated as an output current using Eq. (4).

$$I_j = \sum_i V_i * g_{ij} \quad (4)$$

Next, the output current of each RCN column is detected and converted to the digital value using SAR ADC, which is based on spin neuron devices (shown in **Figure 12**). The performance of the spin neuron device is akin to the current mode comparator functionality. The

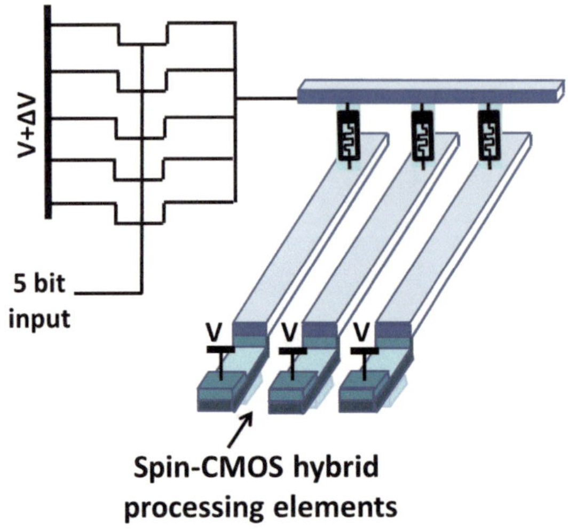

Figure 10. RCN with a single digital input and three spin-neurons [14].

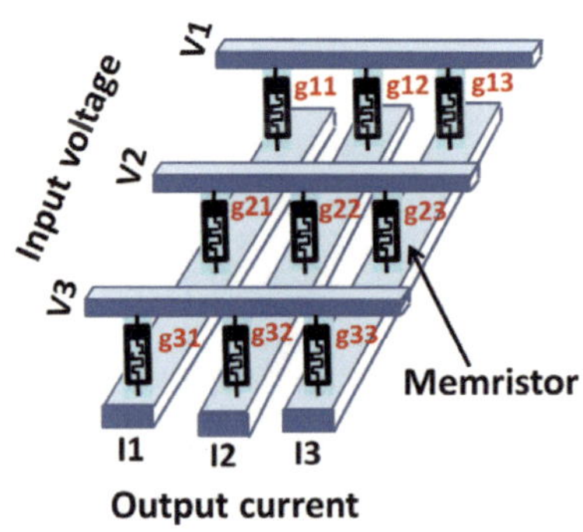

Figure 11. RCN array [14].

spin-neuron may be switched with the particular current flowing through it; therefore it is suitable for the SAR ADC design. In the spin neuron SAR ADC, the DTCS DAC converts the digital value stored in the approximation register to the form of the analog current. Then, this current is compared with the RCN output current produced by the spin-neuron. Finally, a special latch is used to detect output stage. Having a advantage of low power consumption and high resolution, the spin neuron-based SAR ADC enables the conversion of the analog currents from RCN to the digital HTM SP and HTM TM outputs denoted as the input densities over the spatial patterns (HTM SP outputs) and the input densities over the temporal groups (HTM TM outputs) [14]. Finally, the WTA circuit determines the winner of each HTM block. If the HTM block is at the highest hierarchy level (output node), the WTA identifies the class index of an input pattern. Otherwise, if it is located at the non-output node, the WTA determines the winning index of a particular temporal group.

Table 1 shows the comparison of two main implementations of HTM discussed in this Chapter.

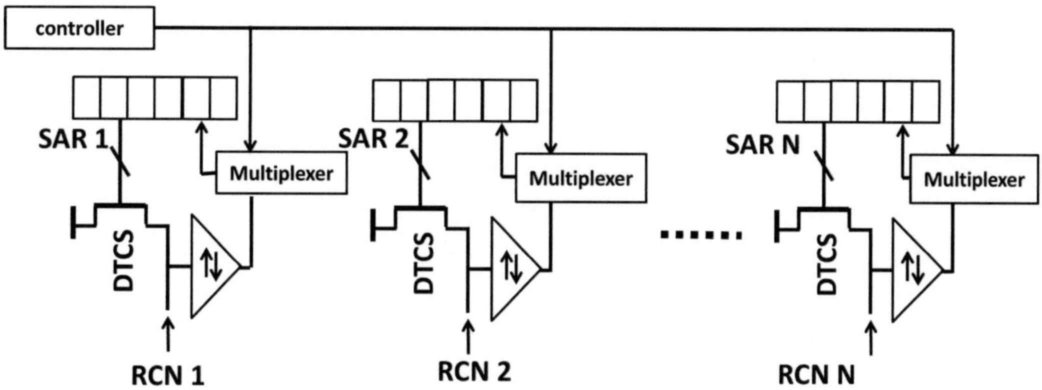

Figure 12. Successive approximation register analog to digital converter (SAR ADC) [14].

	HTM implementation presented in Ref. [14]	HTM implementation presented in Ref. [15]
Algorithm	SP+TM	SP
Hardware implementation	Analog/digital	Purely analog
Technology	Memristors (RCN), 20 × 2 nm spin neuron device (SAR-ADC), spin-CMOS hybrid processing elements based on domain wall neuron (DWN)	50 × 50 nm memristive devices, 180 nm CMOS technology
Architecture	Crossbar	Neuron units
Application	Hand-written digit recognition	Face and speech recognition

Table 1. The comparison of the existing hardware implementations of HTM.

7. Summary

HTM is a type of cortical learning algorithm that aims to resemble the functionalities of the neocortex. The great potential of the HTM for applications related to classification and prediction making pushed for consideration of hardware realizations of the algorithm. The objective of this chapter was to overview the major concepts of HTM and discuss the most recent implementations of HTM in hardware. Currently, there are different hardware implementations of HTM, including the designs based on FPGA and ASIC, that could be found in the literature. However, the discussion in this chapter is focused around the memristor based realizations of HTM. Despite this, for comprehensiveness of the chapter, the authors summarize the general state of the HTM in terms of other hardware implementations [11–13] and provide an interested reader with the references for further reading.

The properties of memristors connected with the small feature size and negligible leakage current of the devices make them very attractive for large-scale circuit designs that reduces the overall on-chip area and power consumption. In addition to that, ability of the memristor to remember its state and change it based on history of applied voltages makes it suitable for neuromorphic designs. Thus, the nanoscale memristive devices could be used to mimic the synaptic connection of the neuron.

After giving an introduction to the HTM concepts and the memritive devices the chapter presents designs of two recent HTM hardware implementations. One of the designs is based on the memristive arrays and spin-neuron devices [14], while the second one integrates the memristor crossbar array and memristor-CMOS circuits [15].

Author details

Alex James*, Timur Ibrayev, Olga Krestinskaya and Irina Dolzhikova

*Address all correspondence to: apj@ieee.org

School of Engineering, Nazarbayev University, Astana,Kazakhstan

References

[1] Hawkins J, Blakeslee S. On Intelligence. New York St. Martin's Griffin: Macmillan; 2004

[2] Hawkins J, George D. Hierarchical Temporal Memory: Concepts, Theory and Terminology. Technical report. Numenta; 2006

[3] Hawkins J., Ahmad S., Dubinsky D. Hierarchical Temporal Memory Including HTM Cortical Learning Algorithms. Technical report, Numenta, Inc, Palto Alto. 2010

[4] Mnatzaganian J, Fokoué E, Kudithipudi D. A Mathematical Formalization of Hierarchical Temporal Memory's Spatial Pooler. Frontiers in Robotics and AI. 2016; 3:81. DOI: 10.3389/frobt.2016.00081

[5] Wu J, Zeng W, Chen Z, Tang XF. Hierarchical temporal memory method for time-series-based anomaly detection. In: 2016 IEEE 16th International Conference on Data Mining Workshops (ICDMW); Barcelona, Spain; 2016. pp. 1167-1172. DOI: 10.1109/ICDMW.2016.0168

[6] Ramli I, Ortega-Sanchez C. Pattern recognition using hierarchical concatenation. In: 2015 International Conference on Computer, Control, Informatics and its Applications (IC3INA); Bandung; 2015. pp. 109-113. DOI: 10.1109/IC3INA.2015.7377756

[7] Farahmand N, Dezfoulian MH, GhiasiRad H, Mokhtari A, Nouri A. Online temporal pattern learning. In: 2009 International Joint Conference on Neural Networks; Atlanta, GA; 2009. pp. 797-802. DOI: 10.1109/IJCNN.2009.5178844

[8] Csapo AB, Baranyi P, Tikk D. Object categorization using VFA-generated nodemaps and hierarchical temporal memories. In: 2007 IEEE International Conference on Computational Cybernetics; Gammarth; 2007. pp. 257-262. DOI: 10.1109/ICCCYB.2007.4402045

[9] Seok K.H., Kim Y.S. A new robot motion authoring method using HTM. In: Control, Automation and Systems, 2008. ICCAS 2008. International Conference on; IEEE; 2008. p. 2058-2061

[10] Zhang S, Ang MH, Xiao W, Tham CK. Detection of activities for daily life surveillance: Eating and drinking. In: HealthCom 2008 - 10th International Conference on e-health Networking, Applications and Services; Singapore; 2008. pp. 171-176. DOI: 10.1109/HEALTH.2008.4600131

[11] Melis WJC, Chizuwa S, Kameyama M. Evaluation of the hierarchical temporal memory as soft computing platform and its VLSI architecture. In: 2009 39th International Symposium on Multiple-Valued Logic; Naha, Okinawa; 2009. pp. 233-238. DOI: 10.1109/ISMVL.2009.11

[12] Zyarah AM. Design and analysis of a reconfigurable hierarchical temporal memory architecture [thesis]. 1 Lomb Memorial Dr, Rochester, NY 14623: Rochester Institute of Technology; 2015

[13] Streat L, Kudithipudi D, Gomez K. Non-volatile Hierarchical Temporal Memory: Hardware for Spatial Pooling. arXiv preprint arXiv:1611.02792; 2016

[14] Fan D, Sharad M, Sengupta A, Roy K. Hierarchical temporal memory based on spin-neurons and resistive memory for energy-efficient brain-inspired computing. IEEE Transactions on Neural Networks and Learning Systems. Sept. 2016;**27**(9):1907-1919. DOI: 10.1109/TNNLS.2015.2462731

[15] James AP, Fedorova I, Ibrayev T, Kudithipudi D. HTM spatial pooler with memristor crossbar circuits for sparse biometric recognition. IEEE Transactions on Biomedical Circuits and Systems. 2017;**PP**(99):1-12. DOI: 10.1109/TBCAS.2016.2641983

[16] Merkel C, and Kudithipudi D. Neuromemristive systems: A circuit design perspective. In: Advances in Neuromorphic Hardware Exploiting Emerging Nanoscale Devices. Springer India; 2017. pp. 45-64

[17] Strukov DB, Snider GS, Stewart DR, Williams RS. The missing memristor found. Nature. 2008;**453**(7191):80-83

[18] Ibrayev T, James AP, Merkel C, Kudithipudi D. A design of HTM spatial pooler for face recognition using memristor-CMOS hybrid circuits. In: Circuits and Systems (ISCAS), 2016 IEEE International Symposium on; IEEE; 2016. pp. 1254-1257

Chapter 11

Review of Recently Progress on Neural Electronics and Memcomputing Applications in Intrinsic SiO_x-Based Resistive Switching Memory

Cheng-Chih Hsieh, Yao-Feng Chang,
Ying-Chen Chen, Xiaohan Wu, Meiqi Guo, Fei Zhou,
Sungjun Kim, Burt Fowler, Chih-Yang Lin,
Chih-Hung Pan, Ting-Chang Chang and Jack C. Lee

Additional information is available at the end of the chapter

http://dx.doi.org/10.5772/intechopen.68530

Abstract

In this chapter, we focus on the recent process on memcomputing (memristor + computing) in intrinsic SiO_x-based resistive switching memory (ReRAM or called memristor). In the first section of the chapter, we investigate neuromorphic computing by mimicking the synaptic behaviors in integrating one-diode and one-resistive switching element (1D-1R) architecture. The power consumption can be minimized further in synaptic functions because sneak-path current has been suppressed and the capability for spike-induced synaptic behaviors has been demonstrated, representing critical milestones and achievements for the application of conventional SiO_x-based materials in future advanced neuromorphic computing. In the next section of chapter, we will discuss an implementation technique of implication operations for logic-in-memory computation by using a SiO_x-based memristor. The implication function and its truth table have been implemented with the unipolar or nonpolar operation scheme. Furthermore, a circuit with 1D-1R architecture with a 4 × 4 crossbar array has been demonstrated, which realizes the functionality of a one-bit full adder as same as CMOS logic circuits with lower design area requirement. This chapter suggests that a simple, robust approach to realize memcomputing chips is quite compatible with large-scale CMOS manufacturing technology by using an intrinsic SiO_x-based memristor.

Keywords: resistive switching, synaptic device, silicon oxide, neuromorphic computing

1. Background

In recent 20 years, emerging memory has drawn a lot of interest and attention as a promising candidate for next generation nonvolatile memory (NVM) [1–3]. Traditional "charge"-based NVM (Flash) will face the potential scaling challenge below the 10 nm node with reliability and power consumption issues [4, 5]. Resistive switching (RS) memory, or we call resistive random access memory (ReRAM), operates by controlling device "resistance" with an external electrical bias [6–9], leading to better electrical performance, smaller design area ($4F^2$), and excellent cycling endurance [10] based on the 2015 International Technology Roadmap for Semiconductors (ITRS) (ReRAM is one of two recommended candidate technologies (the other one is the STT-MRAM) for emerging memory devices) [11]. Moreover, RS-based memories represent a new class of devices compatible with applications that go beyond traditional electronics configurations, for example, three-dimensional (3D) stacking, nanobatteries, neuroelectronics, and Boolean logic operations [12–17].

In 1971, Chua presented the theoretical basis for a passive two-terminal circuit device called a "memristor" (a contraction of memory and resistor) [18]. If realized, the memristor would then join the resistor, inductor, and capacitor to provide four basic circuit elements. In 2010, researchers in HP lab realized the memristor in nanoscale titanium dioxide (TiO_2) cross-point structure [17], and the field has advanced quickly growth over the past decade as a result. Having demonstrated the existence of memristors in the lab, additional research efforts focused on the potential applications that this emerging new circuit element enables [19]. In recent years, memristors have been extensively studied as a nonvolatile memory called resistive random-access-memory (named ReRAM or RRAM) to potentially replace dynamic random-access-memory (DRAM) and flash memory [20]. Memristors have also gained tremendous interest in the field of neuroelectronics and synaptic electronics, which aims to build artificial synaptic devices that emulate the computations performed by biological synapses [21–25]. Jo et al. described possible applications in artificial intelligence using memristors as synapses in neuromorphic circuits [15]. Another interesting application is to use memristors for arithmetic/logic operations, such as an adder circuit or a multiplier circuit.

In the literature, arithmetic operations are proposed using the memristor as a: (1) switch, (2) programmable interconnect, and (3) computational element. In the first approach, crossbar arrays of memristor switches are connected to a row of weighting resistors and sensing logic to build an analog arithmetic processor [26]. The switches control the current flow (ON/OFF) through the weighting resistor, which then controls the analog voltage at the sensing amplifier end. The resistance of the weighting resistor assigns the appropriate bit significance to the each row's current contribution. The memristor-CMOS technology may be used to realize the same types of arithmetic circuits that are developed in CMOS/FPGA (field programmable gate array) technology [27, 28]. Last but not the least, a more universal approach for constructing the logic operations from memristors is via "material implication" (or an "IMP" operation). In 2010, researchers showed that all fundamental Boolean logic functions can be realized by using memristors with the IMP operation [17]. Later work built on these findings to construct larger logic blocks such as adders and multipliers [29–31], linear feedback shift registers [32], and counters [32]. The advantages of memcomputing (memristor + computing) are not only to store and process information on the same physical platform, but also to allow massively parallel computations in a simple crossbar array architecture.

Otherwise, neuroelectronics and synaptic electronics are interesting applications for ReRAM that aim to build artificial synaptic devices that emulate the computations performed by biological synapses [15, 33]. These emerging fields of research potentially have better efficiency in solving complex problems and outperform real-time processing of unstructured data than conventional von Neumann computational systems [34]. There have been many studies of binary metal oxide-based and perovskite oxide-based resistance switching characteristics for synapse-like electronic device development [35, 36], which can have operating instability issues due to difficulty in controlling stoichiometric compositions [37, 38]. Therefore, a simple process that is compatible with conventional complementary metal-oxide semiconductor (CMOS) fabrication allows multilayer compositional engineering and provides good electrical stability and high yield, which are critical requirements for neuroelectronics realization [39]. Silicon oxide (SiO_x) has long been used as gate dielectrics for metal-oxide-semiconductor field-effect transistors. In addition to excellent insulating properties, resistive switching properties have been observed in SiO_x materials as early as 1962 by Hickmott and 1967 by Simmons and Verderber [40–42]. Yao et al. also have reported SiO_x-based RS behaviors in vacuum, indicating that this traditional material can be converted to an active component by controlling the external electrical manipulation [43–45]. Several recent reports describe using SiO_2 as the active switching medium in resistive switching memory devices [46–49]. We have further demonstrated a Si diode (1D) with low reverse-bias current integrated with a SiO_x-based memory element (1R) using nanosphere lithography and deep Si etching to pattern a $P^{++}/N^{+}/N^{++}$ epitaxial Si wafer [50].

2. Introduction

In this chapter, first SiO_x-based resistive switching memory elements (1R) are integrated with Si diodes (1D) using conventional CMOS processing to demonstrate a 1D-1R device with synaptic behaviors. Compared with our previous work (in most cases investigating only the 1R device system), the Si diode provides low reverse-bias current and high power efficiency for future neuromorphic computing array architectures. Unlike other binary or complex metal oxide materials [51], SiO_x has been used in CMOS manufacturing for over 50 years due to its excellent electrical isolation properties, low-cost, high chemical stability, compatibility with mainstream integrated circuit materials, high-throughput processing, and large-area production using chemical vapor deposition (CVD). A 1D-1R architecture fabricated at the wafer-scale using conventional CMOS processing can, therefore, be well controlled in thickness, size, and electrical characteristics by precisely controlling the doping levels of the diode layers and the temperature and flow-rate of the oxide CVD process [52]. Synaptic device performance is characterized in a prototype 1D-1R array configuration. Robust biological synaptic behaviors such as long-term potentiation (LTP), long-term depression (LTD), and spike-timing-dependent plasticity (STDP) are demonstrated with excellent uniformity, low operational variability, and good suppression of static power consumption [51]. A bio-inspired proton exchange resistive switching model is used to help characterize this novel application for SiO_x materials. The SET transition in the resistive switching memory is modeled as hydrogen (proton) release from the $(Si\text{-}H)_2$ defect to generate a conductive hydrogen bridge, and the RESET transition is modeled as an electrochemical reaction (proton capture) that reforms nonconductive $(SiH)_2$. The synaptic behaviors exhibited by the 1D-1R device demonstrates good potential for using a simple and robust approach for large-scale integration of programmable neuromorphic chips using CMOS technology.

Second, the application of SiO_x-based memristors for material implication operations is examined. A bidirectional implication scheme is demonstrated and tested in an actual circuit using SiO_x-based memristors. The symmetric unipolar memristive behavior of the SiO_x-based memristor enables the use of two sets of implication voltage setups, one positive and the other negative, hence the name "bidirectional". Progressing one step further from the initial concept demonstrated by Borghetti et al. and our previous work, a one-bit full adder is realized by using the material implication technique on a crossbar structure with a one-diode one-memristor (1D-1R) array. Several potential application problems such as sneak current paths within an array and using a select transistor as the load resistor are discussed in detail. The results suggest that a memristor-enabled logic circuit is most suitable for applications requiring low-speed, low-power, and high-density.

3. Method and experiment

Secondary electron microscopy (SEM) images show a top-down view of a 1D-1R test structure (**Figure 1a**), a tilted (45°) view of the 1R device (**Figure 1b**) and a cross-section image of the 1R device showing layer information (**Figure 1c**). The devices were fabricated at XFAB in Lubbock TX using the XC06 CMOS process technology. The 1R device was fabricated by first implanting the Si substrate to form an n-type lower electrode. The active SiO_x memory layer was then deposited to a thickness of 40 nm using plasma-enhanced chemical vapor deposition (PECVD). This thickness is known to provide high electroforming yield and good memory endurance [53]. An n-type polysilicon layer was deposited onto the SiO_x layer to form the top electrode. An opening in the polysilicon layer was made after all thermal oxidation and implant anneal steps are complete (**Figure 1b**). A first dielectric layer was then deposited over the polysilicon top electrode. Tungsten plugs were used to make electrical contact to the n-type Si lower electrode and the polysilicon top electrode. After all the back-end dielectrics and a passivation layer were deposited, the back-end dielectric layers were removed using reactive ion etch (RIE) to the Si substrate. This RIE step cleared-out the SiO_x layer inside the hole, and created a SiO_x sidewall where the memory device is formed (**Figure 1c**). Polymer residue that remained after the post-RIE cleaning steps was removed by a 30-s buffered oxide etch (BOE). The pn diode used in the 1D-1R test structures was formed by an implanted p-well inside a deep n-well with 40 V reverse-bias breakdown voltage, 1 nA reverse-bias leakage current and 0.5 V forward voltage. The active memory area of the 1R device is 2 × 2 μm² and the overall size including metal interconnects is 21.9 × 21.9 μm². The overall size of the 1D device is 41 × 19 μm². A lake shore cryotronics vacuum probe chamber (<1 mTorr) and Agilent B1500A device analyzer were used

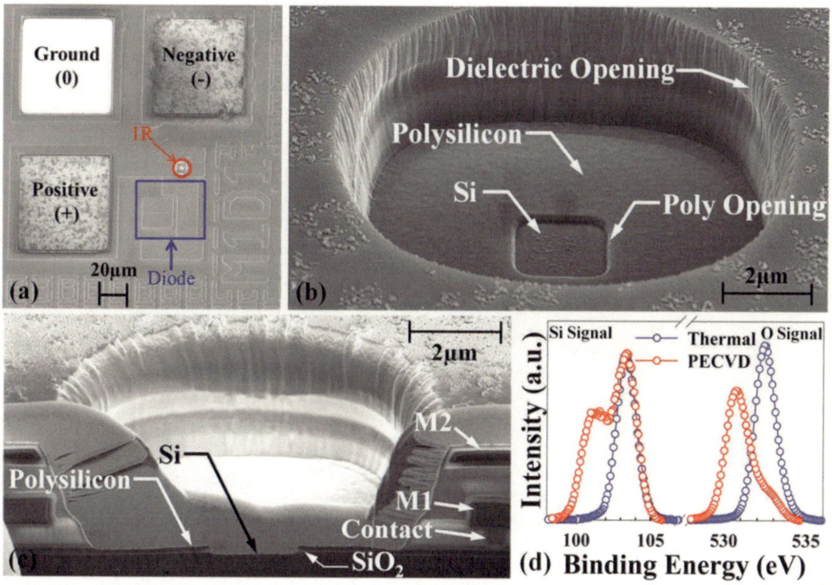

Figure 1. (a) Top-down SEM image of 1D-1R architecture. The 1R is adjacent to the 1D structure. The ground pad (0) is used to bias the substrate, the positive (+) and negative (−) terminals are for applying voltage to the 1D-1R device. (b) Tilted top-down SEM image of resistive memory device. (c) SEM cross-section image showing metal contact to polysilicon top electrode, metal 1 (M1) and metal 2 (M2) layers, and polysilicon/SiO_2/Si 1R device. (d) Si-$2p_{2/3}$ and O-1s XPS spectra for PECVD oxide and thermal oxide. Figure reprinted by [19].

to electroform devices and measure the DC/AC *I-V* response. The SET process programs the device to a conductive, low-resistance state (LRS). The RESET process programs each device to a low-conductance, high-resistance state (HRS). A Kratos Axis Ultra HSA X-ray photoelectron spectrometer (XPS) equipped with a monochromatized aluminum X-ray source was used to analyze several SiO_x materials deposited in our laboratory using different methods. Calibration of the binding energy scale was set by fixing the C-(C,H) peak at 284.4 eV. **Figure 1d** shows XPS analysis results for the O-1s and Si-2p binding energies in thermal oxide grown by low-pressure chemical vapor deposition (LPCVD) and PECVD oxide. The existence of stoichiometric SiO_2 can be observed in thermal oxide (binding energy Si: 103.2 eV; O: 532.5 eV) with essentially no suboxide bonding being detected. In contrast, the PECVD oxide has nonstoichiometric SiO_x (x is about 1.6 based on the peak position and orbital valence) composition in the switching layer, as indicated by the peak-binding energies in the XPS spectra (O: 530.5 eV; Si: 101.9 eV, and 100.9 eV) [54, 55], which may promote low-energy defect generation during the electroforming process.

4. Results and discussions

Figure 2a–d show *I-V* characteristics for DC voltage sweeps applied to the SiO_x-based 1D-1R devices fabricated by the conventional CMOS process. Voltage was applied to the 1D top electrode (p-type Si) with bottom 1R electrode (n-type Si) at ground. All testing was done in

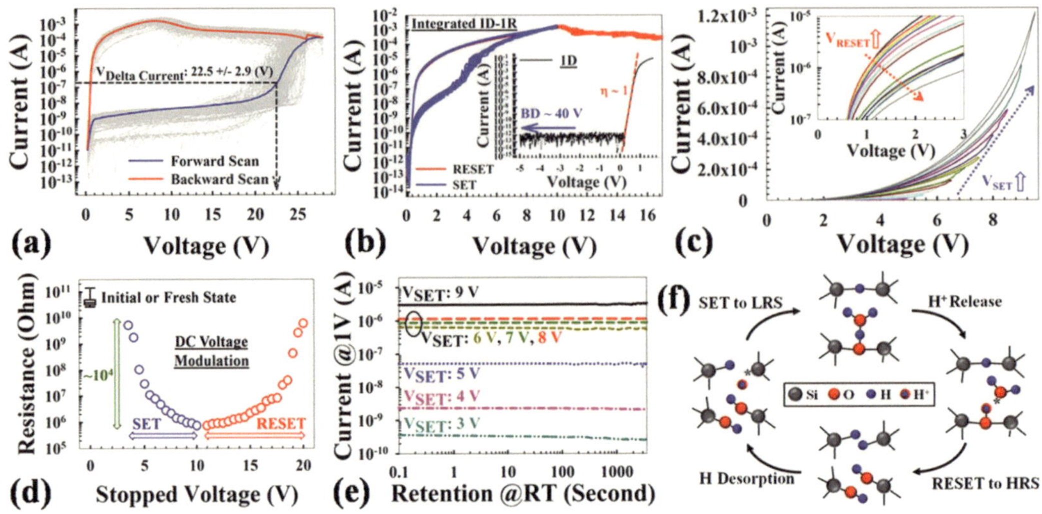

Figure 2. DC sweep resistive switching behaviors of 1D-1R architecture: (a) Forward/backward voltage sweeps during electroforming process averaged for 256 devices in a 16 × 16 array (gray curves). The electroforming voltage ($V_{\text{Delta Current}}$) is defined as the voltage where maximum current change occurs during the forward sweep. (b) 10 I-V resistive switching SET/RESET cycles. The inset shows the average of 100 measurement cycles of diode I-V behavior. (c) Effects of voltage modulation on I-V curves in SET process plotted on linear-scale, where the applied SET voltage sweep increases from 3.5 to 9.5 V in 0.5 V steps. The inset shows effects of voltage modulation on I-V curves in RESET process plotted on log-scale, where the applied RESET voltage sweep increases from 11.0 to 18.0 V in 0.5 V steps. (d) The resistance states of initial fresh device, SET DC voltage modulation, and RESET DC voltage modulation. For SET voltage sweep, increases from 3.5 to 10 V in 0.5 V steps; for RESET voltage sweep, increases from 11 to 20 V in 0.5 V steps. The resistance reads at 1V for each state. (e) Retention measurement results of multi-state programming obtained by controlling the SET voltage. (f) Proton exchange induced resistive switching model and defect transitions. Figure reprinted by [19].

vacuum. To establish reversible resistive switching in each SiO_x-based 1R ReRAM device, a forward/backward voltage sweep (**Figure 2a**) was used to electroform each device, where current is observed to increase dramatically at 22.5 ± 2.9 V during the forward voltage sweep. Electroforming is completed during the backward voltage sweep from the maximum sweeping voltage to 0 V, resulting in the formation of a conductive filament (CF) and setting the device to a LRS. After electroformation, RS performance of 1D-1R can be stabilized by 10 times cycles (**Figure 2b**). For SET process, a 10 V forward/backward sweep is applied without any compliance current limitation (CCL) to change the device from HRS to LRS; for RESET process, a 17 V, single sweep is done to change the device from LRS to HRS. The HRS/LRS resistance ratio can be read out at 1 V bias with satisfying sensing requirements (~10^3) [3, 26]. For diode characteristics, the forward current can reach 100 mA at 2 V (current density 1.15×10^{-5} A/μm^2 at 1 V), which indicates a forward current level high enough to support the RESET process. The reverse current is below 1×10^{-12} A at −5 V. Compared with Schottky diodes (potentially useful for 3D arrays), the advantages of Si-based PN diodes include low reverse current, high reverse-bias breakdown voltage, and fewer stability issues [45]. The quality of the Si-based PN diode can dramatically affect diode reverse or forward current characteristics, as well as power consumption (describe below). Also, the chosen Si-based PN diode configuration has high reverse breakdown voltage (>40 V), which is important for SiO_x-based ReRAM operating in an array. **Figure 2c** demonstrates the gradual change of resistive states by modulating the voltage sweep range continuously during the SET and RESET (inset) process, respectively. Specifically, SET and RESET voltages were changed from 3.5 to 9.5 V in 0.5 V increments and from 11 to 18 V in 0.5 V decrements, respectively, thus potentially enabling multilevel programming in a single memory cell and demonstrate the status stability before/after sweeps. It may be noted that the electroforming voltages measured here (~ 28 V) are somewhat higher than those measured in previous work on metal-oxide-semiconductor device architectures or nanopillar type 1D-1R architectures [50, 56, 57], which may be due to fewer electrically active defects being near the SiO_x sidewall as a result of the fabrication process. For example, several high temperature steps (>650°C) were done after PECVD SiO_2 deposition, namely: polysilicon deposition, thermal oxidation, and implant anneals, which might densify the SiO_2 layer, reduce the as-deposited defect levels, increase the soft breakdown threshold, and thus increase the filament formation energy during the subsequent electroforming process (resulting in forming voltage increase). Interestingly, the RESET voltage (the voltage at which LRS current begins to decrease) has been found to be greater than or equal to the SET voltage (where HRS current increases sharply), which is a unique characteristic of the SiO_x-based ReRAM as compared to other materials systems [36, 58]. The difference between RESET and SET voltages can potentially be controlled by optimizing the series resistance in the circuit, choice of electrode materials, and by doping effects that modulate the interfacial contact resistance [59]. The switching voltage is largely independent of device size and SiO_x thickness. **Figure 2e** shows multilevel retention performance of SiO_x-based 1D-1R devices obtained by controlling the maximum SET voltage from 3 to 9 V. The readout current of LRS and HRS is measured at 1 V every 60 s after each programming operation. Although the state's stability still needs to be improved (no equal split of resistance states), the retention reliability test demonstrates ` operation by using different SET voltages, and no degradation is observed for more than 10^3 s, thus confirming the stable, nonvolatile nature of the SiO_x-based 1D-1R devices. In recent studies, a possible proton exchange model consistent with the observed resistive switching *I-V* response has been proposed, as shown in **Figure 2f** [59, 60]. Several studies have used transmission electron microscopy (TEM) to document the presence of Si nanocrystals within the CF [43, 61, 62], but it is not yet clear whether resistive switching (RS) is the result of an overall increase in nanocrystal size or whether switching occurs in "GAP" regions in between nanocrystals. Most models of ReRAM switching involve the drift or diffusion of O^{2-} ions (or oxygen vacancy defects) [39], but these models cannot explain the unconventional *I-V* response. For example, the backward scan effect (see **Figure 2a**, backward scan) is very difficult to explain using a simple oxygen vacancy-switching model. The backward scan effect is a phenomenon where the duration of the reverse sweep during electroforming or RESET determines whether a state change occurs, and has been characterized using DC and AC pulse response in a previous study investigating our resistive switching model [57]. In addition, ambient effects on resistive switching suggest that the defects responsible for switching are hydrogen-passivated or are in some way protected from direct reaction with ambient oxygen and water until a switching events occurs [56, 63]. The detailed interactions between ambient gases and proton (or cation) mobility is an important topic that may provide a deeper understanding of resistive switching mechanisms [64–68], specifically those in oxide-based valence change memory (VCM)-type ReRAMs [69–71]. The models used here to describe the possible

SiO_x-based RS mechanisms differ from most conventional models by considering that the defects responsible for RS may remain localized within the switching region so that resistive switching occurs when a collection of defects are driven between conductive and nonconductive forms [56]. A thorough review of the reported electrical and structural properties of known SiO_x defects has identified a plausible model for the conductive filament that is similar to models used to describe stress-induced leakage current and breakdown in SiO_x materials, where defect concentration increases as a result of electrical stress to the point where percolation pathways capable of conducting appreciable current (>1 uA) are formed [59]. Incorporating known proton exchange reactions that can dramatically alter the conductivity of specific defects further leads to a model where the LRS has a large concentration of conductive defects within the switching region, and, conversely, when the device is programmed to the HRS, most of the defects are converted to their nonconductive form. The electrically conductive hydrogen bridge (Si-H-Si) is viewed as the most likely defect responsible for the LRS due to the location of its energy levels relative to the oxide conduction band and its small effective bandgap energy [59, 60]. Adding a proton to Si-H-Si forms the nonconductive $(SiH)_2$ defect and proton desorption from $(SiH)_2$ reforms Si-H-Si, which are well-understood electrochemical reactions that could enable localized switching without incorporating ion diffusion or drift mechanisms into the model. The SET transition voltage from HRS to LRS occurs at ~2.5 V in the I-V response, and is very near the activation energy for proton desorption from SiH (~2.5 eV), thus making the defect transformation from $(SiH)_2$ to Si-H-Si a logical assignment for the SET transition [59, 60]. In this model, the proton that is lost from $(SiH)_2$ reacts electrochemically with $(SiOH)_2$, which is simply chemisorbed H_2O, to form the fixed positive charged H_3O^+ defect. The transition from LRS to HRS is modeled as being initiated by electron injection into H_3O^+ that induces proton release and electrochemical reaction with Si-H-Si to reform $(SiH)_2$ [59, 60]. The localized proton exchange switching model can thus be written as $(SiH)_2 + (SiOH)_2 \leftrightarrow$ Si-H-Si + Si_2=O-H_3O^+, where a voltage drop of ~2.5 V across the switching is required to drive the reversible reaction. The RS model not only provides insights into multilevel operational characteristics but also implies a possible biomimetic chemical reaction similar to reactive oxygen species (ROS-like) production for future device characterizations [72].

Figure 3a–h show contour plots of the current-change ratio achieved by modulating the AC pulse height and pulse width applied to 1D-1R devices for both SET and RESET switching events, leading to optimized waveform designs for a biological synaptic device. The current-change ratio is defined as $\log_{10}(I_{FINAL}/I_{INITIAL})$, where $I_{INITIAL}$ and I_{FINAL} are the currents measured at 1 V before and after applying the programing waveform, respectively. The SET/RESET sweeps from same initial resistance state (precondition programming) is to eliminate the accumulating SET/RESET effect after each cycle. One can observe by inspecting the contour lines in **Figure 3** that when larger pulse heights (higher voltages) are applied to the device, shorter pulse widths are needed to achieve a similar current-change ratio. In general, we find that a single 1R device operates at higher speed and requires lower programming voltages as compared to a 1D-1R device. The higher operating voltages and lower operating speed of the integrated 1D-1R device may result from higher parasitic resistance in the Si electrodes, their contacts and the diode, as well as higher parasitic

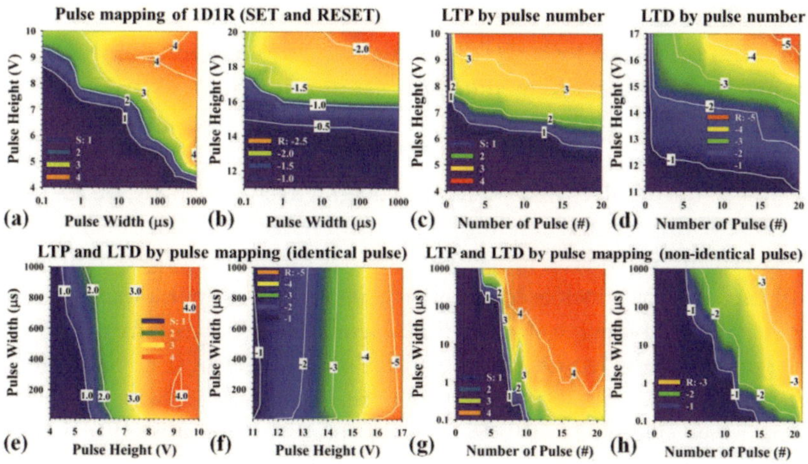

Figure 3. AC pulse mapping contour plots of current-change ratio by modulating pulse height and pulse width to demonstrate synaptic behaviors in 1D-1R architectures: (a) SET (S) and (b) RESET (R) mapping results of 1D-1R device. (c) and (e) Long-term potentiation (LTP) and (d) and (f) long-term depression (LTD) using the identical pulse method as a function of pulse width. For the identical pulse method, pulse height and pulse width are fixed. For LTP, the pulse height modulation changes from 11 to 17 V in 0.3 V increments for each loop, and pulse widths are fixed at 10 μs. The mapping results of using the identical pulse method for LTP are show in (e). By selection of final states (after 20 pulses), the conductance change is highly dependent on the pulse height. For LTD, the pulse height modulation changes from 4 to 10 V in 0.3 V increments for each loop, and pulse widths are fixed at 10 μs. The mapping results (f) are similar and the conductance change for LTD is also highly dependent on the pulse height rather than pulse width. (g) and (h) show the LTP and LTD using the non-identical pulse method as a function of pulse width, respectively. For the non-identical pulse method, pulse height modulation changes continuously from 4 to 10 V in 0.3 V increments (for a total of 21 steps) for LTP, and changes continuously from 11 to 17 V in 0.3 V increments (for a total of 21 steps) for LTD. The initial states for LTP and LTD mapping are determined by fixed DC conditions: a 17 V single sweep for HRS and a 10V double-sweep for LRS, respectively. "S" and "R" denote the increment/decrement of current state changes after applying the AC pulse (defined as Log_{10} (I_n/I_{nitial}), where $I_n/I_{Initial}$ is current ratio measured at 1 V after/before the pulse is applied). Figure reprinted by [19].

capacitance in the diode, all of which can act to degrade the pulse mapping results shown in **Figure 3a** and **b**. It should be noted that current sneak-path issues in arrays and writing disturbance of 1R devices would cause misread problems and state disturbance, and substantially increase standby power consumption and information instability. The 1D-1R devices are used to suppress sneak-path currents, and perform much better than 1R devices in an array architecture (potential 1 Gbit array support in 10% readout-margin at 1V read). From **Figure 3a** and **b**, it can be calculated that the switching energies to achieve at least a one-order-of-magnitude change in resistance in the 1D-1R architecture are about 0.01 pJ for SET and 1.54 nJ for RESET operations. However, due to the suppression of sneak-path current, the standby power during a 1 V read operation can be dramatically reduced in 1D-1R devices (1 pW) as compared to 1R devices (1 μW, due to 1R nonpolar switching behaviors) [73]. Minimizing the total power consumption due to sneak-path current is as crucial as reducing the synaptic dissipation.

Most importantly, the pulse mapping results not only demonstrate the potential for multilevel programming by properly designing the pulse waveforms for SET and RESET operations, but also demonstrate the potential to realize biological synaptic behaviors. **Figure 3c–h** demonstrate the optimization waveform design for biological synaptic behaviors in 1D-1R SiO_x-based resistive switching memories. The long-term potentiation (LTP) and long-term depression (LTD) are a long-lasting enhancement/reduction in signal transmission between two neurons (similar with long-lasting conductance increase/decrease between HRS and LRS for resistive-type memory devices), which can be realized by designing the SET and RESET pulse waveform to use either identical (fixed pulse width and pulse height, as shown in **Figure 3c–f**) or nonidentical (variable pulse width or pulse height, as shown in **Figure 3g** and **h**) pulsing techniques. The trade-offs between high dynamic range and gradual multilevel programming performance (**Figure 3e–h**) needed to be considered, and it was found that the nonidentical pulse waveform method may have the advantages (larger than identical pulse waveform method). Although nonidentical pulsing might require a more complex neuromorphic circuit, our results show that this approach enables more efficient programming to target states while maintaining a larger dynamic range (**Figure 3g–h**). The use of nonidentical pulse heights ranging from 4 to 10 V in 0.3 V increments (for LTP) and ranging from 11 to 17 V in 0.3 V decrements (for LTD) allow the dynamic range to be mapped for pulse widths ranging from 100 ns to 1 ms, thereby realizing biological synapse behaviors in the SiO_x-based 1D-1R architecture (**Figure 3g–h**). The switching energy is defined as $I \times V \times \delta t$, where δt is the pulse width. For $\delta t = 100$ ns, the smallest switching energies are ~6 and ~130 pJ for LTP and LTD, respectively. The larger energy for LTD is mainly due to the lower resistance of the LRS (~93 kΩ) compared to the HRS (~260 MΩ), which results in higher switching current (118.28 μA) for the RESET process than for the SET process (15.38 nA). In order to minimize synaptic energy consumption all three components—programming current (~nA level switching), pulse amplitude (<1 V) and programming time (<10 ns)—need to be minimized. In SiO_x-based ReRAM and in other material systems, an exponential voltage–time relationship is commonly observed. A small increase in programming voltage will decrease programming time exponentially, as shown in **Figure 3a**. For RESET process (both 1R and 1D-1R structures, **Figure 3b**), the process integration may result in certain level of distortion (parasitic resistance/capacitance and possible parasitic depletion region capacitance from 1D) to affect the pulse mapping results. Hence, low programming energy is obtained by minimizing the programming time (traded off by increasing the pulse amplitude slightly) for ReRAM. Further decreases in synaptic energy consumption during the switching process to fJ levels will be challenging but important to build very large-scale systems (the designed pulse waveform optimization and generation is in process).

Such flexible artificial control built with synaptic devices could provide a suitable platform for a broad range of computing applications, as shown **Figure 4**. Some of the advantages that SiO_x-based synaptic devices provide over other resistive switching materials include a higher dynamic range (~10^4) [57] and the potential to achieve as many as 10–60 multilevel states (depend on the stability) in both LTP and LTD by changing the increment/decrement of the voltage step, as shown in **Figure 4a**. These advantages may arise as the result of there being a large number of defects within the switching region of the memory device. Switching is modeled as a change in conductivity of a group of defects within the switching region. In this framework, defects are not created or destroyed, but are simply driven between conductive and nonconductive forms by proton exchange reactions that are known to occur in SiO_x materials (**Figure 2f**) [60]. The SET and RESET switching transitions can be described in more detail with the aid of the electron energy band diagrams shown in **Figure 4b**, which were constructed using the thermodynamic and switching charge-state energy levels reported by Blochl in 2000 [74]. The ideal energy band diagrams in **Figure 4b** represent only a single electron pathway through the memory device, whereas in reality there are likely many such percolation pathways in parallel. The SET transition is modeled as being the result of trap-assisted electron tunneling through $(SiH)_2$ defects (a voltage-triggered mechanism, due to less current flow in the initial stage of SET process) that stimulates H^+ desorption and reaction of H^+ with absorbed water $(SiOH)_2$ to form conductive Si-H-Si and H_3O^+ (**Figure 2f**). Trap-assisted tunneling can only occur when the bias across the switching region is ≥2.6 V, which is the effective bandgap of the $(SiH)_2$ defect and compares well with the observed minimum SET voltage of ~2.5 V in the *I-V* response [59, 60]. The RESET transition is modeled as being the result of Fowler-Nordheim electron tunneling into the H_3O^+ defect (possibly current-induced Joule heating due to large current flow through the filament) that stimulates proton release and electrochemical reactions to reform $(SiH)_2$ and $(SiOH)_2$ (**Figure 2f**) [60]. The band diagrams shown in **Figure 4b** are found to be consistent with measured electron energy barriers [60] and electroluminescence results reported for similar devices [62].

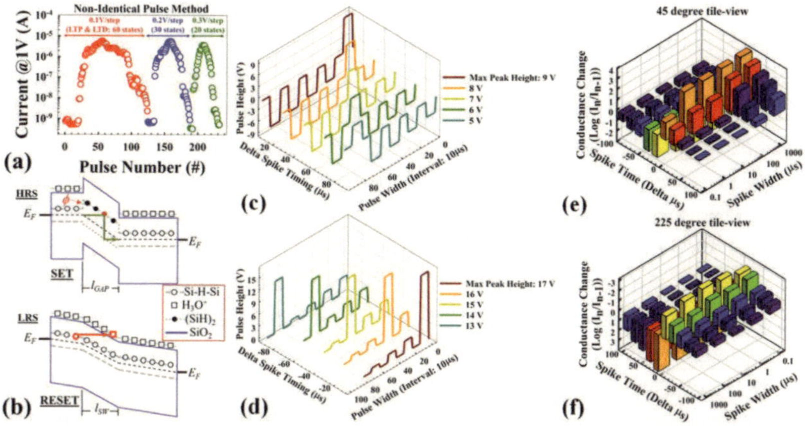

Figure 4. Demonstration of a SiO_x-based synaptic device. (a) Sequential LTP/LTD behaviors as a function of increment/decrement voltage steps (0.1, 0.2, and 0.3 V) by non-identical pulse form. For the non-identical pulse method, pulse height modulation changes continuously from 4 V to 10 V for LTP, and changes continuously from 11 to 17 V for LTD. Pulse width is fixed at 10 μs in both cases. (b) Energy band diagrams: For HRS and SET process, showing theoretical bandgap of $(SiH)_2$ defect within gap region of length l_{GAP}, theoretical bandgap of Si-H-Si defects outside the gap region, and trap-assisted-tunneling SET transition (green arrow). Barrier height to electron transport is ϕ ~ 0.8 eV. For the LRS and RESET process, showing theoretical bandgap of Si-H-Si, H_3O^+ energy level, switching region of length l_{SW}, and Fowler-Nordheim tunneling RESET transition (red arrow). (c–d) A pulse waveform design using the non-identical pulse method for demonstration of spike-timing-dependent plasticity (STDP) as a function of spike pulse width intervals. For the potentiation of conductance strength change, the overall pulse waveform (pulse width fixed at 10 μs in this case) based on the delay of spike timing between neurons is shown in (c). Similarly, for the depression of conductance strength change, the overall pulse waveform (pulse width fixed at 10 μs in this case) based on the delay of spike timing between neurons is shown in (d). (e–f) A demonstration of spike-timing-dependent plasticity (STDP) using the non-identical pulse method with different spike widths. Each colored bar shows the average of 3~5 measurements. (e) Emphasizes potentiation direction of STDP with positive delta time (45° tilted). (f) Emphasizes depression direction of STDP with negative delta time (225° tilted). The definition of conductance change is as $Log_{10}(I_n/I_{nitial})$, where $I_n/I_{Initial}$ is current ratio measured at 1 V after/before the pulse is applied. Figure reprinted by [19].

Figure 4c–f demonstrate that the SiO_x-based 1D-1R architecture can mimic spike-timing-dependent plasticity (STDP), a biological process that adjusts the strength of connections between two neurons in a synapse gap junction region that is an electrically conductive link between the pre- and postsynaptic neurons. Two pulse generator sources are used to simulate the pre- and postsynaptic neurons. This provides the pulse waveforms using the nonidentical pulse method (also used in various types of emerging memory devices or materials systems) for demonstration of STDP. By design of pre-neuron and postneuron spikes in neuromorphic circuits, the strength of the conductance change can be modulated based on the spike-timing delta (Δt) between the two neurons (**Figure 4c–d**). **Figure 4e–f** demonstrates a total of 10 different states of STDP biological behavior for depression and potentiation with $n = 2, 4, 6, 8, 10$ and as a function of spike width modulation, ranging from 100 ns to 1 ms. For example, the depression of conductance change strength can be achieved by using multistep spike heights from −4 to 0 V in the preneuron state and a single spike height fixed at 13 V in the postneuron state, with both neurons having a fixed pulse width of 10 μs and a firing period of 20 μs, as shown in **Figure 4e–f**. When the time delay difference is −10 × (n−1) μs, where n is an even number, the total spike waveform (postneuron spike minus preneuron spike) applied to the synapse gap junction region can adjust the conductance ratio between two neurons over the range from 10^{-3} to 0.1 in the depression direction (RESET process) as compared with the initial LRS conductance (**Figure 4f**). Similarly, the potentiation of conductance change strength can be achieved by using multistep spike heights from 4 to 8 V in the preneuron state and a single spike height also fixed at 13 V in the postneuron state, with both neurons having a fixed pulse width of 10 μs and a firing period of 20 μs. When the time delay difference is 10 × (n−1) μs, where n is an even number, the total spike waveform (postneuron spike minus preneuron spike) applied to the synapse gap junction region can in this case adjust the conductance ratio between neurons over the range from 10^3 to 0.01 in the potentiation direction (SET process) as compared with the initial HRS conductance (**Figure 4e**). It may be noted that the 1D-1R architecture not only avoids sneak-path issues and lowers standby power consumption, but also helps to realize STDP behaviors. Without the 1D rectification characteristics in reverse-bias polarity, the above spiking forms cannot be implemented due to the unipolar nature of the 1R device, specifically in the potentiation behaviors under negative bias. In the 1R case, an applied voltage above the RESET threshold voltage (for example, −9 V) can trigger the RESET process and induce depression behaviors instead of potentiation behaviors. Also, for depression behaviors, when the time delay difference is smaller than the spiking width, the remaining 4 V spike height in this case would not fire the synapse toward a LRS in the depression direction (see **Figure 3h**). Therefore, by carefully designing the firing pulses between neurons in the neuromorphic circuit, a biological synapse behavior can be demonstrated with 1D-1R SiO_x-based resistive switching memories.

The 1D-1R architecture with SiO_x-based resistance switching devices and the structure of artificial neural networks map naturally onto hybrid CMOS/synapse circuits that can be designed on a single chip (**Figure 5**) to provide predictable results with an ultimate scaling potential of CMOS technology to the sub-10-nm level, which could possibly challenge the complexity and connectivity of the human brain.

The other topic is material implication operations by using the same device architecture in SiO_x-based memristor (**Figures 1** and **5**). Based on our recent reports, implication operation

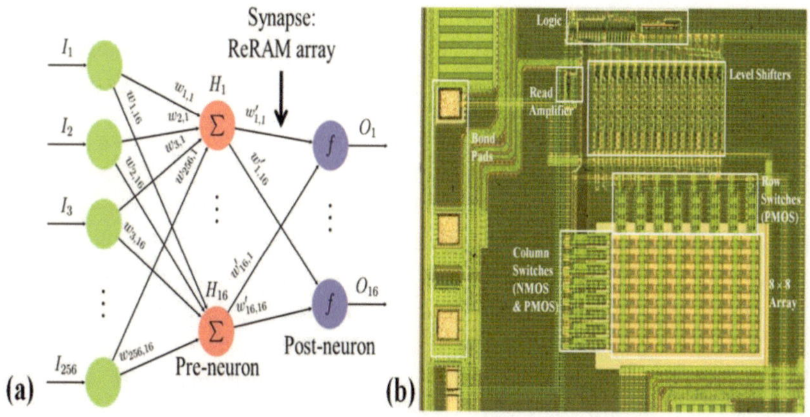

Figure 5. (a) Bio-inspired and mixed-signal information processing: hybrid CMOS/ReRAM circuits may also enable efficient analog dot-product computation, which is a key operation in artificial neural networks and many other information processing tasks. (b) A fabricated 8 × 8 artificial neural network array combined with CMOS transistors and logic control.

(IMP) has been performed by two SiO_x memristors and a 5.7 kΩ standalone resistor are configured as shown in **Figure 6a**. Furthermore, three memristors connected in the circuit shown in **Figure 6b** and two steps of IMP are required to perform a NAND operation. It may be noted

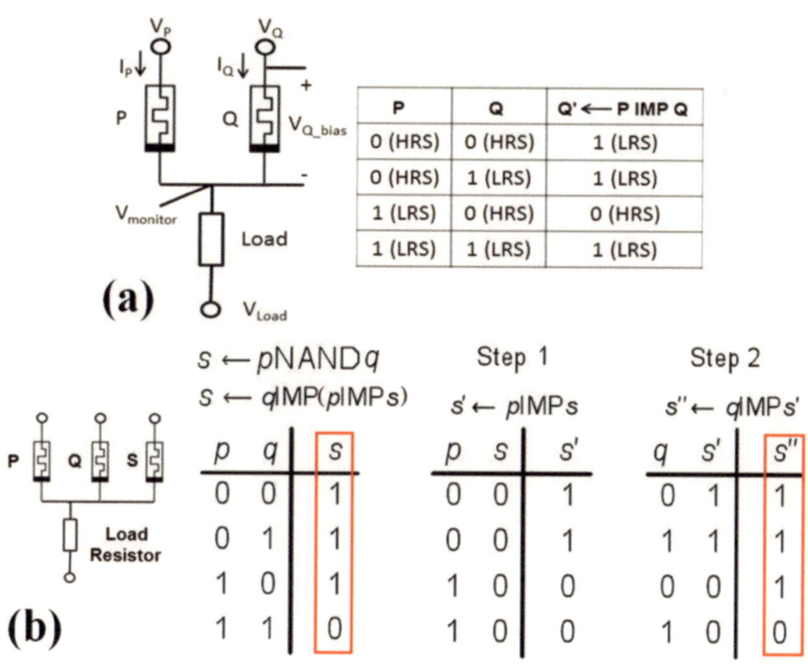

P	Q	Q' ← P IMP Q
0 (HRS)	0 (HRS)	1 (LRS)
0 (HRS)	1 (LRS)	1 (LRS)
1 (LRS)	0 (HRS)	0 (HRS)
1 (LRS)	1 (LRS)	1 (LRS)

Figure 6. (a) Circuit for the implication scheme including two SiO_x memristor and one load resistor, with bias voltages and conducting currents marked out, and truth table for material implication [75]. (b) Circuit to perform NAND operation, and Truth table for NAND operation. Two steps performing NAND operation via implication with final results shown in red square. Figure reprinted by [75].

that the final logic value pNANDq is stored as the last value of memristor s, or s″ in **Figure 6b**. This row of three memristors, namely P, Q, S, can be expanded to a row consisting of more memristors all sharing the same load resistor. Implication operations can be performed on any two memristors in the row, as long as the rest of the memristors are kept unbiased. Since we are able to perform implication on one row, similarly, implication can be done on one column.

However, when we put multiple rows and columns together to form a crossbar array, several problems arise. The first issue is providing multiple voltage signals as well as a common load resistor to an arbitrary pair of memristor on the same row or column. Based on the crossbar RRAM structure, the bit-line/word-line selection transistor can serve as the common resistor. By varying the gate voltage bias of the select transistor, it can serve as an ON state switch, OFF state switch or a resistor with channel resistance of R_{Load}. From **Figure 6**, it is noted that four voltage signals (V_P, V_Q, V_S, and V_{Load}) are required during an implication operation, two different voltages along the same bit-line/word-line. Therefore, a total of four voltage lines, each connected to all NMOS select transistor, will provide voltage signals for implication operation.

The concepts are demonstrated by a 4 × 4 memristor crossbar array (**Figure 7a** and **b**) and a circuit with an 8 × 8 memristor crossbar array. In addition to 1D-1R device arrays (**Figure 5a**), the hybrid CMOS/1D-1R device architecture shown in **Figure 5e** has been successfully demonstrated as shown in **Figure 5f** by the *I-V* resistive switching plots. Using the NMOS/PMOS transistor also fabricated on the same chip (**Figure 5e**), an implication circuit is realized using two 1D1R memory elements and a transistor. In **Figure 7a** and **b**, the design is quite different from the RRAM crossbar array architecture, the circuit consists of two rows of bit select transistors for the same column of memristors, one on the top, and one on the bottom. Similarly, there are two column word select transistors for the same row of memristors, one on the left and one on the right. This redundancy ensures two distinctive voltage signals can be applied on any pair of memristors on the same bit line/word line. The implication voltages (V_P, V_Q, V_R)

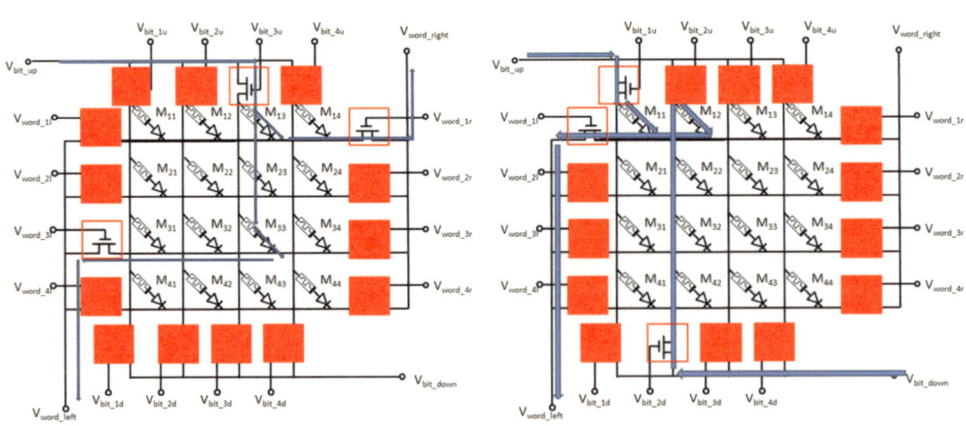

Figure 7. (a) and (b) demonstrate 4 × 4 crossbar structure memristor arrays with select transistors to achieve a one-bit full adder function. The implication circuit performs (a) M_{13} IMP M_{33} and (b) M_{11} IMP M_{12} on a 4 × 4 crossbar structure memristor array. Blue arrows show the current flow directions, and red solid squares cover all OFF-state transistors. Voltage signals and memristor numbers are labeled.

are biased on three of the four lines depending on the configuration, and the voltage applied to each line is labeled as follows, V_{bit_up}, V_{bit_down}, V_{word_left}, and V_{word_right}. The gate of each select transistor is also independently biased, to either isolate the bit lines/word lines from the implication voltages or provide that implication voltage to one particular bit line/word line.

To perform M_{13} IMP M_{33} (negative voltage implication operation performed along bit line 3): Assuming all memristors are initialized to HRS, bias $V_{bit\_up} = 2$ V, $V_{word\_left} = -1.5$ V, $V_{word\_right} = 0$ V, V_{word_1r}, and $V_{word\_3l} = V_{full\_on}$, $V_{bit\_3u} = V_{IMP}$, with all other transistor gate voltages at V_{full_off}. The equivalent circuit is shown in **Figure 5a** with the path of conduction current flow marked. In **Figure 5a–e**, P is M_{13}, Q is M_{33}, and the transistor bit_3u is used as the load resistor. The implication is a negative voltage scheme. All transistors that are biased at fully OFF states are covered by red squares, effectively keeping the voltages of irrelevant columns/rows floating; to perform M_{11} IMP M_{12} (positive voltage implication operation performed along word line 1): Assuming all memristors are initialized to HRS, Bias $V_{bit\_up} = 0$ V, $V_{bit\_down} = 1.5$ V, $V_{word\_left} = -2$ V, V_{bit_1u}, and $V_{bit\_2d} = V_{full\_on}$, $V_{word\_1l} = V_{IMP}$, with all other transistor gate voltages at V_{full_off}. This equivalent circuit is shown in **Figure 5b** with the current flow path marked. In **Figure 5b**, P is M_{11}, Q is M_{12}, and the transistor word_1l is used as the load resistor. In this case, the implication uses a positive voltage scheme. As before, all transistors biased to fully OFF states (covered by red squares) effectively keep the voltages of irrelevant columns/rows floating.

In **Figures 1a** and **5a**, each memristor is placed in series with a pn diode in order to avoid current sneak-path problems. Originating from the crossbar device structure itself, the sneak-path problem has been identified and analyzed by many previous researchers [20, 76–122]. Because the bit line or word line select transistor raises the voltage across the whole bit or word, a group of memristors in the LRS may form a highly conductive path and cause misreading of certain memristors. The solution to the sneak-path problem is using a selection element together with a memory element, as shown in **Figure 5f**. Such a selection element is used to allow current conduction in one direction while suppressing current flow in the other direction. The most common selection element is a low-leakage pn diode, limiting the current flowing through the sneak paths down to reverse the bias leakage current level and reducing the power consumption during implication operations.

5. Summary

In summary, we have demonstrated potentiation, depression and spike-timing-dependent plasticity in a synaptic device built using a SiO_x-based 1D-1R architecture. Proton-induced resistive switching behaviors in the SiO_x memory element were discussed, where the SET threshold is modeled as proton desorption from the $(SiH)_2$ defect to generate the conductive hydrogen bridge, Si-H-Si, and the RESET transition is modeled as proton release and capture to reform nonconductive $(SiH)_2$ [82–89]. The electrical results demonstrate that the technology has good potential for providing a simple and robust approach for large-scale integration of programmable neuromorphic chips using CMOS technology, and represent a critical milestone regarding the potential use of SiO_2-based resistive memory as a synaptic device in future synthetic biological computing applications. Moreover, a logic circuit consisting of a

4 × 4 array of crossbar structure memristor 1D1R memory elements and select transistors are proposed together with bidirectional implication schemes. Then a one-bit full adder is theoretically realized with a total of 48 operation steps performed on the circuit. A comparison between CMOS-enabled logic circuits and memristor-enabled circuits shows advantages in real estate and power consumption, as well as disadvantages in speed. This result suggests the memristor-enabled logic circuit is most suitable for high-speed, low-power, high-density applications. Further study is still required to make a few steps in various implication schemes as well as lower power consumption in synaptic computations.

Author details

Cheng-Chih Hsieh[1], Yao-Feng Chang[1*], Ying-Chen Chen[1], Xiaohan Wu[1], Meiqi Guo[1], Fei Zhou[1], Sungjun Kim[2], Burt Fowler[1], Chih-Yang Lin[3], Chih-Hung Pan[3], Ting-Chang Chang[3] and Jack C. Lee[1]

*Address all correspondence to: yfchang@utexas.edu

1 Microelectronics Research Center, the University of Texas at Austin, Austin, TX, USA

2 Inter-university Semiconductor Research Center (ISRC) and the Department of Electrical and Computer Engineering, Seoul National University, Seoul, Korea

3 Department of Physics, National Sun Yat-Sen University, Kaohsiung, Taiwan

References

[1] Lundstrom M. Science. 2003;**299**:210-211. DOI: 10.1126/science.1079567

[2] Ieong M, Doris B, Kedzierski J, Rim K, Yang M. Science. 2004;**306**:2057. DOI:10.1126/science.1100731

[3] Chen YY, Degraeve R, Clima S, Govoreanu B, Goux L, Fantini A, Kar GS, Pourtois G, Groeseneken G, Wouters DJ, Jurczak M. Techenical Digest. International Electron Devices Meet (IEDM); 2012. p. 482. DOI: 10.1109/TED.2012.2218607

[4] Kahng D, Sze SM. Bell System Technical Journal. 1967;**46**:1288-1295. DOI: 10.1109/T-ED.1976.18468

[5] Chang TC, Jiana FY, Chenc SC, Tsai YT. Materials Today. 2011;**14**:608-615. DOI: 10.1016/S1369-7021(11)70302-9

[6] Lu W, Lieber CM. Nature Materials. 2007;**6**:841. DOI: 10.1038/nmat2028

[7] Heath JR, Ratner MA. Physics Today. 2003;**56**:43. DOI: 10.1063/1.1583533

[8] Sawa A. Materials Today. 2008;**11**:28. DOI:10.1016/S1369-7021(08)70119-6

[9] Terabe K, Hasegawa T, Nakayama T, Aono M. Nature. 2005;**433**:47. DOI: 10.1038/nature03190

[10] Lee MJ, Lee CB, Lee D, Lee SR, Chang M, Hur JH, Kim YB, Kim CJ, Seo DH, Seo S, Chung UI, Yoo IK, Kim K. Nature Materials. 2011;**10**:625. DOI: 10.1038/nmat3070

[11] ITRS International Technology Roadmap for Semoconductors, (2013) edn; http://www.itrs.net

[12] Yu S, Chen HY, Gao B, Kang J, Wong HSP. ACS Nano. 2013;**7**:2320. DOI: 10.1021/nn305510u

[13] Song S, Cho B, Kim TW, Ji Y, Jo M, Wang G, Choe M, Kahng YH, Hwang H, Lee T. Advanced Materials. 2010;**22**:5048. DOI: 10.1002/adma.201002575

[14] Valov I, Linn E, Tappertzhofen S, Schmelzer S, van den Hurk J, Lentz F, Waser R. National Nature Communication. 2013;**4**:1771. DOI:10.1038/ncomms2784

[15] Jo SH, Chang T, Ebong I, Bhadviya BB, Mazumder P, Lu W. Nano Letters. 2010;**10**:1297. DOI: 10.1021/nl904092h

[16] Ohno T, Hasegawa T, Tsuruoka T, Terabe K, Gimzewski JK, Aono M. Nature Materials. 2011;**10**:591. DOI:10.1038/nmat3054

[17] Borghetti J, Snider GS, Kuekes PJ, Yang JJ, Stewart DR, Williams RS. Nature. 2010; **464**:873-876. DOI: 10.1038/nature08940

[18] Chua LO. IEEE Transactions on Circuit Theory. 1971;**18**:507. DOI: 10.1109/TCT.1971.1083337

[19] Chang YF, Fowler B, Chen YC, Zhou F, Pan CH, Chang TC, Lee JC. Scientific Reports. 2016;**6**:21268. DOI: 10.1038/srep21268

[20] Chen Y, Fowler B, Wang Y, Xue F, Zhou F, Chang YF, Lee JC. ECS Journal of Solid State Science and Technology. 2012;**1**:148. DOI: 10.1149/2.013203jss

[21] Carlos ZR, Luis AC, Jose AP, Timothée M, Teresa SG, Bernabé LB. Frontiers in Neuroscience. 2011;**5**:26. DOI: 10.3389/fnins.2011.00026

[22] Demming A, Gimzewski JK, Vuillaume D. Nanotechnology. 2014;**24**:380201. DOI: 10.1088/0957-4484/24/38/380201

[23] Serrano-Gotarredona T, Masquelier T, Prodromakis T, Indiveri G, Linares-Barranco B. Frontiers In Neuroscience. 2013;**7**:2. DOI: 10.3389/fnins.2013.00002

[24] Suri M, Querlioz D, Bichler O, Palma G, Vianello E, Vuillaume D, Gamrat C, DeSalvo B. IEEE Transactions on Electron Devices. 2013;**60**:2402. DOI: 10.1109/TED.2013.2263000

[25] Ambrogio S, Balatti S, Nardi F, Facchinetti S, Ielmini D. Nanotechnology. 2013;**24**:384012. DOI:10.1088/0957-4484/24/38/384012

[26] Hsieh CC, Roy A, Chang YF, Rai A, Banerjee S. 73rd Annual Device Research Conference (DRC). 2015. 101-102. DOI: 10.1109/DRC.2015.7175575

[27] Xia Q, Yang JJ, Wu W, Li X, Williams RS. Nano Letters American Chemical Society. 2009;**9**:3640. DOI: 10.1021/nl901874j

[28] Sills S, Yasuda S, Calderoni A, Cardon C, Strand J, Aratani K, Ramaswamy N. Symposium on VLSI Technology. 2015 T106. DOI: 10.1109/VLSIT.2015.7223639

[29] Chang YF et al. VLSI Technology, Systems, and Applications (VLSI-TSA). 2016. 1-2. DOI: 10.1109/VLSI-TSA.2016.7480497

[30] Guo M, Chen YC, Chang YF, Wu X, Fowler B, Zhao Y, Lee JC. Device Research Conference (DRC), 74th Annual. 2016. 1-2. DOI: 10.1109/DRC.2016.7548460

[31] Chen YC et al. ECS Transactions. 2016;**72**(2):25-33. DOI: 10.1149/07202.0025ecst

[32] Zhou J, Tang Y, Wu J, XFang X, Zhu X, Huang D. ICISEM. 2013. DOI: 10.1109/ICISEM.2013.87

[33] Indiveri G, et al. Frontiers in Neuroscience. 2011;**5**:73-96. DOI: 10.3389/fnins.2011.00073

[34] Yang JJ, Strukov DB, Stewart DR. Nature Nanotechnology. 2013;**8**:13-24. DOI:10.1038/nnano.2012.240

[35] Waser R, Aono M, Nature Materials. 2007;**6**:833. DOI:10.1038/nmat2023

[36] Rainer W, ReginaD, Staikov G, Szot K. Advanced Materials. 2009;**21**:2632-2663. DOI: 10.1002/adma.200900375

[37] Yang JJ et al., Nature Nanotechnology. 2008;**3**:429-433. DOI:10.1038/nnano.2008.160

[38] Szot K, Speier W, Bihlmayer G, Waser R. Nature Materials. 2005;**5**:312-320. DOI:10.1038/nmat1614

[39] Meijer GI. Science. 2008;**319**:1625-1626. DOI:10.1126/science.1153909

[40] HickmottTW. Journal of Applied Physics. 1962;**33**:2669-2682. DOI: 10.1063/1.1702530

[41] Simmons JG, Verderber RR, The Royal Society Proceedings of the London Series. 1967; A **301**:77. DOI: 10.1098/rspa.1967.0191

[42] Dearnaley G, Stoneham A M, Morgan DV. Reports On Progress In Physics. 1970;**33**:1129-1191. DOI:10.1088/0034-4885/33/3/306

[43] Yao J, Sun Z, L Zhong L, Natelson D, J M. Tour. Nano Letters. 2010;**10**:4105. DOI: 10.1021/nl102255r

[44] Yao J, Lin J, Dai Y, Ruan G, Yan Z, Li L, Zhong L, Natelson D, J M. Tour. Nature Communications. 2012;**3**:1101. DOI:10.1038/ncomms2110

[45] Wang G, Lauchner AC, Lin J, Natelson D, Palem KV, Tour JM. Advance Materials. 2013;**25**:4789. DOI: 10.1002/adma.201302047

[46] Lamb DR, Rundle PC, British Journal of Applied Physics. 1967;**18**:29. DOI: 10.1088/0508-3443/18/1/306

[47] Mehonic A, Cueff S, Wojdak M, Hudziak S, Jambois O, Labbé C, Garrido B, Rizk R, Kenyon AJ. Journal of Applied Physics. 2012;**1**:11, 074507. DOI: 10.1063/1.3701581

[48] Mehonic A, Cueff S, M. Wojdak M, Hudziak S, Labbé C, Rizk R, Kenyon AJ. Nanotechnology. 2012;**23**:455201. DOI:10.1088/0957-4484/23/45/455201

[49] Cavallini M, Hemmatian Z, Riminucci A, Prezioso M, Morandi V, Murgia M. Advance Materials. 2012;**24**:1197. DOI: 10.1002/adma.201104301

[50] Ji L, Chang YF, Fowler B, Chen YC, Tsai TM, Chang KC, Chen MC, Chang TC, Sze SM, Yu ET, Lee JC. Nano Letters. 2014;**14**:813-818. DOI: 10.1021/nl404160u

[51] Kuzum D, Jeyasingh RGD, Lee B, Wong HSP. Nano Letters. 2011;**12**:2179. DOI: 10.1021/nl201040y

[52] Cho B, Kim TW, Song S, Ji Y, Jo M, Hwang H, Jung GY, Lee T. Advanced Materials. 2010;**22**:1228. DOI: 10.1002/adma.200903203

[53] Chang YF, et al. Journal of Applied Physics. 2012;**112**:123702. DOI: 10.1063/1.4769218

[54] Dang TA, Chau C N. Journal of Electrochemical Society. 1996;**143**:302-305. DOI: 10.1149/1.1836427

[55] Alfonsettia R, et al. Applied Surface Sciences. 1993;**70**:222-225. DOI: 10.1016/0169-4332(93)90431-A

[56] Zhou F, et al. Applied Physics Letters. 2014;**105**:163506. DOI: 10.1063/1.4900422

[57] Chang YF, et al. Applied Physics Letters. 2013;**103**:193508. DOI: 10.1063/1.4829526

[58] Mehonic A, et al. Applied Physics Letters. 2015;**117**:124505-1245013. DOI: 10.1063/1.4916259

[59] Chang YF, et al. Applied Physics Letters. 2014;**116**:043708. DOI: 10.1063/1.4891242

[60] Chang YF, et al. Applied Physics Letters. 2014;**116**:043709. DOI: 10.1063/1.4891244

[61] Yao J, Zhong L, Natelson D, Tour JM. Scientific Reports. 2012;**2**:242-247. DOI: 10.1038/srep00242

[62] He C, et al. Advanced Materials. 2013;**25**:5593-5598. DOI: 10.1002/adma.201302447

[63] Chang YF, et al. Applied Physics Letters. 2013;**103**:033521. DOI: 10.1063/1.4816162

[64] Tappertzhofen S, Hempel M, Valov I, Waser R. Materials Research Society Symposia Proceedings. 2011;**1330**. doi:10.1557/opl.2011.1198

[65] Tappertzhofen S, et al. ACS Nano. 2013;**7**:6396-6402. DOI: 10.1021/nn4026614

[66] Tappertzhofen S, Waser R, Valov I. ChemElectroChem. 2014;**1**:1287-1292. DOI: 10.1002/celc.201402106

[67] Valov I. ChemElectroChem. 2014;**1**:26-36. DOI: 10.1002/celc.201300165

[68] Wedig A, et al. Nature Nanotechnology. 2015. DOI:10.1038/nnano.2015.221

[69] Messerschmitt F, Kubicek M, Rupp JLM. Advanced Functional Materials. 2015;**25**:5117-5125. DOI: 10.1002/adfm.201501517

[70] Lübben M, et al. Graphene-modified interface controls transition from VCM to ECM switching modes in Ta/TaOx based memristive devices. Advanced Materials. 2015;**27**:6202-6207. DOI: 10.1002/adma.201502574

[71] Jameson JR, Nishi Y. Role of hydrogen ions in TiO_2-based memory devices. Integrated Ferroelectrics. 2011;**124**:112-118. DOI: 10.1080/10584587.2011.573733

[72] Arnold W P, Mittal CK, Katsuki S, Murad F. Nitric oxide activates guanylate cyclase and increases guanosine 3′,5′-cyclic monophosphate levels in various tissue preparations. Proceedings of National Academy of Sciences U.S.A. 1977;**74**:3203-3207. DOI: 10.1073/pnas.74.8.3203

[73] Chang YF, et al. Applied Physics Letters. 2012;**101**:052111-052115. DOI: 10.1063/1.3294632

[74] Blöchl PE. Physics Review B. 2000;**62**:6158-6179. DOI: 10.1103/PhysRevB.62.6158

[75] Zhou F, Guckert L, Chang YF, Swartzlander EE Jr, Lee J. Applied Physical Letters. 2015;**107**:183501. DOI: 10.1063/1.4934835

[76] Liou JJ, Liaw SK, Chung YH. Nano Devices and Sensors, De Gruyter. Walter de Gruyter GmbH & Co KG. 2016. ISBN: 978-1-5015-0153-1

[77] Chang YF, et al. VLSI Technology, Systems, and Applications (VLSI-TSA), 2013. DOI: 10.1109/VLSI-TSA.2013.6545589

[78] Strukov DB, Snider GS, Stewart DR, Williams RS. The missing memristor found. Nature. 2008;**453**:80-83. DOI: 10.1038/nature06932

[79] Pickett MD, Strukov DB, Borghetti JL, Yang JJ, Snider GS, Stewart DR, Williams R S. Journal of Applied Physics. 2009;**106**:074508. DOI: 10.1063/1.3236506

[80] Sun X, Li G, Ding L, Yang N, Zhang W. Applied Physics Letters. 2011;**99**:072101. DOI: 10.1063/1.4934835

[81] Linn E, Rosezin R, Kügeler C, Waser R. Complementary resistive switches for passive nanocrossbar memories. Nature Materials. 2010;**9**:403. DOI: 10.1038/nmat2748

[82] Fowler B, Chang YF, Zhou F, Wang Y, Chen PY, Xue F, Chen Y T, Bringhurst B, Pozder S, Lee JC. RSC Advances. 2015;**5**:21215. DOI: 10.1039/C4RA16078A

[83] Zhou F, Chang YF, Chen YC, Wu X, Zhang Y, Fowler B, Lee JC, Physical Chemistry Chemical Physics. 2016;**18**:700. DOI: 10.1039/C5CP06507K

[84] Chang YF, Fowler B, Zhou F, Chen YC, Lee JC. Applied Physical Letters. 2016;**108**:033504. DOI: 10.1063/1.4940203

[85] WangY, Chen YT, Xue F, Zhou F, Chang YF, Fowler B, Lee JC. Applied Physical Letters. 2012;**100**:083502. DOI: 10.1063/1.3687724

[86] Chen YT, Fowler B, Wang Y, Xue F, Zhou F, Chang YF, Chen P Y, Lee JC. IEEE Electron Device Letters. 2012;**33**:1702. DOI: 10.1109/LED.2012.2218566

[87] Wang Y, Fowler B, Zhou F, Chang YF, Chen YT, Xue F, Lee JC. Applied Physical Letters. 2013;**103**:213505. DOI: 10.1063/1.4832595

[88] Wang Y, Fowler B, Chen YT, Xue F, Zhou F, Chang YF, and Lee Wang JC. Applied Physical Letters. 2012;**101**:183505. DOI: 10.1063/1.4765356

[89] Zhou F, Chang YF, Byun K, Fowler B, Lee JC. Applied Physical Letters. 2014;**105**:133501. DOI: 10.1063/1.4896877

[90] Chu TJ, et al. IEEE Electron Device Letters. 2013;**34**(4):502-504. DOI: 10.1109/LED.2013.2242843

[91] Feng LW, Chang CY, Chang YF, Chen WR, Wang SY, Chiang PW, Chang TC. Applied Physical Letters. 2010;**96**:052111. DOI: 10.1063/1.3294632

[92] Chang KC, et al. Nanoscale Research Letters. 2015;**10**(1):1. DOI: 10.1186/s11671-015-0740-7

[93] ChangYF, Chang TC, Chang CY. Journal of Applied Physics. 2011;**110**(5):053703. DOI: 10.1063/1.3630119

[94] Yang S, et al. Advanced Materials. 2016;**27**(41):6423-6430. DOI: 10.1002/adma.201502386

[95] Feng LW, Chang CY, Chang YF, Chang TC, Wang SY, Chen SC, Lin CC, Chen SC, Chiang PW. Applied Physics Letters. 2010;**96**:222108. DOI: 10.1063/1.3428777

[96] Feng LW, Chang CY, Chang TC, Tu CH, Wang PS, Chang YF, Chen MC, Huang HC. Applied Physics Letters. 2009;**95**:262110-262113. DOI: 10.1063/1.3279131

[97] Zhou F, Chang YF, Fowler B, Byun K, Lee JC. Applied Physics Letters. 2015;**106**:063508. DOI: 10.1063/1.4909533

[98] Zhou F, Chang YF, Wang Y, Chen YT, Xue F, Fowler BW, Lee J C. Applied Physics Letters. 2014;**105**:163506. DOI: 10.1063/1.4900422

[99] Xue F, Jiang A, Chen YT, Wang Y, Zhou F, Chang YF, Lee J. Electron Devices Meeting (IEDM), 2012 IEEE International, 27.5. 2012;1-27.5. 4. DOI: 10.1109/IEDM.2012.6479116

[100] Feng LW, Chang YF, Chang CY, Chang TC, Wang SY, Chiang PW, Lin CC, Chen SC, Chen SC. Thin Solid Films. 2010;**519**:1536. DOI: 10.1016/j.tsf.2010.08.165

[101] Chang YF, Chen YT, Xue F, Wang Y, Zhou F, Fowler B, Lee JC. Device Research Conference (DRC), 70th Annual. 2012. 49. DOI: 10.1109/DRC.2012.6256972

[102] Hsieh CC, Roy A, Rai A, Chang YF, Banerjee SK. Applied Physics Letters. 2015;**106**:173108. DOI: 10.1063/1.4919442

[103] Xue F, Jiang A, Chen YT, Wang Y, Zhou F, Chang YF, Lee JC. IEEE Transactions on Electron Devices.2014;**61**:2332. DOI: 10.1109/TED.2014.2320946

[104] Zhou F, Xue F, Chang YF, Lee JC. Device Research Conference (DRC), 2014 72nd Annual. 2014. 207. DOI: 10.1109/DRC.2014.6872370

[105] Chang YF, Feng LW, Chang TC. Materials Chemistry and Physics. 2011;**131**:262. DOI: 10.1016/j.matchemphys.2011.09.037

[106] Cheng CC, Chien CH, Luo GL, Liu JC, Chen YC, Chang YF, Wang SY, Kei CC, Hsiao CN, and Chang CY, Journal of Vacuum Science & Technology B. 2009;**27**:130. DOI: 10.1116/1.3058724

[107] Xue F, Chen YT, Wang Y, Zhou F, Chang YF, Fowler B, Lee JC, ECS Transactions. 2012; **45**:245. DOI: 10.1149/1.3700959

[108] Chang YF, Tsai YT, Syu YE, Chang TC. ECS Journal of Solid State Science and Technology. 2012;**1**:Q57. DOI: 10.1149/2.020203jss

[109] Chang YF, Tsai YT, Chang GW, Syu YE, Tai YH, Chang TC. ECS Journal of Solid State Science and Technology. 2012;**1**:Q91. DOI: 10.1149/2.003205jss

[110] Chang YF, Fowler B, Zhou F, Lee JC, ECS Transactions. 2016;**69**(5):149-164. DOI: 10.1149/06905.0149ecst

[111] Chang YF, Fowler B, Chen YC, Lee JC, Progress in Solid State Chemistry. 2016;**44**(3):75-85. DOI: 10.1016/j.progsolidstchem.2016.07.001

[112] Chen YT, Fowler B, Chang YF, Wang Y, Xue F, Zhou F, Lee JC. ECS Solid State Letters. 2013;**2**:N18. DOI: 10.1149/2.009305ssl

[113] Hsieh CC, Roy A, Chang YF, Shahrjerdi D, Banerjee SK, Applied Physics Letters. 2016;**109**(22):223501. DOI: 10.1063/1.4971188

[114] Chang YF, Fowler B, Zhou F, Byun K, Lee JC, VLSI-TSA, 2015. 1-2. DOI: 10.1109/VLSI-TSA.2015.7117558

[115] Ji L, et al., IEEE International Electron Devices Meeting. 8.6. 2014. 1-8.6. 3. DOI: 10.1109/IEDM.2014.7047013

[116] Ji L, et al. 72nd Device Research Conference; 2014. pp. 243-244 DOI: 10.1109/DRC.2014.6872388

[117] Chang YF, Fowler B, Chen YC, Ji L, Zhou F, Lee JC, 72nd Device Research Conference, 2014. 1. DOI: 10.1109/DRC.2014.6872349

[118] Zhou F, Xue F, Chang YF, Lee J, 72nd Device Research Conference, 2014. 207-208. DOI: 10.1109/DRC.2014.6872370

[119] Chang YF et al., VLSI-TSA, 2014. 1-2. DOI: 10.1109/VLSI-TSA.2014.6839674

[120] Chang YF, Chen YC, Li J, Xue F, Wang Y, Zhou F, Fowler B, Lee JC, Device Research Conference (DRC), 71st Annual, 2013. 135-136. DOI: 10.1109/DRC.2013.6633830

[121] Wang Y, Chen YT, Xue F, Zhou F, Chang YF, Lee JC. ECS Transactions. 2013;**50**(4):151-156 DOI: 10.1149/05004.0151ecst

[122] Chen YC, Chang YF, Wu X, Zhou F, Guo M, Lin CY, Hsieh CC, Fowler B, Chang TC, Lee JC, RSC Advances. 2017;**7**. DOI: 10.1039/c7ra00567a

Chapter 12

Memristor Neural Network Design

Anping Huang, Xinjiang Zhang, Runmiao Li and
Yu Chi

Additional information is available at the end of the chapter

http://dx.doi.org/10.5772/intechopen.69929

Abstract

Neural network, a powerful learning model, has archived amazing results. However, the current Von Neumann computing system–based implementations of neural networks are suffering from memory wall and communication bottleneck problems ascribing to the Complementary Metal Oxide Semiconductor (CMOS) technology scaling down and communication gap. Memristor, a two terminal nanosolid state nonvolatile resistive switching, can provide energy-efficient neuromorphic computing with its synaptic behavior. Crossbar architecture can be used to perform neural computations because of its high density and parallel computation. Thus, neural networks based on memristor crossbar will perform better in real world applications. In this chapter, the design of different neural network architectures based on memristor is introduced, including spiking neural networks, multilayer neural networks, convolution neural networks, and recurrent neural networks. And the brief introduction, the architecture, the computing circuits, and the training algorithm of each kind of neural networks are presented by instances. The potential applications and the prospects of memristor-based neural network system are discussed.

Keywords: memristors, neural networks, deep learning, neuromorphic computing, analog computing

1. Introduction

Neural networks, composing multiple processing layers, have achieved amazing results, such as AlphaGo, DNC and WaveNet. However conventional neural networks based on Von Neumann systems have many challenges [1]. In Von Neumann computing system, the computing process and external memory are separated by a shared bus between data and program memory as shown in **Figure 1**, which is so called Von Neumann bottleneck. In Von Neumann computing system, a single processor has to simulate many neurons and the synapses between neurons. In addition, the bottleneck leads the energy-hungry data communication when

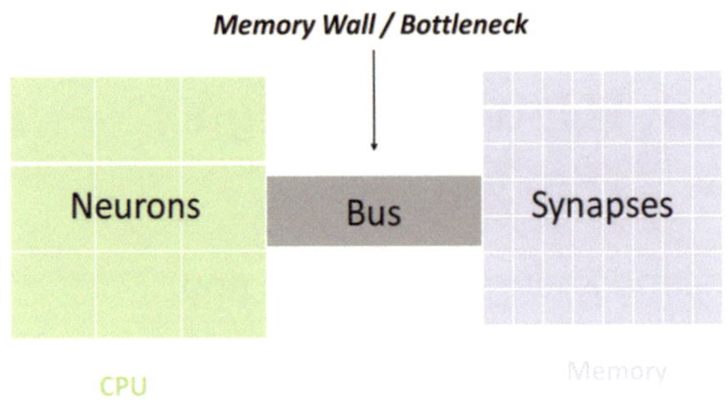

Figure 1. Von Neumann computing system bottleneck.

updating the neurons states and retrieving the synapse states, and when simulates a large-scale neural networks, the massages among processors will explode [2]. These defects make the Von Neumann computing system based neural network power hungrier, low density, and slow speed. In order to overcome these defects, a novel Nano device and computing architecture need proposing. Memristor crossbar is considered to be the most promising candidate to solve these problems [3]. Memristor crossbar is a high density, power efficiency computing-in-memory architecture. Thus, this chapter presents different design paradigm of memristor-based neural networks, including spiking neural networks (SNNs), multilayer neural networks (MNNs), convolutional neural networks (CNNs), and recurrent neural networks (RNNs).

2. Memristor neural networks

2.1. Memristor

Memristor was conceived by Leon Chua according to the symmetry of circuit theory in 1971 [4] and funded by HP lab in 2008 [5]. Memristor is a nano two-terminal nonvolatile device, with a Lissajous' IV curve. In mathematical, the model of memristor can be express as (take an example of HP memristor) [6]

$$i(t) = \frac{1}{R_{ON}w(t) + R_{OFF}(1 - w(t))} v(t) \tag{1}$$

$$i(t) = G(\varphi(t))v(t) \tag{2}$$

Here, w(t) stands for the normalized position of the conduction front between the O^{2-} vacancy-rich and O^{2-} vacancy-poor regions. The range of w(t) is from 0 to 1. $G(\varphi(t))$ is the conductance. The conductance of memristor can be continuous changing when applied control pulse on the memristor. When the negative pulse is applied, the O^{2-} vacancy moves to O^{2-} vacancy-rich region, which cause the conductance decrease, and vice versa. This result is similar to the phenomenon in biological synapse, such that memristor can simulate the dynamic of synapse.

2.2. Memristor merits

Memristor as the forth device, comparing with conventional computing system such as CPU and GPU, has many advantages. First, memristor is a two-terminal nonvolatile device, resulting in the low power consumption [7]. Second, memristor is compatible with the CMOS, and it can be integrated with higher density [4]. Third, the size of memristor is in nanoscale, such that the switching speed fast [8]. These characteristics make memristor become a promising candidate for neuromorphic computing. In recent years, many researchers have performed various experiments in neural network with memristor for synapse and neurons.

2.2.1. Memristor as synapse

Human brain can perform complex tasks such as unstructured data classification and image recognition. In human brain, excitatory and inhibitory postsynaptic potentials are delivered from presynaptic neuron to postsynaptic neuron through chemical and electrical signal at synapses, driving the change of synaptic weight, as shown in **Figure 2**. The synaptic weight is precisely adjusted by the ionic flow through the neurons. In neural networks, this mechanism can be simulated by memristors. There are many samples that memristor used as synapse. In this section, we use SNN as a sample to explain how memristor used as synapse.

As shown in **Figure 3**, a memristor acts as a synapse between two CMOSs neuron, which acts as pre-/postsynaptic neurons, respectively. The input signal of presynaptic neurons reached the postsynaptic neurons through the synapse. When a presynaptic spike is triggered before a postsynaptic spike, equivalently there is a positive voltage applied on the memristor, and then the synaptic weight is increased and vice versa, which is [6] explained as

$$\Delta t = t_{pre} - t_{post} \tag{3}$$

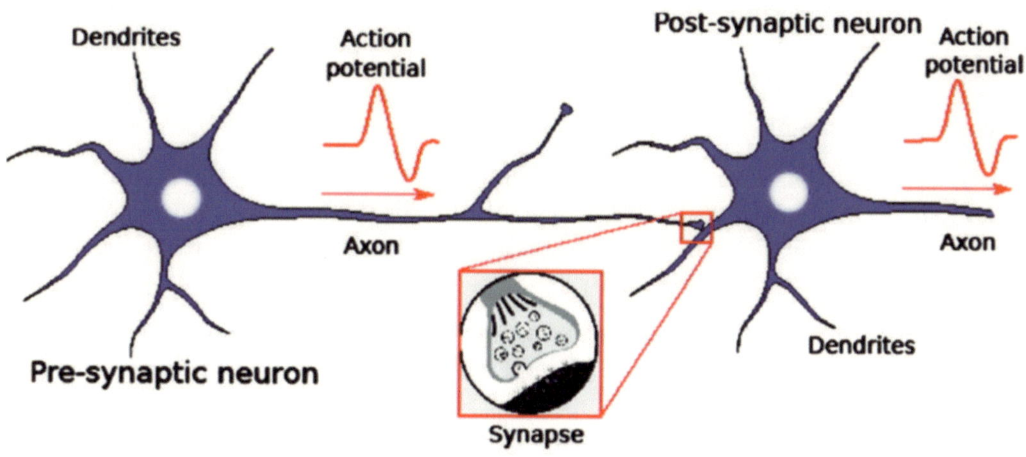

Figure 2. Biological neuron and synapse.

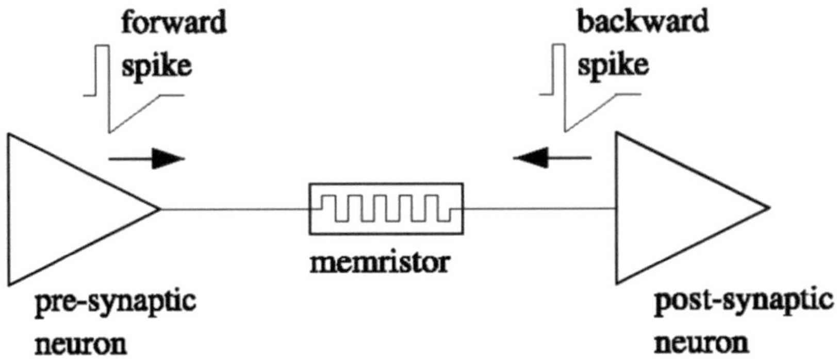

Figure 3. A paradigm of memristor based synapse.

where $t_{pre}(t_{post})$ is the pule weight the presynaptic neuron (postsynaptic neuron) spikes. Δt is the difference between neurons spike time. That means, when $\Delta t > 0$, the synapse weight is increased, and when $\Delta t < 0$, the synaptic weight is decreased.

2.2.2. Memristor as neuron

In biology, the membrane separates the inter-cell ions and enter-cell ions. Based on the electrochemical mechanism, the potential on the sides of membrane is balanced. When the excitatory and inhibitory postsynaptic potentials are arrived, the signals through the dendrites of the neurons and the balance will be destroyed. When the potential surpasses a threshold, the neuron is fired. Emulating these neuronal mechanism, including maintaining the balance of potential, the instantaneous mechanism, and the process of neurotransmission, is the key to implement biological plausible neuromorphic computing system [9].

When a memristor is used to act as a neuron in neural networks, it is not essential that the conductance of memristor implement continuous change, instead to achieve accumulative behavior. When competent pulses applied, the neuron is fired. These pulses can change the conductance state of memristor.

2.3. Memristor crossbar

Memristor crossbar consists of two perpendicular nanowire layers, which act as top electrode and bottom electrode, respectively. The memristive material is laid between two nanowire layers; as a result, memristor is formed at each crosspoint [11]. The schematic diagram of memristor crossbar is shown in **Figure 4**.

Memristor crossbar is suitable for large-scale neural networks implementations. First, it is high density, since crossbar can be vertical stack, and each crosspoint is a memristor. In addition, memristor is nonvolatile, nanoscale and multistate. Second, it is low power consumption, since the crossbar allow memory and computation integrating [10], and memristor is nonvolatile device with a low operation voltage. These advantage of memristor crossbar such that this architecture applied in a wide range of neural networks.

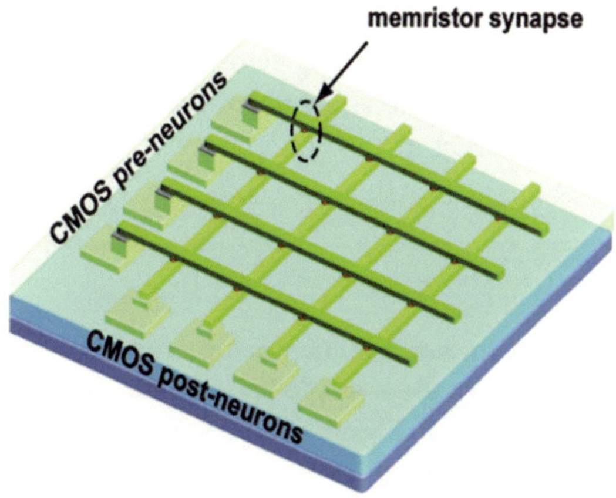

Figure 4. Memristor crossbar.

In neural networks, memristor crossbar has three operations such as read, write, and training. In this section, we use a sample to illustrate how the memristor crossbar read, write and training.

2.3.1. *Read operation*

In memristor crossbar, the conductance of a single memristor can be read individually. As shown in **Figure 5**, we assume that we will read the m_{ij} memristor, which is the crosspoint of i_{th} top wires and j_{th} bottom wires. The voltage V is applied on the i_{th} top wire, and other top wires and bottom wires are grounded. In this situation, only the m_{ij} memristor is applied the V bias, the current i can be collected on the j_{th} bottom wire. According to Ohm's law, the conductance of m_{ij} memristor M is caculated by $M=V/i$ [11].

2.3.2. *Write operation*

Similar to reading operation, the conductance of m_{ij} memristor can be written individually. We assume that we will write the m_{ij} memristor. Different amplitude and duration of writing

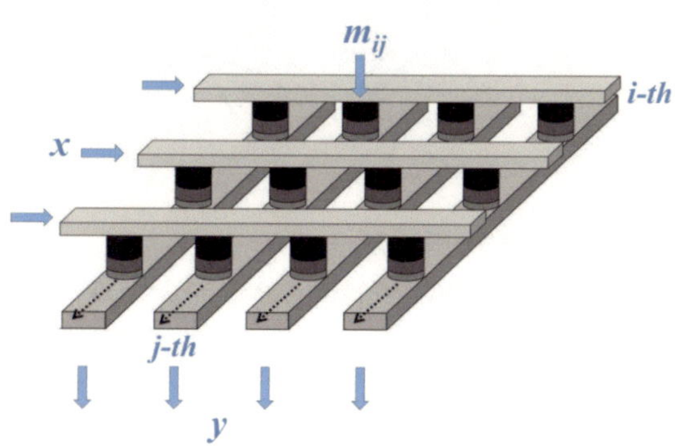

Figure 5. Memristor crossbar readout.

pulses will be directly applied on the target memristor. The i_{th} top wire is applied voltage V, and the j_{th} bottom wire is grounded. Other top wires and bottom wires are applied voltage V/2, then, only the m_{ij} memristor is applied the full voltage V, which is above the threshold and can change the conductance of target memristor. The conductance of other memristors is not changed because the voltage applied on them is 0 [12].

2.3.3. *Training operation*

Based on the read and write operation, the memristor neural networks are trained to implement practical neural networks. We use a single-layer neural network to explain the training process of neural network. As shown in **Figure 6**, the relationship between input vectors ***U*** and output vectors **Y** can be illustrated as [12]:

$$Y_n = W_{n \times m} \times U_m \tag{4}$$

Here, the weight matrix $W_{n \times m}$ represents the synaptic strengths between the two-neuron groups, which are represented by the conductance of corresponding memristors. When we train a memristor crossbar, we first assume we have a set of data. We input the training data, the synaptic weight matrix W is updated repeatedly until the difference between the output y and the target output y^* become minimum. In each repetition, W is adjusted across the gradient of the output error $|y\text{-}y^*|$ as [12]

$$\Delta w_{ij} = \mu \left(\frac{\partial (y - y^*)^2}{\partial w_{ij}} \right) \tag{5}$$

Here, w_{ij} is the synaptic weight in the **W** connecting the neuron i and j, Δw_{ij} is the change of w_{ij} during per update. μ is the training rate.

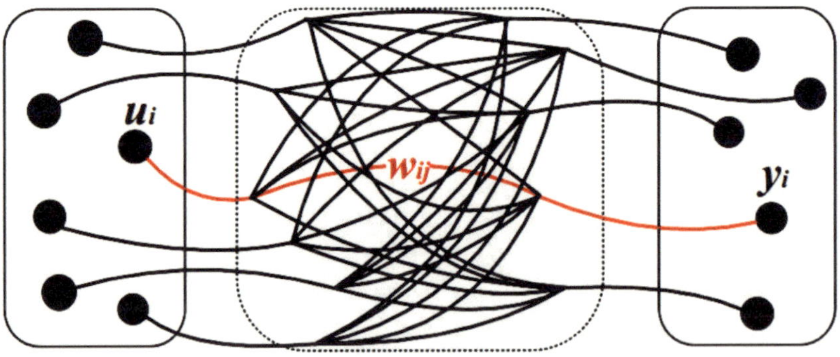

Figure 6. A single layer neural network [12].

3. Design of memristor neural networks

This section discusses different memristor-based neural network design paradigm, including spiking neural networks (SNN), multilayer neural networks (MNN), convolutional neural networks (CNN), and recurrent neural networks (RNN). Each part of these neural networks consists of five subsections, which are the concepts, the architecture, the algorithm, the circuits, and the instance.

3.1. Spiking neural networks

3.1.1. SNN concept

Spiking neural network (SNN), a neural network of neurons interchange information using spikes [13], is neural network based on individual spikes [14]. SNN is a brain-like architecture. The signal in SNNs uses pulse coding rather than rate coding, and allows multiplexing of information as frequency and amplitude. In some electronic SNNs, spikes have the similar waveform shape than biological spikes, but normally in electronic systems spikes are much simpler being represented by a square digital pulse [13]. In SNN, the presence and timing of individual spikes are considered as the means of communication and neural computation. The basic idea on biology is that the more intensive the input, the earlier the spike transmission. Hence, a network of spiking neurons can be designed with n input neurons Ni whose firing times are determined through some external mechanism [14].

3.1.2. SNN architecture

In this section, we use a three-layer neural network to illustrate the structure of SNN. In this structure, as shown in **Figure 7**, the multilayer SNNs are fully connected feedforward networks; all neurons between two adjacent layers are connected. All the input neurons and output neurons are multiple spikes, i.e., spikes trains.

In this structure, neurons have a model. Spike response model describes the response of both the sending and receiving neuron to a spike. In this model, the spikes of sending neuron transmitted from presynaptic neurons via synapses to postsynaptic neurons. When all spikes arrive, a postsynaptic potential is accumulated in receiving neuron. The internal state of neuron is defined as the sum of postsynaptic potential induced by all the spikes and affected by the weights for synapses that transmit these input spikes.

Suppose an input neuron has N input synapses. The i_{th} synapse transmits G_i spikes. The arrival time of each spike is denoted as $\mathcal{g}_i = t_i^1, t_i^2 \ldots\ldots t_i^g$. The time of the most recent output spike of the neuron prior to the current time t (>0) is $t^{(fr)}$. Then the internal state of the postsynaptic neuron is expressed as

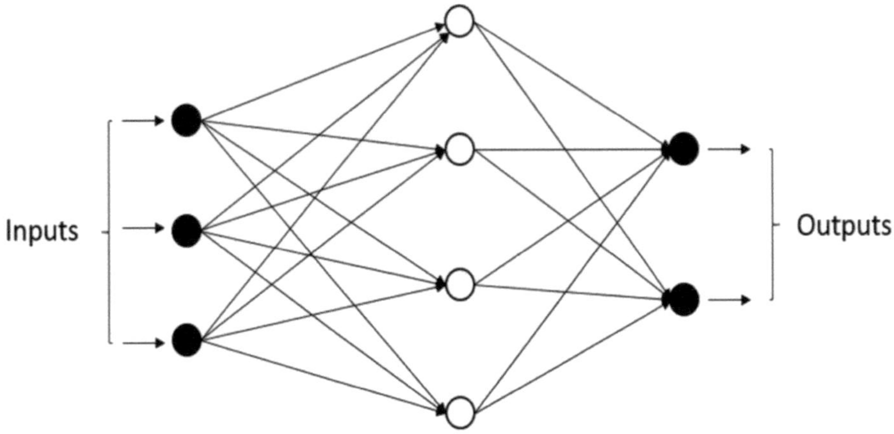

Figure 7. The architecture of SNNs.

$$u(t) = \sum_{i=1}^{N} \sum_{\substack{t_i^{(g)} \epsilon \mathcal{G}_i \\ t_i^{(g)} > t^{(fr)}}} w_i \varepsilon\left(t - t_i^{(g)}\right) + \eta(t - t^{(fr)}) \tag{6}$$

where w_i is the weight for the ith synapse. The postsynaptic potential induced by one spike is determined by the spike response function $\varepsilon(t)$, expressed as

$$\varepsilon(t) = \begin{cases} \frac{t}{\tau} e^{1-\frac{t}{\tau}} & \text{if } t > 0 \\ 0 & \text{if } t \le 0 \end{cases} \tag{7}$$

In additional to the model of postsynaptic neuron, SNN has a model, too. For convenience, we assume that the layers are numbered backwards starting from the output layer numbered as layer 1 to the input layer. Every two neurons in adjacent layers connected by K synapses with different transmit delays and weights. The delay of the kth synapse is denoted as d^k.

We assume that there are N_{l+1} neurons in layer $l + 1$ and neuron i, belongs to the layer $l + 1$, has emitted a spike train composed of F_i spikes, the times of firing are denoted $F_i = t_i$, the time of the t_i spike which through the kth synapse arrive at postsynaptic neuron j which is in layer l is $t_i + d^k$. At time t, the internal state of the jth postsynaptic neuron in layer l can be expressed by

$$u_j(t) = \sum_{i=1}^{N_{l+1}} \sum_{k=1}^{K} \sum_{\substack{t_i^{(f)} \epsilon \mathcal{F}_i \\ t_i^{(f)} + d^k > t_j^{(f_r)} + R_a}} w_{ij}^k \varepsilon\left(t - t_i^{(j)} - d^k\right) + \eta(t - t_j^{(f_r)}) \tag{8}$$

where w_{ij}^k is the weight of the k_{th} synapse between presynaptic neuron i and postsynaptic neuron j; $t_j^{(f_r)}$ is the time of the most recent output spike for neuron j prior to the current time t [15].

3.1.3. SNN algorithm

Spike-Timing Dependent Plasticity (STDP) is the synapse strength changing mechanism according to the precise timing of individual pre- and/or postsynaptic spikes. As illustrate in Section 2, the sign of the difference between the pre-/postsynaptic neurons times determines the synaptic weight whether increased. STDP learning in biology is inherently asynchronous and online which means that synaptic incremental update occurs while neurons and synapses transmit spikes and perform computations. In experiment, the synaptic strength is a function of relative timing between the arrival time of a presynaptic spike and the time of generation of a postsynaptic spike as shown in **Figure 8**.

Although the data show stochasticity, we can infer an underlying interpolated function as shown in **Figure 9**.

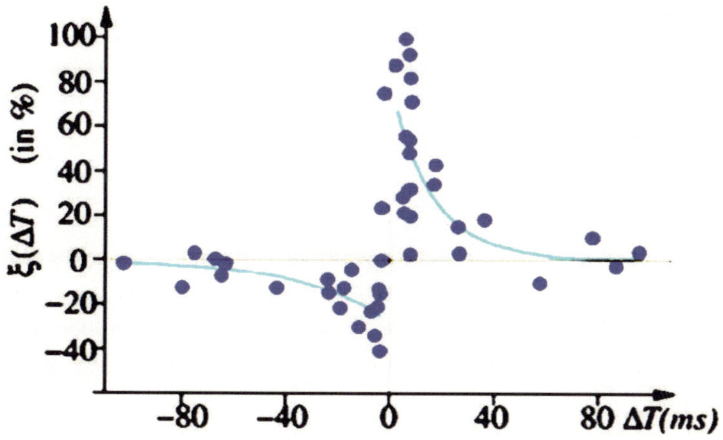

Figure 8. Experimentally measured STDP function on biological synapses [13].

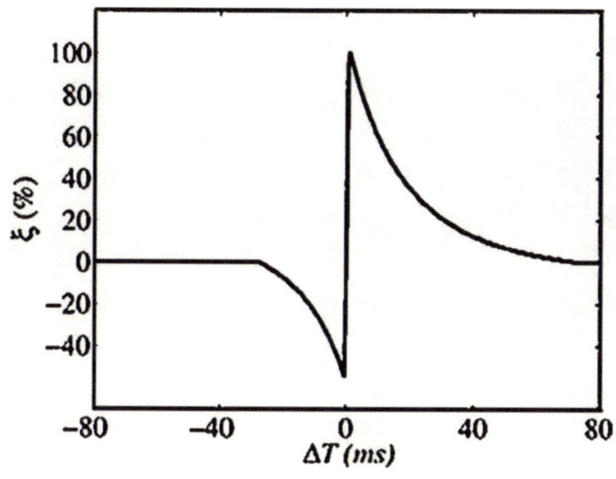

Figure 9. Ideal STDP update function used in computational models of STDP synaptic learning [13].

$$\xi \Delta \mathrm{T} = \begin{cases} a^{+}e^{-\Delta T/\tau^{+}} \; if \; \Delta T > 0 \\ -a^{-}e^{\Delta T/\tau^{-}} \; if \; \Delta T < 0 \end{cases} \tag{9}$$

3.1.4. SNN circuits

SNN with three layers of neurons and two fully connected inter-layer meshes of memristors is shown in **Figure 10**. The neuron layers are fabricated with CMOS devices, and the inter-layer meshes of memristors are made with nanowires on the top of a CMOS substrate [16]. In **Figure 10**, triangles represent the neuron soma, being the flat side its input(dendrites) and the sharp side the output (axon). Dark rectangles are memristors, representing each one synaptic junction. Each neuron controls the voltage at its input and output nodes.

In this SNN circuit, the CMOS-based spiking neurons work basically the same as conventional integrate-and-fire neuron, and use proposed spike shape and specific spike back-propagation. The total current of receiving neuron is given by Ohm's Law by conductance, g, of connected synapses and the voltage drop across the synapses. SNN training process needs building external circuit. In external circuit, the input signals are prepared, and the output signal will be measured in the external circuit.

3.1.5. SNN instances

Memristor behavior is more likely to a bidirectional exponentially grow with voltage, and many mathematical formulations can be used to simulate it. Here, we use a voltage-controlled device as a synapse, whose synaptic weight is represented by the conductance g of memristor. The function of the device is "sinh-like" in the voltage Vmem. The nano device satisfied the formulation as expressed follow

$$\frac{dg}{dt} = Asinh(V_{mem}) \tag{10}$$

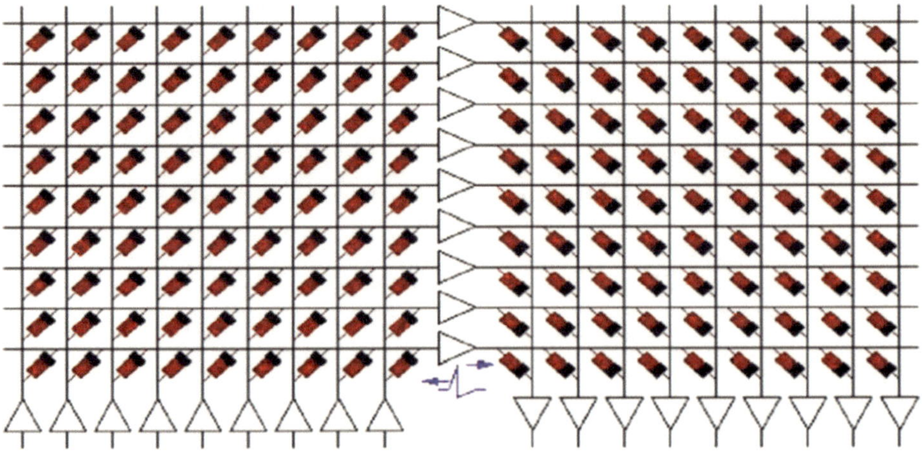

Figure 10. Memristor crossbar based SNNs paradigm [13].

http://dx.doi.org/10.5772/intechopen.69929

A and B are the parameters which depend upon the memristor material, thickness, size, and it fabrication method.

In this section, we verify the STDP properties of the memristor-based synapses. **Figure 11** is the proposed spike shape, which is similar to the biological spikes. **Figure 12** shows the STDP curves produced by the proposed spike shape. In **Figure 12**, the vertical axis shows the average

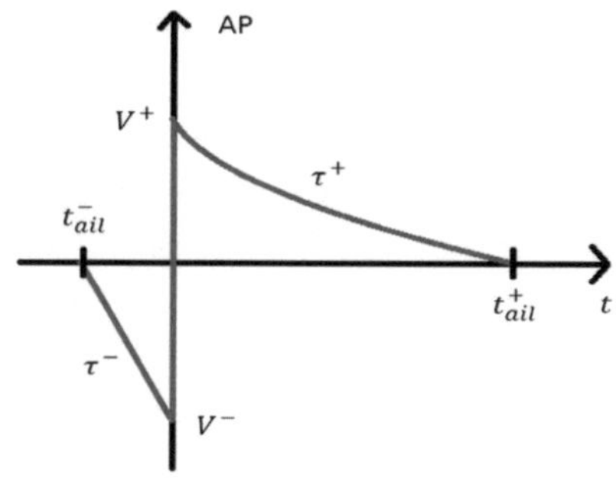

Figure 11. Proposed spike shape used for processing and learning purposed [17].

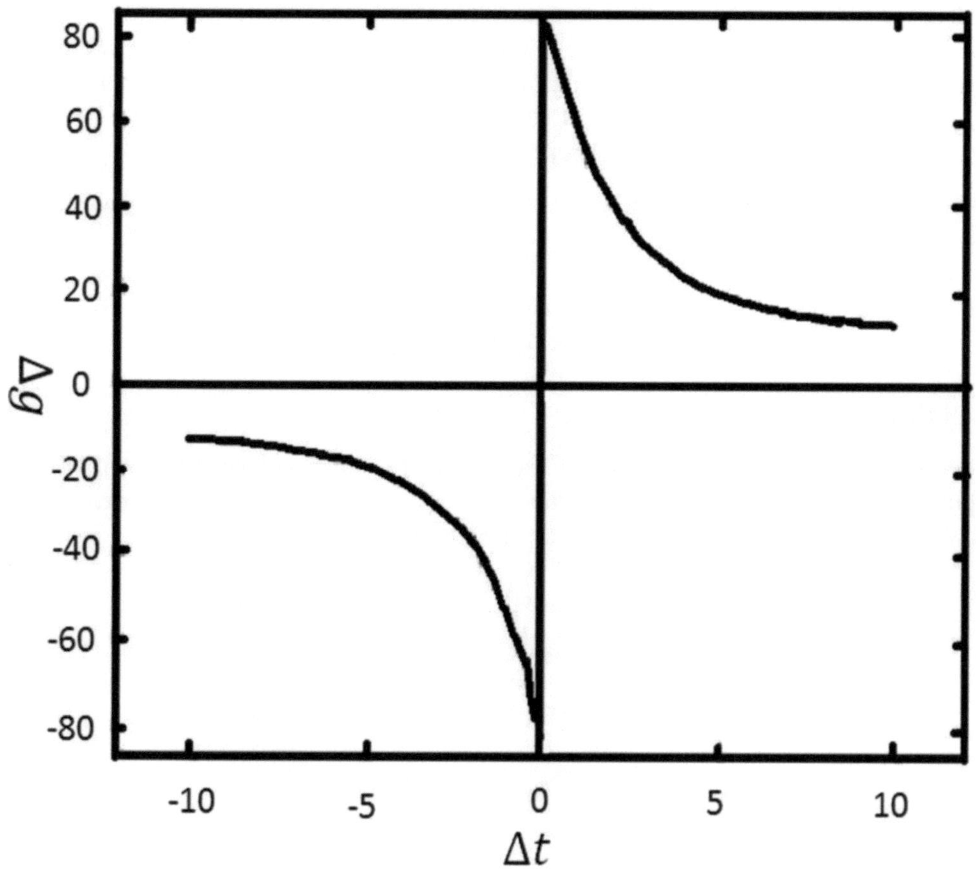

Figure 12. Simulated curve using proposed spike shape [17].

change of memristor conductance. The horizontal axis represents the difference between pre- and postsynaptic spike timings Δt. Here, the default spike parameters are e$V_{\pm} = 0.45$V volt, $t^{+}_{ail} = 11$ ms, $t^{-}_{ail} = 0.3$ ms. The result are provided for memristors with $V_{th\pm} \approx \pm 0.5$ V volt. The value of parameters A and B are 2 and 4, respectively [18, 19].

3.2. Multilayer neural networks

3.2.1. MNN concepts

Multilayer neural networks, also known as multilayer perception, are the quintessential deep networks. The advantage of MNN better than the single-layer perceptron overcomes the weaknesses that the perceptron cannot classify linearly indivisible data. To realize large scale learning tasks, MNNs can perform impressively well and produce state-of-the-art results when massive computational power is available [20, 21]. Learning in multilayer neural networks (MNNs) relies on continuous updating of large matrices of synaptic weights by local rules [22, 23]. The BP algorithm is a common algorithm in local learning, which is widely used in the training of MNNs.

3.2.2. MNN architecture

In MNN architecture, neurons of upper and lower layers are fully connected, no neuron connection exists between the same layer, and no cross layer connects to the neural network. As a quintessential deep network, multilayer neural network consists of an input layer, an output layer, and a hidden layer. MNN is the evolution of the single-layer perceptron. **Figure 13** is a double layer neural network.

The X_1, X_2 may represent the inputs single, W is the value of the weight between layers, Y is the output value. For the two-layer neural network shown above, the input signal is represented as x_1,... x_j, x_n (N represents the number of input neurons), b_i is represented for bias, so the result of the signal from the input layer to the hidden layer is N_{11}=f($x_1 w_{11} + x_2 w_{21} + b$), and Y_1=f ($N_{11} w_{11} + N_{12} w_{21}$+b), in which f is an activation function.

3.2.3. MNN algorithm

In this section, we give a short sketch of the back-propagation technique [25, 23]. The actual output value of the neural network is denoted by y_j and the ideal tag value is denoted by t_j, and we can use the mean square error as an error function

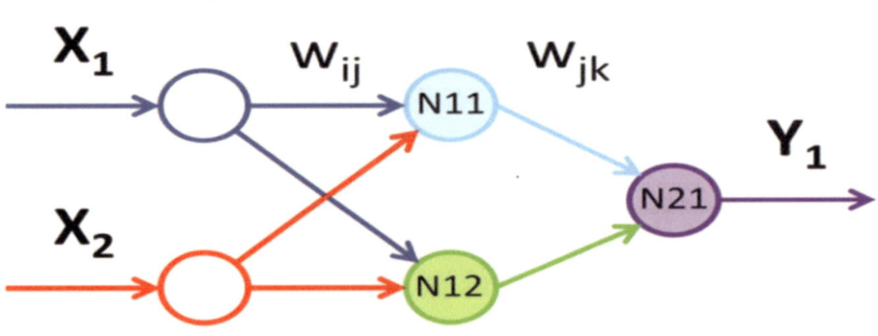

Figure 13. Logic scheme of the implemented neural network with two inputs, two hidden and one output neurons [24].

$$\varepsilon\mathbf{MSE} = \sum\nolimits_j \left(y_j - t_j\right)^2 \tag{11}$$

w_{ij} represents the weight between two layers of neurons, the neurons of the previous layer are indexed with i, and the next layer of neurons is indexed with j. The derivation of the error can be obtained by the following equation:

$$\frac{\partial\varepsilon}{\partial w_{ij}} = \frac{\partial\varepsilon}{\partial y_j}\frac{\partial y_j}{\partial z_j}\frac{\partial z_j}{\partial w_{ij}} = \dot{\in}\left(y_j\right)\dot{f}(z_j)x_i = \delta_j x_i \tag{12}$$

where $z_j = \sum\nolimits_i w_{ij}x_i,\ y_j = f(z_j),\ \delta_j = \dot{E}\left(y_j\right)\dot{f}z_j$

Moreover, it is assumed that the multilayer neural network uses sigmoid as a nonlinear activation function. For Eq. (3) we get

$$\frac{\partial\in}{\partial w_{ij}^{(k)}} = x_i^{(k-1)}\delta_j^{(K)} \tag{13}$$

where $\delta_j^{(L)} \equiv \delta_j = \left(y_j - t_j\right)$, x_i^0 are input signals, and $\delta_j^L \equiv \sum\nolimits_i w_{ji}^{(k)}\delta_i^{(k)}\dot{f}\left(z_j^{(k-1)}\right)$.

3.2.4. MNN circuits

In this section, we enumerate an example of a memristor implementation of a two-layer neural network. As shown in **Figure 14**.

In hybrid-circuit based neural networks [26–28], memristors are integrated into crossbar circuits to implement density-critical analog weights (i.e., synapses). In this scheme, each artificial synapse is represented by memristors, so the weight of the synapse is equal to the conductance of the memristor. For the multilayer neural network mentioned above, each weight is represented by two memristors, so that the memristor crossbar can easily account for both "excitatory" and "inhibitory" states of the synapses. The number of memristor in the hidden layer is arranged in an 8 × 1 grid array as shown in **Figure 14**. The value of each weight $W = G^+ - G^-$, where G^+ and G^- is the effective conductance of each memristor. In the simplest case, neuron output x is encoded by voltages V and synaptic weight w by memristor conductance G. With virtually grounded neuron's input, the current was given by Ohm's law using the potential of postsynaptic V and the corresponding conductance G.

The memristor crossbar combined with CMOS circuitry, which implements neuron functionality and other peripheral functions. The artificial neuron body (soma) was implemented in the circuit by an op-amp based differential adder and a voltage divider with a MOSFET controlled by the output of the summator [24]. This element executed the basic neuron functions in terms of information processing—summation and threshold. The differential summator performing $y = \sum w_i x_i$ function is required to separate different classes of input combinations, where y is the output voltage of the summator, w_i, x_i – the ith input voltage and the corresponding weight respectively.

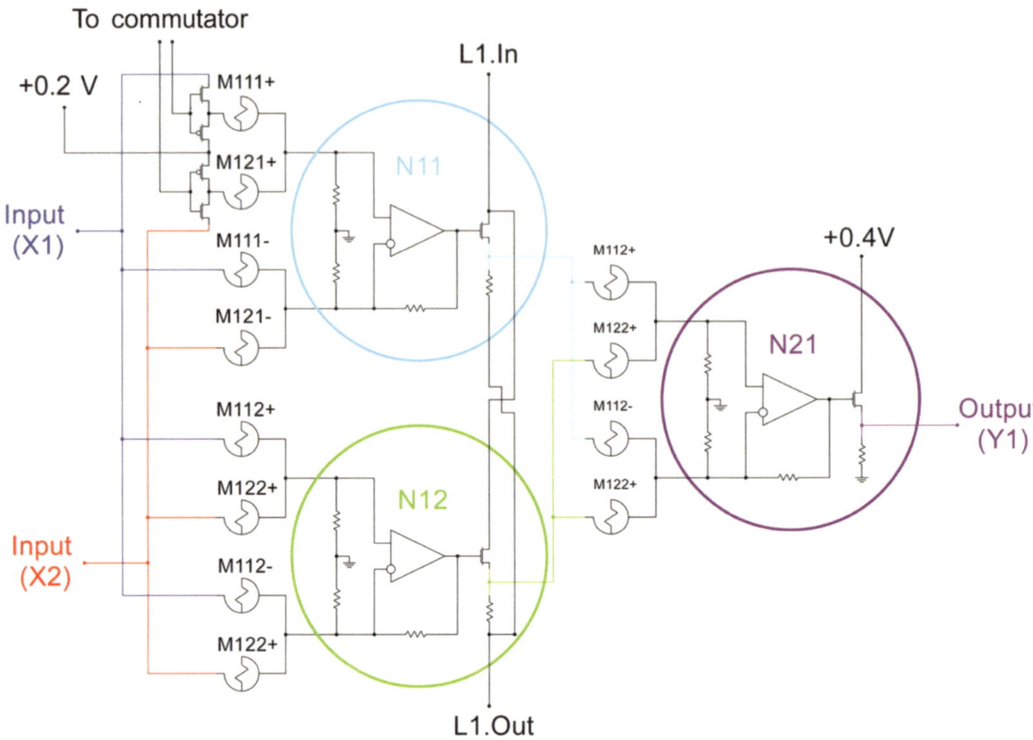

Figure 14. Circuit diagram of the ANN memristor-based hardware.

3.2.5. MNN instance

Conclusion all the experiments, we selected the image data of the MNIST data set to train and test the two-layer neural network, with the batch size 100 to speed up calculations [28]. The initial weights were selected randomly from the uniform distribution; in the experiment, the learning rate is changed depending on the training set error, and the learning rate is only constant at a level close to 0.0035.

3.3. Convolutional neural networks

3.3.1. CNN concepts

Convolutional neural network is taking inspiration from the study of biology neural science. A classical architecture of convolutional neural network was first proposed by Lecun et al. [29, 30]. As a kind of deep learning neural network, several powerful applications of CNNs were reported including pattern recognition and classification, such as human face recognition [31], traffic sign recognition [32], and object recognition [33]. Recently, in the field of image classification accuracy, convolution neural network (CNN) achieved a state-of-the art result, which can classify more than a million images into 1000 different classes [29, 34, 35].

Compared with traditional neural networks, such as fully connected NN, where each neuron is connected to all neurons of the prelayer via a large number of synapses,convolutional neural networks take advantages in weight sharing, which reduces the number of parameters need to be trained [29]. CNNs are inspired from visual cortex structure, where neurons are sensitive to small subregions of the input space, called receptive fields, exploiting the strong spatially local correlation present in images [35]. CNNs, exploiting the spatial structure of input images, has significantly fewer parameters than a fully connected network of a similar size are better suited for visual document tasks than other NN topologies such as fully connected NNs [36].

Software implementations of artificial convolutional neural networks, which require power-hungry CPU/GPU to perform convolution operations, are at the state of the art for pattern recognition applications. While achieving high performance, CNN-based methods is based on computationally expensive sums of multiplications, which is demand much more computation and memory resources than traditional classification methods. This hinders their integration in portable devices. As a result, most CNN-based algorithms and methods have to be processed on servers with plenty of resources [37].

3.3.2. CNN architectures

The overall architecture of a typical CNN consists of two main parts, the feature extractor and classifier [38, 39]. The feature extractor layers composed of two types of layers convolutional layers and pooling layers. A series of convolution and pooling are stacked, followed by fully connected layers (**Figure 15**).

In the feature extraction layers, each layer of the network receives an input from the immediate previous layer [39, 40]. Convolution neural networks are often used to handle image processing and recognition tasks. The image signal was processed by the input layer of the convolutional neural network and then enters the convolution layer for the convolution operation. Convolution operation can be expressed as [37]

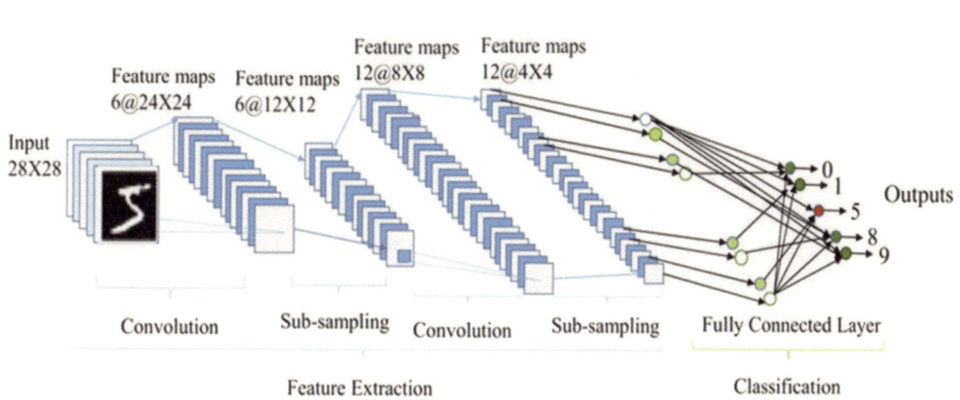

Figure 15. CNN block diagram.

$$g(x, y, z) = \sum_{i=0}^{c-1}\sum_{j=0}^{c-1}\sum_{k=1}^{l} f(x+i, y+j, k) \cdot c_z(i, j, k) = \vec{f} \cdot \vec{c_z} \tag{14}$$

where the vector $\vec{f}$ and $\vec{g}$ respectively represent the input and output feature map in the form of 3D matrix; $\vec{Cz}$ is one convolution kernel with the size of C × C; and i is the channel number of the convolution kernel and the input feature map.

This operation could extract different features of input images when using different convolutional kernels [29]. The input image signal will have dot product operation with kernel, and through the nonlinear transformation, the final output feature map. Then will be the subsampling process. Nonlinear neuron will be operated attached after the convolution kernel. And then, pooling computation is operated after the nonlinear neurons in order to reduce the data amount and keep the local invariance. A typical pooling unit computes the maximum of a local patch of units in one feature map (or in a few feature maps) [41]. Fully connected layers are the final layers of the CNN that all layers are fully connected by weights [37]. A feed forward neural network is usually used as a classifier in this work because it has been shown to provide the best performance compared to neural networks [42, 43].

3.3.3. CNN algorithm

In this section, the backpropagation learning algorithm for CNNs will be introduced [36]. The input of a convolution layer is the previous layer's feature maps, and the output feature map is generated by a learnable kernels and the activation function, which may combine the kernel convolutions with multiple input maps. In general, we have that

$$x_j^l = f\left(\sum_{i \in M_j} x_i^{l-1} * k_{ij}^l + b_j^l\right) \tag{15}$$

We can repeat the same computation for each map j in the convolutional layer, pairing it with the corresponding map in the subsampling layer:

$$\delta_j^l = \beta_j^{l+1}\left(f'\left(u_j^l\right) \circ up\left(\delta_j^{l+1}\right)\right) \tag{16}$$

where up(·) denotes an up sampling operation that simply tiles each pixel in the input horizontally and vertically n times in the output if the subsampling layer subsamples by a factor of n. One possible way to implement this function efficiently is to use the Kronecker product, $up(x) \equiv X \bigotimes 1_{n \times n}$. Since the sensitivities of a given map are known, the bias gradient can be immediately computed by simply summing over all the entries in δ_j^l, $\frac{\partial E}{\partial b_j} = \sum_{u,v} (\delta_j^l)_{uv}$.

Finally, the gradients of the kernel weights are computed using backpropagation. Then, the gradient of a given weight is summed over all the connections that mention this weight

$$\frac{\partial E}{\partial k_{ij}^{l}} = \sum_{u,v} \left(\delta_j^l\right)_{uv} (P_i^{l-1})_{uv} \quad (17)$$

$$\frac{\partial E}{\partial k_{ij}^{l}} = rot180(conv2\left(x_i^{l-1}, rot180\left(\delta_j^l\right), 'valid'\right)) \quad (18)$$

A subsampling layer produces down sampled versions of the input maps. If there are N input maps, then there will be exactly N output maps, although the output maps will be smaller. More formally, $x_j^l = f(\beta_j^l down\left(x_j^{l-1}\right) + b_j^l)$, where down(·) represents a subsampling function, which sum over each distinct n-by-n block in the input image so that the output image is n-times smaller along both spatial dimensions. Each output map has multiplicative bias β and an additive bias b. Since every other sample in the image $\delta_j^l = f'(u_j^l) \circ conv2(\delta_j^{l+1}, rot180\left(k_j^{l+1}\right), 'full')$ can be thrown away, the gradients of b and β can be computed. The additive bias is again just the sum over the elements of the sensitivity map $\frac{\partial E}{\partial b_j} = \sum_{u,v} \left(\delta_j^l\right)_{uv}$. The multiplicative bias β will involve the original down-sampled map generated by the current layer during the forward propagation. Therefore, the maps generated during the forward propagation should be saved, to aviod recomputing them during backpropagation. Defining $d_j^l = down(x_j^{l-1})$, then the gradient of β can be represented as

$$\frac{\partial E}{\partial \beta_j} = \sum_{u,v} (\delta_j^l \circ d_j^l)_{uv} \quad (19)$$

Meanwhile, it is better to provide an output map that involves a sum over several convolutions of different input maps. Generally, the input maps combined to form a given output map are typically chosen by hand. However, such combinations can be learned during training. Let α_{ij} represents the weight given to input map i when forming output map j. Then output map j is calculated by

$$x_j^l = f\left(\sum_{i=1}^{N_{in}} \alpha_{ij}(x_i^{l-1} * K_i^l) + b_j^l\right) \quad (20)$$

where

$$\sum_i \alpha_{ij} = 1, \text{and } 0 \le \alpha_{ij} \le 1 \quad (21)$$

By setting the α_{ij} variables equal to the softmax over a set of unconstrained weights c_{ij}, these constraints can be enforced

$$\alpha_{ij} = \frac{\exp(c_{ij})}{\sum_k \exp(c_{kj})} \quad (22)$$

Since each set of weights c_{ij} for fixed j are independent of all other such sets for any other j, only the updates of a single map need considering and the subscript j can be dropped. Each map is updated in the same way, except with different j indices. The derivative of α_k with respect to the α_i variables at layer is the derivative of the softmax function is given by

$$\frac{\partial \alpha_k}{\partial c_i} = \delta_{ki}\alpha_i - \alpha_i\alpha_k \tag{23}$$

where δ is used as the Kronecker delta.

Use $\boldsymbol{\delta}^l$ represents the sensitivity map corresponding to an output map with inputs $\mathbf{u}$. Again, the convolution is the "valid" type so that the result will match the size of the sensitivity map. Now, the gradients of the error function with respect to the underlying weights c_i can be computed by the chain rule

$$\frac{\partial E}{\partial \alpha_i} = \frac{\partial E}{\partial u^l}\frac{\partial u^l}{\partial \alpha_i} = \sum_{u,v} (\delta^l \circ (x_i^{l-1} * K_i^l))_{uv} \tag{24}$$

In addition, the sparseness constraints on the distribution of weights α_i for a given map can also been imposed by adding a regularization penalty $\Omega(\boldsymbol{\alpha})$ to the final error function. Therefore, some weights will be zero. That means, only a few input maps would contribute significantly to a given output map, as opposed to all of them. The error for a single pattern can be written as

$$\frac{\partial E}{\partial c_i} = \sum_k \frac{\partial E}{\partial \alpha_k}\frac{\partial \alpha_k}{\partial c_i} = \alpha_i(\frac{\partial E}{\partial \alpha_i} - \sum_k \frac{\partial E}{\partial \alpha_k}\alpha_k) \tag{25}$$

$$\widetilde{E}^n = E^n + \lambda \sum_{i,j} |\alpha_{ij}| \tag{26}$$

This will find the contribution of the regularization term to the gradient for the weights c_i. The user defined parameter λ controls the trade-off between minimizing the fit of the network to the training data, and ensures that the weights mentioned in the regularization term are small according to the 1-norm. Again, only the weights α_i for a given output map need considering and the subscript j can be dropped. First, there is

$$\frac{\partial \Omega}{\partial \alpha_i} = \lambda sign(\alpha_i) \tag{27}$$

Combining this result with Eq. (24), the derivation of the contribution is

$$\frac{\partial \Omega}{\partial c_i} = \sum_k \frac{\partial \Omega}{\partial \alpha_k}\frac{\partial \alpha_k}{\partial c_i} = \lambda(|\alpha_i| - \alpha_i \sum_k |\alpha_k|) \tag{28}$$

The final gradients for the weights c_i when using the penalized error function Eq. (11) can be computed using Eqs. (13) and (9)

$$\partial \frac{\widetilde{E^n}}{\partial c_i} = \frac{\partial E^n}{\partial c_i} + \frac{\partial \Omega}{\partial c_i} \tag{29}$$

3.3.4. CNN circuits

This part introduces the construction and operation of the memristor neural networks circuit. First of all, we introduce how a single column within a memristor crossbar can be used to perform a convolution operation. Pooling operation can be seen as a simpler conversation operation [39]. The circuit diagram of each column for the convolution operation of the memristor crossbar structure is shown in **Figure 16**.

Each crosspoint of the circuit was composed of memristors, which is represented for synapses. The kernel (k) was represented by the conductivity value (G) in the crossbar circuit. Some extra manipulation include converting kernel matrix into two parallel column to express the positive and negative value of the kernel and converting kernel matrix to conductivity values ($\delta^{\pm}$) [39] that fall within the bounded range of a memristor crossbar. The op-amp circuit is used to scale the output voltage and implements the sigmoid activation function.

The convolution computation operation in memristor crossbar is the same as the matrix convolution operation. That mainly is a result of the dot-production about the matrixes of kernels and inputs. The first step is the multiplication of voltage (V) and conductance ($G = x^{-1}$) [29], which is following ohm's law ($I = V{\cdot}G$). Second, it will follow Kirchhoff's current law (KCL), which describes that the circuit flowing out the node will be equal to the sum of current flowing into that node. Based on KCL, novel computation architecture for implementing pot-product is implemented [29]. And then, the lower end of the op amp circuit performs activation function. As a result, each neuron of hidden and output layers implements $f(\sum_i (G^+ - G^-)V_i)$, where f is a kind of activation function. **Figure 17** shows the flow chart of the CNN image identification system.

where L is the number of layers of the CNN recognition system, the input layer ($L = 1$) holds a testing set of 500 MNIST images, whose size of data set is 28×28. $L = 2$ is the first convolution layer [39].

step 1. First convolution layer($l = 2$)

The signal size from the front input layer is 28×28. In this layer, an input image will be convolved with six different 5×5 size kernels on the memristor crossbar. According with the front description, each column is the kernel value of 5×5. And the 2D kernel was broken into two arrays in the memristor crossbar to easily account for negative values in the kernel arrays. The total number of a column in the crossbar structure is $2 \times 25 + 1$, in which "1" is the value of bias. Since we are using a memristor crossbar to perform the convolution operations, we can generate all six of these output maps in parallel. So, the crossbar circuit exist six parallel columns in a row. Therefore, this layer requires a 51×6 memristor crossbars.

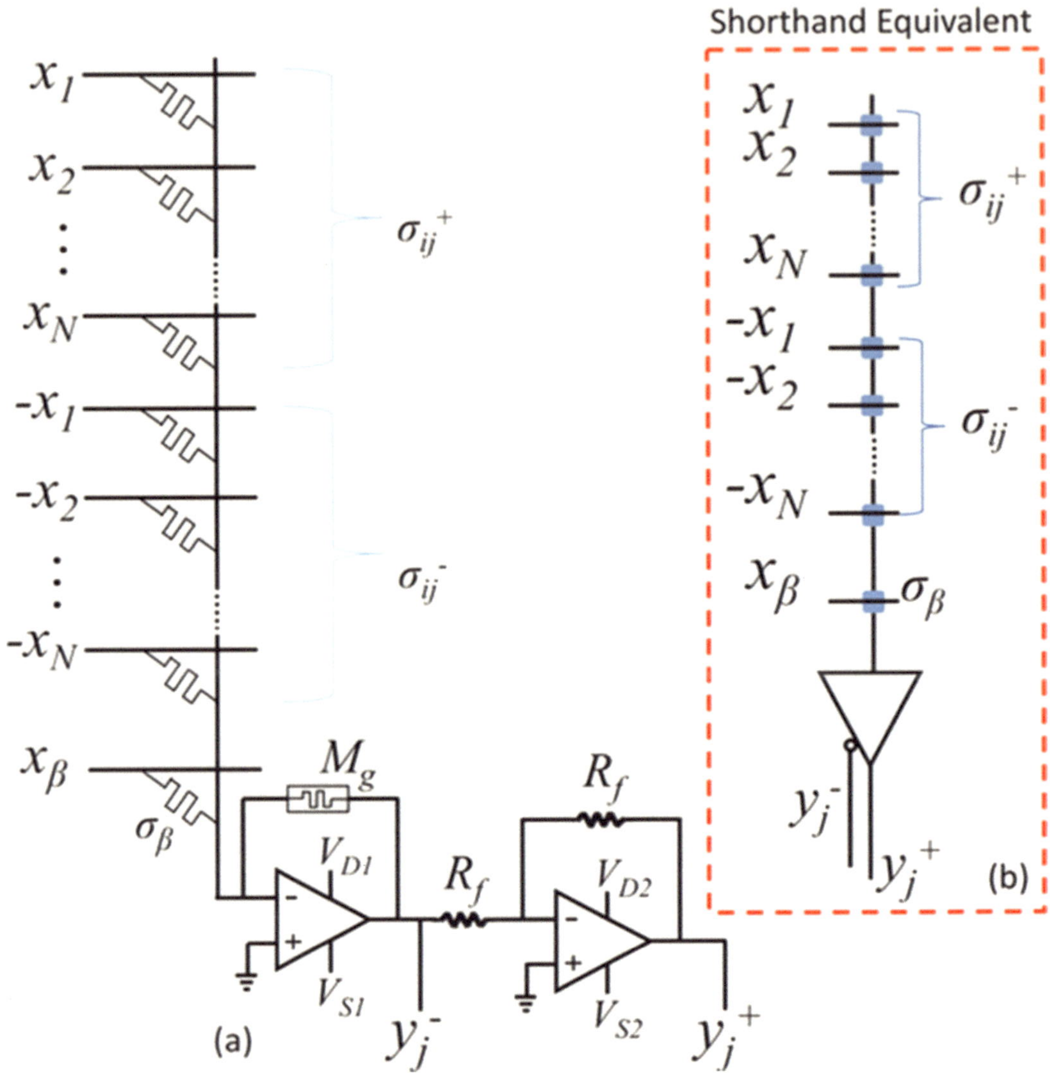

Figure 16. (a) A column circuit of MCNN circuit diagram that is capable of performing convolutional operation and (b) a shorthand depiction for this circuit.

So far, we have got the memristor crossbar structure, which simulates the synapses and stores the value of kernels in it. The circuit perform the first convolution operation is shown in **Figure 18**.

Each image contains 784 pixel, but the image is applied 25 pixels at a time where each 25 pixel section generates a single output value. After these convolution kernels applied, a data array that has a size of 24 × 24 × 6 will be generated in the memristor crossbar and then will be operated in the next layer. For each column in the memristor crossbar structure,memristor is used to simulate synapses of neural networks. And, the circuit simulates neurons to produce

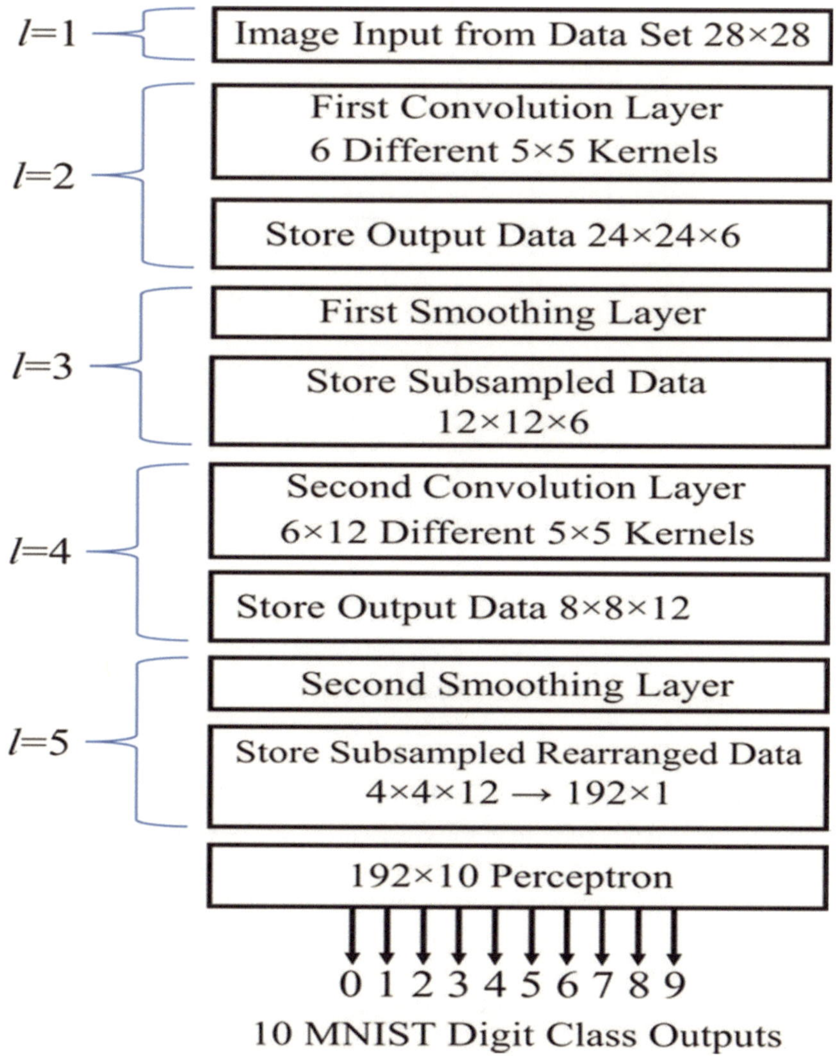

Figure 17. Flowchart describing the CNN recognition system [39].

the summation of all the product of inputs and kernels and operate activation function. According to Ohm's law and Kirchhoff's law, every single output value in this time is the input value and the kernel value of the inner product results. After the signal is input, the memristor and op-amp circuits are output later. When all 6 24 × 24 sizes of feature map are obtained, the first convolution operation was finished,the output is the input value of the next neuron that will be applied in pooling operation process.

Step 2. First smoothing layer ($l = 3$)

Following the first convolution layer, a smoothing operation is performed on the six generated feature maps. Pooling operation can be seen as a simpler conversation operation, with all kernel applied to each feature map is

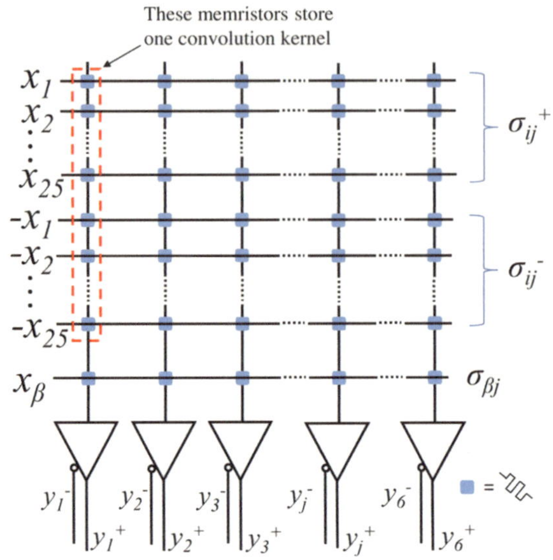

Figure 18. Circuit used to perform the convolution operations for the second ($l = 2$) in the CNN recognition system.

$$K = \begin{bmatrix} 0.25 & 0.25 \\ 0.25 & 0.25 \end{bmatrix}$$

Be similar with the convolution process, each column of the crossbar represents a kernel. So the memristor numbers of a single column of the crossbar is $4 \times 2 + 1$, and six column for with all six feature maps be operated in parallel, Therefore this layer requires a $6 \times (2 \times 4 + 1)$ memristor crossbars. But different with the convolution layers, the conductivities corresponding to negative elements in the kernel matrix in this layer are meaningless because all components of the pooling kernel are positive. The following circuit is shown that has pooling operation on the $6 \times 24 \times 24$ size of feature map which the convolution layer is derived (**Figure 19**).

In the pooling operation, six different feature maps obtained from the convolution layers applied to every corresponding column respectively and obtain another sets of feature maps.

A subsampling operation is performed following each of the smoothing crossbars that reduce the size of each feature map by a square factor of 2. This could be design in to place a single-bit counter on the memory array where the data output from the smoothing operation is stored. The memory address would only update for every other sample so all unwanted data would be overwritten during the smoothing step.

Step 3. Second convolutional layer (l=4)

Following the polling and subsample, operation is the second convolution operation. Different with the first one, inputs of the second convolution layers are six feature maps with 12×12 size, and it exists 12 outputs instead of six in the front one. Because the different number and size of input and output single, the structure of the second layer is distinctly different from the

http://dx.doi.org/10.5772/intechopen.69929

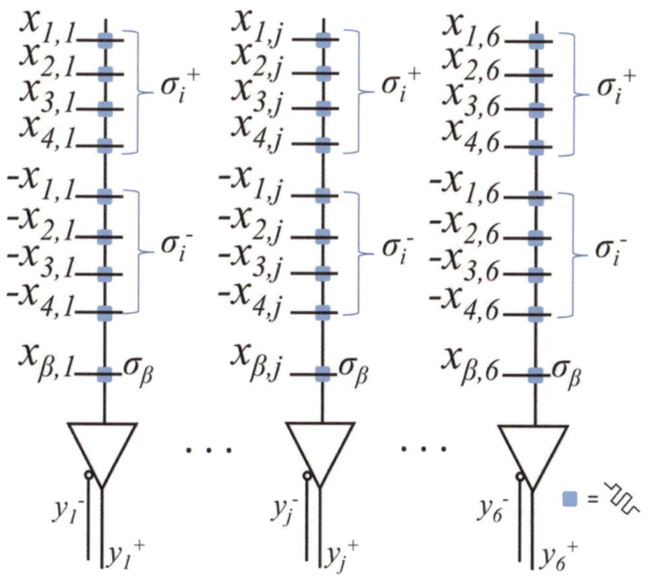

Figure 19. The group of convolution circuits that is used to implement the smoothing operation.

one. The circuit design of the second convolution layer is shown in **Figure 20**. Each column represents six different feature map convolution processes, and will be operated with 12 different kernels in parallel methods.

Step 4. Second smoothing layer($l = 5$)

Following the second convolution layer, another smoothing layer is following the second convolution layer to further reduce the size of the data array. The circuit in this layer will be identical to that displayed in **Figure 7**. With 12 feature maps will be operated, so required 12 parallel single column crossbars. After second layers of pool will produce 4×4 of the size of 12 feature map, the input to the next layer, classification layer ($l = 6$).

Step 5. Classification layer

Following the front feature extraction operations, a fully connected layer is used to classify the feature maps. The classification layer is generally a single layer perceptron or multilayer neural network.

The circuit used to complete this operation can be seen in **Figure 21**. The memristor crossbar used in classification layer is to store a weight matrix, which is different with storing a set of convolution kernels arrays in convolution circuits. The crossbar consists of 192*2+1 rows which represent 192 inputs (one input for each of the 16 value in each of the 12 outputs maps), and 10 columns which represent 10 outputs (one for each MNIST digit). So the total numbers of memristors in this layers is $(192 + 1) \times 10$.

Step 6. Digital storage layers

Following every convolution layer, a digital layer was placed at the output of each convolution. The digital storage layer reduces the amount of analog circuit error that is transmitted

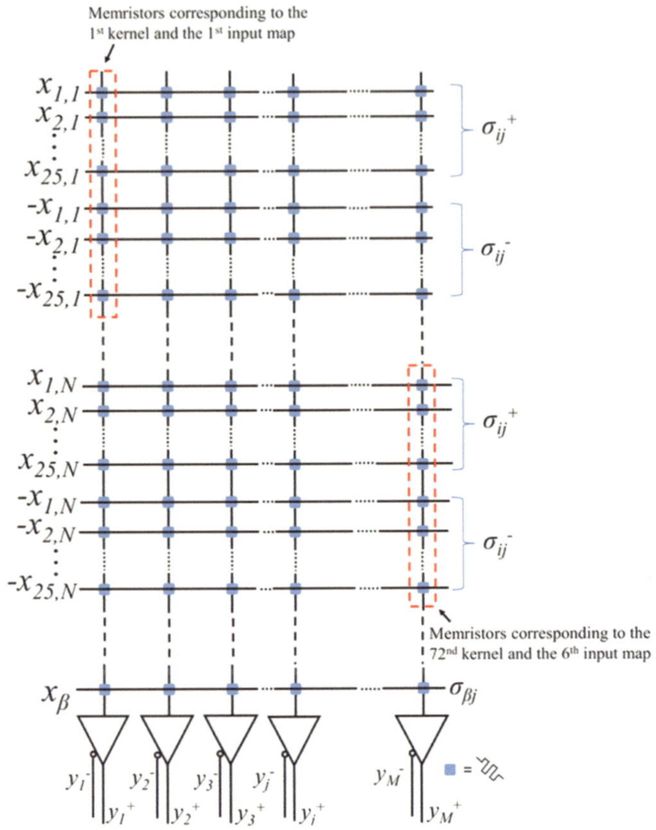

Figure 20. The circuit that is used to implement the second convolution layer.

between layers. We chose to store an entire image between layers because any benefit gained by a systematically reduced memory size would likely be outweighed by the complexity of a data controller of this nature [44].

3.3.4.1. CNN instance

The CNN algorithm purely in simulation under these training conditions results in 92% classification accuracy as shown in **Figure 22**. And, the simulation process is to test the accuracy of the memristor based CNN recognition system described in the previous section. When testing the simulated memristor crossbars, an accuracy of 91.8% was achieved.

3.4. Recurrent neural networks

3.4.1. RNN concept

Recurrent neural networks, or RNNs, are the main tool for handling sequential data, which involve variable length inputs or outputs [40]. Compared with multilayer network, the weights in an RNN are shared across different instances of the artificial neurons, each associated with

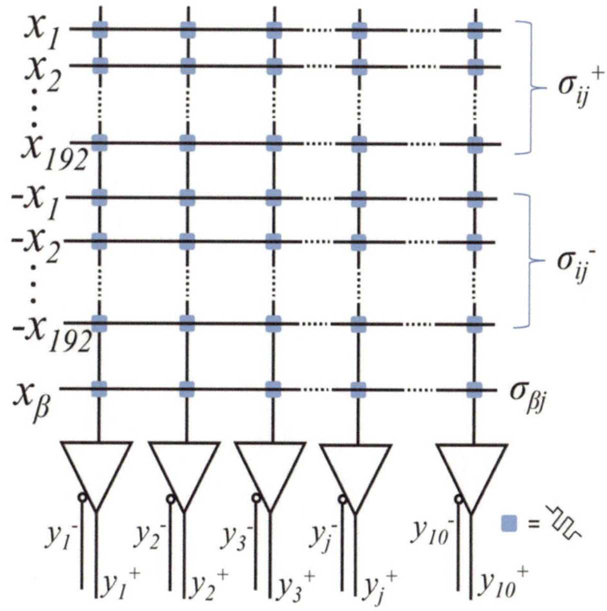

Figure 21. Circuit that is used to implement the classification layer of the CNN recognition system.

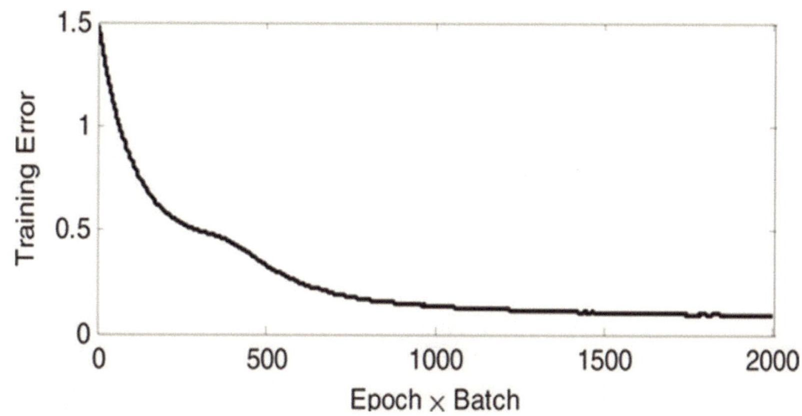

Figure 22. Error present when training the CNN algorithm is software [39].

different time steps [40, 42]. And, others, in recurrent neural networks, lengths history represented by neurons with recurrent connections, and history length is unlimited. Also recurrent networks can learn to compress whole history in low dimensional space, while feedforward networks compress (project) just single word recurrent networks have possibility to form short term memory, so they can better deal with position invariance [45] RNN architecture.

The simplest architecture of RNNs is illustrated in **Figure 23** [40]. The left of **Figure 24** shows the ordinary recurrent network circuit with weight matrices U, V, W denoting three different kind of connection (input-to-hidden, hidden-to-output, and hidden-to-hidden,

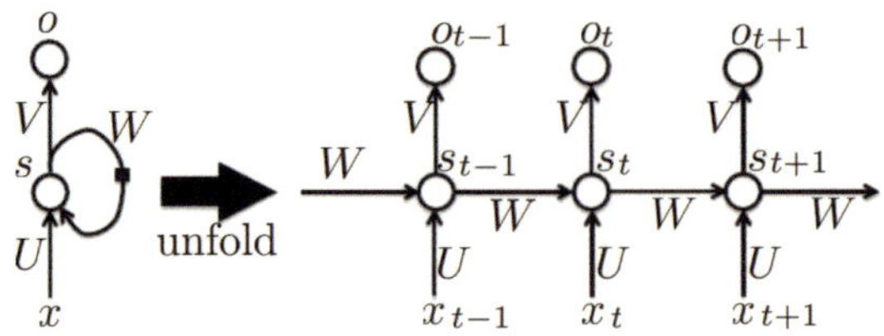

Figure 23. The architecture of recurrent neural networks.

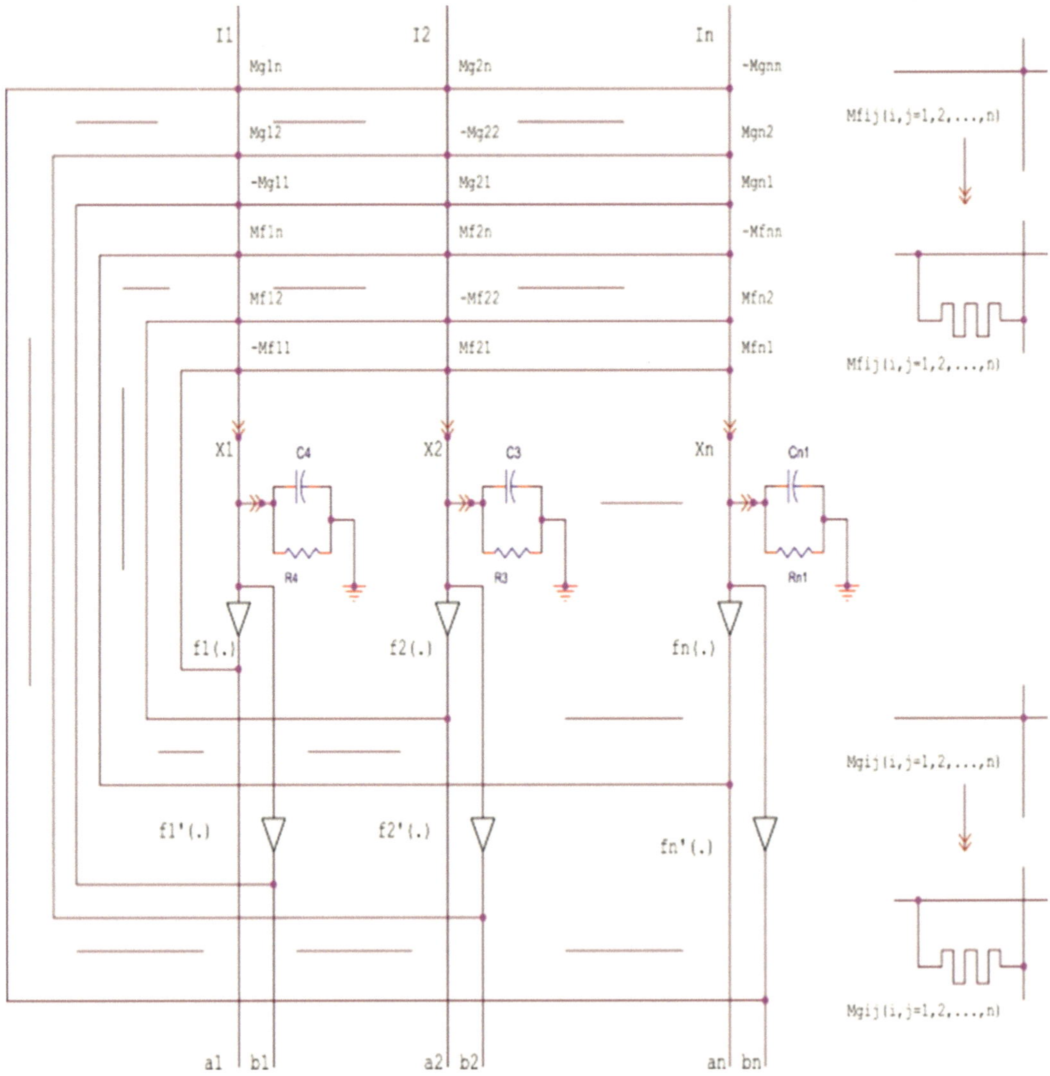

Figure 24. General class of recurrent neural network circuit.

respectively). Each circle indicates a whole vector of activations. The right of **Figure 24** is a time-unfolded flow graph, where each node is now associated with one particular time instance.

3.4.2. *A Hopfield neural network design*

Memristor-based Hopfield networks (MHN), which is an ideal model for the case where the memristor-based circuit network exhibits complex switching phenomena, and is frequently encountered in the applications [46]. A Hopfield network consists of a set of interconnected artificial neurons and synapses. In this case, a nine synapses Hopfield network is realized with six memristors and three neurons. As shown in **Figure 25**, the artificial neuron has three inputs and each input, Ni = ($i = 1, 2$, and 3), is connected to a synapse with synaptic weight of w_i. The output of the three-input binary artificial neuron is expressed as

$$y = \text{sign}\left(\sum_{i=1}^{3} w_i N_i - \theta\right) \tag{30}$$

where y is the neuron's threshold; and the sign function is defined as

$$\text{sign(N)} = \begin{cases} 1 & if N \geq 0 \\ 0 & if N < 0 \end{cases}$$

An artificial neuron was constructed, as shown in **Figure 26**. An operational amplifier is used to sum the inputs. The switches, S_1, S_2, and S_3, are controlled by external signals to obtain positive or negative synaptic weights. The synaptic weights corresponding to input N_1, N_2, and N_3 are $w_1 = \pm\frac{M_1}{M_1+R}$, $W_2 = \pm\frac{M_2}{M_2+R}$ and $W_3 = \pm\frac{M_3}{M_3+R}$, respectively ($M_1$, M_2, and M_3 are the resistance of the memristors, respectively, and the resistance of R is fixed at 3 MΩ). In the circuit shown in **Figure 26**, transmission gates B_1, B_2, and B_3 reform signals without modifying its polarity, inverters I_1, I_2 and I_3 generate negative synaptic weights.

The architecture of a 3-bit MHN implemented with nine synapses is shown in **Figure 27**. The synaptic weight from neuron i to neuron j is denoted as $w_{i,j}$, which is mapped to resistance of the corresponding memristor $M_{i,j}$. $M_{i,j}$, and $w_{i,j}$ are represented by the resistance matrix, respectively

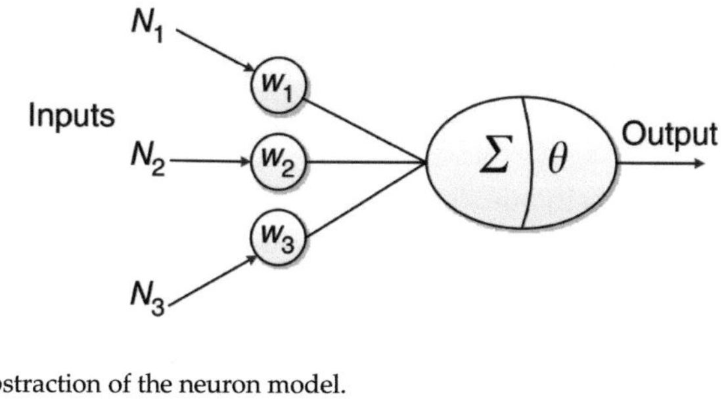

Figure 25. Mathematical abstraction of the neuron model.

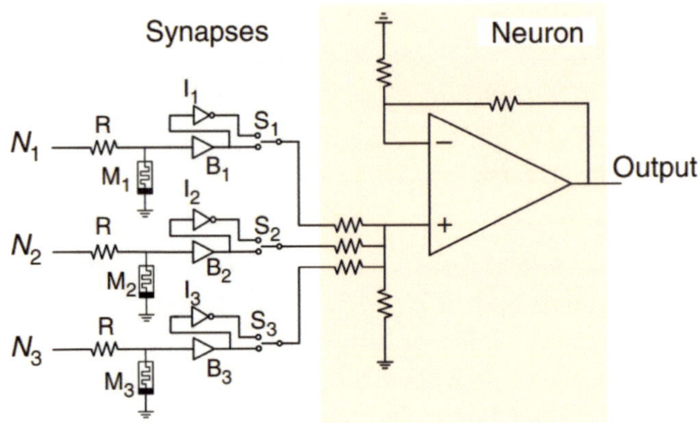

Figure 26. Circuit schematic of the designed 3-bit neuron.

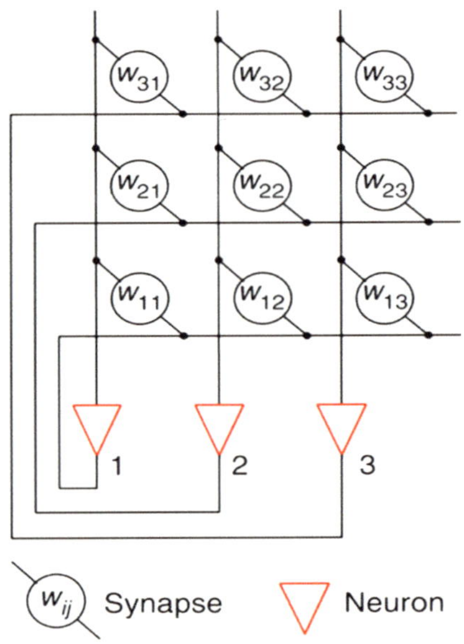

Figure 27. Architecture of the 3-bit MHN consisting of nine memristors.

$$\mathrm{M} = \begin{bmatrix} M_{11} & M_{12} & M_{13} \\ M_{21} & M_{22} & M_{23} \\ M_{31} & M_{32} & M_{33} \end{bmatrix}, \ \mathrm{W} = \begin{bmatrix} W_{11} & W_{12} & W_{13} \\ W_{21} & W_{22} & W_{23} \\ W_{31} & W_{32} & W_{33} \end{bmatrix},$$

Due to the symmetry of Hopfield network, $M_{12} = M_{21}$, $M_{23} = M_{32}$, and $M_{13} = M_{31}$, the implementation of the network only needs six memristors. The schematic of this circuit is shown in **Figure 28**, and all the demonstration below is based on this circuit. The threshold vector $\mathbf{T} = (\theta_1, \theta_2, \theta_3)$ represents the threshold of the artificial neurons (neurons 1, 2, and 3), and the state vector $\mathbf{X} = (X_1, X_2, X_3)$ represents the states of the three neurons, respectively. In each updating cycle, new states of the neurons are updated by the following function

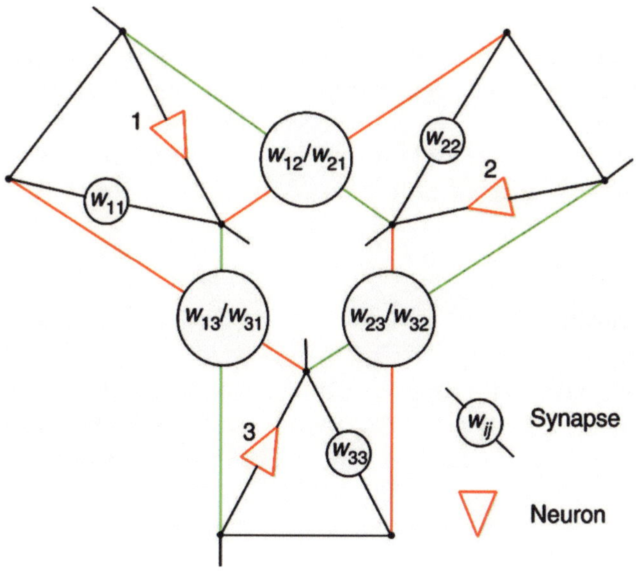

Figure 28. Architecture of the MHN with symmetrical configuration consisting of six memristors.

$$\mathbf{X}(\mathrm{t}+1) = \mathrm{sign}(X_{(t)} \cdot \mathbf{W} - \mathbf{T}) \tag{31}$$

where t represents the number of updating cycles and when $t = 0$, $\mathbf{X}(0)$ represents initial states vector. In one updating cycle, new states of the neurons are asynchronously updated from X_1, X_2 to X_3 in three stages, which are defined as stages a, b, and c, respectively [46].

4. Potential applications and prospects

Hardware implementation of deep neural networks is accomplished by using neuron-synapse circuits and future devices can make deep neural networks (NNs) design and fabrication more efficient. The full power of NNs has not yet been realized, but the release of commercial chips implementing arbitrary neural networks, more efficient algorithms will no doubt be realized in these domains where neural networks can improve the performance dramatically. Memristor-based NNs promote and solve many A.I. problems such as machine translation, intelligent question-and-answer, and game play, and in the future, memristor-based NNs can be used in neuromorphic computation, brain-computer interface or computer-brain interface, cell phone A.I. application, autopilot and environment monitor.

5. Conclusions

Different memristor-based neural network design paradigms are described. With regard to neural network systems, the current neural network implementations are not sufficient but fortunately, memristor-based systems provide the potential solution. The basic concepts of memristor-based implementation, such as memristor-based synapse, memristor-based neuron, and memristor crossbar based neuromorphic computing engine, are discussed. The memristor-based neural networks, including SNNs, MNNs, CNNs, and RNNs, are possible and efficient and are expected to spur future development of A.I. It is expected that memristor-based neural networks will take the lead.

Acknowledgements

The work was jointly financially supported by the National Natural Science Foundation of China under grant nos. 11574017 and 51372008, and the Special Foundation of Beijing Municipal Science & Technology Commission (Grant No. Z161100000216149).

Author details

Anping Huang*, Xinjiang Zhang, Runmiao Li and Yu Chi

*Address all correspondence to: aphuang@buaa.edu.cn

School of Physics and Nuclear Energy Engineering, Beihang University, Beijing, China

References

[1] Rothenbuhler A. A memristor-based neuromorphic computing application [Dissertation]. Boise State University; 2013

[2] Merolla PA, Arthur JV, Alvarezicaza R, et al. A million spiking-neuron integrated circuitwith a scalable communication network and interface. Science. 2014;**345**(6197): 668-673

[3] Shahsavari M, Falez P, Boulet P. Combining a volatile and nonvolatile memristor in artificial synapse to improve learning in Spiking Neural Networks. In: IEEE/ACM International Symposium on Nanoscale Architecture; 2016. pp. 67-72

[4] Chua LO. Memristor–The missing circuit element. IEEE Transactions on Circuit Theory. 1971;**18**(5):507-519

[5] Strukov DB, Snider GS, Stewart DR, et al. The missing memristor found. Nature. 2008;**453** (7191):80-83

[6] Jo SH, Chang T, Ebong I, et al. Nanoscale memristor device as synapse in neuromorphicsystems. Nano Letters. 2010;**10**(4):1297-1301

[7] Ali S, Bae J, Lee CH, et al. Ultra-low power non-volatile resistive crossbar memory based on pull up resistors. Organic Electronics. 2017;**41**:73-78

[8] Li Y, Zhong Y, Xu L, et al. Ultrafast synaptic events in a chalcogenide memristor. Scientific Reports. 2013;**3**:1619

[9] Wu C, Kim TW, Guo T, et al. Mimicking classical conditioning based on a single flexible-memristor. Advanced Materials. 2017;**29**(10):1602890

[10] Burr GW, Shelby RM, Sebastian A, et al. Neuromorphic computing using non-volatile memory. Advances in Physics: X. 2017;**2**(1):89-124

[11] Indiveri G, Linares-Barranco B, Legenstein R, et al. Integration of nanoscale memristor synapses inneuromorphic computing architectures. Nanotechnology. 2013;**24**(38):384010

[12] Liu B. Neuromorphic System Design and Application. University of Pittsburgh; ProQuest Dissertations Publishing, 2016

[13] Liu B. Memristor-based analog neuromorphic computing engine design and robust training scheme [Dissertation]. University of Pittsburgh; 2014

[14] Serrano-Gotarredona T, Masquelier T, Prodromakis T, et al. STDP and STDP variations with memristors for spiking neuromorphic learning systems. Frontiers in Neuroscience. 2013;**7**:2

[15] Paugam-Moisy H, Bohte S. Computing with spiking neuron networks. In: Handbook of Natural Computing. Berlin Heidelberg: Springer; 2012. pp. 335-376

[16] Prezioso M, Bayat FM, Hoskins B, et al. Self-adaptive spike-time-dependent plasticity of metal-oxide memristors. Scientific Reports. 2016;**6**:21331

[17] Xu Y, Zeng X, Han L, et al. A supervised multi-spike learning algorithm based on gradient descent for spiking neural networks. Neural Networks. 2013;**43**:99-113

[18] Linares-Barranco B, Serrano-Gotarredona T. Memristance can explain spike-time-dependent-plasticity inneural synapses. Nature Precedings. 2009;**1**:2009

[19] Afifi A, Ayatollahi A, Raissi F. Implementation of biologically plausible spiking neural network models on the memristor cross bar-based CMOS/nano circuits. In: 2009 European Conference on Circuit Theory and Design (ECCTD); 2009. pp. 563-566

[20] Soudry D, Di CD, Gal A, et al. Memristor-based multilayer neural networks with online gradient descent training. IEEE Transactions on Neural Networks & Learning Systems. 2015;**26**(10):2408

[21] Rosenthal E, Greshnikov S, Soudry D, et al. A fully analog memristor-based neural network with online gradient training. In: IEEE International Symposium on Circuits and Systems. IEEE; 2016. pp. 1394-1397

[22] Chung J, Park J, Ghosh S. Domain wall memory based convolutional neural networks forbit-width extend ability and energy-efficiency. In: International Symposium on LowPower Electronics and Design. ACM; 2016. pp. 332-337

[23] Kataeva I, Merrikh-Bayat F, Zamanidoost E, et al. Efficient training algorithms for neural networks based on memristive crossbar circuits. In: IEEE International Joint Conferenceon Neural Networks; 2015. pp. 1-8

[24] Emelyanov AV, Lapkin DA, Demin VA, et al. First steps towards the realization of a double layer perceptron based on organic memristive devices. AIP Advances. 2016;**6**(11): 111301

[25] Yang C, Kim H, Adhikari SP, et al. A circuit-based neural network with hybrid learning of back propagation and random weight change algorithms. Sensors. 2016;**17**(1):16

[26] ZhangY,LiY, Wang X, et al. Synaptic characteristics of Ag/AgInSbTe/Ta-basedmemristor for pattern recognition applications. IEEE Transactions on Electron Devices. 2017;**64**(4): 1806-1811

[27] Yakopcic C, Hasan R, Taha TM. Flexible memristor based neuromorphic system for implementing multi-layer neural network algorithms. International Journal of Parallel, Emergent andDistributed Systems. 2017 DOI: http://dx.doi.org/10.1080/17445760.2017.1321761

[28] Negrov DV, Karandashev IM, Shakirov VV, et al. A plausible memristor implementation of deep learning neural networks. Computer Science. 2015

[29] Zeng X, Wen S, Zeng Z, et al. Design of memristor-based image convolution calculationin convolutional neural network. Neural Computing & Applications. 2016:1-6

[30] Lecun Y, Bottou L, Bengio Y, et al. Gradient-based learning applied to document recognition. Proceedings of the IEEE. 1998;**86**(11):2278-2324

[31] Lawrence S, Giles CL, Tsoi AC, et al. Face recognition: A convolutional neural-network approach. IEEE Transactions on Neural Networks. 1997;**8**(1):98-113

[32] Lau MM, Lim KH, Gopalai AA. Malaysia traffic sign recognition with convolutional neural network. In: 2015 IEEE International Conference on Digital Signal Processing (DSP). IEEE; 2015. pp. 1006-1010

[33] Wang J, Lu J, Chen W, et al. Convolutional neural network for 3D object recognition based on RGB-D dataset. In: 2015 IEEE 10th Conference on Industrial Electronics and Applications (ICIEA). 2015. pp. 34-39

[34] Krizhevsky A, Sutskever I, Hinton GE. ImageNet classification with deep convolutional neural networks. In: International Conference on Neural Information Processing Systems. 2012. pp. 1097-1105

[35] Wang Y, Wen W, Song L, et al. Classification accuracy improvement for neuromorphic computing systems with one-level precision synapses. arXiv. 2017;arXiv:1701.01791

[36] Bouvrie J. Notes on Convolutional Neural Networks. Neural Networks. 2006. Unpublished. http://web.mit.edu/jvb/www/papers/cnn tutorial.pdf

[37] Wang Y, Xia L, Tang T, et al. Low power convolutional neural networks on a chip. In: IEEE International Symposium on Circuits and Systems; 2016. pp. 129-132

[38] Garbin D, Bichler O, Vianello E, et al. Variability-tolerant convolutional neural network for pattern recognition applications based on OxRAM synapses. In: 2014 IEEE International Conference on Electron Devices Meeting (IEDM); 2014. pp. 28.4.1-28.4.4

[39] Yakopcic C, Alom MZ, Taha TM. Memristor crossbar deep network implementation based on a convolutional neural network. In. International Joint Conference on Neural Networks; 2016. pp. 963-970

[40] Simard PY, Steinkraus D, Platt JC. Best practices for convolutional neural networks applied to visual document analysis. In: International Conference on Document Analysis & Recognition (ICDAR), vol. 3; 2003. pp. 958-963

[41] LeCun Y, Bengio Y, Hinton G. Deep learning. Nature. 2015;**521**(7553):436-444

[42] Mohamed AR, Dahl GE, Hinton G. Acoustic modeling using deep belief networks. IEEE Transactions on Audio, Speech, and Language Processing. 2012;**20**(1):14-22

[43] Nair V, Hinton G. Rectified linear units improve restricted boltzmann machines. In: Proceedings of the 27th International Conferenceon Machine Learning (ICML). 2010. pp. 807-814

[44] Mathiyalagan K, Anbuvithya R, Sakthivel R, et al. Non-fragile H8 synchronization of memristor-based neural networks using passivity theory. Neural Networks. 2016;**74**: 85-100

[45] MikolovT, Karafiát M, Burget L, et al. Recurrent neural network based language model. In: Interspeech Interspeech, Conference of the International Speech Communication Association, Makuhari, Chiba, Japan; 2010. pp. 1045-1048

[46] Hu S G, Liu Y, Liu Z, et al. Associative memory realized by a reconfigurable memristive Hopfield neural network. Nature Communications. 2015;**6**:7522

Chapter 13

Spike-Timing-Dependent Plasticity in Memristors

Yao Shuai, Xinqiang Pan and Xiangyu Sun

Additional information is available at the end of the chapter

http://dx.doi.org/10.5772/intechopen.69535

Abstract

The spike-timing-dependent plasticity (STDP) characteristic of the memristor plays an important role in the development of neuromorphic network computing in the future. The STDP characteristics were observed in different memristors based on different kinds of materials. The investigation regarding the influences of device hysteresis characteristic, the initial conductance of the memristors, and the waveform of the voltage pulses applied to the memristor as preneuron voltage spike and postneuron voltage spike on the STDP behavior of memristors are reviewed.

Keywords: Memristor, Spike-timing-dependent plasticity

1. Introduction

The state-of-the-art artificial intelligence based on traditional von Neumann computation paradigm has shown remarkable learning and thinking abilities, for instance, AlphaGo created by the Google-owned company Deep Mind beat the top Go player Lee Sedol by 4:1 recently [1]. However, the information processing through the digital von Neumann computation paradigm is much less efficient as compared to human brains, which is the major bottleneck of von Neumann computation paradigm. Synapse plays the key role in learning, thinking, and memorizing for a human being, and there are approximately 10^{14} synapses in a human's brain [2]. A synapse is formed between two neuron cells [3], and the synapse weight can be precisely tuned by the ionic flowing through them. It is well known that the adaptation of the synapse weight between two neurons it connects with makes the biological systems functional [4]. In order to build up a system that behaves in a much more efficient way like a human brain, people have never stopped searching for an electrical element that mimics the basic function of a synapse until "the miss memristor found [5]."

Similar to a biological synapse, memristor is a two-terminal device whose conductance can be changed by the input pulses or by controlling the charge through it [4, 6] and in such a way, a memristor works as an artificial electronic synapse. Electronic synapses based on memristor devices are around three orders of magnitude smaller than a prominent CMOS design [2]; thus, the memristor has a great potential for scalability as compared to the electronic synapse made by traditional complex circuits [7].

Synapses have different kinds of plasticity, which have been realized and investigated in different memristors [8]. And the research on the application of memristors with the common synaptic plasticity in some kind of neural networks has also been conducted. For instance, HfO_2-based memristors were used in a Hopfield neural network to implement associative memory [9]. The relationship between the resistance of the memristor and the synaptic weight was defined. And the resistances of the memristors were tuned to the target resistances through the application of the voltage pulses on the memristors as the training process [9]. Prezioso et al. realized pattern classification by using the neural network based on memristors with synaptic plasticity [10]. The 12 × 12 crossbar with Pt/Al_2O_3/TiO_{2-x}/Ti/Pt memristors at each cross point was fabricated, which is illustrated in **Figure 1(a)**. Sixty memristors among them were used to realize the function. The relationship between synaptic weight and conductance of the memristors is shown in Eq. (1). The synaptic weight was changed by applying fixed voltage pulses with the amplitude of ±1.3 V on the memristors, and the change of conductance under different voltage pulses is shown in **Figure 1(c)**.

$$W_{ij} = G_{ij}^{+} - G_{ij}^{-} \tag{1}$$

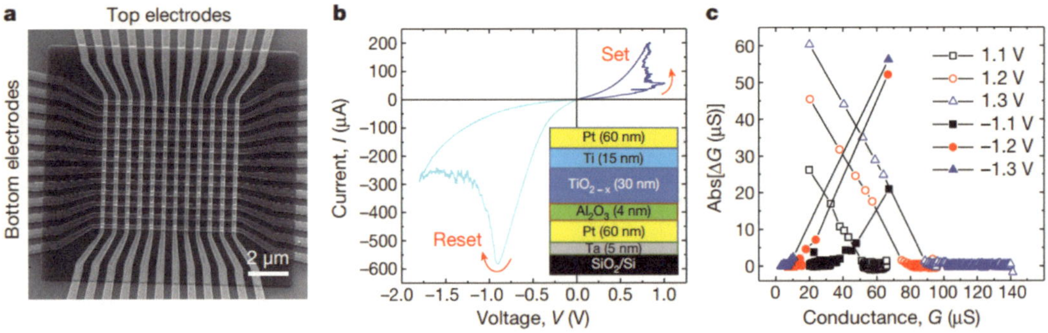

Figure 1. Memristor crossbar. (a) Integrated 12 × 12 crossbar with an Al_2O_3/TiO_{2-x} memristor at each cross point. (b) I–V curve of the memristor. Inset (b): the cross-sectional structure of the memristor device. (c) Absolute values of the change of memristor's conductance under voltage pulses (with the width of 500 μs) of two polarities, as a function of the initial conductance, for various pulse amplitudes [10].

2. STDP in memristors

In the common synaptic plasticity mentioned above, the change of the conductance (weight) is only related to one voltage pulse applied on the memristors. Another kind of plasticity of the synapses is spike-timing-dependent plasticity (STDP). STDP is one of the most important synaptic characteristics. STDP modulates synapse weight based on the activities of the so-called pre- and postsynaptic neurons [11]. The spikes from both preneuron and postneuron arrive at the synapse occasionally in the opposite direction [7]. In STDP, the change of the synaptic weight is the function of relative neuron spike timing Δt ($\Delta t = t_{pre} - t_{post}$), where t_{pre} is the time when the presynaptic neuron spike arrives and t_{post} is the time when the postsynaptic neuron spike arrives [4]. In a typical STDP behavior, if postsynaptic neuron spike arrives after presynaptic neuron spike ($\Delta t < 0$), the synaptic weight increases. If postsynaptic neuron spike arrives before presynaptic neuron spike ($\Delta t > 0$), the synaptic weight decreases. In electronic synapse based on memristor, voltage spikes or pulses are applied on the memristor through the two electrodes, which modulates the conductance of the memristor, and the change of conductance is related to the relative timing of voltage spikes or pulses. Memristors can realize STDP function which is similar with that of biological synaptic systems, which is shown in **Figure 2** [4].

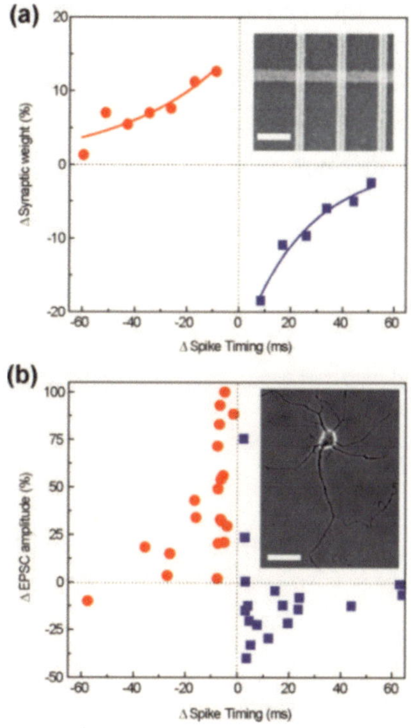

Figure 2. (a) The relationship between change of the memristor synaptic weight and the relative timing Δt of the neuron spikes. The synaptic change was normalized to the maximum synaptic weight. Inset (a): SEM image of the crossbar structure of memristors. (b) The relationship between the change in excitatory postsynaptic current (EPSC) of rat hippocampal neurons after repetitive correlated spiking (60 pulses at 1 Hz) and relative spike timing. The figure was reconstructed with permission from Ref. [8, 12]. Inset (b) is the phase contrast image of a hippocampal neuron, which was adapted with permission from Ref. [4, 13, 26].

STDP have been intensively investigated in the different memristors with different materials. The memristors are usually composed of two electrodes and memristive materials sandwiched between two electrodes. Metals such as Au, Pt, Ag, Cu, conductive nitrides such as TiN, and conductive oxides such as ITO are usually used as the materials of electrodes. The memristive materials can be grouped into binary oxides, ternary and more complex oxides, polymer, and other kind of materials.

The STDP of binary memristive materials such as TiO_x [6], WO_x [3], Al_2O_3/TiO_2 [14], CeO_x [15], TaO_x/Ta_2O_5 [16], and HfO_2 [17, 18] have been investigated very intensively; Seo et al. tested the STDP function of the memristor based on TiO_x, and they demonstrated the potential of such memristor as electronic synapses in neuromorphic network. The results are shown in **Figure 3**. Matveyev et al. demonstrated the STDP functionality of HfO_2-based memristor with the structure of $TiN/HfO_2/Pt$ [17]. The function relationship between the relative change of the conductance ΔG and the spikes' delay time Δt was obtained from the 4-nm-thick HfO_2 40 × 40 nm^2 device, which is shown in **Figure 4**. Tan et al. conducted investigation on the memristor with the structure of $Pt/WO_3/Pt$. The STDP behavior was demonstrated in such WO_3-based memristor, which is illustrated in **Figure 5(b)** [3]. Wang et al. carried out investigation on memristor device of $Pt/HfO_x/ZnO_x/TiN$. The STDP characteristics of the memristors were measured with voltage pulses with the amplitude of the $V^-/V^+ = -1.0$ V/1.0 V. Those voltage pulses were applied on the top electrode and bottom electrode as presynaptic and postsynaptic spikes. The relationship between the relative change of the synaptic weight and relative spike timing is illustrated in **Figure 6(b)**, which is basically consistent with the STDP behavior of biological synapse.

Memristors based on ternary and more complex oxides such as $BiFeO_3$ [19], InGaZnO [20], and so on, were also investigated.

Wang et al. reported that STDP was observed in the memristors based on amorphous InGaZnO. As shown in **Figure 7(c, d)**, a pair of voltage spikes with amplitude of $V^+/V^- = 5$

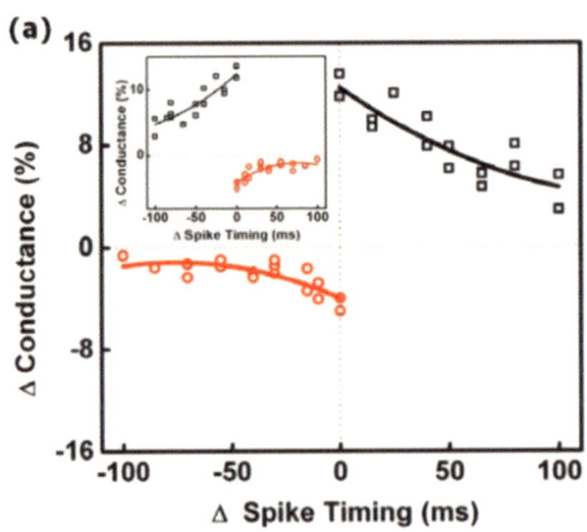

Figure 3. STDP synaptic characteristic of the memristor. Inset shows the anti-STDP synaptic characteristic of the memristor [6].

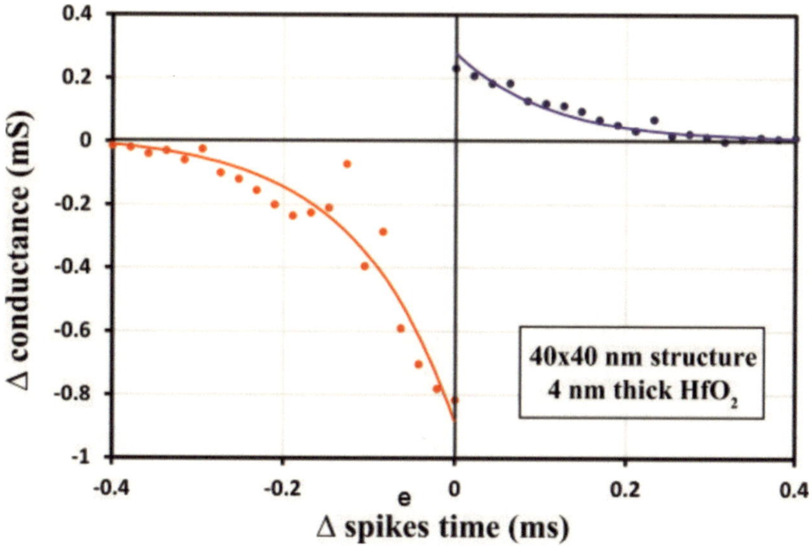

Figure 4. Asymmetric STDP characteristic emulated in crossbar 4-nm-thick, 40 × 40 nm² HfO_2-based memristors [17].

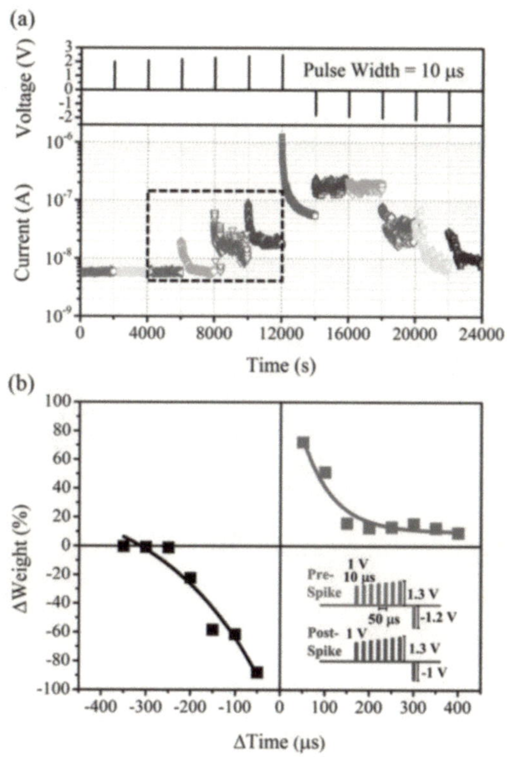

Figure 5. Experimental results of the STDP characteristic of $Pt/WO_3/Pt$ memristor. (a) Current decay after the application of a sequence of positive and negative pulses was measured with reading voltage with the amplitude of 0.05 V. The transition from volatile to nonvolatile is indicated in the dotted square. (b) The relationship between the change of the synaptic weight and the relative timing of the prespike and postspike. Inset (b): waveform of prespike and postspike [3].

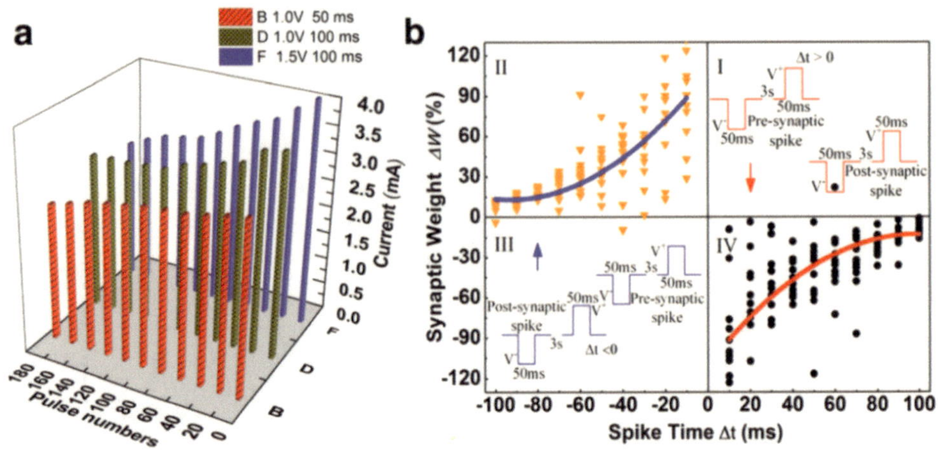

Figure 6. Nonlinear transmission characteristics and STDP of the memristor device. (a) Response of a memristor to different pulses; (b) emulation of STDP characteristics of memristor with the structure of Pt/HfO_x/ZnO_x/TiN—the relationship between the relative change of the memristor synaptic weight (Δ*W*) and the relative spike timing (Δ*t*). And the solid line is the exponential fitting curve to the experimental data. The insets (b): schematics of various spikes.

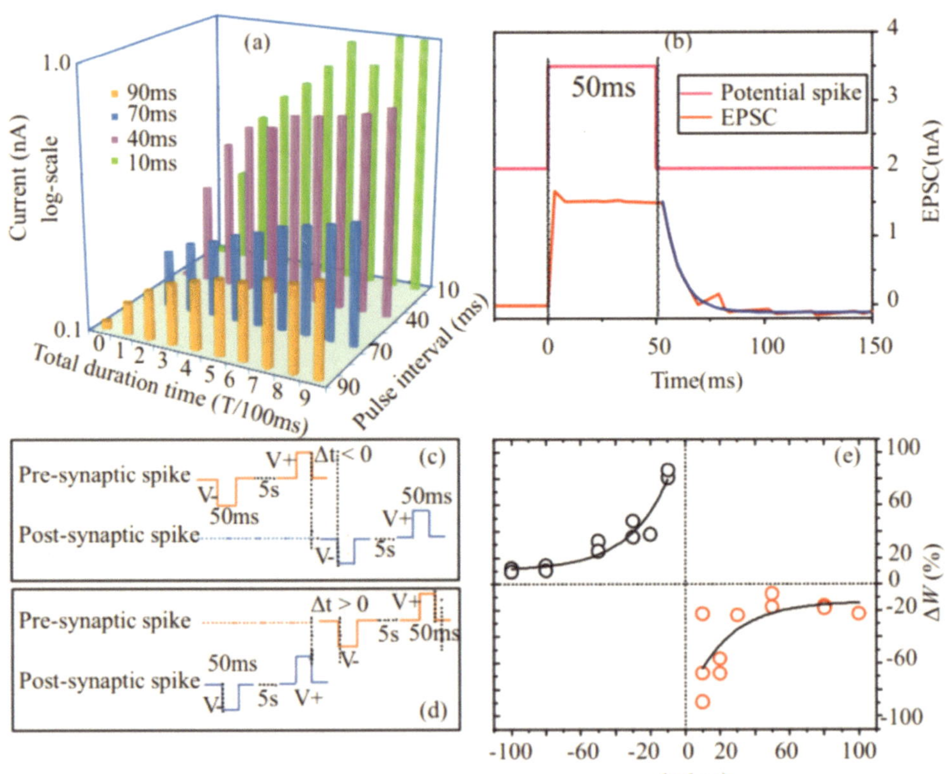

Figure 7. Demonstration of STDP characteristics of memristor. (a) The variation of the current with the interval of voltage pulses. (b) The formation and decay of spike-induced EPSC. (c and d) The preneuron spike and postneuron spike applied on the memristor for STDP. (e) The relationship between the relative change of the memristor synaptic weight (Δ*W*) and the relative spike timing (Δ*t*). The exponential fitting results for the experimental data are illustrated by the solid lines in the graph.

V/−5 V was applied on the two terminals of the memristors with relative timing Δ*t* to test the STDP characteristics. As shown in **Figure 7(e)**, the Δ*W* changed with Δ*t*, which is a typical STDP characteristic of biological synapses.

The STDP behavior was also observed in polymer such as poly(3,4-ethylenedioxythiophene): poly(styrenesulfonate) (PEDOT:PSS) [21], $EV(ClO_4)_2$/BTPA-F [22], and so on. Li et al. imitated the STDP of Ag/PEDOT:PSS/Ta structure [23]. A pair of temporally correlated voltage pulses with amplitudes $V^+/V^- = 2$ V/−2 V was used as presynaptic spikes and postsynaptic spikes, which was applied to the memristors, respectively. The change of the synaptic weights related to the precise timing between pre- and postsynaptic spikes is shown in **Figure 8(c)**.

In addition, the investigations on the STDP of the memristors based on other kind of materials such as Si/Ag mixture [4], polycrystal $CH_3NH_3PbI_3$ [24], have also been conducted.

Some factors in the STDP measurements can change some characteristics of the STDP, for example, the waveform of voltage spikes used to imitate the presynaptic neuron spike and postsynaptic neuron spike influences the STDP behavior significantly. It has been reported that the STDP function can be strongly influenced by the shape of the input voltage spikes [25]. The shape of voltage spike generated from presynaptic neuron is the same with that generated from postsynaptic neuron. Zamarreño-Ramos et al. investigated the influence of the shape of the voltage spikes (spk(*t*)) on STDP learning function ξ (Δ*T*). The results are shown in **Figure 9**. The results reveals that the voltage spikes with a narrow short positive pulse of large amplitude and a longer relaxing slowly decreasing negative tail are needed in order to obtain the STDP function similar with the behavior of the biological synapses [25].

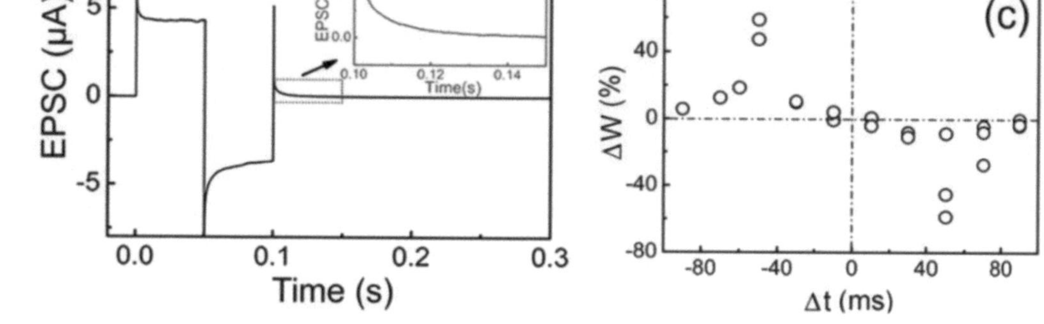

Figure 8. Simulation of STDP. (a) EPSC. The preneuron spike was $V^+/V^- = 2$ V/−2 V. The current value gradually decayed back to zero within 50 ms after the spike. A pair of temporally correlated pulses with amplitudes $V^+/V^- = 2$ V/−2 V was applied to the TE and BE as preneuron spikes and postneuron spikes, respectively. (b) Δ*t* is the interval between the beginning of the preneuron spikes and the beginning of the postneuron spikes. (c) STDP characteristics. The relationship between the change of synaptic weight and Δ*t* defined in (b).

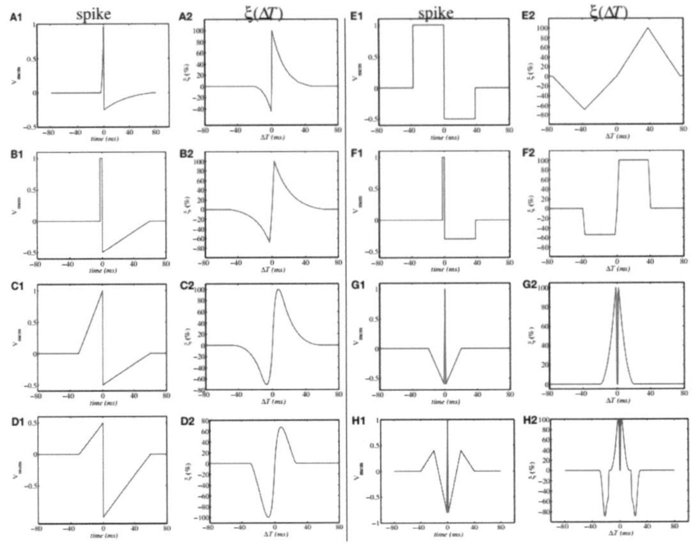

Figure 9. Illustration of influence of shape of waveform of the voltage spikes on the STDP learning function $\xi(\Delta T)$. X1 is spike waveform applied on the memristor, and X2 is resulting STDP learning function, where X goes from A to H [25].

Cederström et al. investigated the role of device hysteresis characteristic of the memristors played in the operation of its STDP function. Hysteresis characteristics of memristors based on $BiFeO_3$, Ag/Si, TiO_2, and chalcogenide (PCM) were compared. STDP characteristics were simulated with different models of different memristors, and the results are shown in **Figure 10**. The influence of switching characteristics on the operating region used for STDP was discussed. A smooth switching characteristics leads to a much wider operation region, and a steep switching characteristics leads to a much narrower operation region [26].

Du et al. reported that the learning time constant can be adjusted through changing the duration of the voltage spikes. The scheme of the voltage spikes is shown in **Figure 11**, and pulse width (t_p) is one of the parameters of the voltage spikes. The range of the delay time Δt where the normalized current is larger than 50% is called learning window. As shown in **Figure 12**, learning window decreases from 25 ms to 125 μs with the decrease of pulse width (t_p) from 10 ms to 50 μs. In addition, energy consumption of the memristors was also discussed in this work, the authors showed that energy consumption of the Au/BFO/Pt/Ti memristor is 4.7 pJ. A method to reduce the energy consumption was proposed and tested, and the results indicate by decreasing the pulse width (t_p) energy consumption can be reduced to 4.5 pJ.

Xiao et al. reported the STDP characteristics of the memristor with the structure of Au/polycrystal $CH_3NH_3PbI_3$/ITO/PEDOT:PSS. Different waveforms were used as presynaptic neuron voltage spike and postsynaptic neuron voltage spike, which are shown in **Figure 13(b–e)**. Four different kinds of STDP characteristics, including asymmetric Hebbian rule, asymmetric anti-Hebbian rule, symmetric Hebbian rule, and symmetric anti-Hebbian rule, were obtained corresponding to four different waveforms applied to the memristor as shown in **Figure 13(f–i)**. And the four kinds of STDP behaviors were fit by different equations [24].

http://dx.doi.org/10.5772/intechopen.69535

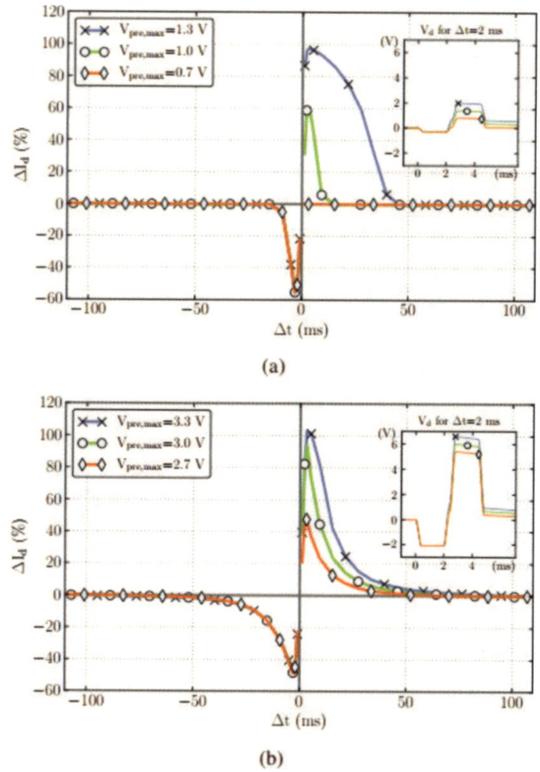

Figure 10. STDP simulations by the implementation of SPICE models, and for each Δt, a sequence of 60 pulses has been used to change the conductance. The waveforms used were adapted (a) for the TiO_2 device model and (b) for our BFO device model [26].

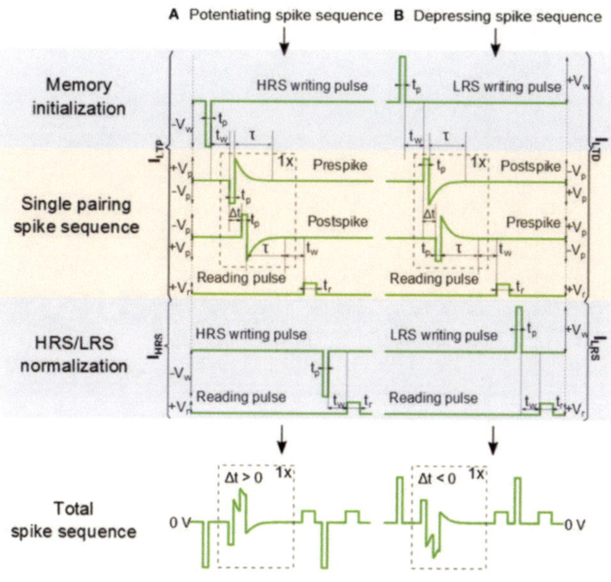

Figure 11. Schematic of the waveforms for memristor initialization, single pairing STDP, and memory consolidation. (A) A pre-post spike order is used for long-term potentiation (LTP). (B) A post-pre spike order is used for long-term depression (LTD) [19].

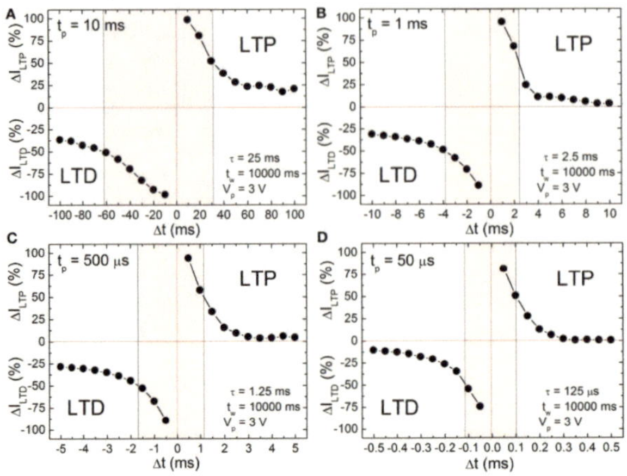

Figure 12. STDP characteristics of a BFO-based memristor with single pairing pulse width (A) t_p = 10 ms, (B) t_p = 1 ms, (C) t_p = 500 μs, and (D) t_p = 50 μs, measurement waiting time t_w = 10,000 ms, pulse amplitude V_p = 3.0 V, reading pulse amplitude V_r = +2.0 V, and reading pulse width t_r = 100 ms. The memristor was preset in HRS and LRS with a writing pulse amplitude of V_w = −8.0 V and V_w = +8.0 V, respectively [19].

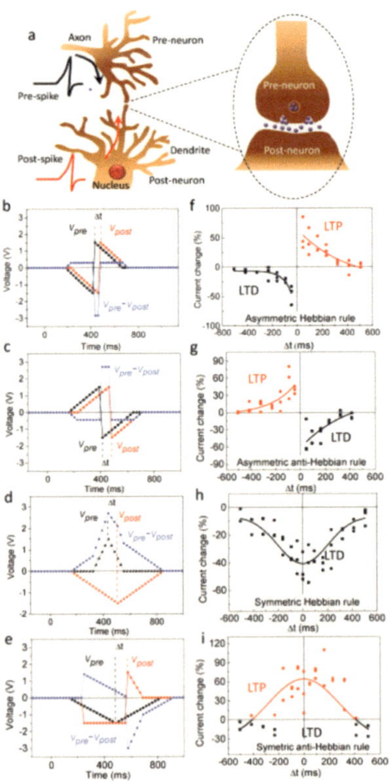

Figure 13. STDP characteristics of memristor: (a) schematics of a biological synapse. The voltage spikes for (b) asymmetric Hebbian rule, (c) asymmetric anti-Hebbian rule, (d) symmetric Hebbian rule, and (e) symmetric anti-Hebbian rule. (f-i) The current change with the applying of corresponding voltage spikes. The conductance of the synaptic device was read with a reading pulse amplitude of −0.75V before and after the applying of the voltage spikes with the interval of 3 s [24].

$$\Delta W = A\exp(-\frac{\Delta}{\tau}) + W_0 \quad (2)$$

$$\Delta W = A\exp(-\frac{\Delta t^2}{2\tau^2}) + W_0 \quad (3)$$

Prezioso et al. investigated the STDP characteristics of the memristor with the structure of $Pt/Al_2O_3/TiO_{2-x}/Ti/Pt$. Three pairs of preneuron spike and postneuron spike with different waveforms, which are shown in **Figure 14(a–c)**, were applied on the memristor. Three different STDP behaviors were observed, which are illustrated in **Figure 14(g–i)**. The results demonstrated the dependence of STDP window on the waveform of preneuron spike and postneuron spike. The investigation regarding the influence of the initial conductance (G_0) on the STDP behavior was also conducted. In this set of tests, the waveform shown in **Figure 14(a)** was used. The STDP functions for different initial conductance G_0 = 25, 50, 75, and 100 μS were measured and compared. The results shown in **Figure 15** indicate the influence of the switching dynamics' saturation of the memristors on the STDP property. All the memristors have their own dynamic range of the conductance. When G_0 is close to its maximum value, the increase of the conductance is very low. And when G_0 is close to its minimum value, the decrease of the conductance is very low [14].

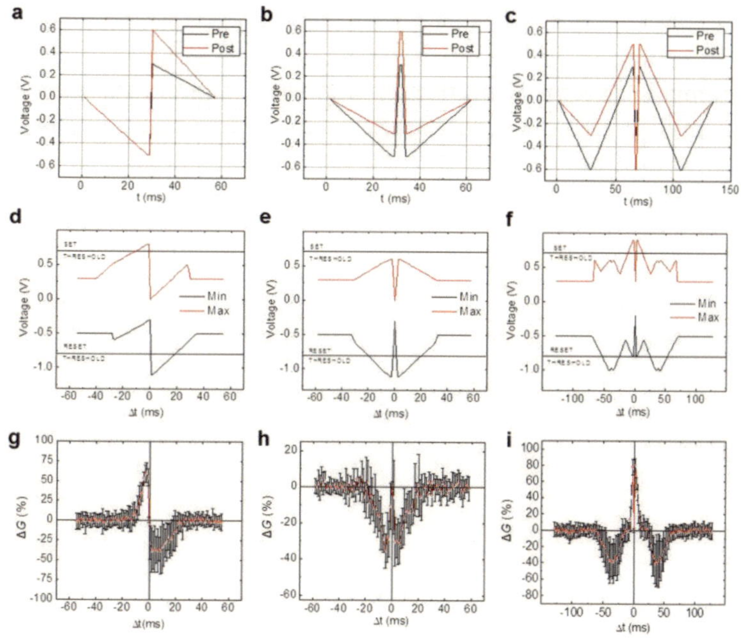

Figure 14. Experimental results for STDP characteristics. (a–c) The shapes of presynaptic and postsynaptic voltage pulses, marked by black lines and red lines, respectively (d–f) The time maxima and minima of the net voltage applied to the memristor, as functions of the time interval Δt between the pre- and postsynaptic pulses. (g–i) STDP characteristic of the memristors: the relationship between the changes of memristor's conductance and Δt. The initial memristor conductance G_0 was always set to about 33 μS in all the experiments mentioned above [14].

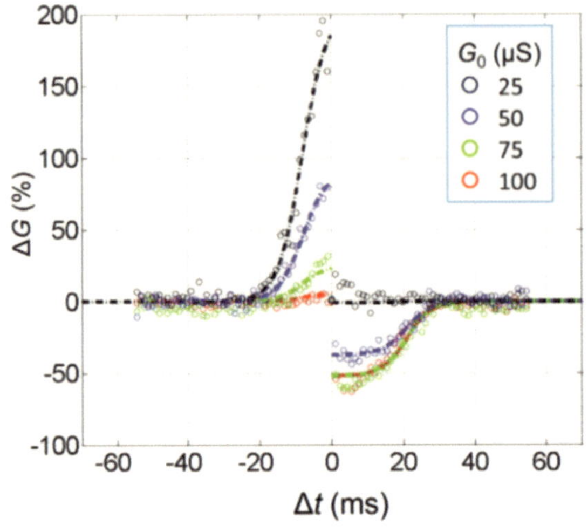

Figure 15. The experimentally measured STDP window function with several initial values G_0 = 25, 50, 75, and 100 μs together with the results of its fitting with equations (dash-dot lines) [14].

3. Conclusions

In summary, the STDP characteristics have been observed in different memristors based on different kinds of materials, which make memristors become promising in the bio-inspired neuromorphic application. Great efforts have also been made in the investigation on the influence factors of the STDP characteristics such as device hysteresis characteristic and the waveform of the voltage pulses applied to the memristor as preneuron voltage spike and postneuron voltage spike. Different kinds of waveform were used, and different kinds of STDP characteristics were observed.

Acknowledgements

This work was supported by the National Natural Science Foundation of China (No. 51402044, 51602039 and U1435208).

Author details

Yao Shuai*, Xinqiang Pan and Xiangyu Sun

*Address all correspondence to: yshuai@uestc.edu.cn

State Key Laboratory of Electronic Thin Films and Integrated Devices, University of Electronic Science and Technology of China, Chengdu, China

References

[1] Gibney E. Artificial intelligence. What Google's winning Go algorithm will do next. Nature. 2016;**531**:284-285

[2] Snider GS. Spike-timing-dependent learning in memristive nanodevices. IEEE, New York, NY 10017 USA In: 2008 IEEE International Symposium on Nanoscale Architectures. Anaheim, CA. 2008. pp. 85-92

[3] Tan ZH, Yang R, Terabe K, Yin XB, Zhang XD, Guo X. Synaptic metaplasticity realized in oxide memristive devices. Advanced Materials. 2016;**28**:377-384

[4] Jo SH, Chang T, Ebong I, Bhadviya BB, Mazumder P, Lu W. Nanoscale memristor device as synapse in neuromorphic systems. Nano Letters. 2010;**10**:1297-1301

[5] Chua LO. Memristor—the missing circuit element. IEEE Transactions on Circuit Theory. 1971;**18**:507-519

[6] Seo K, Kim I, Jung S, Jo M, Park S, Park J, et al. Analog memory and spike-timing-dependent plasticity characteristics of a nanoscale titanium oxide bilayer resistive switching device. Nanotechnology. 2011;**22**:254023

[7] Yu SM, Wu Y, Jeyasingh R, Kuzum DG, Wong HSP. An electronic synapse device based on metal oxide resistive switching memory for neuromorphic computation. IEEE Transactions on Electron Devices. 2011;**58**:2729-2737

[8] Jang JW, Park S, Jeong YH, Hwang H. ReRAM-based synaptic device for neuromorphic computing. IEEE, New York, NY 10017 USA. In: 2014 IEEE International Symposium on Circuits and Systems (ISCAS). Melbourne, Australia. 2014. pp. 1054-1057

[9] Hu SG, Liu Y, Liu Z, Chen TP, Wang JJ, Yu Q, et al. Associative memory realized by a reconfigurable memristive Hopfield neural network. Nature Communications. 2015;**6**:7522

[10] Prezioso M, Merrikh-Bayat F, Hoskins BD, Adam GC, Likharev KK, Strukov DB. Training and operation of an integrated neuromorphic network based on metal-oxide memristors. Nature. 2015;**521**:61-64

[11] Mostafa H, Khiat A, Serb A, Mayr CG, Indiveri G, Prodromakis T. Implementation of a spike-based perceptron learning rule using TiO_{2-x} memristors. Frontiers in Neuroscience. 2015;**9**:357

[12] Bi GQ, Poo MM. Synaptic modifications in cultured hippocampal neurons: Dependence on spike timing, synaptic strength, and postsynaptic cell type. Journal of Neuroscience. 1998;**18**:10464-10472

[13] Kaech S, Banker G. Culturing hippocampal neurons. Nature Protocols. 2006;**1**:2406-2415

[14] Prezioso M, Merrikh Bayat F, Hoskins B, Likharev K, Strukov D. Self-adaptive spike-time-dependent plasticity of metal-oxide memristors. Scientific Reports. 2016;**6**:21331

[15] Hsieh C-C, Roy A, Chang Y-F, Shahrjerdi D, Banerjee SK. A sub-1-volt analog metal oxide memristive-based synaptic device with large conductance change for energy-efficient spike-based computing systems. Applied Physics Letters. 2016;**109**:223501

[16] Kim S, Choi S, Lu W. Comprehensive physical model of dynamic resistive switching in an oxide memristor. ACS Nano. 2014;**8**:2369-2376

[17] Matveyev Y, Kirtaev R, Fetisova A, Zakharchenko S, Negrov D, Zenkevich A. Crossbar nanoscale HfO_2-based electronic synapses. Nanoscale Research Letters. 2016;**11**:147

[18] Covi E, Brivio S, Serb A, Prodromakis T, Fanciulli M, Spiga S. HfO_2-based memristors for neuromorphic applications. IEEE, New York, NY 10017 USA; In: IEEE International Symposium on Circuits and Systems. Montreal, Canada. 2016. pp. 393-396

[19] Du N, Kiani M, Mayr CG, You T, Burger D, Skorupa I, et al. Single pairing spike-timing dependent plasticity in $BiFeO_3$ memristors with a time window of 25 ms to 125 μs. Frontiers in Neuroscience. 2015;**9**:227

[20] Wang ZQ, Xu HY, Li XH, Yu H, Liu YC, Zhu XJ. Synaptic learning and memory functions achieved using oxygen ion migration/diffusion in an amorphous InGaZnO memristor. Advanced Functional Materials. 2012;**22**:2759-2765

[21] Chen Y, Liu G, Wang C, Zhang WB, Li RW, Wang LX. Polymer memristor for information storage and neuromorphic applications. Materials Horizons. 2014;**1**:489-506

[22] Liu G, Wang C, Zhang W, Pan L, Zhang C, Yang X, et al. Organic biomimicking memristor for information storage and processing applications. Advanced Electronic Materials. 2016;**2**:1500298

[23] Li S, Zeng F, Chen C, Liu H, Tang G, Gao S, et al. Synaptic plasticity and learning behaviours mimicked through Ag interface movement in an Ag/conducting polymer/Ta memristive system. Journal of Materials Chemistry C. 2013;**1**:5292

[24] Xiao Z, Huang J. Energy-efficient hybrid perovskite memristors and synaptic devices. Advanced Electronic Materials. 2016;**2**:1600100

[25] Zamarreno-Ramos C, Camunas-Mesa LA, Perez-Carrasco JA, Masquelier T, Serrano-Gotarredona T, Linares-Barranco B. On spike-timing-dependent-plasticity, memristive devices, and building a self-learning visual cortex. Frontiers in Neuroscience. 2011;**5**:26

[26] Cederstrom L, Starket P, Mayr C, Shuai Y, Schmidt H, Schuffny R. A model based comparison of $BiFeO_3$ device applicability in neuromorphic hardware. IEEE, New York, NY 10017 USA; In: 2013 IEEE International Symposium on Circuits and Systems (ISCAS). Beijing, China. 2013. pp. 2323-2326

Chapter 14

Neural Network-Based Analog-to-Digital Converters

Aigerim Tankimanova and Alex Pappachen James

Additional information is available at the end of the chapter

http://dx.doi.org/10.5772/intechopen.73038

Abstract

In this chapter, we present an overview of the recent advances in analog-to-digital converter (ADC) neural networks. Biological neural networks consist of natural binarization reflected by the neurosynaptic processes. This natural analog-to-binary conversion ability of neurons can be modeled to emulate analog-to-digital conversion using a set of nonlinear circuit elements and existing artificial neural network models. Since one neuron during processing consumes on average only about half nanowatts of power, neurons can perform highly energy-efficient operations, including pattern recognition. Analog-to-digital conversion itself is an example of simple pattern recognition where input analog signal can be presented in one of the 2^N different patterns for N bits. The classical configuration of neural network-based ADC is Hopfield neural network ADC. Improved designs, such as modified Hopfield network ADC, T-model neural ADC, and multilevel neurons-based neural ADC, will be discussed. In addition, the latest architecture designs of neural ADC such as hybrid complementary metal-oxide semiconductor (CMOS)-memristor Hopfield ADC are covered at the end of this chapter.

Keywords: neural networks, analog-to-digital converters, Hopfield network

1. Introduction

This chapter presents a review of the advancements in the application of neural network (NN) systems in analog-to-digital converter (ADC) design. Analog-to-digital (A/D) conversion is an essential part of all microelectronic systems design that serves as a link between analog sensors and digital-processing circuitry [1]. The dominant period of the ADC design development came with the maturity of complementary metal-oxide semiconductor (CMOS) technologies [1]. At present, there is a huge variety of high-speed and high-resolution ADCs based on the most advanced CMOS processes that are applicable for different applications [1]. In fact, even though the ADC design field is mature, the complexity of the construction of properly operating ADC system that fits certain applications is still high. In conventional CMOS ADCs, a number of appropriately designed analog circuitries, such as switches, operational amplifiers, voltage converters, and so on, are required [2]. However, with modern advancements in computational systems and processing applications, the demand for faster processing and more flexible architectures that can perform a variety of tasks in the most efficient manner has increased. Artificial neural network (ANN) technology is a well-known candidate that can resolve such demands in high-performance A/D conversion as it divides the task between a number of simple processing elements (neurons) [3]. Further, neurons can perform highly energy-efficient operations of pattern recognition, in particular, one neuron during processing consumes on average only about half nanowatts of power [4].

Since the early twentieth century, scientists and engineers have been trying to explain how human brain functions, and a number of models that are aimed to mimic some features of the biological neural networks were proposed. The work presented by McCulloch and Pitts [5] is one of the first examples of mathematical modeling of ANN that is based on a two-state neuron model. The information processing that is performed in biological neural networks incorporates memorization, learning, classification, and so on and is performed by natural binarization mechanism reflected by the neurosynaptic processes. Brain associative property that is used in processing information is being discussed widely since the 1960s and later. Based on the works presented by [5–8], Hopfield proposed a neural network model that incorporates associative memory property. The idea that he presented is actually a model of content addressable memory (CAM) that can be implemented in hardware [9–11]. He discovered that such a type of network has collective computational properties so that it can be used in solving different optimization problems [9–11].

One of the applications of such CAM-based neural network (NN) that was introduced by Hopfield and Tank includes solving simple optimization problem such as analog-to-digital (A/D) conversion, where the dynamics of the system is described by an energy function (or cost function) [9]. The main concept behind the proper operation of the Hopfield NN is based on minimization of the energy function, so that when the minimum value is achieved, the network reaches its stable state [9–12]. In general, A/D conversion can be classified as an example of simple pattern recognition where input analog signal can be presented in one of the 2^N different patterns for N bits. In Hopfield NN-based ADC, these digital patterns are stored as a memory and are retrieved when the network reaches stable state after conversion period [11].

The NN model proposed by Hopfield represents a network of interconnected processing units (neurons) connected through a symmetric connection matrix with zero diagonal elements [9–11, 13]. The interconnection nodes between neurons can be viewed as synaptic strength values. The strength of each synapse is represented by the conductance value at each node. The network dynamics is governed by the behaviour of energy function, E, so that when the energy function is of the minimum value, the network reaches stable state and gives digital output [9–11, 13].

Therefore, in Section 2, a comprehensive discussion on Hopfield NN in general and the ADC based on the Hopfield NN design is presented. The section addresses such topics as the theory of the Hopfield NN, the description of how to construct an ADC structure and the problems that appear in the Hopfield NN ADC. In Section 3, a review of different designs based on original Hopfield ADC such as modified Hopfield neural ADC, NN-based ADCs with non-symmetrical weight matrix, NN-based ADC with multilevel neurons and level-shifted neural ADC is presented. In Section 4, recent CMOS-memristor-based ADC architectures are reviewed. The last section summarizes and gives a conclusion for this chapter.

2. Hopfield neural network ADC

2.1. The Hopfield ADC theory

In his early works, Hopfield introduced the ideas behind the emergent collective computational properties of highly interconnected associative networks [9, 10]. The neural network models that were presented earlier were of Perceptron type and were implemented by feedforward architecture [13]. By contrast, Hopfield presented a different type of architecture with fully interconnected neurons, where each neuron translates its output to the inputs of the remaining neurons through feedback connections [9, 10]. The strength of each feedback connection is represented by its weight (or synapse). In a later work, Hopfield and Tank [11] presented methods of how the network can be applied in solving optimization problems, such as A/D conversion, signal decomposition and linear programming.

One of the earliest works on artificial neural networks (ANNs) by McCulloch and Pitts [5] described a two-state (on-state and off-state) stochastic neuron model that simplifies biological neural function to simple logical operation. However, this model was not applicable for analog processing as it did not have the continuous behaviour as of biological neurons [10, 11, 13]. Hopfield proposed the NN model with continuous neuron response [10, 11, 13], which has computation properties of the stochastic model [9] that can be implemented in hardware. Continuous neuron response in Hopfield NN can be interpreted as an analogy of graded dependence of firing rate produced by the soma of biological neuron as the input signal to the neuron membrane [10, 11, 13] without considering action potential signal details. Two states in neuron model are considered as '0' for not firing state and '1' for firing at a maximum rate [10, 11, 13]. The graded response function that describes such dependence is neuron's activation function $g_i(u_i)$ that is represented by monotonically increasing sigmoid function (Eq. (1))

$$g_i(u_i) = \frac{1}{1 + \exp(u_i)} \quad (1)$$

where u_i is the input voltage to neuron, so the neuron's output signal will be equal to $V_i = g_i(u_i)$.

The neuron output V_i can be either logic high or logic low depending on whether the effective input voltage to neuron u_i is higher or lower than the neuron threshold, as it can be observed from **Figure 1**.

The hardware implementation of 4-bit Hopfield NN ADC proposed in [11] is shown in **Figure 2**. As it is described in [11], at each analog input level, the network creates an energy function surface that consists of local minima states with one global minimum for this particular analog input. The global minimum for each input level represents the correct digital representation for the input signal [11]. The dynamics of the system can be viewed as a flow in energy state space that tends to minimize E, so that when the network reaches minimum it stops searching process [10, 13]. When the ADC network arrives at an energy minimum state, it should produce an output code that best represents the corresponding analog input. Thus, the E function is a Lyapunov stability function of the system [10]. The proper operation of the Hopfield ADC is achieved when the voltage level of the output code is equal to the value of the analog input, Eq. (2).

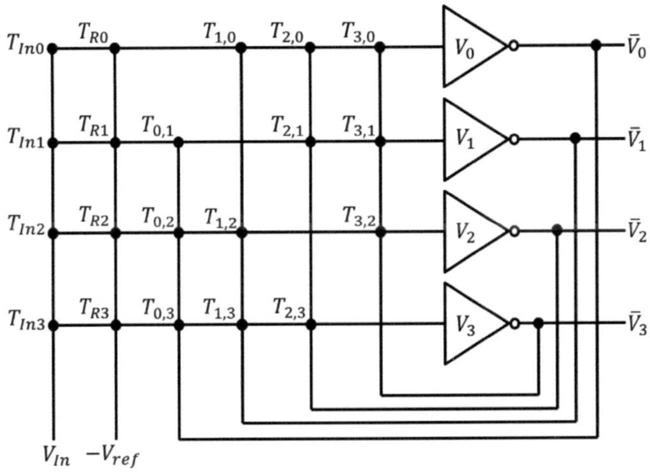

Figure 1. Neuron sigmoidal transfer function.

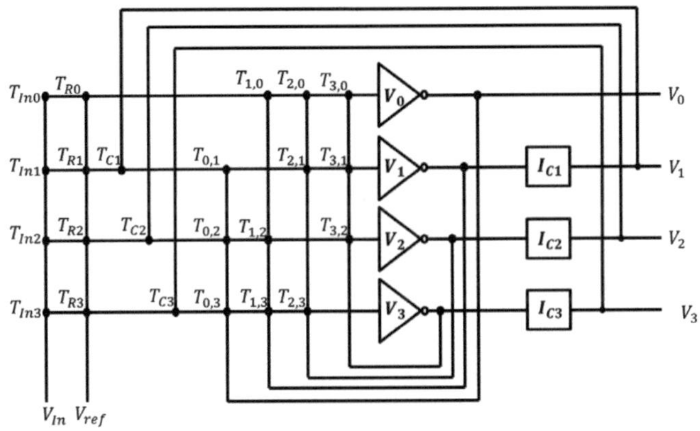

Figure 2. 4-bit Hopfield neural network ADC.

$$V_{In} = \sum_{i=0}^{N-1} 2^i V_i \tag{2}$$

The ADC network consists of four neurons that are interconnected by a synaptic weight matrix. The network dynamics is highly dependent on the values of synaptic matrix elements. This dependency was analysed by Hopfield in his work [9, 10], where it is deduced that for the system to reach a stable state two conditions should be maintained: (1) the symmetrical synaptic weight matrix $T_{ij} = T_{ji}$ and (2) the diagonal synaptic weights that correspond to feedbacks from neurons to their own inputs should be equal to zero $T_{ii} = 0$. Following this condition, as it is shown in [9–11, 13], the Hopfield neural network should converge to a stable state. The energy function for the Hopfield network with symmetric weight matrix is shown by Eq. (3)

$$E = -\frac{1}{2}\sum_{i,j} T_{ij} V_i V_j + \sum_i 1/R_i \int_0^{V_i} g_i^{-1}(V)\, dV - \sum_i I_i V_i \tag{3}$$

where the term $g_i^{-1}(V)$ is equal to the neuron input potential u_i and R_i is the neuron input resistance [10, 13].

The NN proposed by Hopfield has the features that correlate with biological NNs and so it represents a simplified analogy of biological NNs. The system dynamic change can be described by the first-order differential equation of the rate of change of i_{th} neuron input potential, Eq. (4). The capacitance C that is present at the neuron input is a circuit representation of neuron cell membrane capacitance, while the term $T_{Ini} + T_{Ri} + \sum_i T_{ij} = {}^1/_{R_i}$ in which R_i can be viewed as neuron cell transmembrane resistance [6]

$$C\frac{du_i}{dt} = \sum_j T_{ij} V_j - \left(T_{Ini} + T_{Ri} + \sum_i T_{ij} \right) u_i + T_{Ini} V_{In} + T_{Ri} V_{ref} \tag{4}$$

From Eq. (4), it is seen that i_{th} neuron is charged by integrating the current flowing into the neuron with charging RC time constant [10, 13]. The current that flows into the neuron consists of three components formed prior to the neuron input, which are postsynaptic current $T_{ij}V_j$ from neuron j, analog input current $T_{Ini}V_{In}$ and constant reference current $T_{Ri}V_{ref}$ [10, 13].

The ADC operation also can be described by the energy function shown by Eq. (5) [11]. The first term of Eq. (5) shows the squared difference between analog input voltage and the corresponding digital output voltage. As it was previously assumed, the value of analog input voltage should be close to the voltage level of the corresponding output code, see Eq. (2). If for particular V_{In} the output code $V_3V_2V_1V_0$ is the most correct digital representation, the first term of Eq. (5) should be equal to zero [11]. The second term in Eq. (5) is added to ensure that the digital output voltages V_i will be of logic '0' and '1' [11]

$$E = \frac{1}{2}\left(V_{In} - \sum_{i=0}^{N-1} V_i 2^i \right)^2 - \sum_{i=0}^{N-1} \left(2^i\right)^2 [V_i(V_i - 1)] \tag{5}$$

After expanding and rearrangement of the above equation, we get the expression shown in Eq. (6). By using Eq. (6), the expressions for synaptic weights calculation can be obtained, Eq. (7)

$$E = -\frac{1}{2}\sum_{\substack{i=0\,j=0\\ i\neq j}}^{N-1}\left(-2^{i+j}\right)V_iV_j - \frac{1}{2}\sum_{i=0}^{N-1}\left(-2^{(2i-1)} + 2^iV_{In}\right)V_i \tag{6}$$

$$T_{ij} = -2^{(i+j)} \quad T_{refi} = -2^{(2i-1)} \quad T_{Ini} = 2^i \tag{7}$$

Therefore, four-bit Hopfield NN ADC can be designed by using Eqs. (2)–(7).

2.2. The local minima problem

As it is already discussed, the stability of the Hopfield NN is achieved when the energy function is at its minimum in the state space. The dynamics of the system is moving towards decreasing the energy function. Thus, for the Hopfield NN the energy state space will have multiple local minima, where each of these local minima states is able to stabilize the system dynamics. In theory, the ADC structure proposed by Tank and Hopfield [11], which is based on the Hopfield NN with symmetric weight matrix, has to retrieve correct digital response of the analog input voltage by means of the energy local minima states that are assigned for each correct digital output. However, in practice, this concept does not work as is expected. It appears that the local minima states corrupt the correct operation of the network [14–19].

In the original Hopfield's work [11], it was proposed to implement neurons with the CMOS operational amplifiers. The results that were obtained exhibit not ideal ADC behaviour with incorrect output states (**Figure 3**).

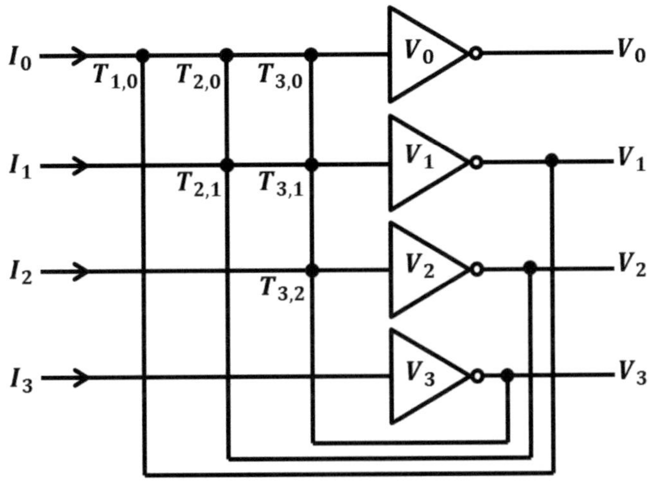

Figure 3. Hopfield NN ADC transfer characteristics with digital errors.

It is found that after each A/D conversion cycle, the threshold voltage of each neuron circuitry differs from the pre-set value of $u_{th} = 0$ V [11], such that the response of comparators exhibits offset. The authors in [11] proposed that the behaviour caused by the hysteresis of CMOS neurons in addition to the local minima states is a dominant contributor to the wrong network response. This hysteresis change in thresholds makes the system to stabilize at the local minima state, which is located closer to the network's present energy state at the moment of conversion [14–19]. In order to solve this problem, one of the solutions is to reset the neuron state to the initial threshold value after each conversion [11]. However, the main disadvantage of this method is that it requires more power.

Alternatively, in the works [11–16], the authors proposed to change the Hopfield ADC network architecture itself in order to eliminate the local minima states, which cause errors in the ADC outputs. Thus, different methods on eliminating local minima problem are proposed in [14–19], which are discussed in more detail in Section 3.

3. Hopfield neural network-based ADCs

The design presented by Hopfield and Tank is a first example of ADC task implementation with neural networks. This idea became very popular later, as it appeared very simple compared to the conventional designs and, moreover, it opens up the possibilities to explore its phenomenological computational abilities which is a good contribution for science and engineering by itself.

As it was previously described, the existence of local minima in the dynamics of the original Hopfield network ADC design corrupts its digital output by generating spurious states. This problem was addressed by several works that presented the ways of eliminating the local minima states by changing the structure of the ADC network [14–19]. In the following subsection, the two methods that are claimed to eliminate the problem of local minima of the energy function are presented.

3.1. Eliminating the local minima problem of Hopfield ADC

3.1.1. Modified Hopfield architecture with correction currents

In the study by [14], the authors analyzed the stability of the output codes of Hopfield network ADC in terms of overlap of input currents between two adjacent output codes which is defined as *GAP*. According to Lee and Sheu [14], in order to avoid the local minima state, this parameter should be higher or equal to zero. Thus, it was deduced that in order to eliminate this current overlap condition, the correction currents can be applied back to the inputs of Hopfield network through the additional set of conductance weights [14].

The modified Hopfield network ADC schematic diagram is shown in **Figure 2**. The correction currents are generated by inverting amplifiers in order to compensate the overlap and to maintain system dynamics converging to a stable state. In Eq. (8), the dynamics of network in a stable state with applied correction current, I_{iC}, is described.

$$T_i u_i = \sum_{\substack{i=0 \, j=0 \\ j \neq i}}^{N-1} T_{ij} V_j + I_i + I_{iC} \tag{8}$$

The energy function of the modified Hopfield network can be described by adding an additional term that represents the correction currents, Eq. (8). The correcting energy eliminates the local minima states and gives the network one global minimum energy state [14].

$$E_C = -\frac{1}{2} \sum_{\substack{i=0 \, j=0 \\ i \neq j}}^{N-1} T_{ij} V_i V_j - \sum_{i=0}^{N-1} I_i V_i - \sum_{i=1}^{N-1} I_{iC} V_i \tag{9}$$

There are certain conditions, according to [14], that should be followed while selecting the correction currents and conductance values. The first condition is to avoid the state when the GAP_C parameter is less than zero so that to avoid the two adjacent codes be stable simultaneously. The second condition states that the network dynamics must be sustained in the operation that minimizes energy function of the system. The last condition is to maintain the input current range in appropriate for the global minimum value. For the detailed description of the method, please refer to [14].

3.1.2. Non-symmetric Hopfield architecture

The type of architecture based on Hopfield network is built with non-symmetric connection weight matrix, which is another example that is aimed to solve the local minima states problem. In the designs by [15–19], the properties of the triangular connections are analyzed. In [19], the authors prove that by triangular interconnection matrix the network operates without spurious states and that this type of architecture can be a good alternative for the original Hopfield design. Similar network type was analyzed by Sun et al. [18], and it is proven that the local minima problem can be mitigated by using this architecture. Taking into account the structure of the model [18], the learning component can be applied to the network making this type of architecture advantageous over the original one.

In **Figure 3**, the non-symmetric T-model ADC is shown. The input current at each raw represents the current flowing from the external analog input source and from the reference.

This section presents an overview of the designs of neural network ADC of Hopfield network type that solves the problem of the local minima of energy function that creates the digital error at the output of the ADC. We introduced a brief explanation of the two methods of elimination of the local minima.

3.2. Hopfield ADC with multilevel neurons

An interesting alternative design is proposed by [20, 21] in which the authors focus on implementing analog neurons to be of multiple states. The design named as *Multilevel Neural*

Network is applied to the original Hopfield neural network ADC by replacing the conventional two-state sigmoidal neurons by multiple-state (or multiple threshold) neurons [21]. The motivation under this idea is to create a type of neural ADC with better resolution but with the same number (or even less number) of synaptic weights as in the original Hopfield ADC design [18]. This method reduces the complexity of weight matrix and makes it easier to implement the ADC with improved resolution in hardware [21].

The schematic diagram of the ADC proposed in [21] is shown in **Figure 4**. Being a distinguishable alternative neural networks-based ADC design, it still does not solve the problems of the local minima states of the Hopfield associative network. In [21], the authors considered this case and proposed to solve the local minima by additional correction current method [14].

The multilevel neuron dynamics is described by the block diagram shown in **Figure 5** [21]. In the original Hopfield ADC, continuous neuron model dynamics is described by the first-order differential equation (Eq. (4)). The two-state neuron activation function is expressed by Eq. (1). The neuron output is then equal to $V_i = g_i(u_i)$, and it can take two states logic high and logic low (refer to Section 2). In multilevel neuron model, a two-state activation function neuron is replaced with the multiple-state nonlinearity block (Eq. (10)) (**Figures 6** and **7**)

$$V_i = M_i(u_i) \tag{10}$$

The nonlinearity function $M(u)$ shown in Eq. (10) is described as a sum of monotonically nondecreasing step functions $f_j(.)$ with different threshold values θ_j, where the state of the

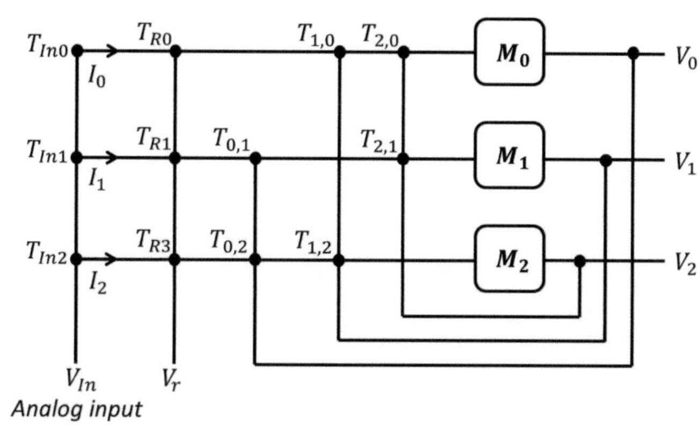

Figure 4. Schematic representation of modified Hopfield network ADC.

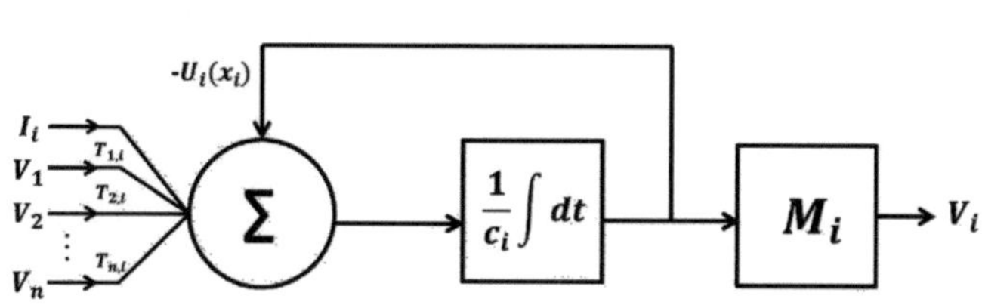

Figure 5. Non-symmetric T-model ADC.

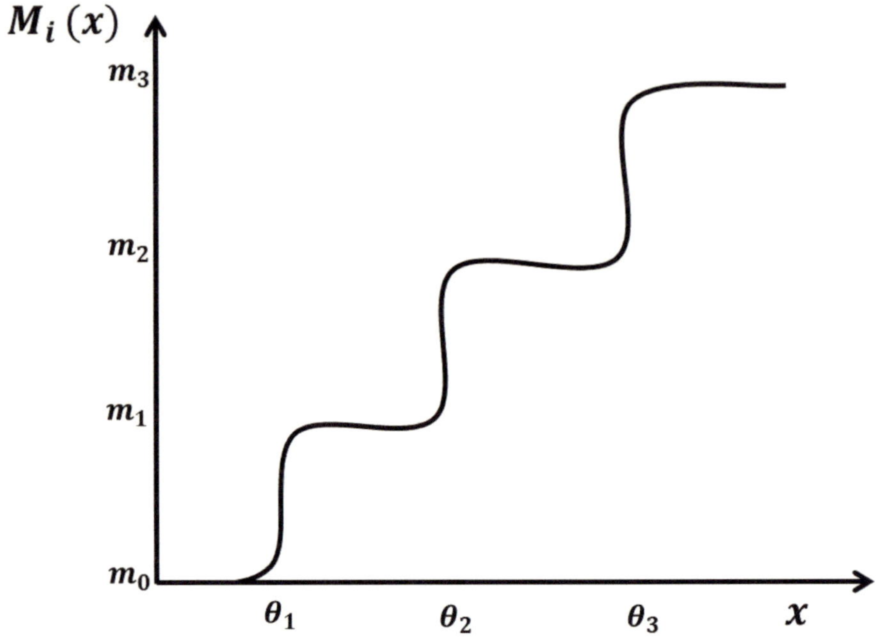

Figure 6. Multilevel neural ADC.

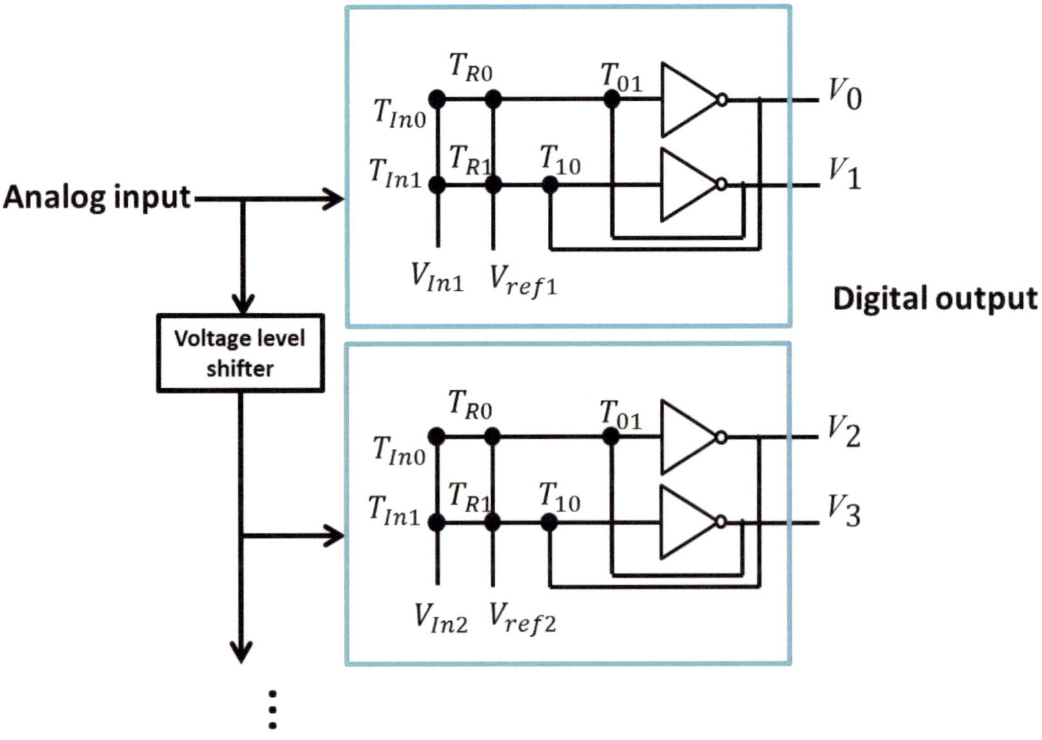

Figure 7. Multilevel neuron block diagram.

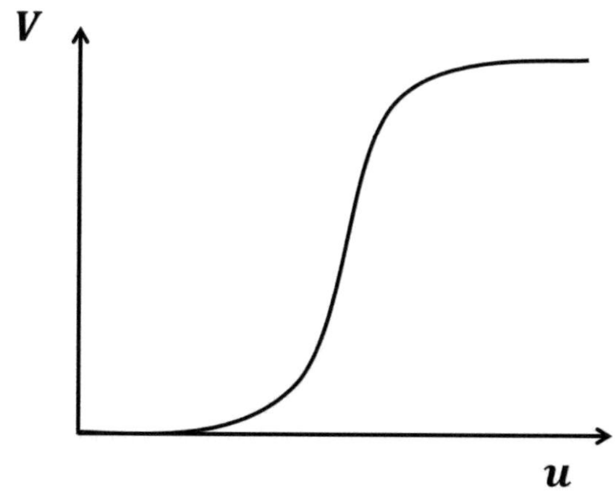

Figure 8. Sigmoidal multilevel nonlinearity.

neuron changes. Each step function is multiplied by the positive coefficient parameter that can be seen as an offset parameter b_j. The sigmoidal multilevel nonlinearity can be observed in **Figure 8**

$$M(u) = \sum_{j=0}^{l-1} b_j f_j(u - \theta_j) \tag{11}$$

The neuron dynamics can be expressed by the block diagram shown in **Figure 7**. The term $X_i(u_i) = G_i u_i$ translates information about the current state to its own input so that when the input current value I_i is higher than the $X_i(u_i)$, the state of the neuron is increased. In this design, the additional G_i value is present as a diagonal element in the weight matrix [18]. Therefore, the system is described by Eq. (12)

$$C_i \frac{du_i}{dt} = \sum_{j=0}^{n-1} T_{ij} V_j - G_i u_i + I_i \tag{12}$$

$$u_i = M^{-1}(V_i) \tag{13}$$

The energy function for the multilevel ADC architecture can also be found by the square of difference expression, Eq. (14). The number of levels in the multilevel nonlinearity block of the neuron is $m = 0, 1, 2, \ldots, l-1$ and l represents the base of conversion [21]. The system tends to find the correct digital representation with base l of analog input signal with the minimum energy function value [21]. After expanding Eq. (14), Eq. (15) is obtained, which gives the synaptic weight values of the network, Eq. (16)

$$E = \frac{1}{2}\left(V_{In} - \sum_{i=0}^{N-1} l^i V_i\right)^2 \tag{14}$$

$$E = -\frac{1}{2} \sum_{\substack{i=0\, j=0 \\ i \neq j}}^{N-1} \left(-l^{i+j}\right) V_i V_j - \sum_{i=0}^{N-1} l^i V_{In}\, V_i + \frac{1}{2}\sum_{i=0}^{N-1} l^{2i} V_i^{\,2} \tag{15}$$

$$T_{ij} = -I^{i+j} \tag{16}$$

In the ADC with multilevel neurons, the design system suffers from the local minima problem, which they solve by applying a similar technique that was proposed by [14] described in the previous subsection [21]. Another method of eliminating incorrect output response for multilevel neuron-based ADC was presented in [19], where the parallel hardware-annealing technique was introduced.

3.3. Hopfield neural network-based level-shifted ADC

In the previous subsections, we discussed various types of architectures that are the modified versions of Hopfield ADC, such as the ADC with correction current, the ADC with non-symmetric weight matrix and the ADC with multilevel neurons. All these designs are based on the original Hopfield ADC structure. However, in this subsection we discuss a type of Hopfield-based ADC that is different from the earlier architectures discussed. The level-shifted neural ADC [23] is a new type of architecture that is constructed with multiple 2-bit Hopfield ADCs and voltage level shifters (**Figure 9**). The ADC design proposed by Hopfield and Tank [11] produces a 4-bit digital output, which is not very much practical in modern technologies. In order to increase the number of neurons in Hopfield NN ADC [11], the corresponding scaling of input and output voltages should be made according to Eq. (2). Therefore, if the goal is to increase the resolution by increasing the number of neurons of Hopfield ADC, the binary output voltage values from neurons will be reduced. Furthermore, the resolution change will require appropriate scaling of the weight matrix. These two problems were addressed in [20–22] and methods that solve these problems were presented. The level-shifted neural ADC is another method that can solve the resolution improvement issue of Hopfield NN ADC.

The operation principle of the proposed level-shifted neural ADC [23] is not very complicated compared to the designs in [14–22]. As it was mentioned, the design consists of multiple 2-bit

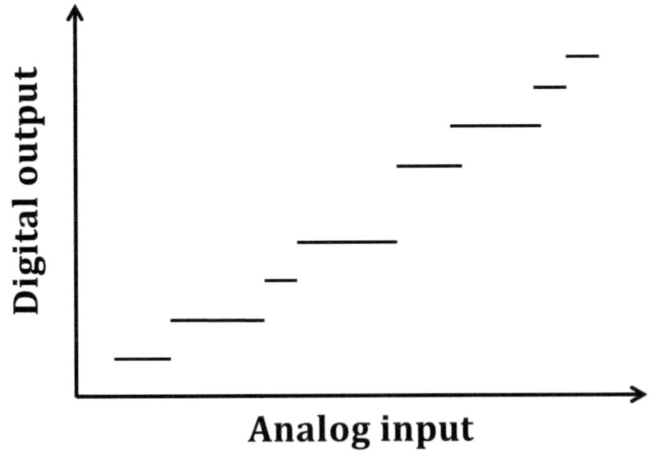

Figure 9. Level-shifted neural ADC.

Hopfield ADC blocks that operate in parallel. Each successive 2-bit ADC block receives input signal that is DC-shifted to some small positive voltage level. The design parameters can be adjusted depending on the application of the ADC.

The preliminary results of the level-shifted neural ADC for 16-quantization level ADC are presented in [23]. As the design consists of multiple operation in parallel 2-bit Hopfield ADCs, the number of output bits in the digital code is larger compared to the conventional Hopfield ADC. Therefore, it is proposed to use a feedforward neural network encoder so that the digital output will be of a 4-bit format and also to reduce the error in computation due to the local minima and circuit nonidealities.

4. CMOS/memristor hybrid network-based ADC

Since memristor, the fourth fundamental circuit element [24], was discovered by HP Labs in 2008 [25], the device is receiving very high attention as it has a potential to emulate the functionality of biological synapses. During the past decade, many scientists have shown a variety of methods of memristor application in hardware design of ANN systems. For instance, in [26] the hybrid CMOS-memristor Hopfield network-based associative memory is demonstrated. While in the work conducted by Guo et al. [27], the CMOS-memristor hybrid architecture is applied in the design of 4-bit Hopfield neural ADC. **Figure 10** reflects the schematic of the system proposed in [27].

The CMOS-memristor hybrid Hopfield ADC [27] consists of memristor-based weight matrix and sigmoidal CMOS neurons. The advantage of implementing constant synapses (in Hopfield NN for ADC design synaptic weights a preset and kept unchanged [11]) with memristors is that being a nanoscale device, memristors consume much less power [27]. Moreover, they significantly reduce the on-chip area compared to CMOS-based synaptic weights [27]. In their work, Guo et al. [27] demonstrated the simulation of the proposed system and also successfully implemented their circuit in hardware.

The tuning of memristors is performed by applying either voltage or current pulses with gradually changing amplitude (and/or width) continuously until the device reaches a desired resistance state [27]. In order to sustain the pre-programmed resistances in memristive weight matrix, the network-operating region (analog input and neuron maximum output voltage) was scaled down so as to prevent any resistance state fluctuations in memristors [27]. The CMOS-memristor hybrid ADC applied resetting the neuron states technique similar to that demonstrated in [11] for reduction of the effects of the local minima states.

Another type of CMOS-memristor hybrid neural ADC is a T-model neural ADC architecture proposed by [2]. In the design by Wang et al. [2], the additional least mean square (LMS) training algorithm is applied in order to optimize the system operation to certain conditions. The LMS algorithm that was used in [2] allows flexibility to ADC in terms of voltage operation region. The training algorithm is implemented by means of digital training block connected to the T-model weight matrix. The works presented in [2, 27] introduce architectures of neural

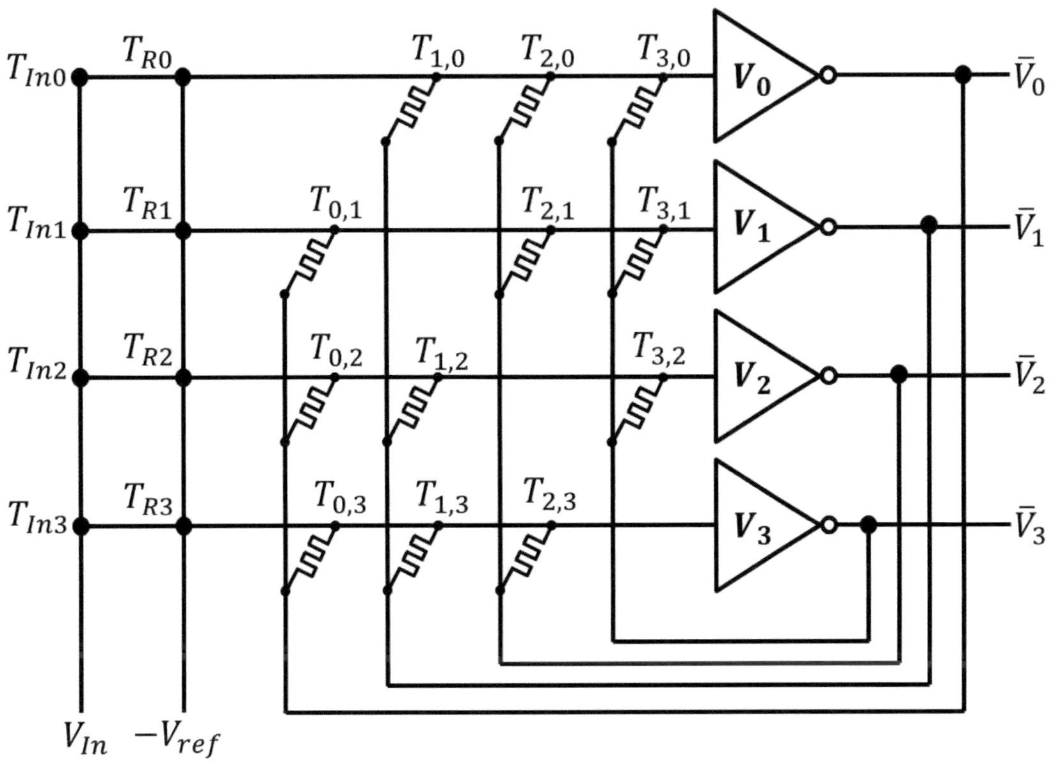

Figure 10. CMOS-memristor hybrid neural ADC.

ADC that utilize memristors as a synaptic weight elements. They demonstrate that the lower power consumption of the memristive devices can be applied in the Hopfield NN ADC design. By contrast, the Hopfield network still requires additional circuitry to eliminate the local minima-related errors.

5. Discussion

The Hopfield network-based ADCs represent a compact approach for the implementation of analog-to-digital conversion task. However, if trying to implement the model in hardware, the multiple circuit nonidealities create errors in the digital output that somehow must be corrected. For instance, as it was discussed previously, the offset response (hysteresis) of comparators after each conversion creates condition for the network to develop incorrect patterns. The possible solution for eliminating offset is to reset the comparators periodically after each conversion to the initial 0-V threshold state, as it was already mentioned [11]. However, this method is not preferable in terms of circuit implementation, as such circuit requires more power. Another problem, as it was previously discussed, was the local minima behaviour of Hopfield network that creates spurious states so that the output does not correspond to the desired response. The existence of local minima of the network is deduced by circuit analysis techniques in [14], and it was proposed to add a feedback current that will balance the network and create a single energy minimum for the whole system dynamics. Thus, the Hopfield NN-based ADC examples discussed in this chapter are still not adapted into practical use. Even though the local minima problem was mitigated, there is not much analysis on resolution improvement. In [20–22] by means of multilevel neuron structure, the 8-bit of resolution was achieved. However, ADC structure becomes much more complex since it incorporates multilevel nonlinearity blocks in each neuron and also uses correction current technique as in [14]. Therefore, in order to achieve performance as better as possible from such type of designs as Hopfield network-based ADCs, the complexity of system components must be increased and many parameters must be taken into account, such as circuit mismatches and offsets since they can affect the output significantly. In addition, the analog structure of Hopfield network-based ADCs creates limitations to resolution improvement and thus makes these designs difficult to be implemented and to be compatible with conventional ADCs.

The alternative ADC structure based on Neural Engineering Framework (NEF) was demonstrated in [28], where it is proposed to shift system parts as much as possible into the digital domain, and only the front end of the ADC incorporates feedforward-type neural network encoder that passes signal to analog neurons, and the rest of the processing is done in digital form. Since the design uses a huge population of neurons in the input, even some amount of neurons will fail and the system is robust to such failures. Moreover, the stability issue is no longer valid in this type of architecture, as the neural network used in the design is purely feedforward. The NEF ADC is generally flexible and scalable, as it mostly consists of digital circuitry, and therefore, it can be adapted to any system requirements and technologies. However, the unresolved issue of the design is a very high power consumption of the network [28].

6. Conclusion

This chapter presents a review of existing technologies of neural network-based ADC designs. A/D conversion is an essential process in microelectronic systems that create a connection between analog systems (e.g., sensors) and digital-processing circuitry [1]. With the modern advancements in submicron CMOS technologies, a variety of high-speed and high-resolution ADCs that are used in different applications have increased [1]. In fact, considering the maturity of the field, the complexity of building an ADC has not been reduced. Moreover, due to the applications that require higher performance and flexibility, the resources of conventional ADC architectures may not be enough. Artificial intelligence is considered to tackle such high requirements on speed and performance. The A/D conversion is not excluded from the list of operations that can be done by means of ANN.

In classical works presented by Hopfield [9, 10], he proposed a mathematical CAM model that consists of a group of two-state neurons interconnected between each other that exhibit collective computational behaviour. He further presented the design that can solve optimization problems [11]. The A/D conversion in his work [11] was considered as a simple optimization problem in which it was desired to minimize the value of energy function that describes the dynamics of the ADC system. He presented a 4-bit NN ADC architecture that can be implemented in hardware

[11]. However, the ADC architecture has intrinsic imperfection due to multiple local minima of energy function that creates digital error in the output of the ADC [14–19].

To solve the local minima problem, several methods are proposed in [14–19]. As it is discussed in Section 3, there are two main methods of eliminating the local minima states and obtaining one global minimum. In the modified Hopfield ADC design, it is proposed to apply correction currents back to the input of each neuron in order to reduce the overlapping current occurring between adjacent output codes [14]. This method eliminates local minima and creates one global minimum towards which the network flow is attracted [14]. Another interesting method that also reduces the effects of local minima is the neural ADC with non-symmetrical weight matrix connection [15–19]. According to this method, ADC architectures with non-symmetrical weight matrix do not create multiple energy minima states; as a result, such networks are also attracted to a global minimum energy state [15–19].

Multilevel neural ADC architecture [21] is based on the original Hopfield ADC structure but with modified neuron model. The authors in [21] proposed a multiple-state neuron implementation that is aimed to improve the resolution of the ADC. A similar goal, to improve resolution, was pursued by the level-shifted neural ADC architecture [23] that is built with multiple Hopfield ADC blocks and voltage level shifters.

In addition to the presented CMOS-based neural ADC structures in Section 3, examples of CMOS-memristor-based neural ADC architecture [2, 27] are discussed in Section 4. The memristor device is a promising technology that is aimed to expand the capabilities of traditional CMOS-based systems. The application of memristors in neuromorphic circuits and the development of new memristor-based architectures are currently being widely discussed. However, in [2, 27], traditional implementation of neural ADC architecture was modified by the addition of memristors. Thus, the demonstrated results in [2, 27] have shown that there is a potential in the application of memristors in CMOS-based systems, as memristors consume less power and save on-chip area, which makes memristor-based neural ADC an attractive alternative to traditional NN-based ADC designs that are discussed previously. To sum up, a general overview on the NN-based ADC design area is presented in this chapter.

Author details

Aigerim Tankimanova* and Alex Pappachen James

*Address all correspondence to: atankimanova@nu.edu.kz

Nazarbayev University, Astana, Kazakhstan

References

[1] Van de Plassche RJ. CMOS Integrated Analog-to-Digital and Digital-to-Analog Converters. 2nd ed. Netherlands: Kluwer Academic Publishers; 2003. 588 p

[2] Wang W, You Z, Liu P, Kuang J. An adaptive neural network A/D converter based on CMOS/memristor hybrid design. IEICE Electronics Express. 2014;**11**(24):1-6

[3] Yang H, Sarpeshkar R. A bio-inspired ultra-energy-efficient analog-to-digital converter for biomedical applications. IEEE Transactions on Circuits and Systems I: Regular Papers. 2006;**53**(11):2349-2356

[4] Aiello L. Brains and guts in human evolution: The expensive tissue hypothesis. Brazilian Journal of Genetics. 1997;**20**(1):141-148

[5] McCulloch WS, Pitts WH. A logical calculus of the ideas immanent in nervous activity. Bulletin of Mathematical Biophysics. 1943;**5**:115-133

[6] Cooper L. A possible organization of animal memory and learning. In: Lundquist B, Lundquist S, editors. Proceedings of the Nobel Symposium on Collective Properties of Physical Systems. New York: Academic Press; 1973. pp. 252-264

[7] Warren S, Pitt M, Pitt W. A logical calculus of the ideas immanent in nervous activity. Bulletin of Mathematical Biophysics. 1943;**5**(4):115-133

[8] Longuet-Higgins HC. The non-local storage of temporal information. Proceedings of the Royal Society of London B: Biological Sciences. 1968;**171**(1024):327-334

[9] Hopfield J. Neural networks and physical systems with emergent collective computational abilities. Proceedings of National Academy of Sciences of the United States of America. 1982;**79**(8):2554-2558

[10] Hopfield J. Neurons with graded response have collective computational properties like those of two-state neurons. Proceedings of National Academy of Sciences of the United States of America. 1984;**81**(Biophysics):3088-3092. DOI: 10.1073/pnas.81.10.3088

[11] Tank D, Hopfield J. Simple "neural" optimization networks: An A/D converter, signal decision circuit, and linear programming circuit. IEEE Transactions on Circuits and Systems. 1986;**33**(5):533-541

[12] Rosenblatt F. The perceptron: A probabilistic model for information storage and organization in the brain. Psychological Review. 1958;**65**(6):386-408

[13] Hopfield J, Tank D. Computing with neural circuits: A model. Science, New Series. 1986; **233**(4764):625-633

[14] Lee B, Sheu B. Modified Hopfield neural networks for retrieving the optimal solution. IEEE Transactions on Neural Networks. 1991;**2**(1):137-142

[15] Chande V, Poonacha P. On neural networks for analog to digital conversion. IEEE Transactions on Neural Networks. 1995;**6**(5):1269-1274

[16] Avitable G, Mannetti S. Some structures for neural based A/D conversion. Electronic Letters. 1990;**26**(18):1516-1517

[17] Gray D, Michel A, Porod W. Application of neural networks to sorting problems. 27th IEEE Conference on Decision and Control; 7-9 Dec; IEEE; 1988. pp. 350-351

[18] Sun CL, Tang Z, Ishizuka O, Matsumoto H. Synthesis and implementation of T-model neural-based A/D converter. In: IEEE International Symposium on Circuits and Systems; 10-13 May; IEEE; 1992. pp. 1573-1576

[19] Avitabile G, Forti M, Manetti S, Marini M. On a class of nonsymmetrical neural networks with application to ADC. IEEE Transactions on Circuits and Systems. 1991;**38**(2):202-209

[20] Yuh J, Newcomb R. Circuits for multi-level neuron nonlinearities. In: International Joint Conference on Neural Networks; 7–11 June; IEEE; 1992. pp. 27-32

[21] Yuh J, Newcomb W. A multilevel neural network for a/d conversion. IEEE Transactions on Neural Networks. 1993;**4**(3):470-483

[22] Bang SH, Chen O, Chang J, Sheu B. Paralleled hardware annealing in multilevel Hopfield neural networks for optimal solutions. IEEE Transactions on Circuits and Systems II: Analog and Digital Signal Processing. 1995;**42**(1):46-49

[23] Tankimanova A, Kumar Maan A, James A. Level-shifted neural encoded analog-to-digital converter. In: 24th IEEE International Conference on Electronics, Circuits and Systems (ICECS 2017)

[24] Kumar Maan A, Ai JD, James AP. A survey of memristive threshold logic circuits. IEEE Transactions on Neural Networks and Learning Systems. 2016;**PP**(99):1-13

[25] Strukov DB, Snider GS, Stewart DR, Williams RS. The missing memristor found. Nature. 2008;**453**(7191):80-83

[26] Hu SG, Liu Y, Liu Z, Chen TP, Wang JJ, Yu Q, Deng LJ, Yin Y, Hosaka S. Associative memory realized by a reconfigurable memristive Hopfield neural network. Nature Communications. 2015;**6**:7522

[27] Guo X, Meririkh-Bayat F, Gao L, Hoskins DB, Alibart F, Linares-Barranco B, Theogarajan L, Teuscher C, Strukov DB. Modelling and experimental demonstration of a Hopfield network analog-to-digital converter with hybrid CMOS/memristor circuits. Frontiers in Neuroscience. 2015;**9**:488

[28] Mayr CG, Partzsch J, Noack M, Schuffny R. Configurable analog-digital conversion using the neural engineering framework. Frontiers of Neuroscience. 2014;**8**:201